MORE

COURAGEOUS
CONVERSATIONS
ABOUT RACE

"All our philosophy is dry as dust if it is not immediately translated into some act of living service."—Gandhi

This book is dedicated to the courageous leaders who passionately, practically, persistently, and purposefully usher in the Courageous Conversation About Race in their classrooms, schools, and districts and are getting the results.

You know exactly who you are and so do our children!

This book is also dedicated to President Barack Obama who provided for me a much-needed second wind as well as the audacity to keep on hoping!

MORE
COURAGEOUS
CONVERSATIONS
ABOUT RACE

GLENN E. SINGLETON
Foreword by James P. Comer

CORWIN
A SAGE Company

FOR INFORMATION:

Corwin

A SAGE Company

2455 Teller Road

Thousand Oaks, California 91320

(800) 233-9936

www.corwin.com

SAGE Publications Ltd.

1 Oliver's Yard

55 City Road

London EC1Y 1SP

United Kingdom

SAGE Publications India Pvt. Ltd.

B 1/I 1 Mohan Cooperative Industrial Area

Mathura Road, New Delhi 110 044

India

SAGE Publications Asia-Pacific Pte. Ltd.

3 Church Street

#10-04 Samsung Hub

Singapore 049483

Copyright © 2013 by Glenn E. Singleton

Printed in the United States of America

A catalog record of this book is available from the Library of Congress.

ISBN 978-1-4129-9266-4

Acquisitions Editor: Dan Alpert

Associate Editor: Megan Bedell

Editorial Assistant: Heidi Arndt

Production Editor: Cassandra Margaret Seibel

Copy Editor: Jackie Tasch

Typesetter: C&M Digitals (P) Ltd.

Proofreader: Susan Schon

Indexer: Judy Hunt

Cover Designer: Michael Dubowe

Permissions Editor: Karen Ehrmann

This book is printed on acid-free paper

Certified Chain of Custody
Promoting Sustainable Forestry
www.sfiprogram.org
SFI-01268

SFI label applies to text stock

12 13 14 15 16 10 9 8 7 6 5 4 3 2 1

Contents

Foreword

Can We Talk About Race?

The United States of America is a remarkable nation. Birthed in two polar-opposite beliefs—freedom and slavery—and possibly a bit of genocide, it has moved slowly and fitfully to become the largest and most powerful, diverse, and compassionate democracy in the history of the world. But it is now being challenged for its leadership position by other nations, and currently is limited by a growing sense of confusion within (or perhaps an identity crisis). The long-term downside of this quandary could be a reduction in the commitment to freedom that has made our nation exceptional.

Aspects of our economic situation are both the probable problem and the potential solution. Throughout human history, achieving a state in which most people could survive and thrive most of the time has had limited success. As a result, human nature has often led to aggressive and destructive interactions such as man's (or humankind's) inhumanity to man (humankind), from minimal to extreme. But despite slavery, the abuse of Native Americans, and the stigmatization of certain groups of immigrants, and because of a slow but sustained effort to live up to the principles of our founding documents, we Americans established an identity of inclusion, belonging, a commitment to human rights, and opportunity for all. This accomplishment made us not only the economic leader but also a moral leader in the world. This combination and the resultant stability were mutually beneficial, making us a global, economic, and human rights "safe haven."

The challenges to our leadership began to arise in large part from the effects of rapid global, scientific, and technological changes coupled with an inadequate effort to prepare a large majority of our young people to function well in this new and future world. The new economy and open technology-based society requires not only well-educated but also well-developed and well-functioning people among all our diverse groups. Yet we allowed too many to fall behind over the past 50 years, and the students who are falling behind are disproportionately poor and marginalized African Americans, American Indians, and Hispanics and poor Whites and Southeast Asian Americans. The American students not among those groups are achieving above most other students in the world.

Academic underperformance closes the mainstream workforce pipeline and invites able young people to engage in illegal financial and lifestyle activities, thus engendering the all-too-familiar list of social problems that threaten our nation's overall well-being. And while many economic and political leaders worry about the failure of our top students to compete with others, the real danger lies in the fact that too many able students are not getting a chance to compete in our own economic mainstream, much less the global economy. The resultant social problems are the real threat to America's future.

During the same 50 years that the gap in preparation and performance has been growing, the evidence that most poor and marginalized young people can achieve at a significantly higher level has also been growing. But instead of building on this evidence, our nation has been focusing on accountability issues—and without widespread success. To promote what we need nationwide, we must make urgent, very significant, and complex political, technological, and social changes. This is more urgent than raising standards and exacting penalties on parents and educators who are not prepared to do what we are asking them to do.

And before we can elevate student performance overall, we are going to need to answer some basic questions about the issues that both stabilize and move or paralyze our society: Who are we? What do we want to become? How do we get there? To do so, *we are going to have to talk about race*—without blame or finger-pointing, but in the service of understanding and problem solving.

We have already come a long way over a unique and hugely difficult path. Because of this, we should be proud; and we should ask ourselves how we did it. The American experience is a real-life social and historical petri dish of one of the most successful efforts to manage the human potential for good and evil that has ever existed. But despite what we might learn that could help us help create a better world, we don't want to think or talk about one of the most critical, if not central, features of our American experience.

I don't welcome the idea of talking about race. Most parents—Black, White, and others—use a version of "don't ask, don't tell" when discussing the issue of race with their children. We don't talk about race in a useful way in our education system(s), and even scholars have difficulty talking about it. In schools, it is a short history discussion that rarely if ever focuses on discussions of the psychosocial effects of race on all people and society at large. Often we do not even acknowledge that it is an issue at all or why it is so difficult to talk about.

In the 1980s, when I discussed racial issues while interviewing my mother for our family history, titled *Maggie's American Dream,*[1] she turned the tables on me and asked a question: "When did you get to be so *Black?* When you were a little boy in school [I attended a significantly White-majority school], you said that if you were not a Negro, you would not have any problems." It was obviously a statement that had given us both pain, and it had remained with her over many years. I admit to a moment of unease upon hearing about the comment before I allowed the immaturity and underdeveloped identity process of my childhood to bear the responsibility for it.

A few years after the interview with my mother, I was in a study group composed largely of White social and behavioral science scholars when I suggested that the growing problems in African American communities were due in part to the fact that economic changes and under-education were contributing heavily to the creation of dysfunctional families. Generation after generation, I continued, the most dysfunctional of these families, those least able to thrive in the American mainstream, were having the most children. Subsequently, their numbers were growing geometrically while the highest-functioning Black families had fewer children than the national average. My colleagues erupted into a short period of disagreement and called for lunch early. It was the only time in all the meetings of this very collegial group that nobody invited me to join them for lunch. After lunch, we moved on as if nothing had happened, never revisiting the idea.

These incidents point to the pain and sensitivity of the American racial situation for children, parents, thought leaders, and policymakers. But why not let bygones be bygones? Why not just move to higher social and moral ground without wading through the muck, mire, and pain of past and even present transgressions?

The reason is that *race is not the underlying and central problem.* As real, omnipresent, pervasive, and destructive as the issue has been and continues to be, it obscures the real problem: that critical flaw in human nature or *the very frequent tendency of the privileged to exploit the vulnerable less privileged.* Without understanding the complex ways race obscures this underlying and generative problem, we cannot adequately address it.

Throughout a human history rarely committed to democracy, slavery was largely a product of conquest. It was a way to promote privilege and to get hard work done. As an aspiring democracy influenced greatly by theocratic principles, the United States could not continue to enslave human beings without a powerful justification. The most useful argument, particularly after most Africans became Christians, was that Africans were inferior, particularly intellectually. This argument played into the ongoing struggle between the White "haves" and "have-nots." It was helpful to many among both groups. There were psychological, social, and economic benefits to it and a resultant widespread receptivity among many have-nots, particularly after slavery and during the heavy influx of White immigrants competing for opportunities.

During slavery, Blacks experienced the three conditions most harmful to good mental health and well-being: the loss of organizing and sustaining African cultures and the imposition of a slave culture; an imposed condition of inferiority; and the absence of opportunity to work toward and hope for a better future. Many African Americans created protective and supportive conditions powered by group-made religious, fraternal, and family cultures that promoted high-level functioning. But too many experienced hopelessness, despair, and depression—the source of many demeaning stereotypes. Too many others exhibited troublesome acting-out behaviors. The proof of this inferiority pudding was in both these troublesome outcomes. And while most groups had access to the economic, political, and social keys needed to improve their lot immediately or within a generation of coming to America, it was the 1960s before most Blacks could vote and utilize the enormous amounts of energy that other groups used for economic and overall group development.

Throughout our nation's history, the inferiority designation strategies and perspectives of America's White population, established and new, became increasingly entrenched. In *De Bow's Review,* the most influential pre-Civil War periodical in the South, editor J. D. B. De Bow was explicit, writing: "The poor white laborer at the North is at the bottom of the social ladder, whilst his brother here has ascended several steps and can look down upon those who are beneath him, at an infinite remove." Also, for reasons that are not clear to historians, many Whites came to America seeking wealth, and they typically identified with the rich and powerful even when they themselves were not. Identification with captors, concentration camp guards, and slavery overseers are derivatives of the same human tendency. Research has shown that, even today, American children identify with the apparently powerful.

These widely held convictions and conditions created a powerful mindset of Blacks as bottom dwellers, legitimate scapegoats, and losers for life—people to be excluded, despised, and abused. The identification-with-the-powerful phenomenon often makes it difficult for non-Black and nonprivileged people to join with Blacks to improve their own conditions. Most troublesome of these results is that the victimized Blacks often internalize these perspectives.

For example, although my parents helped me play "doctor" by buying me a toy doctor's kit, a Black neighbor asked them, "Why are you encouraging him to be a doctor? We are poor [Black] people. You know he will never be a doctor!" Several academic leaders working with excellent Black students have wondered why these students often do not view themselves as smart. Steele and Aronson's elegant 1995 study, "Stereotype Threat and the Intellectual Test Performance of African-Americans," strongly suggests that this internalization of inferiority has created a serious problem (one for which they presented a pilot solution, by the way).[2]

Most of us would like to think of ourselves as rational thinkers who act on the basis of objective observations and information. But our thinking and doing is influenced greatly by at least five powerful factors that often cause us to do otherwise: human nature; history; experience; culture; and external and internal situations, both personal and institutional. And we all are carriers of the dominant cultural norms that are established and influenced by all these conditions. As a result, despite enormous political, economic, and educational progress, too much of that early thinking persists, particularly at an unconscious but still potently harmful level. And it plays out in ways about which we often are not aware.

Because economic well-being affects all other types of well-being, and because education and the economy are both the energy pipeline and the engine, let's think now about how our perceptions influence our institutional and individual behavior in both. I'll illustrate with the following examples. A White father of a Black adopted son attending a highly regarded public school once spoke twice by telephone to the youngster's White teacher to indicate that he felt his son could do better in school. The father offered to be helpful in this regard, but the teacher said the child was doing fine. When the flustered father went to the school to discuss the matter, the teacher, upon seeing that the father was a White man, said, "Oh, oh, *now* I understand!" and was willing to discuss improvement strategies. She did not realize that she had been saying that the boy was doing fine—for a *Black* child!

In another case, a very affluent African American mother whose son attended an elite private school felt that her son's athletic prowess, and *maybe* his race, might be keeping him out of the highest-level mathematics course. Ignoring suggestions from school administrators that it was "better" for the boy to be "well rounded and happy," she insisted on the move. Her son subsequently achieved the highest scores in the top-level math class. Thus, the school got it wrong. Appropriately challenged, well-rounded students—of all races—can be happy.

Any gathering of well-educated, middle- and upper-income Blacks often produces similar stories. To be fair, however, there are many unbiased White educators. I myself had all White teachers until I went to medical school, and I can think of only three incidents in which I am certain race was a contributing factor. Indeed, the unspoken negative perception of Blacks at the time was so apparent that I can recall some White teachers going out of their way to allow me and other Black students at my schools to demonstrate their high levels of excellence to their White classmates. But poor children of color and even marginalized White children, then and now, often have no one to protect or promote them similarly.

As a nation, we have utilized many of the traditionally useful, large-scale, culture-change methods to address race-based problems: the passage of laws, the dissemination of the best scientific evidence, passionate advocacy for justice and equity, and more. But our greatest successes—support for the education of and athletics for women, the huge reduction in smoking, and other wins—did not have to deal as deeply with issues of identity trauma, unconscious guilt and shame, myth-generating protective and reinforcing institutions, and more, with troublesome behavioral consequences resulting from all. And, it is important that they did not address the historical absence of significant power among the victims of these inequities and their limiting impact on self- and group protection and promotion.

This unique situation suggests where it will be most helpful to start and, in a way, points to sources of increased power. That is why, I presume, *MORE Courageous Conversations About Race* focuses mostly on young people. They are the hope.

The young of all races are groping for their own identity and demanding an opportunity to live in a country where they can experience their own humanity and have the best chance to modify and then change entrenched political, economic, and social structures and beliefs that generate the conditions that are holding our nation back. Their personal questions intersect with our national questions: Who are we? What do we want to become? How do we get there?

The so-called "Arab Spring" of the contemporary era is much more than that. It is a worldwide search by young people, fueled by visions that modern science and technology have made possible, to improve the human condition generally and their own specifically. It has spawned continuing, worldwide efforts to reject long-standing and excessive privilege that promotes harmful ideologies and to replace them with efforts to move toward a focus on the common good and on what all human beings will need to survive and thrive, live with dignity and decency, and reduce conflict and exploitation.

For example, the young are breaking down the long-standing left-versus-right political model because they believe it distracts us from the question of how to create real-world systems that provide the level of community and family security that will facilitate high-level adult functioning among the most people, including child rearing that prepares the young for success in the next generation. Social science has long suggested that this is possible, and modern neuroscience also supports this perspective.

The African American young have a particularly critical role to play in our future. Just as resistance to increased opportunity for African Americans was justified by an argument of inferiority, the stereotyping of Blacks in the United States, particularly males, as criminals, along with continued claims of their limited intellectual ability, are now being used for that purpose. Even sincere efforts to close the academic achievement gap in education do not address the consequences of a difficult history; indeed, the latter is at the root of the former. Fortunately, there are teenaged, young adult, and even long-mature Black men and women creating programs in and outside of schools across the country that understand and address the particular challenge, not only of Black males but also of all Blacks.

But what we Blacks are doing outside of school must also prepare our young for school success. And to be successful, that effort must thoughtfully involve people from all groups who realize that *we are all in this together.* This nation will not achieve true success until we all realize that *when the boat sinks, ALL will go down.*

Missing are the institutional and organizational structures that will promote coherence and optimal impact for this effort. To create those structures, we must have widespread understanding of the underlying problem and how it presents itself in our day-to-day lives, and we must gain this understanding in societies where many continue to work to prevent this from happening. Thus, beyond understanding the problem, we must understand why human nature (both individual and group), political dynamics, and economics often work against change designed to promote opportunity for all. In that regard, it is important not to romanticize the young or to simplify the task. Our young people will need the full support and guidance of the adults and institutions that facilitate their development and learning.

But we cannot create better and more supportive institutions and experiences for the young without first *talking about the role of race* and the other obstructive issues confronting world society in a mature and problem-solving way. *MORE Courageous Conversations About Race* is designed to facilitate that process. It discusses in depth some of the issues outlined in this introduction. It considers educational systems and how they can change to meet the needs of those who populate them. And, most important of all, it presents the voices of the adults and students who must move us through this pivotal period of American history on to interactions and institutions that can make us better people and create a better world.

James P. Comer, M.D.
Maurice Falk Professor of Child Psychiatry, Yale Child Study Center
Associate Dean, Yale School of Medicine
New Haven, CT

first black psychiatrist in '50s

Preface

Yes. We. Can.

Three simple words came to represent the most significant change I have ever seen in my entire life. Not in my wildest dreams could I have imagined that one day I would see a Black man become president of the United States of America. And yet, on January 20, 2009, I stood side-by-side with millions of former disbelievers on the National Mall in Washington, D.C., and witnessed Barack Hussein Obama's swearing-in ceremony as he became the nation's 44th commander-in-chief. That day was also one of the coldest days, temperature-wise, that I have ever experienced in my life, but the fire burning in my soul out there on the mall provided a warmth that no coat or coffee could match.

That extraordinary day began and ended in my mother's home in Baltimore. I got up at 5 a.m. to drive quite a distance to catch the bus that took me to a Washington-area Metro stop. From there, I hopped on a subway that delivered me just steps away from the Washington Monument. Months earlier, I had secured tickets from my state senator to enjoy the historic ceremony in a reserved section near the Capitol, but as I arrived in the nation's capital, I felt a strong desire to be in the thick of it—in the midst of the vast numbers of everyday Americans who braved the subzero temperatures to watch the inauguration live or on the giant screens dotting the mall.

Clearly, the fact that a Black man was being inaugurated president was the sole reason I had made this challenging journey. The multiple obstacles involved, including the logistics and expenses associated with getting to D.C. and onto the mall, the brutal weather, and the crowds were encouragement enough for anyone, except the most diehard and fanatical, to stay home. But I wanted to be there—with our new president and his beautiful family and with all the other Americans who desperately wanted and needed CHANGE.

I once believed that no other pageantry could outdo the pomp and circumstances of my Ivy League convocation and commencement. The flags, costumes, and instrumentation of that larger-than-life experience, with all its carefully and precisely choreographed pageantry, left deep and lasting impressions on my psyche that I believed no other event could top. I was wrong. The inauguration of a U.S. president is truly the apex of ritual in the Western world. All of the symbols and rituals of our nation's long-held and all-too-often unattained principles are all bundled into a brief yet compellingly significant program designed to propel our citizenry seamlessly from one notable era to the next.

That day, however, I suspected that even veteran onlookers and those who were intimately familiar with the changing of the guard might have been a bit disoriented by the rare and glorious spectacle of this particular moment. The incoming president's coterie was preceded by the usual, seemingly all-White cascade of lawmakers, judges, diplomats, and dignitaries. When we finally got our first glimpse of the First Family-elect, Mrs. Obama's brilliant yellow coat and green gloves provided the first indication that real change was indeed coming to Washington.

As awe-inspiring as was the thought of a Black man taking the helm of leadership of the free world, equally moving were the faces of those in the crowd assembled before him, a mosaic of expressions of joy, relief, liberation, and vindication—and of curiosity and complaint. The mood was not overly political; rather, it was more of a feeling of over-whelming humanitarianism, of human-ness in the best sense of the word. And regardless of the social, political, and economic station of those in the crowd that day on the mall, each and every one of us believed that a new day was dawning.

Crowds of Black folk, some quite elderly and others held tight in the arms of their mothers or sitting on the shoulders of their fathers, seemed not to notice the bitter cold of the January wind as they sang spirituals from the African American tradition like "His Eye is on the Sparrow" or more contemporary renditions such as "Ain't No Stopping Us Now" in four-part, *a capella* harmony. Brown people chanted "*Si Se Puede!*" providing a reminder to all that Obama's powerful slogans had broad significance to Americans of all origins. Whites in the crowd joined people of color in the chorus of "boos" that heralded the arrival of officials from the outgoing administration on the dais. Seemingly everyone—people across our nation's more typical racial, economic, linguistic, and generational divides, and perhaps in defiance of them—added their jubilant voices to the masses, singing Kool and the Gang's hit, "Celebration," as the president and his procession settled on the stage.

Then came the deafening silence as the "queen of soul," Aretha Franklin, stepped up to the microphone to belt out the national anthem. Tears poured from my eyes and quickly froze on my cheeks. I tell you, I felt more alive at that moment than I have ever felt before, as if my very humanity was being completely affirmed. I could not believe that the event I was attending was actually happening.

At any given moment, however, I feared that my fears would overtake my joy. Thoughts of the day ending tragically encircled my mind and would not let go. I prayed that no one would mar this momentous event with reckless violence and mayhem. I wanted no one, misunderstanding the need for this governmental transition to take place in a peaceful way, to decide—individually or in conspiracy—to do harm to the new president or his family.

At last, the camera honed in on the image of my newest hero strutting through the Capitol rotunda. Moments later, President-elect Barack Hussein Obama stood before the massive, frozen crowd, poised and prepared to change the course of history. As the new president spoke, it was clear that many who had not previously held a place at the so-called table of wealth and freedom were about to dine.

As I stood, frozen yet fixated, I could not help but wonder what Obama's election would mean for the nation's schools and schoolchildren. Whenever our new president referenced education in his speech about change in America, I could not help but scan the crowd for representatives from our public schools. I am certain that there were thousands of teachers and administrators in the crowd that day who, like me, were trying to hold on to Obama's every word about the plight of the nation's failing schools.

My heart sank, however, as I searched unsuccessfully in the crowds to locate the American Indian, Black, and Brown students who would depend most on this president to lead our school transformation efforts. My joy in that moment was replaced by sadness as I realized that this inauguration might be yet another missed opportunity for our lowest-performing children to experience hope.

I wish I could say that I remember the specific words spoken by President Obama in his riveting inaugural address. I do not. Perhaps my powerful emotions, or the blistering cold, wiped clear all my recollection. What I do remember was the powerful presence of a courageous, intelligent, relentless, and relentlessly patriotic Black man addressing the world and everyone listening intently, as if our futures hinged on every word he spoke. My own memory may have blurred, but Obama's language, themes, meanings, and intentions were crystal clear: it was the dawning of a new day in the United States.

I often replay that glorious day, scene by scene, in my mind to remind me of the simple fact that all things are possible. Rebroadcasts of the inauguration only sharpen my determination not only to orchestrate change in schools but also to understand racism as a force to be reckoned with and surmounted.

Thank you, President Obama, for giving me and millions of others in America and throughout the world *Change We Can Believe In!*

Glenn E. Singleton
San Francisco

Acknowledgments

I would like to acknowledge the following for their generous assistance, support, and dedicated efforts in helping this book come to fruition:

Eden Prairie Schools
Pacific Educational Group, Inc.
Portland Public Schools
San José State University, Urban High School Leadership Program
Saint Paul Public Schools
Spence School
The Park School

Janet Perkins

Devon Alexander

Dan Alpert

Kamili Anderson

Marlecia Autrey

Sandro Backer

Maureen Benson

Michelle Bierman

Stewart Blackburn

Jeff Blaskower

Bodie Brizendine

Dan Cohen

Diane Cowdery

Nancy Dome

Patrick Duffy

Malcolm Fialho

Jay Frazier

Anthony Galloway

Gabriel Gima

Ivan Hart

Elaina & Yudi Hershowitz

Niels Hooper

Charles Hopson

Connie Hytjan

Andrea Haynes Johnson

Marion Kickett

Melissa Krull

Chris Lim

Nichole Maher

Donna Marriott

Akemi Matsumoto

Michael McGregor

Graig Meyer

Kehaulani Minzghor

Nanette Missaghi

Mathew J. Morton

Moisés Nascimento

Pam Noli

Ariel Pippo

Matais Pouncil

Carla Randall

Jackie Roehl

Scott Sellman

Valeria Silva

John W. Singleton, Sr.

Wendell Singleton & Family

Carole Smith

Jimmy Smith	Carrie Streeter	Pablo Vega
Sanford Smith	Jackie Tasch	Luis Versalles
Elona Street-Stewart	Donna Hart Tervalon	Lee Mun Wah

I extend a very special acknowledgment to James Comer for his lifelong dedication to improving the circumstances of our nation's most vulnerable populations. Meeting and having an opportunity to work with you was truly an important moment of inspiration in my life. I am forever grateful to you for your support.

PUBLISHER'S ACKNOWLEDGMENTS

Corwin gratefully acknowledges the contributions of the following reviewers:

Bonnie M. Davis, Educational Consultant
Educating for Change

Randall B. Lindsey, Educator and Emeriti Professor
California State University, Los Angeles

Ignacio Lopez, Director of Outreach and Professor of Education
National College of Education, National Louis University, Chicago IL

About the Author

 **Glenn Eric Singleton** hails from Baltimore, Maryland. A product of public elementary and independent secondary school, Singleton earned his bachelor's degree from the University of Pennsylvania and his master's degree from the Graduate School of Education at Stanford University. Singleton began his career as an Ivy League admissions director. In 1992, he founded Pacific Educational Group (PEG), Inc., to support families in their transitions within and between K–12 and higher education. His company rapidly grew into a vehicle for addressing systemic educational inequity by providing a framework, guidance, and support to K–12 systems and institutions of higher education focused on meeting the needs of under-served students of color. He is now its president and chief executive officer.

Singleton and his associates at PEG design and deliver individualized, comprehensive professional development for educators in the form of training, coaching, and consulting. Working at all levels, from beginning teachers to superintendents at local, state, and national levels, PEG helps educators focus on heightening their awareness of institutional racism and implementing effective strategies for eliminating racial achievement disparities in schools. In 1995, Singleton developed Beyond Diversity, a widely recognized seminar aimed at helping administrators, teachers, students, parents, and community stakeholders identify and examine the intersection of race and schooling. The Beyond Diversity seminar is the foundation for the PEG Systemic Racial Equity Framework and its theory of transformation, which focuses on leadership development, teacher action-research, and family/community empowerment. Today, participants around the world use Singleton's Courageous Conversations Agreements, Conditions and Compass, introduced to them in Beyond Diversity, as they strive to usher in culturally proficient curriculum, instruction, and assessment. Over its 20-year history, PEG's scope of work has expanded to include online professional learning, independent school partnerships, and international efforts in Canada and Australia that focus on educational equity for indigenous populations. PEG hosts an annual Summit for Courageous Conversation, in which scholars, educators, community members, and other stakeholders convene to identify strategies and best practices for creating high-level, equitable learning environments for all students.

In 2003, Singleton received the prestigious Eugene T. Carothers Human Relations Award for outstanding service in the fields of human rights and human relations from the National School Public Relations Association. He has hosted and produced educational programs for television and has written numerous articles on the topics of equity, institutional racism, leadership, and staff development. He is the author of *Courageous Conversations About Race: A Field Guide for Achieving Racial Equity in Schools*, which earned "Book of the Year" recognition from both the National Staff Development Council and ForeWord Magazine in 2006.

Singleton serves as an adjunct professor of educational leadership at San José State University where he instructs graduate-level students on developing the requisite will, skill, knowledge and capacity to lead for racial equity. He has also lectured at the University of California, Berkeley, on the topic of educational equity. Singleton is an internationally recognized keynote speaker and consultant to a variety of school reform organizations and educational consortia. In May 2009, Singleton was selected to serve on the California State Board of Education's African American Advisory Committee, where he participated in shaping policy that promoted equitable education for the state's lowest-performing students.

Singleton currently resides in San Francisco, California. He is the founder of the Foundation for a College Education (FCE) and currently serves on the FCE Advisory Board.

ONE

Why Do We Need Another Book on Courageous Conversations About Race?

I do not see how we will ever solve the turbulent problem of race confronting our nation until there is an honest confrontation with it and a willing search for the truth and a willingness to admit the truth when we discover it.

—Martin Luther King Jr.[1]

IT'S (STILL) A QUESTION OF WILL!

In December 2005, at the National Staff Development Council's annual conference in Philadelphia, I felt a kind of excitement and joy such as I had never experienced before. I was back in the city where I had struggled through many courses, and occasionally fallen into doubt about my graduation possibilities, while attending the University of Pennsylvania. Despite those early challenges, I also experienced accomplishment there, completing the first of a series of college degrees that would lead me further and more deeply into my chosen field of education. Now I was there again, pen in hand, books stacked neatly around me, sitting proudly beside a bright and beautiful orange poster of the cover of *Courageous Conversations About Race: A Field Guide for Achieving Equity in Schools.*

I had invited friends and family to join me at what would become the first of many signings and discussions about a book that would later define a small movement in education. I must admit that I was a bit overwhelmed that afternoon in Philadelphia by the attention *Courageous Conversations* was getting. More and more, the book was appearing in the hands of and generating discussion among my professional development colleagues, many of whom had gathered from around the country for updates on professional learning communities, responses to intervention, and positive behavior intervention and support efforts. Although "Beyond Diversity," the international face-to-face and online training program on which the book was modeled, had been (and remains) extremely popular and successful, I never imagined that *Courageous Conversations* would become an award winner, let alone a bestseller for my publisher, Corwin.

I felt that way especially because the book was being introduced into a society that categorically denied the very presence of racism at the same time it was calling out, with some urgency, for a protocol to examine and address the myriad manifestations of racism evident in its schools. I certainly was not anticipating such mass approval for a work stemming from two simple premises. The first of these is that to address racial achievement disparities in schools, educators must first gain permission from their institutional leadership to engage in conversations about race. The second is that educators must develop the will, skill, knowledge, and capacity to sustain and deepen the dialogue about the impact of race on leadership, learning and teaching, and family/community empowerment. Still, educators by the thousands had purchased the book by then, and scores had spoken about the importance of the Four Agreements, Six Conditions, and specialized Compass introduced in its pages to assist educators in navigating and negotiating issues related to race in their professional as well as their personal lives.

I was then and remain truly humbled by the entire author experience. Even today, given my comparatively modest writing experience, I am simply amazed how authors such as Michael Fullan and Linda Darling-Hammond (or heck, even Danielle Steele!) can produce so many books in a single lifetime. This second book was, for me, a 2-year effort, and it took nearly everything out of me that the first book left behind. It also often depleted the patience of my family and friends and the members of my staff at Pacific Educational Group (PEG), Inc. The latter often had to cover for me when I would just disappear to Tahoe National Forest or Hawaii's Big Island to unplug, concentrate, and compose this narrative, which is designed to provoke, inspire, challenge, and support the growing band of school leaders striving for racial equity. I am grateful to all for their love and support, and I remain committed to accompanying my courageous colleagues around the world on a journey to discover ways to make the so-called "achievement gap"—or what I now refer to as "racial achievement disparities in education"—a thing of the past.

■ ■ ■

I learned in crafting my first book that writing about race for a U.S. audience requires that I first state exactly what must be said to enlist the confidence of and maintain my credibility among racially conscious people of color. It next demands that I craft a revision that does not overwhelm or alienate my majority White readership. This is because, alongside my critical and targeted audiences, there exists a powerful and largely White body of critics who will indiscriminately challenge any attempt I make, meaningful or otherwise, to elevate the conversation and consciousness about race and racism in this country to a higher and more urgent level. As a result, in my writing, I spend much of my time and energy defending my right to examine and discuss the intersection of race and schooling. I strive also to carefully illustrate the importance of that investigation while simultaneously pointing out the racism of my potential detractors. Striking this peculiar balance of language and tone, while ensuring that I continue to convey my personal and deep feelings of pride, authenticity, and integrity—chapter after chapter—is both a litmus test and a goal.

WRITING IN DIFFICULT TIMES

This second book, *More Courageous Conversations About Race,* was a much harder project for me to complete because I wrote it in what I would define as a far more racially pernicious time. As you will see over the course of this book, while the election of the nation's first president of color seemed to signal a positive moment in the history of U.S. race relations, his term in office has nevertheless left educators of today confronting racial issues more compatible with the era of segregation and outright oppression. As an author, I have struggled long and hard with the content and tone of this book to avoid being labeled angry or negative about race relations in the United States. At the heart of this struggle was the challenge I faced of expressing, in an explicit and unapologetic way, my opinion on this matter—which is that our nation has taken, as far as I am concerned, the figurative two steps forward and three steps back.

Of course, all of this has taken place amid a deafening silence about the issue of race itself. Who would have thought, for example, that education officials would ever find themselves in a quandary over whether their students should or should not be allowed to watch a televised message delivered by the president of the United States about the importance of studying hard and staying in school? And yet, when arrangements were made so that classrooms across the nation could tune in via the White House website to the president's speech at an Arlington, Virginia, high school, there was an enormous outcry from conservative pundits, Republican leaders, and White parents, even in some of the most equity-focused school districts. The gist of the complaint was that Obama was attempting to indoctrinate students with his political—read socialist—viewpoints. I do not believe, however, that such resistance to the president and his message was just politics, when other recent presidents—of both political parties but only one color—have addressed the nation's school-age children without a similar furor.

Bigotry aside, the mere fact that some of the nation's lowest-performing students, Black males, were prevented from this most important moment in education because of adult cowardice is one of several realities that fueled me to press on and complete this book. Those students especially desperately needed to absorb the president's message and see themselves reflected in his image in the highest position of authority in the land.

In the past three years, corresponding with the bulk of Barack Obama's first term as president, this nation has fallen backward with regard to race relations and its willingness and ability to challenge racism. Some people simply cannot believe a Black man is president and refuse to accept his worthiness, intelligence, or leadership. Former President Jimmy Carter was right on point when he spoke out against this type of racist resistance in a television interview on September 15, 2009. According to Carter:

> When a radical fringe element of demonstrators and others begin to attack the president of the United States as an animal or as a reincarnation of Adolf Hitler or when they wave signs in the air that said we should have buried Obama with Kennedy, those kinds of things are beyond the bounds. I think people who are guilty of that kind of personal attack against Obama have been influenced to a major degree by a belief that he should not be president because he happens to be African American. It's a racist attitude . . . based on the fact that he is a black man.[2]

That the White House issued a statement disagreeing with Carter shortly after his interview was not surprising, given the first president of color's inability or strategic unwillingness to address race head-on, much less to call out racism and survive in his leadership. Unfortunately, President Obama's statement served only to exacerbate the national confusion around the topic. Conversely, the statement offered by the African American leader of the Republican National Committee, Michael Steele, was not at all confusing. Steele rose in quick defense of his constituencies, many of whom were the subject of President Carter's conjectures about racism.

Equally confounding is the growing number of people in schools and society today who believe that we as a nation have somehow entered an era of post-racialism. That era, in their view, is highlighted by the election of our first Black president. It is further "colored" by his appointment of the first Brown American woman to the Supreme Court (Sonia Maria Sotomayor); by his selection of Eric Holder, another Black man, to be the nation's attorney general; and by his appointment of other officials of color to high positions of government authority.

Not surprisingly, however, despite this growing perception that both race and racism are behind us, hardly a day goes by in which some politician, media pundit, or everyday American fails to express publicly some racially insensitive remark that other supposedly more racially conscious citizens fail to point out or oppose. The outcome of this scenario is a racially dangerous one in which the Obamas, our nation's First Family, appear to lead gracefully while suffering unprecedented personal attacks and in which increasing numbers of onlookers interpret the bigoted encroachments against them as nonracist in character. Worse still, those onlookers typically characterize the civil deportment of the Obamas as appropriate and somehow "normal."

I realize that it would be political suicide for the President, Justice Sotomayor, Attorney General Holder, and others of color in such high positions to launch into a lesson on racism at every turn or slight as a means of defending themselves, their perspectives, or their actions in office or of challenging the characters, perspectives, or actions of others. Nevertheless, to move the Courageous Conversations approach from theory to practice, racial equity leaders must be aware of, acknowledge, and address the racism displayed by those otherwise well-meaning people who incorrectly posit that we in this nation have evolved beyond our own individual and collective racial struggles in the span of a single national election cycle.

No matter how one perceives or spins what is occurring in our nation today, the election of Barack Obama clearly represents the most racially significant event in modern times. Regardless of how one may feel about President Obama's politics or party affiliation, however, his era as leader of the free world presents either our nation's greatest opportunity or simply a missed opportunity to deepen its educators' understanding of and ability to talk about race. For that reason, this book will delve into the Obama presidency multiple times.

■ ■ ■

In the minds of our children, the inability of our nation's educators to recognize and grab hold of the increased opportunities to engage in courageous conversations about race further cements the idea that racism no longer represents a battle that they will need knowledge and skills to wage. Often, those who believe that we in this country have overcome our racial struggles cite the success of Barack Obama (or of me, for that matter) as evidence enough that we are living in a brave, new, racially just society and world. The vast difference in perspective among various racial groups regarding our so-called national post-racialism is cause for discussion—one that I will join in a later chapter.

For now, as I set you, the readers of this book, off on a course of moving Courageous Conversations from theory to practice, let it suffice to say that I believe nothing is more dangerous, especially for children of color, than to be taught that racism no longer exists. This is especially dangerous when, in fact, racism continues to be the most devastating factor contributing to the inability of those same children to achieve at their highest levels.

Now I certainly do not wish to be perceived as overlooking or downplaying the many and obvious advancements that have taken place with regard to race relations in America in recent years. However, the modicum of racial progress realized is, to me, largely a nuanced one. It is also one that has given rise to newfound racial conflicts as well the ugly specter of the nation's unfortunate racial history. Both still mar our overall progress, and those of us who are progressive educators and racial equity leaders may be fooling ourselves by asserting that the United States is much further along in addressing either than it actually is.

So much of the school reform literature, theory, and corresponding frameworks have focused on *how* to change our schools. Yet when focusing on how to achieve racial equity, educational researchers, theorists, policymakers, and practitioners have, for the most part, limited themselves to describing the pathologies of an ill-functioning system and offering strategies for surmounting them rather than getting at the root causes of those challenges.

In some ways, the *Courageous Conversations* field guide followed this formula. In it, my coauthor Curtis Linton and I suggested that the nation's public education system, suffering as it does from institutional racism, plays an instrumental role in preserving and perpetuating racial achievement disparities. We offered a compelling case for the argument that the American school system was designed, from the very beginning, to exclude, then marginalize, and then under-educate children of color while simultaneously mis-educating *all* children of *all* races. Contemporary data, we contended, indicates that this design has proved itself effective and has achieved its intended results.

Throughout the book you now hold in your hands, I will share multiple sources of contemporary data that reveal and reconfirm my point that our current school system fails to meet the needs of the growing number of students of color within it. Our educators' collective failure to do little more than recognize this condition—and specifically their refusal to directly speak to the plight of Black, Brown, and American Indian students, much less work toward discovering solutions to their challenges—is the most compelling evidence of systemic racism. Ironically, as those educators fail under-served student of color populations at escalating rates, historically higher-performing White students increasingly are also achieving at lower levels. Later in this book, I will review current and critical achievement data that substantiate my claims that the racial disparities in education outcomes persist in all types of school systems.

BUILDING ON THE FIELD GUIDE

To counteract the fundamental intentions of the early framers, the first *Courageous Conversations* book focused on assisting educators of all colors to develop their ability and capacity simply to begin talking about racial matters. The result of this interracial discourse, my coauthor and I postulated, would be a more racially conscious, and thus racially knowledgeable, cadre of teaching professionals. Such teachers, we asserted, could, in turn, have a greater impact on the educational outcomes of the growing populations of children of color in America. They could also influence and elevate the social and intellectual development of White American students.

Although the specifics of our philosophy and of the protocols described in the field guide may be unique to the field, perhaps even groundbreaking, clearly our conjecture that race matters and that we educators need to talk about race are not revolutionary. Rather, we believe that facilitating open and honest dialogue among educators, students, and their families about the impact of race and racism on learning and teaching, although often controversial, is nothing short of . . . *courageous!*

A few years after the *Courageous Conversations* field guide was published, I felt the gravitational pull of the racial equity field drawing me toward the possibility of offering yet another "here-is-the-problem-and-here's-how-to-fix-it" book. Strong was my resistance to that pull, however. Although I knew that such a book would sell, I was also painfully aware that books alone cannot instigate deep, sustainable, systemic transformation in a system that is well-programmed to destroy the intellectual curiosity, cultural foundations, and social imagination of children of color and, by extension, their White counterparts.

As much as I wanted to answer the call to provide advanced-level support to educators on the front lines of the racial equity leadership battle, I was at a loss to find a contemporary and embraceable way to address what I, and my great teacher mentors who had journeyed on this path before me, believe to be the real problems of schooling in this country since its inception.

Until now.

■   ■   ■

Each chapter in this book, like those in the preceding volume, provides you, my readers, with a number of opportunities for reflection. Some chapters also present challenging prompts to help you personalize the themes discussed within them and apply the research outlined in each to your own work. The examination and explanation of the multiple theories, tools, and perspectives in this book are deeper and much more encompassing than those presented in the field guide. This is because my goal in these pages is to engage you in narratives that compel you to synthesize your knowledge and transform it into direct and measurable action. In this way, we can together close the professional "knowing-doing" gap in education.

Before writing this book, I spent several months reflecting on the tremendous work that leaders in the field of racial equity have been and are doing in schools and other settings around the country. But rather than provide mere racial autobiographies detailing how other educators arrived at deeper understandings of the impact of race in their personal, professional, and organizational lives, I wanted to showcase some unique efforts to implement courageous racial equity leadership. Thus, I conclude each of this book's chapters with a section titled "Voices From the Inside," written by education leaders who "walk the walk" and "talk the talk" of racial equity work. These first-person vignettes detail the real-life efforts of those who daily face race-relations challenges in their classrooms, schools, and districts. They show how the authors engage in thoughtful and effective racial equity leadership practices with passion and unyielding persistence. They also provide concrete pathways to guide you in challenging systemic racism, uncovering racial landmines and barriers to success for under-served children of color, and offering hope for the achievement of racial equity in all schools for all students. Last, they share, I believe, the very perspectives that can enable you to move the Courageous Conversations approach from theory to practice with greater precision—and yes, speed.

That said, I do not intend in this book to restate the narrative of race and racism in public education that Curtis Linton and I offered in our first book. Rather, I will assume that you have examined that earlier work and have reached the point at which you can effectively translate into practice the theories it advocated. This second book will focus on demonstrating how you can use the Courageous Conversations Protocol to transform your school leadership, learning, and teaching as well as your engagement with families and communities of color.

This book will also provide you with a candid view of racially unjust schooling via a number of well-constructed counternarratives documenting the work of my organization, PEG, in school systems across the country for the last 15 years. These counternarratives detail some of the "monumental moments" in public education, incidents that will facilitate a deep understanding of the tangible factors that contribute to the academic failure of students of color but also highlight the ways in which our educational system continues to advantage White, middle-class, monolingual children. They further reveal how that same system also advantages those who are willing and able to embrace the cultural beliefs, behaviors, and perspectives of the White dominant group.

A hallmark distinction between the field guide and this book is that the earlier work is primarily descriptive and theoretical, while the book you now hold in your hands (or are viewing on your electronic reading device) focuses on implementation. This second book is, in effect, a response to the first book's call to action. Its objectives, thus, are twofold: to help White educators move beyond guilt and rhetoric to a place of purposeful action and to support educators of color in finding the courage and language to name the individual and systemic racism around them, accept the challenge to speak their truth, and feel empowered to hold the system accountable for providing quality education for *all* children.

Curtis Linton and I began the *Courageous Conversations* field guide with a question posed in some form or fashion by the late Asa G. Hilliard III, the late scholar of educational psychology and African history, to each and every group of educators he encountered. That question: Do we—teachers, administrators, parents, and other education stakeholders—have the *will* to educate *all* children? Linton and I challenged our readers to consider Hilliard's question before presenting them with the assemblage of histories, narratives, frameworks, and strategies that we believed might bring urgent and lasting care and repair to our education system. For some, this challenge alone was effective. As proponents of racial equity, those leaders are today seeing remarkable results in their districts, schools, or classrooms. For the lion's share of our early readers, however, such noteworthy successes have not yet been realized. This book, I believe, presents the "missing link"—it calls out the specific situations and circumstances that will benefit from skillfulness in courageous conversations about race, and it challenges racial equity leaders to bridge understood theory with bold and courageous practices.

As I was writing this book, I found myself facing an enormous dilemma. On one hand, many of the readers of the field guide told me that they wanted Book Number Two to present another, albeit more advanced strategy to help them move the Courageous Conversations approach from theory to practice. Others wanted some "feel-good words" about what they were already doing. Still others indicated that racial autobiographical narratives, with complementing exercises and prompts, would be helpful. Thus, it became increasingly clear to me that this book would have to be remarkably different; that it would have to challenge the "willing" to reconsider whether they are indeed *truly willing* to do whatever is necessary to educate *all* children. But what, exactly, constitutes *will*?

In the field guide, Linton and I suggested that it involves passion, practice, and persistence—that is, it requires educators to care deeply about meeting the needs of underserved children of color. It further demands that we educators manifest our depth of concern through our commitment to a likewise deep and continuous engagement in new learning about ourselves and our craft over time. This charge resonates closely with Dr. Hilliard's timeless message and meaning. As he once wisely wrote:

> The knowledge and skills to educate all children already exist. Because we have lived in a historically oppressive society, educational issues tend to be framed as technical issues, which denies their political origin and meaning.... There are no pedagogical barriers to teaching and learning when willing people are

prepared and made available to children. If we embrace a will to excellence, we can deeply restructure education in ways that will enable teachers to release the full potential of all our children.[3]

Like Hilliard, I still believe that the dysfunction evident in our nation's education system today is less about a dearth of skills and knowledge and more about educational practitioners' and policymakers' will and purpose. Having thus reminded you, the readers of this second *Courageous Conversations* volume, of this underpinning philosophy—basic yet difficult though it may be to embody in mind and deed—I feel compelled to reiterate this book's central premise. Quite simply, it is that we, the self-proclaimed or perhaps even publicly acknowledged leaders for racial equity in education, have yet to demonstrate or determine our own individual or collective will to educate *all* children. (Indeed, our individual and collective plights and purposes to rectify the racial ills and injustices in our educational systems are fraught with conditions and self-imposed detours.)

For most of us, whether our work is in public or private schools, preK–12 or higher education, the first step in moving Courageous Conversations from theory to practice is not to determine what we should do next, but rather to ask ourselves: Why haven't we yet done what we already know we need to do? Too often, the need to preserve adult employment trumps the need to provide effective schooling of children. Protecting the adults in our nation's schools continues to be more important than serving our children. The lack of courage on the part of some educators simply to *speak truth to power* locks all educators in a holding pattern, in which we fail to embrace and amplify existing best practices.

Our cowardice also causes us to fall woefully short in discovering and developing essential, innovative strategies for achieving equity. The resulting inadequate habits of mind and work, among even the most racially conscious of educators, result in our tiptoeing around the racist philosophies, policies, programs, practices, and (especially) feelings of our most racist colleagues while trampling on the spirit, souls, and thus, the future possibilities for success, of our most needy children.

■ ■ ■

I believe that education is the fundamental method of social progress and reform . . . Education is a regulation of the process of coming to share in the social consciousness; and that the adjustment of individual activity on the basis of this social consciousness is the only sure method of social reconstruction.

—John Dewey[4]

Since John Dewey first presented his views about the purpose of education—still a centerpiece of conversation and coursework in our graduate schools of education today—lively debates about preserving the status quo versus creating and inventing new possibilities for future transformations in society have abounded. However, the rhetoric about how schools should help students to use their minds well so that they can address the social, political, economic, and cultural challenges of today and tomorrow—whether real or imagined—plays like a broken record, or rather, like a scratched CD.

Still, many educators, especially those of us in the academy, continue to feel good about the articles we submit cementing our progressive ideology because, somehow, putting our ideologies into practice is not as concrete as writing about them. Fortunately for them, but not for their students, those educators are rarely graded on the practicality of their ideals. Given our nation's currently challenged economy and its increasingly poorly funded schools, I do not doubt that many students would prefer that educators be held accountable for moving democratic education theories into practice so that schools can become the engines of social transformation that Dewey envisioned.

When I launched my teaching career at San José State University nearly a decade ago, I set out to challenge the status quo regarding how school leaders are developed. I insisted that my students, all of whom were hoping to earn a master's degree and an administrative credential at the conclusion of their 2-year academic pursuit, not only put racial equity theories into practice but also attain mastery of that practice. The only possible grade I offered them was 100 percent mastery—that is, no one got out of my classes with a passing grade until they got it right, in practice. Until then, they and their grades, in my view, were incomplete.

I took this admittedly strict approach because I believed then, and believe still, that the only real way to effect lasting transformation of what school leaders do in their classrooms, schools, and district or university offices is to enable them to imagine, see, touch, embrace, and practice the reforms to which they are introduced as pre-service teachers, via their own studies and apprenticeships, or as in-service professionals via staff development exercises. Certainly, nothing was more demoralizing to my students, as practitioners, or to me as their professor than when we discovered alumni of our program who had found their way back to the status quo, sometimes even becoming leaders of the status quo, a year or two after graduation. When that happened, I could only ask myself: What more can I do in my classroom or in my in-service work with our school and university partner-educators to ensure that what my students know about racial equity and what they are able to do to achieve systemic equity transformation has greater lasting power?

THE "MORE" IN MORE COURAGEOUS CONVERSATIONS

From the outset, this book assumes that you already know enough about what needs to be done. But rather than ask, "Why aren't you doing it?" and inundate you with data points and decontextualized exercises to convince you that our nation (the world, actually) has an equity problem, each chapter presents a contextualized discussion, followed by a series of "essential questions," concluding with a personal narrative or vignette ("Voices From the Inside"). The questions posed (i.e., "Why have I failed to act?" "What prevents me from internalizing the Four Agreements and Six Conditions?" and "What is my next and more significant level of courageous leadership?") are intended to summon readers from a place of earned praise for theoretical mastery of the Courageous Conversations basics to a more adaptive and transformative space, in which you can engage in effective racial equity practices in and beyond your own sphere of influence and control. Then, to ensure that readers clearly "see" the possibilities inherent in such transformational leadership, each chapter ends with a "practicing" racial equity leader's personal narrative providing details, in his or her own voice, about how they helped to move the Courageous Conversations program from theory to practice.

Many racial equity leaders and readers of the *Courageous Conversations* field guide have expressed the importance of becoming acquainted with exemplars or systems that have experienced notable and measurable success through application of the Courageous Conversations Protocol. To my knowledge or understanding, no racially diverse school district has, as yet, eliminated racial disparities completely. Several, however, have made extraordinary progress toward that end. Although a collection of narratives on the racial equity journeys of governing boards, superintendents, principals, and teachers should not be viewed as prescriptive, it can offer essential nourishment to sustain educators as they experience the productive disequilibrium that is sure to result from the strategic insubordination required to stare down institutional racism. Their shared "equity experiences" will invite you to take immediate action in your own workplace and guide you to define and assess your practice and its impact.

It is my hope that, together, the racial equity theory, essential questions, and narratives in this book can help to elevate you to a place of more effective equity practice, where you can attain more tangible and measurable results for *all* children in *all* classrooms. I also hope that the combined voices in this book, focused as all are on combating the problem of systemic racism, will provide you, as a co-leader in the battle for racial equity, with the language and knowledge base you need to uncover, examine, address, and eradicate barriers to academic success for under-served students of color.

I challenge you, however, to *put this book aside right now* if you have not read and internalized its precursor, *Courageous Conversations About Race: A Field Guide to Achieving Equity in Schools.* I do this because it seems to me a bit disingenuous, as well as unproductive, for anyone to assert that he or she has the will to put a theory into practice when he or she is unfamiliar with the very basics of that theory. I have been using the *Courageous Conversations* field guide as a primary text in my course at San José State and with PEG's preK–12 and higher education clients for more than 5 years, and I am continually amazed by the large numbers of students and clients who show up for my class or training without ever cracking the spine of that book. However, it is my steadfast view that the first text is effective only when readers carefully consider the narratives contained within it, complete the book's exercises, and apply its Protocol to their personal, professional, and organizational racial equity challenges.

Therefore, if you have studied and committed to the field guide's basic premise that a civil and productive way to dialogue about race is desperately needed, and you have attempted yourself to lead such dialogues with limited success, *MORE Courageous Conversations About Race* is definitely *your* book.

■ ■ ■

Chapter 2 will feel familiar as you are called on to refocus on your existing level of will and moral imperative and to authenticate your resolve for achieving racial equity in your institution. Recognizing the struggle many Courageous Conversation practitioners face, especially when summoned to *speak truth* to power in critical, perhaps job-threatening situations, this chapter also introduces the Personal Racial Equity Purpose (PREP) tool as a means of inviting you to develop, intensify, and fortify your courageous leadership pursuits.

In Chapter 3, I briefly reintroduce the components of the Courageous Conversations Protocol before exploring some of the common barriers school leaders encounter as they internalize and apply that Protocol's Four Agreements, Six Conditions, and specialized Compass to everyday, racialized situations in schools. These tools provide educators with a way *into* understanding how careless focus on other aspects of human diversity (i.e., economic status, gender, religion, or sexual orientation) can fortify racial inequity. This chapter examines these important intersections and explains how our society's multiple cultural layers can serve as both strengths and challenges when educators set out to facilitate the discovery of racial meaning for themselves and for others.

Critical race theorists point to gradualism and incremental change as the means by which American society addresses race. Thus, Chapter 4 explores what is different and what is the same in the racial landscape of our schools since the field guide was published in 2006. In this chapter, I point out how the language that racial equity leaders commonly embrace (language that includes terms such as *achievement gap*) and our ingrained omissions (such as excluding American Indians from data sampling and equity programming) serve as primary methods for perpetuating racism. I also squarely examine the nature and scope of the resistance that racial equity leaders face in their efforts to create schools that work for *all* children, and I explore strategies for engaging those who need alternative points of entry into racial equity work. Before exiting this discussion, I also specifically name and identify people who intentionally block racial equity efforts.

Chapter 5 presents an exploration of what seem to be some of the hottest topics in the racial equity arena—those issues and circumstances that urgently command educators' highest level of will, skill, knowledge, and capacity to effectively employ the Courageous Conversations Protocol. In this chapter, I submerge my readers, going into great specificity, in information about what is happening to a particularly challenged and challenging population in our nation's schools: Black males. This chapter also offers a critique of liberalism and exposes the devastating consequences that accompany the "soft bigotry" of well-meaning White educators who disproportionately refer students of color to highly restrictive environments such as special education or English-language development classes.

My racial equity friends and critics alike have suggested that my previous writings and fieldwork have focused too much on Black and White racial issues to the exclusion and perhaps detriment of other groups of color. Thus, Chapter 6 illustrates my efforts to deepen my understandings about how the processes of dispossessing Brown students of their language, American Indian students of their history, and most students of color of their culture have direct and negative impacts on their achievement. By mindfully engaging with these multiple and critical perspectives, I reached my own place of disequilibrium, and this chapter traces my personal and professional, yet still unfinished, racial equity journey. Thus, in the truest sense of moving Courageous Conversations from theory to practice, I also recognize in Chapter 6 my own personal struggle with respect to the Agreement: *Expect and accept nonclosure.*

In Chapter 7, I describe PEG's belief and purpose. I also detail its signature Systemic Racial Equity Framework as a compelling and comprehensive model that can lead educators away from engaging in the "random acts of equity" that are, I believe, the primary response to racial disparities in our schools and school systems. This framework demonstrates how important it is for preK–12 educators in our nation's schools to challenge racism in a way that is systemic, consistent, and coherent—in every classroom, every day, and all the time. It also underscores the importance for those educators to develop the critical competencies they need to effectively engage educators at institutions of higher education and independent schools, who also perpetuate (and in some ways exacerbate) racial inequality in public schools, as partners in their racial equity efforts.

Chapters 8, 9, and 10 examine critical components of the PEG Systemic Racial Equity Framework. These chapters go deeper into what leadership, learning and teaching, and family and community empowerment look and feel like in school systems that are focused on achieving racial equity. Together, the three chapters serve to fortify readers' understanding of how the Courageous Conversations Protocol can be used to strengthen school leaders' adaptive skills and help them construct equitable environments that produce educators who are proficient in culturally relevant teaching and effective in creating meaningful partnerships with parents of color.

My penultimate chapter, Chapter 11, is devoted entirely to a case study illuminating the educators and efforts of Eden Prairie Schools in suburban Minneapolis, a public school district that truly is pushing the boundaries of equity leadership and learning. In the 12th and final chapter, I offer my deepest and most current thinking on the overall state of our national efforts to transform systems of education into democratic and more equitable environments that intentionally work to eradicate racism. I do so because I realize that I am completing this second book during one of the most racially charged and fascinating times in U.S. history. As our nation stands poised to witness the possible re-election of the nation's first Black president, while confronting a rapid escalation of racial hate crimes and the skyrocketing dropout and incarceration rates of young men of color, I am compelled to reflect more intensely on what more and different I can and must do to raise the consciousness and embolden the actions of the growing forces of racial equity leaders across this country and in various places around the world. Given how fast and vehemently resistance has mounted to PEG's equity efforts in the various systems with which we partner, my final chapter is also where I comment on the up-to-the-moment characteristics and dynamics of the terrain on which I anticipate future racial equity leaders will more intentionally and boldly move *Courageous Conversations About Race* from theory to practice in their personal, professional, and organizational spheres of influence.

At times when I was growing up, my wise grandmother—we called her "Nana"— would tell me, "Glenn, when you know better, you should do better." I believe this was her way of telling me that good theory is useful only when put into effective practice. It is my hope that this book will provide you, my readers, and educators everywhere with a deeper understanding of how and where we all, as leaders for racial equity, can identify and apply the most effective protocols for talking about race. Thus, beyond its usefulness as a technical resource, I envision this book as an advanced sourcebook for courageous leaders who are poised to take bolder actions and insist on results that are more substantial.

I believe it can arm you with a sufficient supply of racial equity language, understanding, and leadership examples to allow you to challenge the status quo and instigate systemic transformation—that is, if *and only if* you truly have the *will!*

ESSENTIAL QUESTIONS

Now might be a good time for you to stop and consider what defines the racial culture and climate in the system where you work. Take a minute to answer the following Essential Questions:

1. How would you characterize the racial culture and climate of the region/district in which you are engaging in your Courageous Conversations work?

2. How have these racial culture and climate characteristics influenced and affected your racial equity leadership profile and/or style?

TWO

From Will and Passion to Purpose

Passion is not an event, but an energy; and it's an energy that exists in all of us, all the time. The question is not whether we have it but whether we access it, and how we channel it . . . In essence, passion can be the fuel that powers the ethical engine. An ethical life is usually also a passionate life.

—Dr. Derrick Bell[1]

S ix years after authoring the *Courageous Conversations* field guide, I still believe that *will*—fortified by passion, practice, and persistence—is the only fuel that can propel Courageous Conversations from theory to practice. But providing all students with legitimate opportunities to learn also requires purpose and an unfailing, unapologetic determination that is personal, local, and immediate. This is especially the case in the present era of shrinking resources, escalating greed, and diminishing compassion for children from all strata of society. Educators must possess something more than desire if they are to challenge, and challenge effectively, a public system of schooling that, contrary to popular opinion, was never designed to meet the needs of all.

Given the sheer number of in-service and pre-service hours education researchers, practitioners, and policymakers devote to a so-called examination of the problems of practice, why are schools still so radically segregated by race, class, and culture in this nation? Why have we not yet universally implemented a way to educate English language learners (ELL students) effectively? Why are teachers and administrators who lack the cultural agility and proficiency to meet the needs of Black, Brown, and American Indian students still hired and promoted in schools in which these populations predominate? Finally, why has our education system—one that clearly and unapologetically advantages White community interests—been allowed to continuously and smugly ignore or dismiss parents' and students' charges of racism while blaming those protestors of color for their inability to navigate these racially unjust environments effectively?

I have met countless educators over the years, many of whom have demonstrated the will to engage, sustain, and deepen the courageous conversations about race as long as the time, place, mood, and resources were just right. I have found, however, that the vast majority increasingly have faced a good deal more than their fair share of challenges. Their school budgets have been reduced or eliminated, and they often are confronted with both subtle and overt resistance from powerful, and typically White, constituencies.

In these fairly typical circumstances, only those who embrace and embody what I call a Personal Racial Equity Purpose (PREP) have demonstrated that they have the courage, determination, and fortitude to hold out a lifeline to our children, no matter what, and rescue them from a system designed and developed to destroy them. Armed with their PREPs and focused on creating a refuge from racism, such courageous school leaders work tirelessly to rewrite policy, institute rigorous and innovative programming, and engage in culturally relevant instructional practices that ensure success for *all* children and especially our Black, Brown, and American Indian males.

COURAGE REQUIRES PERSONAL PURPOSE

In November 1995, I was contracted by the California School Leadership Academy (CSLA) to co-facilitate, with filmmaker and educator Lee Mun Wah, a 3-day racial and cultural competency training in San Francisco for that organization's statewide directors. CSLA was then a professional learning and development agency that trained and certified school leaders to be decision makers, change agents, and instructional leaders by implementing new leadership and instructional theories and strategies. Although based in California, CSLA's directors and contracted trainers (like me) conducted workshops and shared materials nationwide. I was already known to several of these directors for launching The Transitions Project, an initiative aimed at linking the University of California and California State University systems with restructuring high schools to ensure greater racial equity in college admissions.

During the course of the project, I worked closely with the director of CSLA's San Diego office, Dr. Elaina Hershowitz, for several months. I soon developed a close friendship with Elaina and members of her family. Elaina struggled initially, however, to view me in the capacity of a racial equity trainer. But given her clear demonstration of leadership in what ultimately became a profound and pioneering movement to propel racial equity from theory to practice, I naturally called on Elaina for guidance in writing this book.

Now retired for several years and greatly disappointed by a system she deemed unwilling to change, Elaina took a few moments to offer the following reflections on her early equity journey and accomplishment to the readers of *More Courageous Conversations About Race.*

> I met Glenn [Singleton] at a conference in San Francisco in the summer of 1994. He and I happened to be sitting at the same table. That meeting was the beginning of a deep, complex, close, and sometimes turbulent relationship.

During the day, Glenn and I talked on and off. When the conference ended, I mentioned to him that if there was anything I could do for him in San Diego, I'd be happy to help. He handed me his business card, and we said our farewells. I was quite sure we'd never see each other again.

I received a call from Glenn several days later. Figuring that I knew most of the school administrators in my region, he asked if I would introduce him to five or six high school principals in the San Diego area. I assured him I would, wrote down their names, and told him that I'd call them within the next day or so to tell them to expect a call or visit from him. Glenn responded that this was not what he needed; he needed me to make the actual appointments and then go with him to the meetings with each principal. Although I thought his request to be the height of chutzpah, I wound up saying yes. That heralded the beginning of a close and loving friendship that continues to this day.

During the few days that Glenn and I spent visiting the identified principals, I had the opportunity to listen to him present his proposal for a new way to evaluate high school students—a way that didn't rely exclusively on grades, seat time, Carnegie units, and colleges admissions test scores. Glenn impressed each of the principals, but he impressed none more than me. At the end of his stay, I offered him a contract to work with me in training all of the school leadership teams in San Diego, which has the largest secondary school district in California.

Over the next year, Glenn and I worked together for at least 3 days a month. My husband, our two grown sons, and I insisted that Glenn stay with us at our home, where, over the next 12 months, we enjoyed meals together and spent many hours in the evening talking. And we talked about everything! No topic was off limits. Glenn soon became like a member of our family.

The following summer, all CSLA directors were told to set aside 3 days for antiracism training. I was not at all happy about having to attend. Being a New York-raised, Jewish liberal, with two best friends who were Black, I felt the 3 days were going to be a complete waste of my time. On the first day, I walked into the training room and was surprised to see Glenn there. He was the antiracism trainer. I was stunned.

I asked him—"What do you know about racism?"—to which he replied: "Oh, I know a few things." He asked me to just join in and see how the day went and told me that we could talk in the evening.

In that first day of antiracism training, I focused on some fundamental areas such as the "racial nomenclature" of American social relations and theories of racial identity development. I also engaged the workshop participants in conversations about power, privilege, and Whiteness. I kicked off the day by offering, for the first time I'd ever done so publicly, a version of my life story as it has been affected by race. (This discussion marked the genesis of the Racial Autobiography Exercise that I have since introduced to thousands of educators as a means of developing authentic and trusting interracial relationships with colleagues and with students and their families.)

After the first day's work, I reached out to Elaina to gauge her reactions because I deeply cared about and trusted her critique of my work. What she told me then is exactly what she included in the following reflection that she crafted for this book:

By the end of the first day, I was confused and distressed. I learned that there were volumes of information that I just did not know about the situation of people of color in America, and that racism was alive and well in our country.

Elaina also confided that she simply was not ready to talk more about what she was feeling and thinking with me that evening. The next day's training session turned out to be even more difficult for her than the first, while the third day, in her view, was the most difficult.

During Day 2, I had the group watch Lee Mun Wah's video-documentary, "The Color of Fear." This moving story chronicles eight men's journeys into and through a difficult interracial dialogue about race. I was viewing the film for the very first time myself, and I too was riveted by the depth of emotional, moral, intellectual, and relational energy each of the men had expended to arrive at greater mutual understanding and collective meaning.

In one of several emotional scenes in the film, David, a White man living in a remote part of the state, struggles to believe that men of color still experience racism in present-day California. As he continues to question the validity of the other men's racial narratives—as well as to excuse, deny, and redefine their experiences—his own narrative offers concrete examples of the everyday racism the others had experienced. The film also focuses on an African American man named Victor, who eventually erupts into a profane indictment of racially unconscious White men. Victor proclaims that White men rob people of color not only of their artifacts but also of their dignity and souls.

By the film's end, many of the CSLA directors' eyes were red from crying. Some of the White directors expressed a high level of discomfort with the film, which I would later determine to be a manifestation of their resistance and lack of passion and purpose for exploring the topic the film and workshop addressed.

My friend Elaina, the self-proclaimed Jewish liberal, found herself vacillating between extraordinary pain and anger. To my dismay, but not surprise, she directed the latter, along with her feelings of betrayal, toward me. In her workshop evaluation, which she shared with her CSLA colleagues after viewing Mun Wah's film, Elaina said she felt betrayed because I had never previously revealed my racial autobiography to her, even though I had been working with her and staying in her home with her family almost every month for 2 years:

I realized [both from the film and Glenn's discussion] that I had been living in a fantasy world, believing that racism no longer existed in America, and that, if it did, it certainly did not exist in California! In contrast to what I believed, I learned that a majority of African American people were living a very different life experience than I imagined.

As we all left the training room on the last day, Glenn came up to me and asked when we were going to get together. I told him that I was very angry with him, and that I wasn't at all sure we could ever be friends again. I challenged him to explain how we could have spent so much time talking with each other without the topic of race or racism ever coming up. I wanted to know how, if we were so close, he could have managed to avoid that topic. I told him that I was very unhappy, depressed almost, about that and that I needed to rethink our relationship.

Over the next month, I talked with my family and with each of my Black friends about this. I struggled with the matter, wanting to know how I could miss the racism in front of my eyes. How could I have been so blind to it, and how could my friends allow me to remain that way?

I will return later to Elaina's story and to the pioneering racial equity work that she and I have since developed and offered to educators in San Diego and Imperial Counties. That work represents and illustrates a significant example of how an educational leader can collaborate to clarify and fortify her PREP as a way of moving Courageous Conversations from theory to practice. But first, I want to discuss what has happened in some of the other dozen or so counties throughout California where I have presented similar workshops.

In most instances, on reporting back to me after they had returned home, my CSLA participant-leaders described their experiences in the workshops as both profound and intensive. The vast majority indicated that they felt an immediate need to incorporate their learning into the central work of their respective school leadership centers, but they feared that they lacked the understanding, knowledge, skill, and capacity to do so. When I shared these expressed concerns with CSLA's statewide director, Karen Kearney, she responded promptly to her colleagues' calls for additional training and technical support around this critical work. So, together with my good friend and colleague Pam Noli, another self-proclaimed White liberal, and CSLA's Bay Area (San Francisco) center director (and also agency director) Franklin Campbell Jones, I went to work on recrafting the diversity module of CSLA's Foundations Program to make it more explicit about race and racism.

When the resulting new module, which eventually morphed into the Pacific Educational Group (PEG) Inc.'s signature training program, Beyond Diversity, was introduced, many CSLA directors, for a variety of reasons, found it difficult to offer it to educators in their regions. A few White directors never accepted the premise that race or racism affects student outcomes in schools. For them, addressing personal and institutional racism was not a critical aspect of learning and development for the school leaders under their supervision. By contrast, most directors of color, as well as several White directors, were genuinely committed to implementing programmatic reform that addresses racial equity in some way. This latter group, however, expressed concern and some anxiety over how the school leaders in their regions would respond to such efforts.

In California's Orange and Santa Clara Counties, the local CSLA directors moved quickly to embed Beyond Diversity into their Foundations Program so that those educators who saw the need for this type of professional development could obtain certification in that area. (Regrettably, both directors told me that they had to engage in constant battles with their county education offices to keep this work "out in front" of school leaders.) Despite a growing demand from the CSLA directors who had received Beyond Diversity certification to continue and deepen the racial equity work they had begun in their regions, when those educators retired, this type of work in all CSLA centers diminished. Eventually, the California state government ended funding to CSLA altogether, and thus the Beyond Diversity trainings virtually disappeared.

However, I learned a key lesson from my 10-year adventure with CSLA, one that has greatly influenced my beliefs and behaviors insofar as moving Courageous Conversations from theory to practice is concerned. That lesson was about understanding the importance of differentiation, not only as it pertains to the content of racial equity training but also as it pertains to the instructions provided for the implementation of such training in various regions.

DIFFERING APPROACHES TO DIVERSITY

For example, when Pam, Franklin, and I began our work on the CSLA diversity modules, our initial thinking was that we could roll out a standardized racial equity training in the exact same way across the state. That proved to be a grave mistake. Nonetheless, we began by assuming that educators working in the San Francisco Bay Area would enter into courageous conversations about race in a similar way and with similar tools and experiences to draw on as, say, educators from a more rural and less racially diverse area like Shasta County. This misjudgment revealed a major problem in our early theory-to-practice design. I have since realized that the workshop participants from these extraordinarily different regions needed to develop different banks of knowledge, skill, and capacity to lead effectively. Indeed, what I may have defined as resistance to this kind of work at the time may actually have been evidence of the need for more effective differentiation in the way that we provided access and opportunities for our participants to learn about race and become leaders for racial equity.

Over a decade later, my team at PEG and our trained affiliates in school districts across the country continue to use just one format, the (since greatly improved) Beyond Diversity seminar, to introduce the concepts and applications detailed in the *Courageous Conversations* field guide. That format still serves as the foundation for racial equity work in schools, but my team members are now trained to pay very close attention to how regional racial culture and climate can affect educators' will and ability to connect to theory. They also know how to differentiate training styles to accommodate such distinctions. Currently, each time we are called into a school district or region to introduce Courageous Conversations through our Beyond Diversity seminar, we carefully select to lead that training a team member who embodies the most compatible demeanor and disposition to address that district's participants, based on what we know about the culture and climate of our target audience and their community.

■　■　■

I want to return now to a closer investigation of how my early CSLA racial equity work unfolded in the San Diego/Imperial County region under the direction of my friend Elaina Hershowitz, as I believe it is both enlightening and instructive to the theory-to-practice goal of this book. To date, the San Diego area is where I have witnessed some of the most advanced, deepest, and longest-lasting regional racial equity transformation.

Beginning in 1996, San Diego's county, district, site, and classroom equity leaders engaged in professional learning that not only provided essential knowledge about the intersections of race, teaching, and learning but also permitted them to develop and share practices that they deemed effective in better meeting the needs of under-served student of color populations. The efforts of selected San Diego/Imperial County educators—who so passionately, skillfully, and tirelessly still work today at all levels to address systemic racism and to "re-culture" and restructure the way in which schooling is presented to *all* their students—have given me cause to celebrate on many occasions and levels. My work with Elaina, beyond helping me to recognize the importance of differentiation in my content and processes to adapt to various groups and locales, drove home for me the need to ensure that school leaders in areas where racial equity work is taking place have a personal stake or *purpose* in that work. It also confirmed my view that although it is the professional responsibility of *all* educators to ensure a high-quality, free, and appropriate education for *all* students, leaders working for racial equity must draw on a deeper purpose—one that is grounded in a strong moral conviction or imperative—if they are to be successful in that effort.

As I mentioned earlier, Elaina's initial introduction to racial equity work created a strong reaction in her heart and soul. At first, those feelings incapacitated her emotionally, to the point where she no longer desired to be friends with me, let alone partner with me in her critical work in San Diego. Yet, by doing work to clarify and fortify her own PREP, Elaina was able to move from hopelessness and despair to action and impact, as evidenced in her continuing narrative:

> Eventually, it all became so much clearer to me. No one talks about race because it's a very difficult conversation to have. Either people get angry—a typical response would be, "Sure, put the blame on White people"—or they deny the experiences Black people have as real, as in "I can't believe it!" or "You're just being sensitive and imagining things!" or any number of other reactions that make it the last conversation people of color want to have with White people, especially with their White friends. As one of my closest friends and colleagues, a Black woman, told me when I berated her for not starting a conversation with me about the racism she had experienced, "Elaina, I wouldn't have been able to take it if you didn't believe me."

If a White person who is to be the leader of a racial equity project needs to be convinced of the existence and permanence of racism, if that leader must be convinced that racism permeates and is embedded in the interactions and systems and institutional designs of virtually everyone and everything in our nation, then that leader should not be charged to get out in front of the "racially unconscious" masses. Lacking such understanding, leaders can never truly develop the essential and authentic types of interracial friendships and professional relationships needed to do this kind of work. Why? Because those leaders simply do not "get it"—that White people's disbelief about the lived racial experiences of people of color serves only to slow the progress of racial equity and weaken the bonds between the races.

Months later, after many talks with her family, friends of color, and colleagues, Elaina found her own essential place, as a human being first and as a school leader second, by mounting a fight to achieve racial equity in the schools and thus in society. As she concluded in her narrative:

> Glenn and I put our relationship back together a few months after the workshop ended. I decided that, with his help, I was going to devote the remaining years of my career to ensuring that conversations of the type he correctly calls "Courageous Conversations" would happen at the San Diego center every month among educators from throughout our county.

Boldly, Elaina decided for herself that no educator in her CSLA region would receive leadership certification without successfully completing my Beyond Diversity workshop. But she did not stop there. Jointly recognizing that a 2-day workshop was not nearly enough to make significant or lasting strides in the racial equity arena, Elaina and I created a series of advanced-level seminars for school administrators, teachers, and family and community members in the San Diego/Imperial County area. While she was establishing requirements for those seeking CSLA basic and advanced certification, she also often provided funding for the teachers and administrators in the two counties under her supervision who were not enrolled in CSLA programs so that they too could take the racial equity seminars and engage deeply in the kinds of actions the seminars prescribed. The resulting racial equity curriculum—the product of Elaina's PREP—was an extensive and intensive one. Those important efforts served as a launch pad for my later, nationally recognized work in the Sweetwater, Lemon Grove, and Grossmont school districts in the San Diego area, as well as in the Juvenile Court and Community Schools (JCCS) and in a number of other school districts throughout the state of California.

PURPOSE AT EVERY LEVEL

Some may argue that expecting all school leaders or even a majority of them to develop Elaina's level of PREP is unrealistic. I contend that not only *must* school leaders—be they superintendents, principals, teachers, or food services and transportation workers—be held accountable and evaluated on their efforts to achieve racial equity, but their PREP must be nurtured and developed within the essential organizational processes of each school district's continuous improvement program. Furthermore, if we are ever to truly improve the culture, climate, and results of schooling in the United States, districts must begin to prioritize and assess their potential leaders' PREP as a part of their hiring criteria. I believe we can identify characteristics and qualities—and seek them in beginning educators—that indicate they will, at the very least, embrace racial equity transformation rather than resist it. Moreover, given that most school districts already have a wealth of veteran educators who are gifted at *subverting* reform, why make the job more difficult by increasing their ranks with new hires?

Indeed, Elaina's PREP created the safe and supportive space for me and my team to begin developing a framework and curriculum for challenging systemic racism in the nation's schools. Even more important, her unfailing *will* to place this work in front of any educator who would listen and learn about it cultivated a crop of racial equity leaders who now work at all levels of the education system to ensure that the children whose lives they touch do not grow up with the same harmful racial beliefs and attitudes, and perhaps some new ones.

Another important lesson that I learned from my early work with Elaina in San Diego is that purpose and leadership capacity for racial equity work must be developed at the state, county, and district levels as well as at the site level if it is to survive and be sustained during times of extraordinary change, such as budget reductions, personnel transitions, or political backlash. Just 5 years after Elaina's retirement, too little evidence remains of her focused, systemic equity efforts in San Diego and Imperial Counties. When the state stepped in and cut the funding to CSLA, she needed the buy-in of her county superintendent, her immediate supervisor, and her peer managers to keep her programs viable. Lacking that, no matter how impressive Elaina's PREP and racial equity programming were, the work of the numerous teachers who attended Beyond Diversity—some of whom went on to lead larger scale work in their respective districts and many of whom spoke of remarkable improvements in their instruction and student achievement results for Black and Brown students in particular—has been abandoned. That is why my emphasis in this work has shifted away from "random acts of equity" (which I will also discuss later in greater detail) and toward systemic transformation.

ESSENTIAL QUESTIONS

These questions relate to your personal preparation for engaging in courageous conversations and the related work to bring racial equity to our schools.

1. The *Courageous Conversations* field guide introduces the reader to the importance of passion, practice, and persistence in leading for racial equity. What evidence suggests that you possess a requisite level of each to advance conversations about race in your personal and professional spheres of influence?

2. Chapter 2 explores a notion of racial equity purpose and posits that leaders will need to clarify and assert their own personal purpose in order to advance this work. What is your PREP, and what factors do you feel serve as the greatest threat to you not achieving your purpose?

Voices From the Inside: Macarre Traynham

I enter this conversation as a Black woman awakened—awakened about the events in my life that have led me to where I am today, personally and professionally, in this work. When I started, I didn't know what I didn't know, and I had no idea about the fire, desire, and will that *Courageous Conversations About Race* would spark within me.

I grew up talking about race. It was a common topic in my household. My grand-mother never missed an opportunity to remind my sisters and me about how impor-tant it was to take education seriously. We needed it, she said, to be better than our White counterparts, not as good as [they were], but better—if we were going to make it, that is. I understood my grandmother, but I didn't understand my grandmother. And although I attended an HBCU (historically Black college or university); filled my per-sonal library with books by Black authors; and engaged in fist pumping, fight-the-power conversations with friends and family, my own consciousness and perspicacity about race and White privilege was challenged and sparked when I started reading the *Courageous Conversations* field guide.

The work began for me in 2007, when I was sitting in a large banquet room with all the district's administrators, and we were together digesting the question: Why do Black and Brown students consistently fail in our district? It was the first time anyone had presented the district's data so clearly and pointedly, shining a light on our persistent failure with students of color. It was also the first time that race was identified as the glaring outlier without apology or fear. This approach was new to me, and I welcomed the method. Apparently, others in my district felt the same way because the Courageous Conversations approach, as a way to improve student achievement, was adopted.

The trainings began and so did my fascination with this work. I showed up to each training ready to tell my story and get things off my chest. Every time I participated, my learning and understanding expanded, and I became more empowered. The train-ings consistently provided me with food for thought. The program gave me permission to talk openly about race with White people and supplied me with ample discussion topics, no matter what the occasion. And yet, each time I left a training, I went back to my building and did nothing with the work until the next scheduled session.

I struggled to lead courageous conversations in my building, but I couldn't because I had not fully internalized the Courageous Conversations framework. I morally believed in antiracist leadership and that systemic racism was the most serious imped-iment to Black and Brown students' success, but I had not internalized the Courageous Conversations Protocol to the point that I could lead real change.

In my initial attempts to lead my E-Team, I had content overflowing—articles, vid-eos, books, and talking points—but I did not have the facilitation skills I thought I needed to reproduce the format and momentum that Glenn's team brought to train-ings. So I spent the majority of my time doing book and article studies with my team. The discussions were safe, with everybody at the table nodding their heads in agree-ment, allowing themselves to be preached to and allowing little if any disagreement or challenge to what was being said or shared. Meetings would end with everyone agreeing to engage more before the next meeting and no one actually doing so. We never once presented to the staff. I never prepared properly for our meetings, and no other members stepped forward in a desire to facilitate. The prevailing thought seemed to be that I, the Black lady, was probably the best to lead conversations about race, but attending the trainings together did allow us to further our conversations.

It was during the trainings that we would get excited again. We'd go deeper in our conversations. We'd try to plan our next steps—a kind of "where do we go from here" effort. We knew a couple of the Agreements and could place ourselves on the

Compass, but no one in our group could ever recite all Six Conditions at any one time. We never thought much about that, though; we focused our discussions on next steps and implementation. Each time we'd leave the training with a new commitment—one that would fall flat as soon as the next school day presented itself. So my work as a vice principal to move Courageous Conversations into practice was a failure.

In retrospect, I can see that my participation in the beginning was self-fulfilling and how that period of time illuminated my lack of commitment to the work. My failure to commit came from an unwillingness to devote time to fully reading the *Courageous Conversations* field guide. I read the first two chapters and then referred to the other chapters as needed. I couldn't write my own racial autobiography because, when I listened to the autobiographies of others, their memories of race seemed to have started young, they spoke of "in-your-face" situations and occurrences, and I just couldn't relate. I didn't recognize my own Whiteness, and probably wouldn't have done so if my principal at the time, a White woman, hadn't pointed it out to me. I also didn't know or fully understand the Six Conditions. My connection with the Courageous Conversations Protocol was all based on my experiences. My experiences had allowed me to connect from an emotional and moral place. There was a lot of hurt that had been tucked away.

My only outlet was with family and friends, people that looked like me. With them, I was allowed to go to that place and would find comfort, support, and alliance. But Courageous Conversations gave me permission to unpack those feelings, to put it all on the table with all people, not just those who shared my story. These were the reasons I embraced Courageous Conversations right from the beginning.

I have since come to realize that I could never fully immerse myself in Courageous Conversations if I didn't understand and internalize the Conditions, not just the Agreements and the Compass, but the Conditions because that is the piece that changes all conversations and truly makes them courageous. The Agreements and Compass feel natural to acquire and implement. They can also be applied without regard to the conversation's topic. My journey has taught me that the Compass and the Agreements are the "hows" of the conversation; they create the parameters by which we operationalize the conversations. The Conditions is the "what" of the conversations; they keep you focused so you can go deeper.

I fully began to internalize the Six Conditions when I understood that even as a Black woman, Condition 6 applied to me. From the moment my former boss said to me, "You grew up pretty White. You had both parents in the house, they were educated and owned their home, you lived in the suburbs, you went to predominately White schools...," Condition Six became clear to me. It also became my fascination. My Whiteness wasn't that I had both parents in the household or that they were educated or even that we owned our house—those are qualities all ethnic groups appreciate, model, and live out. That's not a "White thing." My realization of my Whiteness was understanding how my views and beliefs, my perspective, were all shaped and impacted through my immersion in White culture at school, in my neighborhood, and through my education.

Until my Whiteness was called out, I only attached that Condition to the dominant culture—that is, to White folks who needed to know how they perpetuated systematic racism. It never occurred to me that I too was a donor and beneficiary of that system. Conditions 1 and 2 were natural and easy to internalize. It took more time for me to digest the remaining four conditions.

Attending the 2011 Summit for Courageous Conversations in San Francisco, California, gave me the final dose of what I needed to move the framework from theory to practice because it gave me a clear view of my Whiteness and forced me to admit my true commitment. I was finally able to chart myself around the Compass and truly engage in processing my commitment, using the Conditions to address how I would tackle systemic racism in my position. What began as a superficial piece—of "here's how I will engage and what I will do because I was given this assignment to complete"—turned into deep-rooted beliefs about my responsibility, determination, and devotion to being a change agent.

I understood my Whiteness after watching a video and making huge assumptions about the people speaking. It was in that moment that I recognized my own Whiteness more clearly than ever before. I understood that for years I had written people off just because they didn't look and sound the way I needed them to. My Whiteness prevented me from giving people the benefit of the doubt because they showed up epitomizing certain stereotypes—from clothing to vernacular. I dismissed some people before they ever had a chance to show themselves. In that instant, I saw how I upheld systemic racism and knew that there was nothing more important than doing this work and becoming an antiracism leader.

Courageous Conversations About Race begins with a self-awakening, an awakening that is triggered through the internalization of the Six Conditions and the realization of how Whiteness shows up in each Condition for you. The work is the mastering of the Protocol. The Conditions, more specifically, engage, sustain, and deepen conversations about race and give direction. They create a space that is open to hearing how we internalize race and allows multiple perspectives, correction, and growth.

You can only move Courageous conversations from theory to practice once your eyes are open through consistent and persistent self-evaluation of your beliefs, values, assumptions, and whiteness. That's when you see everything differently and when nothing exists without examination. When the focus is on equity and antiracist leadership, deficiencies in reading, writing, graduation rates, student access, and achievement can and will be addressed. Until you are able to see how you perpetuate and benefit from systemic racism, you will continue to maintain and perpetuate a social construct that was created to circumvent our best instincts.

Macarre Traynham is a high school principal in the Portland (Oregon) Public Schools. She also serves as a representative on that district's Administrators of Color Steering Committee. She is Black American.

THREE

Revisiting the Courageous Conversations About Race Protocol

As human beings, our greatness lies not so much in being able to remake the world—that is the myth of the atomic age—as in being able to remake ourselves.

—Mahatma Gandhi

One spring afternoon in 1990, I was waiting in line to board a flight to Portland, Oregon, when a curious thought popped into my head. I realized, right then and there, that I had never—from the very first day I entered seventh grade at the predominantly White Park School in my hometown of Baltimore to that day in the airport—engaged in authentic dialogue about race with anyone who was not, like me, a person of color. Of course, the ideas that I had been turning over in my head had not yet quite congealed, but they were moving rapidly to the forefront of my consciousness.

I remember thinking at the time that my failure to be fully self-expressed in interracial conversations about race was the result of the powerful socialization I had received growing up a Black male in the United States. That socialization, which, to some extent, had buffered me from a number of the slights and onslaughts of racism, had also encouraged me to keep my mouth shut and my beliefs and perspectives about race private. This "stay silent on race" message had been pounded into my head not only by family and friends but also by educators, clergy, and employers—yet somehow, it never seemed to mesh with my own ideals or the ideals of a nation that preached mightily about freedom of expression, truth, justice, and the pursuit of happiness.

Perhaps I was predisposed to be racially sensitive and curious. Indeed, my personal educational journey led to the discovery of a way to navigate a topic that has caused wars, denied millions basic human dignity, closed doors of employment, and deprived innocent children of their inalienable right to learn. What has long been clear to me, however, is that this nation's collective (and my own individual) silence about matters racial is more than simply incongruent with our national values. It is also a challenge to our intellectual and social evolvement as human beings.

The Courageous Conversations Protocol, a tool for navigating the turbulent terrain of race and race relations as it relates to schooling, emerged from a very deep and personal place. I developed it because I believe that so many of us, people of all races and creeds, have suffered unnecessarily. We have missed too many opportunities to connect with or dispute that terrain and thereby experience true freedom. I developed it because for too long we have lacked a way to engage safely in dialogue about the contrasting perspectives that stem from our divergent racial experiences. The result: Instead of meaningful inter-action, peace, and truthfulness among the races, we have allowed the landmines of our existing and potential relationships to become "weapons of mass destruction" that can terminate friendships and other connections.

In the past, no matter how many times and ways I tried to facilitate in-depth and far-reaching dialogues about race with my White colleagues and friends, my good intentions to do so typically were met with accusations that I was being overly aggressive or delu-sional at best, or engaging in race-baiting and fear-mongering at worst. I cannot begin to count the number of White people who are no longer in my life because I attempted to discuss race with them in relation to education, politics, the arts, or sports. This is because in addition to the extraordinary number of "casualties" I can actually count, there is an unknown quantity: those Whites whom I am certain simply chose to avoid me after such an encounter rather than to let me know I had offended them or violated their "right" to not talk about race.

As time went on, I discovered more and more that Black folks had also learned how *not* to talk about race. On occasion, my Black friends and members of my own family would chastise me for even bringing up the topic. "Oh, there he goes again . . . young Malcolm X!" they would say, referencing me as a Black radical, racial separatist, or, oddly enough, as racist—simply because I refused to remain silent on some racial matter or the other in the way I had been taught.

Being so deeply misunderstood, and having such a profound desire to better under-stand this thing called race, I found it increasingly impossible to calm my curiosity or quiet my voice. If nothing more, I felt that discovering a way to address racial differences and similarities would liberate me and the many others who lacked a vocabulary and a process for humanely articulating the personal meanings surrounding our racial experi-ences. And that is why, working collaboratively with Pam Noli and Elaina Hershowitz, and driven by this thirst to defuse the power of race to divide, I developed the Courageous Conversations Protocol.

Perhaps I could have been clearer about the rationales and driving forces behind this Protocol in my first book, but I chose instead to focus on introducing the tool. Indeed, many educators who have attempted to implement Courageous Conversations have indicated that they struggled to gain proficiency with it simply because they could not grasp its intended purpose. For sure, the Protocol serves as a strategy for uncovering and examining the intersection of race and schooling. It is also a tool for negotiating the vestiges of racism in our nation's education policies, programs, and practices. Even more important, the key elements of the Courageous Conversations Protocol—the Four Agreements, Six Conditions, and the Compass—are essential if educators are to gain access to, and then articulate, their own personal beliefs and perspectives about race. It is important that all parties who engage in courageous conversations about race first understand why each of the Protocol's key elements exists. Then it is up to each participant to monitor continuously how those elements are playing out for themselves and others throughout the resulting dialogue.

Far from being a strategy that tells educators *what* to think, the Courageous Conversations Protocol is a technology that enables us to process personal racial meanings and thus deepen our understandings about how race influences our lives—and those of our students and their families—inside and outside of school. Because of the fluency I and others have gained by using the Courageous Conversations Protocol, we have arrived at this deep-seated, personal meaning. Still, some early critics of the *Courageous Conversations* field guide accused me of attempting to "brainwash" educators. They claimed that adopting and implementing the Courageous Conversations Protocol forced educators to believe that racism is the sole reason children of color struggle in school. Although I do believe that racism is the most devastating systemic factor contributing to the school performance of children of color (I believe racism diminishes the capacity of White children as well), it has been difficult for me to engage with such critics. Why? Because I do not believe they have even the basic tools they need to truly articulate what they believe about race, much less to truly listen to and authentically understand my perspectives on the topic.

■　■　■

In the field guide, Curtis Linton and I proposed that engaging, sustaining, and deepening educators' understandings and conversations about race must be at the center of our strategy for deinstitutionalizing racism and eliminating racial achievement disparities in schools. That is why when I first enter a new partnering district, the primary message I attempt to transmit to my audiences is that I do not know the extent to which race and racism affect student achievement in their schools. What I do know, I tell them, is that they and I will never be able to determine this impact if we do not begin to talk about race or if we allow ineffective "racial emergency" conversations to continue to be the norm.

My simple premise here is that we as educators need to *understand race* before we can begin to identify the racism in our systems of education. We must also be equipped to have meaningful *conversations about race* before we can understand it. Unfortunately, this theory remains a hotly contested one for many school leaders. Furthermore, it takes courage to challenge a culture in which race is off limits as a topic of discussion, or one in which race, as a topic, has been deemed irrelevant to the issue of racial disparities in education.

Thus, the act of moving Courageous Conversations from theory to practice begins with the establishment of an unshakeable personal belief that racism diminishes the academic potential and possibilities of *all* children. It continues with the defining of one's Personal Racial Equity Purpose or PREP. It concludes with individual educators making a commitment to memorize, internalize, and apply the Courageous Conversations Protocol, which enables them to uncover, examine, and address structural racism. It includes personal racial biases and institutional racial inequities whenever and wherever they appear.

I am often asked if it is essential that the Protocol be practiced exactly as it is presented. My response is always the same: absolutely. Each of the components of the Courageous Conversations Protocol must be fully understood, appropriately recalled, and employed to ensure that racial discourse among school leaders will lead to the desired transformation.

Over the years, I have watched school administrators, teachers, and graduate students—those who are both passionate and sincere in their quest to defeat racism—struggle to internalize and apply the Courageous Conversations Protocol in their daily practice. The Protocol is outlined carefully and comprehensively in Chapters 4 through 10 of the *Courageous Conversations* field guide. In this book, rather than offer a more detailed account of the Protocol, I will articulate the philosophy behind its core components: the Four Agreements, Six Conditions, and the Compass. It is important that all parties who engage in courageous conversations about race first understand why each of the Agreements exists. Then it is up to each participant to monitor how each is playing out for themselves and others continuously throughout the resulting dialogue. I will then revisit the fundamental aspects of the Conditions and illuminate some of the stumbling blocks educators have informed me that they encountered in their efforts to operationalize the Courageous Conversations Protocol in its entirety. I hope that, by going into such depth, school leaders who wish and need to apply the Protocol will better understand why it was developed in the first place.

GETTING BEHIND THE PROTOCOL'S AGREEMENTS, CONDITIONS, AND COMPASS

The Four Agreements

The Four Agreements of the Courageous Conversations Protocol provide a means of setting the stage for safer and more deeply transformative interracial conversations about race. They should not, however, be viewed as rules to be enforced; rather, they serve as markers to be embraced by educators as they strive to engage in courageous conversations about race. You will also note that the Agreements are neither sequential nor ordered. This is because they are, and purposely are intended to be, interconnected and overlapping.

OK, here's how it goes: When you *stay engaged* in conversations about race, you are not only physically active in the discussion but also drawing fully on your intellectual, moral, and emotional being. Given the "heat" that often accompanies race talk, offering your whole self to that conversation heightens the likelihood that you will become uneasy or uncomfortable. When you *experience discomfort* in your racial discourse, however, it is

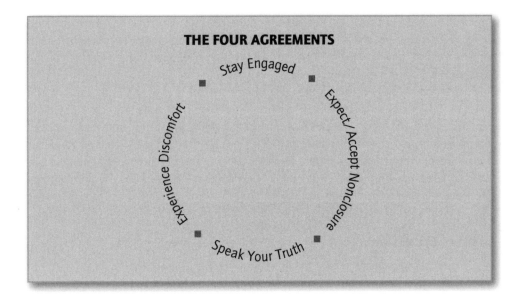

normal to shut down—yet that is *precisely* the time when you must remind yourself to stay engaged!

That is also when you must think to yourself: What exactly is making me so uncomfortable? Is it my own thoughts or the expressions of another? In addition, it is when the Agreements challenge you—a teacher, administrator, student, or parent—to *speak your truth*. The decision to talk or *not* to talk about how racial matters affect each of us spiritually, emotionally, morally, and intellectually, in both conscious and unconscious ways, is what I believe lies at the heart of the quest to achieve racial equity in our schools.

Last but also important, given the multitude of racial issues that surface in our commonplace schooling philosophies, policies, programs, and practices, the Courageous Conversations Protocol invites educators to *expect/accept nonclosure*. For many classroom teachers, this is the most difficult Agreement, as they are looking for an immediate and precise cure to the challenge of successfully educating students of all racial groups.

So what is the rationale behind the Four Agreements? Educators often find themselves in the middle of conversations about race without ever planning to go there. However, given the heightened focus on race spurred initially by the mandates of No Child Left Behind (NCLB) and more recently, Race to the Top, and their insistence on disaggregate data reporting, school leaders have found the topic virtually impossible to escape. Unfortunately, the demands placed on educators to negotiate race in their classrooms, boardrooms, and professional learning spaces do not come with permission to talk about race, nor are the norms for effectively managing the challenging terrain of racial discourse explicit or easily accessible.

For some educators, the racial disaggregation of student achievement data prompts feelings of discomfort, triggering a deafening silence that makes engagement on the issue challenging. For others, such data merely uncover racial truths that are obvious to them but not well received by their colleagues, causing them to feel the need to defend themselves. Still others believe that talking about racial disparities in achievement is a waste of time, prompting them to sit silent on the sidelines of the discussion.

Each of these responses, however, calls out for educators to thoughtfully and expertly practice the Four Agreements if they wish to truly transform a system in which academic success is predictable by race into one of success for all students regardless of race. The practice of introducing the Agreements before commencing all professional development learning exercises, regardless of their intended content, and of pausing to point out when educators veer away from these Agreements, helps educators internalize this foundational aspect of the Courageous Conversations Protocol.

The Six Conditions

As a White woman deeply committed to interrupting racial disparities in public education, I often found myself focused on external, technical solutions (such as changing discipline policies, bell schedules, professional development planning, etc.) to address this essential issue. However, it wasn't until I went through the painful experience of deeply confronting how my Whiteness (e.g., guilt, shame, technical solutions, linear thinking, and, most importantly, the prioritization of my comfort over the comfort of the most marginalized children in our school) was perpetuating the racism I was deeply committed to interrupting, that I was able to be deeply effective as an educator. My entire lens transformed. Rather than hide my Whiteness, I was more passionately committed to examining it within (and ideally modeling it for others to encourage their own exploration) in order to interrupt my own thinking that perpetuated the oppression of Black and Brown children so that others could build consciousness and confidence to do the same. It was then that I turned to the Six Conditions of Courageous Conversations to guide my personal and professional development. It was then that I, and consequently our community, really started to transform.

—Maureen Benson, former principal,
Oakland (California) Unified School District

Although most of my students at San José State University and many of the district educators who partner with my Pacific Educational Group (PEG) can boast of knowing, understanding, and practicing the Four Agreements, it is less likely that they can boast a similar relationship to the Six Conditions. The question of why the Courageous Conversations Protocol's Six Conditions pose such a tremendous problem, in theory as well as practice, for educators who otherwise express tremendous desire to engage in deeper racial discourse is one that I pondered long and hard in writing this second book. That strenuous review has led me back to my initial conclusion: A conversation about race fails to be courageous if all six Conditions are not satisfied.

THE SIX CONDITIONS

1. Getting Personal, Right Here and Right Now

2. Keeping the Spotlight on Race

3. Engaging Multiple Racial Perspectives

4. Keeping Us All at the Table

5. What Do You Mean by Race?

6. Let's Talk About Whiteness

From *Courageous Conversations About Race: A Field Guide for Achieving Equity in Schools*, by Glenn Singleton and Curtis Linton, 2006, Thousand Oaks, CA: Corwin.

In the *Courageous Conversations* field guide, I stressed the importance of understanding the scope and sequence of the Six Conditions. I devoted a chapter to each Condition because I believe that each lies at the heart and soul of how to navigate the conversations from inception to fruition. In this book, in the following discussion, I reiterate my position that the logical starting point for all such racial discourse is understanding and defining oneself as a racial being. I also repeat the first book's assertion that any "race talk" that does not touch on the issue of Whiteness and racial power is an incomplete one.

Unlike the Four Agreements, the Six Conditions follow a logical order. They must be learned, practiced, and applied in sequence. However, when uncovering, examining, or addressing an issue, event, or circumstance involving some racial aspect or another, you simply cannot advance, one by one, through the Conditions and then rest. Rather, you must learn to cycle continuously through the Conditions, each time using your newly acquired meaning and understandings about race to develop even deeper meanings, even broader understandings, and even more appropriate solutions to the challenges that arise.

That being said, I want to begin this deeper exploration of the Six Conditions with some exercises. How you "do" on these exercises should not be viewed as a grade or rating of your Courageous Conversations proficiency. Rather, it should inform you as to whether you should proceed in your reading and use of this book or if you need to revisit all or selected chapters of the *Courageous Conversations* field guide to "get up to speed" on the Courageous Conversations Protocol.

My point here is that if you do not have a firm grasp of the Six Conditions, it is highly unlikely that you will be successful in applying them to the racial challenges present in your school system. Conversely, if your responses to the exercises reveal a deep personal understanding of all Six Conditions, you are indeed prepared to take on the topics and engage with the narratives presented here in *MORE Courageous Conversations About Race.*

LEVEL 1 PROTOCOL EXERCISE: MEMORIZATION

On six separate sheets of paper, write the heading, "Courageous Conversations Condition" and a number, 1 through 6, on the top of each page. Next, without consulting any references, write out the definition of each Condition using language that closely matches that provided in my text.

LEVEL II PROTOCOL EXERCISE: INTERNALIZATION

On each of the numbered pages, beneath your rendering of the "textbook" definition of the Six Conditions, provide an explanation of what each Condition means *in your own words*. Also explain the significance of each in advancing courageous conversations about race.

LEVEL III PROTOCOL EXERCISE: APPLICATION

Think of an occasion when you have engaged the Courageous Conversations Protocol. At the bottom of each page, explain how you applied each Condition to navigate into and through that conversation.

I am aware of the obvious and transformative process of enlightenment that has occurred for members of my staff, my students, and the school leaders who have participated in my Courageous Conversations workshops. I am deeply gratified when they advance from the seemingly compliant act of memorizing the Conditions to a deeper commitment to internalizing and then applying them to everyday racialized circumstances in their personal and professional spheres of influence. Not only do these newly courageous conversationalists express an awesome sense of efficacy in addressing race and racism but those who "live" the Conditions in their daily professional and personal lives have also demonstrated an impressive confidence and competence in leading themselves and others from complex racial meanings toward antiracist educational solutions.

I cannot overstate the importance of school leaders being able to use the Six Conditions expertly as guides for navigating the difficult American racial terrain. I once believed that merely mentioning the word *race* in a multiracial setting would create hysteria far beyond my ability to remain present, much less engaged, in the conversation. Indeed, school leaders who are inclined to engage in such discussions often discover that some of their colleagues simply do not have the capacity to consider how race affects their beliefs and behaviors related to their teaching and their students' learning. In those circumstances, a very slow-paced, careful, and methodical progression through the material on the Six Conditions is warranted. Convincing such race-shy educators to capture in writing the very first and most recent instances in which race entered their thinking or actions (events that I refer to as racial autobiography "bookends") may seem an overwhelming task, and their trying moments of struggle should not be minimized. Ultimately, those who do not first personalize race or discover how to focus their thinking on the impact of race in their lives will never be able to formulate and espouse their own racial beliefs and perspectives, nor will they ever fully comprehend the ways that their behaviors perpetuate racism. Yet, once they have committed to take that journey toward discovery of their own personal racism—the racism within—the hardest and most courageous work truly begins.

In the next few sections, I will invite you to venture further in mastering the three tiers of the Six Conditions—*Engaging, Sustaining,* and *Deepening*—at the level of application. Of course, to apply the Conditions effectively, clearly you must understand and internalize them. But this vision of educators as having routine and normative interracial conversations about race is one that has the power to positively (and perhaps, radically?) transform operational and instructional practices as well as to transform school and district organizational cultures and climates. It requires only that you recognize the predictable challenges that line the path toward your ultimate destination, which is improved achievement for *all* students.

■ ■ ■

The first tier, that of *engaging* in courageous conversations, relates to the first and second Conditions. It begins with your individual willingness to discover your own personal, local, and immediate racial meaning. For many, this involves the writing of a racial autobiography. Your racial autobiography, however, is but the first step in a challenging yet clarifying odyssey that opens up the dialogue among family, friends, and colleagues. Too often this process, which culminates with educators sharing their narratives in site-level teams or district office departments, is the end of their formal discovery of how race affects their everyday life experiences and perspectives.

It is essential that you view your own racial autobiography not as an event but rather as a *process.* You must make public updates to your autobiography frequently, until such time that you no longer feel the pressure to function in a racially unconscious or colorblind manner. As race becomes, for you, one of the permanent lenses through which you view and understand the world, you can begin to incorporate the many other lenses, such as those of diversity, including class, gender, religion, and sexual orientation, into your analysis of events and circumstances taking shape in school. With race permanently "on the table," understanding how race interacts, intersects, or overlays the other dimensions of our being becomes critical. Later in this chapter, I will expand on this phenomenon, which I call *cultural layering.*

A focus on the second tier of *sustaining* courageous conversations about race, which involves Conditions 3 and 4, reveals and addresses the myriad perspectives educators hold about everyday racial occurrences. Healthy courageous conversations are those that engage multiple perspectives—mine, yours, and those of others. After engaging in courageous conversations about race that include perhaps as many racial opinions as people in the room where those conversations are taking place, interracial dialogue is, at best, difficult to navigate if not predictably doomed to fail. Therefore, parameters must be put in place not only to provide guidelines for participants but also to ensure that the topic survives the interaction.

Specifically, Condition 3 requires that we accept the reality that race is not real. Rather, it is a social/political construction that has enabled people to classify one another based on physical traits and to associate meaning and a gradation of power to each classified group. I have found that this "normalized" behavior, at least in every society on the six so-called continents that I personally have visited, introduces a predictable challenge: How do we negotiate such varied perspectives and experiences, all of which are subject to multiple interpretations?

When, for example, a frustrated teacher in the Ann Arbor (Michigan) School District told me that she and her colleagues struggle with the Courageous Conversations process and typically engage in "cowardly conversations" instead, her point struck an important nerve. It also illuminated a predictable challenge to sustaining interracial dialogues about race. Using the Courageous Conversations Compass to navigate the chasms between the way individuals view racialized events or circumstances and the way they respond to them can determine whether a learning community becomes galvanized or balkanized in that process. Also, when we are "mindful" about how we listen and respond to each other in these predictable places of difference, we can "get centered" and thus get to work discovering adaptive solutions to systemic racial disparities.

Truly, what makes the Courageous Conversations approach different from so many other forms of diversity training is its singular focus on race as a way of unlocking educators' ability to tackle not only this difficult phenomenon but also many other human diversity topics that challenge their effectiveness. Even more distinctive, however, is the purposeful surfacing of multiple perspectives and specific directions for proficiently navigating them that the Courageous Conversations approach provides.

The third tier, which encompasses Conditions 4 and 5, addresses how to *deepen* your courageous conversations about race by bringing your own and others' authentic racial perspectives, along with a new sense of personal and collective empowerment, to the dialogue. For some educators, disentangling the words *race, ethnicity,* and *nationality*— and assigning specific meaning to the ways in which color, culture, and consciousness shape their racial beings—prompts an awakening that immediately translates into new behaviors in their classrooms. For others, critical race theory provides a useful schema and some well-researched ideas for deepening their understandings about how race predictably influences our lives.

With respect to deepening courageous conversations about race, perhaps the most relevant part of critical race theory for school leaders to explore in greater depth and detail, given that the vast majority of them are White, is the construct of Whiteness. Although many can speak to what they perceive to be the pathological challenges of under-served children of color, engaging, sustaining, and deepening conversations about the impact of the White presence and perspective in schools is often seen as threatening to an overwhelming number of White educators. Clearly, these educators cannot develop a deep understanding of race or advanced skills for addressing racism without considering how being, acting, and reasoning White influences both student learning and their teaching.

For those of us who are educators of color, how we negotiate the dominant racial culture and consciousness often determines whether or not we experience professional success or failure, not to mention the degree to which we are embraced or marginalized by our colleagues, students, and their parents. Our own Whiteness—that is, the extent to which we align ourselves, intellectually, emotionally, or physically with the prevailing White power structure in education and society—can be the primary determinant of if, how, and when we give voice to our authentic racial thinking, feelings, beliefs, and experiences.

The Compass

Roughly 6 months after the *Courageous Conversations* field guide was published, I began noticing the leaders expressed preference for the Doing quadrant, suggesting that responses from there carried greater significance than those stemming from the Feeling, Believing, or Thinking quadrants. Believing that the simple power of the word *doing* prompted this invalid hierarchical perspective, with respect to this tool, I revised the Compass simply by replacing the word *doing* with *acting*. My point is that some educators may choose to *act* on new racial information, perhaps sign a petition, whereas others will choose to search for additional information, or *think* on it. And, these and all other initial responses represent nothing more or nothing less than that: an initial response.

The Courageous Conversations Compass is based on social intelligence theory and provides a means by which racial equity leaders can monitor their own and others' engagement in courageous conversations about race. The Compass resembles a Chinese compass, which has five coordinates: east, west, north, south, and center. It also has two hemispheres: right and left. Patterned on modern brain research, two of the Compass's cardinal points—the Intellectual/Rational and Relational/Practical—are plotted on the left side of the Compass, while the other two—the Moral and the Emotional—are plotted on the right side. The center of the Compass is where the two sides converge. It is in this coalescent space or frame of mind—in which all participants are engaged intellectually, relationally, emotionally, and morally—that productive, interracial dialogues about race can occur.

The Compass is not only a tool to help racial equity leaders understand what they are experiencing in an interracial dialogue, it also supports their development of "empathic accuracy"—that is, the ability to determine what others are feeling and thinking in such dialogues. An acceptance of the legitimacy of all forms of human cognitive expression is an essential aspect of the Courageous Conversations Protocol. For many, mastery of the Courageous Conversations Compass opens the doorway to personal racial introspection and more effective racial equity leadership. But only one part of this mastery involves locating oneself within the dialogue. "Getting centered," or balancing one's initial racial response with other dimensions of one's feelings, thoughts, beliefs, and acts, is also critical.

For example, when I began my quest toward courageous conversations about race, I initially found myself floundering in the Feeling quadrant. That is, most of my reactions to racially charged statements or actions were similarly racially charged and personalized. My efforts to steer my responses toward the Thinking quadrant marked the beginning of my ability to get centered and balance what I understood intellectually about race with what I knew and experienced about it on an emotional level.

Let's look at another example. Early in his term, President Obama set out to address the nation's school-age children, only to be criticized and censored by school leaders acting under the influence of, primarily, White conservative parent and community constituencies. Obama's refusal to confront the racist responses to his address—actually, the resistance simply to his desire to address those students—is evidence of his centering ability as president and as a person. His centered response in that instance forced me to center my initial response—from one that the president was unwilling, unable, or afraid to confront White racism—to conclude that it would not have been wise, in the long term, for this powerful Black man, so early in his tenure, to challenge the aggressions of resentful White people who felt threatened by his power.

Racial equity leaders must recognize that our initial responsibility in racialized discourses is to locate ourselves on the Compass and then navigate our way to the center, thus touching on the more distant quadrants. Only then can we assist others to locate themselves within the context of the conversation and then to get centered in their public responses to the given racialized circumstances. More than being acutely aware of race and of their own feelings, thinking, and beliefs about it, racial equity leaders must be able to listen, question, and ultimately respond to others, or to act on such matters in such a way that all feel validated and affirmed. If those who partner with you in courageous conversations about race feel validated and affirmed, that is evidence of your willingness to engage more deeply in clarifying and understanding your own perspectives and, in turn, authentically inviting others to share your perspectives and provide counternarratives of their own. Some of the common and predictable stumbling blocks racial equity leaders and Courageous Conversations champions encounter when attempting to internalize the theory and apply it to their everyday personal and professional practices will be the focus of the following section.

ISOLATING RACE: INTERSECTIONALITY AND CULTURAL LAYERING

The *Courageous Conversations* field guide, which is the basic text for PEG's Beyond Diversity seminars, states clearly that racial equity leaders, in manifesting Condition 2, must learn to "isolate race while acknowledging the broader scope of diversity and the variety of factors that contribute to a racialized problem." Still, many years ago, I noticed that when some of my White participant-trainees returned for Day 2 of my workshops, they seemed to be struggling with the way I presented this Condition, "Keeping the Spotlight on Race."

As those educators explained to me, neither the realities of racial injustice nor even the concept of White privilege were stumbling blocks for them. What was particularly challenging for them, however, was what they perceived as my emphasis on "isolating race" and placing it at a level of greater importance than other aspects of diversity. Some of the White women participants, for example, told me that they interpreted Condition 2 to mean that gender oppression and the obstacles women faced due to sexism were less significant or important than the challenges facing people of color due to racism. White gay men and lesbians in my workshops offered similar perspectives relating to their struggles with homophobia and heterosexism vis-à-vis racism. But perhaps the loudest and most widely voiced concerns came from those of my White workshop participants who grew up poor. They strongly asserted that issues associated with poverty—more specifically, the need to confront classism in our society—were more significant in their minds than issues relating to race and racism. In almost all these cases, regardless of whether the trainee's issue was gender, sexual orientation, or class, the voices emanating from my White participants were charged with passion and certainty.

The Theory of Intersectionality

Clearly, for some White educators, moving Courageous Conversations from theory to practice will be a struggle because of their perceptions that the quest for racial equity diminishes other more salient aspects of their being or, essentially, who they are. That is why, at the outset of this book's explorations of the complex, overlapping, and intersecting elements of our various cultural markers and determinants, I want to present a clearer definition of the Courageous Conversations Protocol's Condition 2 to offset such misunderstandings of its intention and importance.

In that earlier text, Curtis Linton and I maintained that by focusing *explicitly* and *intentionally* on race, educators of all races will develop not only a deeper understanding of the subject but also the courage, skills, and knowledge they will need to examine other diversity topics in more sophisticated and comprehensive ways. Due to societal pressures, the fears most people have of talking about race, coupled with the problematic belief that race is not a critical or pressing issue, typically leads to less than desirable outcomes. It often means, for example, that educators plunge into conversations about socioeconomic status, language differences, and immigration and nationalism without recognizing how race filters through these topics and influences our perspectives, experiences, and outcomes. The danger of minimizing or eliminating the racial aspect of any circumstance or situation, however, is that we inevitably arrive at a distorted interpretation of what is happening around us. Consequently, the actions, remedies, or solutions we pursue to address race or racism will be limited as well.

Even more interesting is how much more important race becomes when boundless energy and effort are placed on suppressing it as a topic of conversation or aspect for analysis. According to Micah Pollack, writing in her book, *Because of Race: How Americans Debate Harm and Opportunity in Our Schools*:

> Whenever naming precisely some everyday acts that harm and some opportunities that are necessary on a daily basis inside schools and districts, advocates can take care to say explicitly that the current conversation pinpointing particular school- and district-based harms and opportunities does not imply that additional harms and opportunities are to be ignored, nor that demanding particular opportunities from actors outside schools and districts (and expecting efforts from students and parents) is somehow unnecessary. Rather, the goal is a running conversation on *who* needs to provide *which* opportunities and make which

efforts. . . . Accusations of discrimination "because of race" prompt people to defend their intentions morally and personally, thus clouding any analysis of unintended bias or unwitting participation in harm.[1]

The second Courageous Conversations Condition is not meant to minimize or eliminate any other aspect of human diversity. Instead, its purpose is to guide school leaders in the practice of viewing each and any of our diverse ways of being *through the ever-present prism of race.* Given this, it is essential that racial equity leaders not view diversity factors as hierarchical. Rather, we need simply to practice looking at our world, and specifically our work, through a lens that many have never even considered, much less grappled with or implemented.

All too often, we in the United States have been encouraged to apply racial analyses late or last in our considerations of any given circumstance or only when it is impossible *not* to do so. For example, many of us, both White people and people of color, felt it important not to make race an issue in the 2008 presidential election campaign. How odd this was, not to mention exhausting and diminishing, to not feel welcome to speak openly about the fact that our nation's more than 200-year-old tradition of electing and being led by White presidents had come to an end. What meaning did this silencing have for various individuals and groups in the United States and abroad? Then again, why had this tradition lasted so long, and what enabled this particular person of color to be successful when numerous others in the past had not? Furthermore, how would those who had never had a conversation with a Black man, let alone been governed by one, adjust to this change? Does this "breaking of the color barrier" signal progress, even if new forms of racism surface and old views of racial hatred resurface? These and so many additional questions are born out of Condition 2, and our careful examination of them does not preclude our questions about other factors brought to light in the election of Barack Obama, such as the economy, unemployment, and health care.

For years, I have struggled with how to create synchronicity between what critical race theory scholars have referred to as intersectionality and my own explanations of the seemingly converse logic of Condition 2. At the heart of my dilemma are two concurrent beliefs. First is the belief that racial equity leaders must recognize and acknowledge that in societies like the United States, where meaningful and fruitful conversations about race are rare, issues and challenges pertaining to race are neither freely nor authentically addressed. A prime example of this observation is the shocking state and condition of Black boys in American public education. The absence of courageous, intentional, high-level engagement on this important topic reinforces, if not fosters, a kind of illogical understanding of it as well as distorted perceptions about the meaning and significance of race in resolving the issues confronting these students. Any number of other issues, however, when viewed through the mythical lens of racelessness or racial insignificance, prompts a similar and truly unfortunate, if not dangerous, distortion. This must be balanced with my competing belief that no single diversity factor, including race, functions in a vacuum or is disconnected from other human characteristics and real or imposed traits.

The circumstances surrounding the 2008 presidential primaries present a case in point. In that contest, Hillary Clinton's supporters often failed to acknowledge the significance of their candidate's race, preferring instead to offer powerful observations on the roles gender and sexism were playing in the campaign. In truth, both Obama and Clinton had aspects of privilege and oppression working for and against their bids for the White House. Of course, as a Black man, Obama challenged the racialized construct of who could become president but, as a man, he would occupy an office designed by and for men as well as one held only by men since its inception. Clinton, on the other hand, would have broken the gender barrier to the highest office in the land, but she would also have joined the Whites-only presidential ranks had she been elected to the office.

Much was said and written during the campaign about the perceived changes that might occur if a woman became president. Perhaps even more was written and said about the implications for the office of the First Lady should Obama win, given the strong female leadership and outspokenness exhibited by Michelle Obama. I struggle to recall any mainstream commentary on either of these two women's racial status, however, or on the possible role race played in their actions or in our nation's interpretations, reactions, or responses to them. Although Clinton was compelled to negotiate a terrain that, for centuries, had excluded women, she could draw on her "insider status" as a White woman, thus enlisting the wisdom and experience of former U.S. presidents since the 1700s. How her being White served as an indicator of the unchangeable direction of national policies, programs, and practices is just as important as how her being a woman might have led to significant transformation in the governance of this country.

That this nation still struggles to see the importance and significance of having elected a Black president to office for the very first time in history remains a troubling reality with, perhaps, some increasingly dangerous possibilities. According to various government reports, Obama has had more threats made against his life than any other American president. He even required Secret Service protection before winning the Democratic Party's nomination, a special government provision that—if properly acknowledged, examined, and discussed—offers even more revealing insights into the lingering vestiges of racism in our society today. The galvanization of a viable third party during Obama's presidency, the so-called Tea Party, which is even less racially diverse than the virtually all-White Republican Party, merits an additional conversation about race in America. Instead, we as a nation typically avoid visiting the "race place." We hastily credit ourselves for viewing the intersection of race and gender, as in the aforementioned example involving Hillary Clinton, when offering perspectives on such matters, believing we are being fully conscious and balanced. In truth, however, we are effectively distorting the truth due to omission.

The more productive and, yes, *courageous* conversation in which we can engage, is one that features accurate and detailed analysis of the multiple aspects of diversity playing out in any given scenario. To do so—that is, to examine thoroughly these intersections or layers—demands a similarly thorough understanding of the nature and degree to which meaning about each issue has been constructed. If either or any diversity characteristic is off limits in our discussions or is in some way distorted in terms of how we access or define it or them, the meaning that we construct at their intersection will be limited or distorted. Operationalizing Condition 2 compels us to take time out to intentionally factor race into those instances in which, consciously or unintentionally, it has been omitted by or prematurely conflated with another pressing factor.

Digging deeper into my discussion of the issues surrounding Black male youth in America's schools should solidify your understanding about the notion of intersectionality and the critical role it plays in moving Courageous Conversations from theory to practice. In 2007, *Time* magazine published a cover story about the experience and condition of boys in school.[2] In several pages, the author of that article shared data and provided explanations on why males are, for the first time in U.S. history, falling behind females academically. The story documented a condition that was voiced as serious and encouraged the nation to examine it with a sense of urgency and purpose.

When I first glimpsed the cover of this magazine at an airport newsstand, my initial response was: Now that White boys are struggling in school, *Time* finds it important to offer a report. My curiosity prompted me to purchase the magazine, and as I perused the article, I fully suspected that I held in my hands some outstanding curriculum material for my trainings. I was right.

Nowhere in that article did the writer or researchers explicitly consider race. This was not surprising to me, for had they not omitted race, they would have been compelled to explain why their article did not merit publication two decades ago, when national disaggregated data first begin to reveal how Black males were becoming disproportionately represented at the lowest academic achievement levels in the nation, behind Black females and everyone else. This new gender phenomenon applied to White people only.

Unfortunately, the distortions resulting from failure to isolate race did not stop at that one omission. Later in the article, the authors included two photographs of young Black males with a caption that alludes to these boys' lack of a father figure in their lives, speaking only briefly to the extraordinary circumstances surrounding Black boys and academic achievement. The message of that imagery was quite clear to me, however: Despite the obscure yet stereotypically loaded visual references to Black boys, this story was mainly about White boys. It was not about exploring the complex intersection of race and other human diversity factors that critical race theorist Richard Delgado suggests are at the heart of the struggle against racism.

Delgado's excellent research around this concept of intersectionality is especially helpful for educators who seek to understand and extract authentic racial meaning from their lived experiences, given that multiple cultural aspects are always at play in any situation. Delgado is also clear in his theory that inviting such multiple perspectives or allowing for too much focus on factors other than race can serve as a way of granting permission to avoid addressing race in favor of issues embraced more favorably by our society. In my work with educators, I have noticed how, in their insistence on adding meaningful categories for analysis, they often fail to get to the conversation about racial disparities, given that they devote so much time to each of the other factors, which require a kind of meaning making unto themselves. According to Delgado:

> One problem with intersectionality is what I call the so-what question. Once you point out that a category contains subcategories, what follows? Presumably, one begins paying more attention to those in the subgroup if they have been feeling neglected. . . . But then, suppose that certain members of that very subcategory emerge clamoring for attention—black women lesbians, say. They want to be recognized as a new subcategory. Categories are, potentially, infinitely divisible.[3]

Another question that surfaces for me with respect to Delgado's intersectionality theory is that it seemingly allows for the possibility that diversity factors can operate independently as well as congruently. Figure 3.1 illustrates how three diversity classifications—race, gender, and class—intersect in the case of a middle-class, White female teacher. Delgado's powerful theory helps us to see the opportunities where such an educator would view a student's behavior through an overlapping prism and emerge with a more comprehensive understanding of why American Indian males, for example, struggle in her classroom. It is also possible, however—and, in my experience, quite plausible and typical—that this same educator may neglect to recognize one or more of her own diversity characteristics influencing her perspective. Lacking consciousness about her race, in this case, may cause her not to see how her Whiteness informs her engagement with the student in the same way that she recognizes her being female as having impact.

According to Figure 3.1, this teacher, on entering into a courageous conversation about race, would be expected to frame her racial analyses in terms of her intersecting diversity characteristics. What is unfortunate (and typical, in my experience) is that far too many middle-class, White female teachers neither consciously nor intentionally acknowledge all of these factors, nor do they often possess proficient understandings of each characteristic. For example, let's imagine a conversation about the challenges Black boys from low-socioeconomic-status families face in the classroom. How would this

Figure 3.1 Intersectionality and the Typical American Teacher

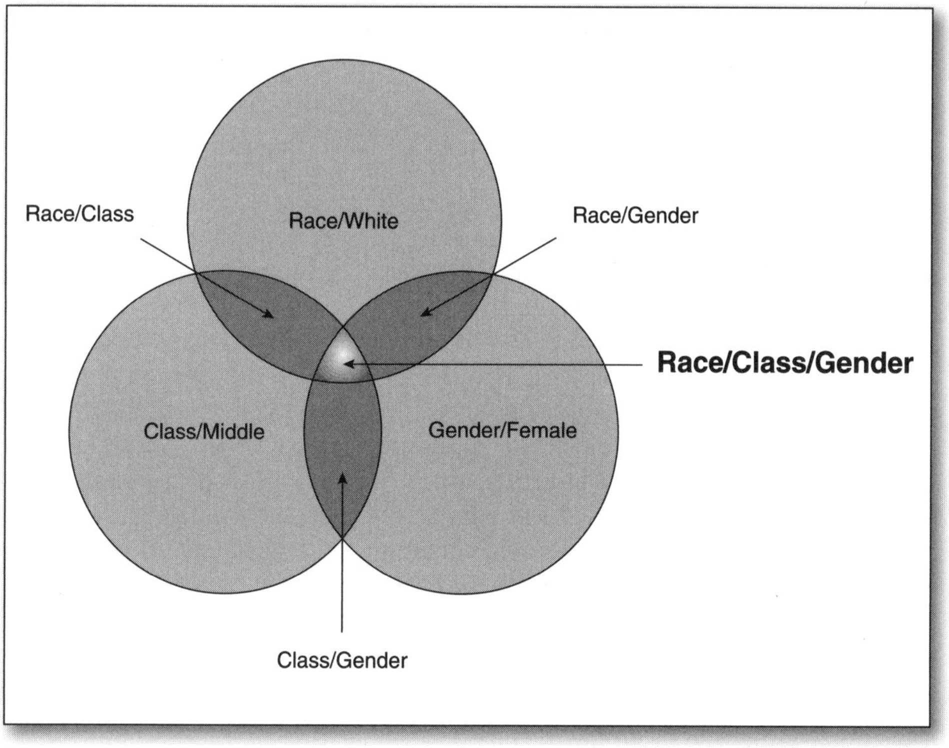

teacher's contribution differ if she started with a careful and comprehensive analysis of her own race, class, and gender and how they contributed to her success—and White, middle-class woman most often are the teachers of low-income males of color from kindergarten through 12th grade? Now, I would never suggest that these women cannot be successful teachers of Black boys. What I am saying, however, is that any teacher who is unaware or unconscious about her own cultural layers will likewise be unable to recognize how those learned and practiced ways of viewing the world have an impact on both her teaching and his learning.

No leadership strategy for dismantling racism in schools can afford to alienate the very people who offer the best chance of moving racial equity work from theory to practice. That is not what I am suggesting. Instead, I assert that White women, White gay men, White people who have experienced poverty, White educators with disabilities—they and others who have experienced and can recognize injustices related to sexism, heterosexism, classism, and able-ism, respectively or collectively—have potentials for empathy that uniquely situate them to reference racism authentically. Racial equity leaders must recognize, however, the significance of each person's diversity factors or characteristics, especially their significance to the person who embodies them. We also need to recognize that some diversity characteristics, such as socioeconomic status and sexual orientation, can be muted or obscured, whereas race is immutable. Thus, to some degree, this reality influences how the culturally targeted and their victimizers interact.

Without disputing the value of Delgado's theory of intersectionality as not only critical for this analysis but also accurate in terms of how individuals show up at their "race place" wearing multiple cultural lenses, I am left with a dilemma. How can we simultaneously isolate race as a focus and truly recognize the ways in which other cultural factors get layered into our meaning and response? I will address this critical matter in the following section.

Cultural Layering

Each of us embodies many diversity factors that influence our analysis of and response to everyday life situations. We are unique not only in which diversity factors—which layers of our beings—we're aware of, but also in how we define those layers independently and in which order of importance and significance we place those layers in our examination of the events taking place in our world. In moving Courageous Conversations from theory to practice, educators, and especially classroom teachers, first must become keenly aware of which cultural layers they themselves project and protect. Second, they must be clear and able to articulate the meanings they have affixed to each of those layers—for example, some must be able to comprehend and convey what it means to be middle class, White, and female in their society, school community, and classroom. Third, they must understand which layer serves as their primary aspect of analysis, the one through which all the other layers or characteristics are viewed.

Let's make this more personal: I am a middle-class Black man. My primary diversity layer, the one through which I have been acculturated to view all of my other human diversity factors, is race. Thus, I understand and define both my middle class-ness and maleness (along with any number of other characteristics) through the filter of my experiences as a Black person, particularly one raised and living in the United States. And because I layer my perspectives in order from race to class to gender and so forth, I perceive myself to be more closely connected to the perspectives and experiences of poor Black women than to middle-class White men.

So, let's be clear: to move Courageous Conversations from theory to practice, it is not essential that race be your *primary* diversity-factor lens, although using that lens can help you to get a clearer view of the omnipresent nature of racism. What is critical is that, as a racial equity leader, you must have a clear sense of which diversity factors you yourself manifest, in what order those factors are layered, and what impact those factors and their order have on how your own racial perspectives and understandings are shaped.

CULTURAL-LAYERING EXERCISE

Answer the following questions in the order presented:

1. Which diversity factors define you?

2. How are these factors layered?

3. Where is race located in your cultural layering?

4. How does this order shape your personal racial perspective and understanding?

5. Would your perspective change if race was your primary layer? How?

6. What happens to your perspective when race is your ultimate layer, or the layer that is viewed through all of your other cultural characteristics (e.g., physical disability, age, sexual orientation, etc.)?

GETTING CENTERED IN A MINDFUL WAY

The power of the Courageous Conversations Compass as a tool rests with your ability to locate your initial response to a racialized circumstance—be it to the political, ideological, cultural, or philosophical left or right—and then navigate toward the center, which represents a broadening of that response. How, though, do you determine your initial location? The answer: By listening carefully to the unarticulated narrative you immediately associate with the racialized event.

I find that writing about my responses often helps me to understand more clearly what I am feeling, believing, or thinking when first confronted with such an event. For example, I wrote the following after watching a television news report showing a confrontation between President Obama and a Tea Party supporter:

> I feel demoralized and unsafe when President Obama fails to stand up and challenge racist White Americans when they display aggression [toward him] in

ways they never have done previously to a sitting U.S. president. I believe he [President Obama] is hurting all people of color, if not greatly setting us back by not standing up to White racial aggression, as this becomes the expectation for us all when faced with similar disrespect and outright racial hatred.

The words I used in this reactive statement provide the strongest clues about which quadrant of the Compass my initial responses occupied. After I wrote it, I realized that my feelings were still "camped out" on the right side of the compass, where beliefs and feelings are clarified. I needed assistance in venturing left toward the intellectual and relational quadrants.

My work with diversity consultant Lee Mun Wah has shown me the importance of "mindful facilitation" as a way of assisting educators to have effective courageous conversations about race. Mun Wah asserts that healthy communication requires mindfulness, or active awareness, and careful attention to the feelings, beliefs, motives, and attitudes of others—both spoken and unspoken. Mindful interrogation of one's own feelings, beliefs, and so forth is another useful tool during courageous conversations, and Mun Wah suggests a number of important points of entry for racial equity school leaders as they engage in listening, inquiring, and responding to racialized situations.

NINE HEALTHY WAYS TO COMMUNICATE

1. Reflect back on what is being said. Use their words, not yours.

2. Begin where they are, not where you want them to be.

3. Be curious and open to what they are trying to say.

4. Notice what they are saying *and* what they are *not* saying.

5. Emotionally, relate to how they are feeling. Nurture the relationship.

6. Notice how you are feeling. Be honest and authentic.

7. Take responsibility for your part in the conflict or misunderstanding.

8. Try to understand how their past affects who they are and how those experiences affect their relationship with you.

9. Stay with the process and the relationship, not just the solution.

Listening, Inquiring, and Responding

- What I heard you say was . . .
- Tell me more what you meant by . . .
- What angered you about what happened?
- What hurt you about what happened?
- What's familiar about what happened? (How did it affect you? How does it affect you now?)
- What do you need/want?

Source: The Art of Mindful Facilitation by Lee Mun Wah, 2004, Berkeley, CA: StirFry Seminars and Consulting, www.stirfryseminars.com.

When I applied Mun Wah's techniques to the circumstances I wrote about earlier, it caused me to probe more deeply and ultimately to uncover the assumptions and personal meanings that supported my belief about President Obama's silence on racism. I asked myself a series of questions:

- What triggers my feelings of demoralization or lack of safety?
- Given my recognition of Barack Obama as a very intelligent and racially astute man prior to becoming President, why do I think he is taking this position on race?
- For whom, racially speaking, is his message intended?
- What might the response of that intended audience be, should he respond in a way that feels more authentic to me?

These and similar questions caused me not only to explore the emotional quadrant of my reactions at a deeper level but also to advance my understanding toward the other Compass quadrants and thereby center myself. As a result of this process, I came to the conclusion that Barack Obama, as the president, must be, of necessity, especially cautious in how he navigates race, as his detractors (and many of his supporters) neither value his commentary on racism nor see it as appropriate. In many ways, I concluded, Obama entered office with an unspoken pledge *not* to engage the nation in a process of racial introspection, and the country now *expects* him to uphold that promise. I hold true, however, to my beliefs and to what seems to me to be morally correct: that because this racially astute Black President is a lightning rod for new and hidden racial meaning to surface in this country, following in his masterful lead, we all must be intentional when *acting* on this new meaning in both our work and our personal interactions.

Once you have attained a level of proficiency in the mindful facilitation process and in the use of the Courageous Conversations Compass, you can support the similar development of others at both the interpersonal and organizational levels. Indeed, the ability to listen, inquire, and respond mindfully to educators as they struggle to uncover, examine, and address racism in their personal lives and professional practices can make all the difference. Without mindfulness, we are likely to experience a systemic breakdown due to theoretical misunderstandings, hurt feelings, and poorly articulated beliefs. Through mindful courageous conversations about race, we are likely to usher in a wave of systemic transformation resulting from the formation of professional learning communities that can engage in compassionate yet authentic dialogue.

EXAMINING THE PRESENCE AND ROLE OF WHITENESS

At the end of day one of my 2-day Beyond Diversity training sessions, I instruct the participants to read a very short article I wrote in 1997, titled "White Is a Color." I wrote the piece in hopes that it would help educators to better understand not only the concept of White privilege but also the broader construct of Whiteness or, as I referred to it at that time, *Whiteism*. The following is an excerpt from that article:[4]

> I highlight a recent business trip to New Orleans because I believe it illuminates the presence and reality of Whiteness. My adventure began Saturday morning

at San Francisco Airport, where I decided to upgrade to first class on a rather large plane. Twenty-three of the twenty-four seats in first class were occupied by White people (perhaps this is the new definition of "White flight!"). Quickly into the trip, one of the six White flight attendants circulated throughout the cabin to take our meal requests. When the attendant arrived at my row, I was offered both options. My choice of an omelet limited the selection of the White gentleman seated beside me to the fruit plate. He became instantly irate. He reprimanded the flight attendant for servicing him last and threatened to stop flying United . . .

Although I have witnessed similar situations before, I was far more attuned to the racial dynamic of this particular episode. I believe the gentleman assumed his flying status was higher than mine was, which, incidentally, was not the case. His assumption, however based, suggested his belief that I, rather than he, should be served last. To pacify his soon-to-be "pain" of reverse discrimination or political correctness—two White-created phenomena—I offered him my omelet. Without hesitation, he accepted my meal without offering me so little as a "thank you." At the end of the flight, I politely asked the Entitled One "if he should not be served last, who should?"

Many White people will individualize this man's indecencies and suggest that "his being a jerk has nothing to do with his being White." Conversely, I insist that his behavior is "typically White." In fact, the ability to individualize the countless episodes like this that people of color document daily is what enables White people to not notice that someone is always last, excluded, or ignored. Perhaps those least accustomed to being "passed over" sometimes should be last in our multiracial "democracy."

. . . I suspect that White people are the last to recognize that White is a color. This realization undeniably shatters the White belief that theirs is a universal human experience—one that is color-blind, socially prudent, and economically just. "Whiteism" is as defining for White people as are injustice, struggle, and inequality for non-White people of color!

When I returned home to San Francisco on Tuesday, I was greeted by a phone call from my best White friend, Eric. "How was your trip?" he asked. As I instantly reflected on my racism-filled adventure and then thought about how foreign my racial reality still is to even my closest White friends, I sighed and simply uttered, "It was great!" Why did I lie to Eric? Because, in my experience, Eric and other White people tend to redefine these patterns of White behavior as individuals' personal foibles or character flaws. Clearly, White people more often than not do not consider themselves to be part of a White collective experience or group.

Frankly, I am simply too exhausted sometimes to shatter another White person's belief that his is a universal human experience. But because I realize that as long as Whiteism is a defining reality for White people, injustice, struggle, and inequality will continue to erode the spirit of non-White people of color. The very next day, I mustered up the energy and humility to tell Eric my personal truth about New Orleans—and San Francisco too, for that matter!

When I wrote that article, I had not yet discovered the tools that later would help me to explain the importance and significance for all educators of developing a deeper understanding of the way Whiteness affects every aspect of schooling. Today, with the help of Peggy McIntosh, Judith Katz, Janet Helms, and Cheryl Harris, to name but a handful of the contemporary scholars who have studied and written extensively about this fundamental aspect of race, I believe I truly "get it."

With the exception of Harris, who in my mind, stands tall and alone in defining how Whiteness functions like physical property in a racialized society, I will reference only White scholars in support of my conjectures about Whiteness here because clearly they, their research, and their ideas on the subject have received less scrutiny–not only by White people but also by less racially conscious people of color. Long before these White voices on Whiteness rose to prominence, however, scholars and laypersons of color had developed significant and detailed understandings about the distinctions between the racial experiences, perspectives, beliefs, and behaviors of White people and people of color. Notably, when W.E.B. Du Bois wrote in 1903 that "the problem of the twentieth century is the problem of the color line, the relation between the darkest and lightest men in Asia, Africa, the Americas and the Islands in the sea," he was, in essence, positing that the distinctive experiences and perspectives of White people are not only racially unique but also a primary source of human struggle.

In the American school setting, nothing causes greater disequilibrium than insisting on an examination of the presence, role, and impact of Whiteness on education as a strategy for improving the academic achievement of all students, especially for under-served student of color populations. The mere mention of the word *Whiteness* in what might have been an otherwise relatively calm discussion about race is too often cause for White educators to put up walls of defense and for the hopes of racially conscious educators of color for meaningful engagement on the topic to be dashed against those walls. Indeed, the power of Whiteness allows White people to deny the existence of White privilege, despite voluminous research and examples to the contrary. It also allows otherwise racially conscious people of color to tiptoe around their profound ignorance of Whiteness as well as their often aggressive resistance to exploring the topic. Unfortunately, in a system of education such as that of the United States, which initially was developed and designed to educate White children exclusively, no sustainable reform can be achieved unless the vestiges of this foundational bias are identified and deinstitutionalized.

Too often, when courageous conversations about race turn to discussion of White privilege, White supremacy, and White racial dominance—especially when the participants are asked to venture outside of their intellectual quadrants and visit any of the remaining four locations on the Courageous Conversations Compass—those conversations, unless they are properly facilitated, quickly escalate into unproductive posturing or deafening silence. Facilitating conversations about race takes courage, but going deeper to unmask issues associated with the racial power dynamic, particularly the impact and role of Whiteness, takes even more. It takes purpose!

To move Courageous Conversations from theory to practice, racial equity leaders must be equipped with the specific knowledge, language, and dialogic skills to guide educators effectively along the path to uncovering, examining, and addressing Whiteness. In addition, racial equity leaders must help their fellow educators recognize the three distinct levels at which race functions in our society: color, culture, and consciousness.

At the color level (which is, ironically, the most basic and yet still most controversial level), Whiteness presents itself as White skin privilege. That is, for the most part, the experience of being awarded unearned advantages in a number of everyday circumstances solely because of one's light complexion is limited to White people. What makes this relatively simple phenomenon more complex is that some people of color appear White in skin tone. As the African American critical race theorist Cheryl Harris explains in the introduction to her groundbreaking essay, "Whiteness as Property," some lighter complexioned people of color, recognizing the social and economic advantages afforded to their White-skinned peers, actively or passively allow society to categorize them as White. Harris notes that her own grandmother spent a lifetime "passing" for White so that she could remain gainfully employed during the 1950s:

> Every day my grandmother rose from her bed in her house in a Black enclave on the south side of Chicago, sent her children off to a Black school, boarded a bus full of Black passengers, and rode to work. No one at her job ever asked if she was Black; the question was unthinkable. By virtue of the employment practices of the "fine establishment" in which she worked, she could not have been. Catering to the upper-middle class, understated tastes required that Blacks not be allowed.
>
> She quietly went about her clerical tasks, not once revealing her true identity. She listened to the women with whom she worked discuss their worries—their children's illnesses, their husbands' disappointments, their boyfriends' infidelities—all of the mundane yet critical things that made up their lives. She came to know them but they did not know her, for my grandmother occupied a completely different place. That place—where white supremacy and economic domination meet—was unknown turf to her white co-workers. They remained oblivious to the worlds within worlds that existed just beyond the edge of their awareness and yet were present in their very midst.
>
> Each evening, my grandmother, tired and worn, retraced her steps home, laid aside her mask, and reentered herself. Day in and day out, she made herself invisible, then visible again, for a price too inconsequential to do more than barely sustain her family and at a cost too precious to conceive. She left the job some years later, finding the strain too much to bear.[5]

Understanding and addressing Whiteness and its prominence at the cultural level holds great promise for creating schools that not only offer all children equitable opportunities to learn but also ensure that students develop the skills, knowledge, and capacity to navigate effectively and fearlessly in an increasingly multicultural world. Therefore, it is critical that all educators, both White educators and educators of color, recognize and examine the ways in which they behave in a "White way" or favor White norms and characteristics over other ways of being and doing.

Sociologist Judith Katz, in her research on White culture in the United States, offers an extensive list of characteristics and behavioral norms to which many, but certainly not all White Americans adhere:

Components of White Culture: Values and Beliefs

Rugged Individualism

Individual is primary unit

Individual has primary responsibility

Independence and autonomy highly valued and rewarded

Competition

Winning is everything

Win-lose dichotomy

Action Orientation

Master and control nature

Pragmatic utilitarian view of life

Decision Making

Hierarchical

Pyramid structure

Majority rule when Whites have power

Communication

Standard English

Written tradition

Direct eye contact

Control of emotions

Time

Adherence to rigid time schedule

Time viewed as a commodity

History

Based on European immigrants' experiences

War is romanticized

Protestant work ethic

Working hard brings success

Progress and Future Orientation

Plan for the future

Delayed gratification

Value continual improvement and progress

Emphasis on Scientific Method

Objective, rational, linear thinking

Cause-and-effect relationships

Quantitative analysis

Dualistic thinking

Status and Power

Measured by economic possessions

Credentials, titles, and positions

Believe "own" system is best

Family Structure

Nuclear family is the ideal social unit

Man is the breadwinner and head of household

Woman is primary caretaker of children

Patriarchal structure

Aesthetics

Women's beauty based on blonde, blue-eyed, thin, and young

Music and art based on European cultures

Source: White Culture and Racism: Working for Organizational Change in the United States (Whiteness Paper No. 3, p. 44), by Judith H. Katz, 2009, Roselle, NJ: Crandall, Dostie, & Douglass Books.

Armed with understandings such as these, we educators must ask ourselves: To what degree do our classrooms, schools, and districts support individual accomplishment over effective collaboration, silence over verbal expression, or delayed over immediate gratification? Understanding strongholds of White culture can also focus educators on discovering whether rigid time schedules and implicit requests to hide one's emotions, for example, make gaining access to curriculum and instruction a greater challenge to students of color who are unfamiliar with or choose not to embrace these and other dominant racial patterns. We must be careful not to view one group's cultural norms as better or worse than those of another. Alternately, when we do not recognize how and to what extent White cultural norms pervade our district policies, school behavioral codes, or classroom instruction, we fail to see how those dominant norms challenge the engagement and achievement of children of color. We also fail to understand how this narrow focus unfairly advantages White children, whose home and family norms are more likely to be congruent with those of the schools.

Katz and several other sociologists speak about the importance of observing and understanding the distinctive racial meanings that White people and people of color attribute to effort and its relationship to reward. For example, from the White cultural perspective, reward is viewed as the direct and commensurate result of effort, thus giving way to commonly asserted teacher mantras like "hard work pays off in the end." Although sociologists of color such as Mano Singham do not dispute this premise—that those who work harder will get farther—my interpretation of Singham's commentary suggests that, for children of color, the relationship between effort vis-à-vis school and societal rewards are often complicated by racial biases and White privilege. That is, for White students, less effort is required to thrive in a school culture dominated by White norms; subsequently, White schoolchildren are rewarded more frequently.

Students of color, on the other hand, often are doubly tasked: (1) to navigate the distance between the White-dominated cultural norms of the school and their own family/ community values *and* (2) to put forth the effort needed to succeed academically. Their efforts in the first regard usually go unrecognized, are rarely rewarded, and may be punished. Their efforts in the latter typically are complicated and made much more challenging by the former. Thus, moving Courageous Conversations from theory to practice demands that racial equity leaders thoroughly assess their schools and school systems to determine the degree to which students of color are required to master White culture as a prerequisite to achieving success.

Of course, this notion of White cultural dominance becomes even more confusing to children of color when an educator of color is the enforcer or arbiter of White school norms in circumstances when children of color fail to adhere, embrace, or even celebrate Whiteness. Too often, in their roles as disciplinarians, educators of color take the lead in punishing those children of color who cannot or choose not to "act White."

Perhaps the most devastating aspect of Whiteness, in terms of its impact on the engagement and achievement of children of color, functions at the consciousness level. Janet Helms's research on White identity development equips us with a clearer understanding of how our racial socialization influences our perspectives about race. Helms offers racial equity leaders a more precise way to determine the dimensions of White perspective, beginning with perceptions of racial neutrality and beliefs in the existence and desirability of color blindness. She also identifies the phases and the necessary and predictable points of development that mark White people's journey from the mythological color-blind and "to be White is normal" perspectives toward becoming antiracist.

HELMS'S WHITE RACIAL IDENTITY DEVELOPMENT MODEL

Two Phases: Abandonment of Racism and Defining a Non-Racist Identity

1. **Contact.** People in this status are oblivious to racism, lack an understanding of racism, have minimal experiences with Black people, and may profess to be color-blind. Societal influence in perpetuating stereotypes and the superior/inferior dichotomy associated between Blacks and Whites are not noticed, but accepted unconsciously or consciously without critical thought or analysis. Racial and cultural differences are considered unimportant and these individuals seldom perceive themselves as "dominant" group members, or having biases and prejudices.

2. **Disintegration.** In this stage, the person becomes conflicted over unresolvable racial moral dilemmas that are frequently perceived as polar opposites: believing one is nonracist, yet not wanting one's son or daughter to marry a minority group member; believing that "all men are created equal," yet society treating Blacks as second class citizens; and not acknowledging that oppression exists while witnessing it (à la the beating of Rodney King in Los Angeles). The person becomes increasingly conscious of his or her Whiteness and may experience dissonance and conflict between choosing between own-group loyalty and humanism.

3. **Reintegration.** Because of the tremendous influence that societal ideology exerts, initial resolution of dissonance often moves in the direction of the dominant ideology associated with race and one's own socioracial group identity. This stage may be characterized as a regression, for the tendency is to idealize one's socioracial group and to be intolerant of other minority groups. There is a firmer and more conscious belief in White racial superiority and racial/ethnic minorities are blamed for their own problems.

4. **Pseudo-Independence.** A person is likely to move into this phase due to a painful or insightful encounter or event, which jars the person from Reintegration status. The person begins to attempt an understanding of racial, cultural, and sexual orientation differences and may reach out to interact with minority group members. The choice of minority individuals, however, is based on how "similar" they are to him or her, and the primary mechanism used to understand racial issues is intellectual and conceptual.

(Continued)

(Continued)

An attempt to understand has not reached the experiential and affective domains. In other words, understanding Euro-American White privilege, the sociopolitical aspects of race, and issues of bias, prejudice, and discrimination tend to be more an intellectual exercise.

5. **Immersion/Emersion.** If the person is reinforced to continue a personal exploration of himself or herself as a racial being, questions become focused on what it means to be White. Helms states that the person searches for an understanding of the personal meaning of racism and the ways by which one benefits from White privilege. There is an increasing willingness to truly confront one's own biases, to redefine Whiteness, and to become more activist in directly combating racism and oppression. This stage is marked with increasing experiential and affective understanding that were lacking in the previous status.

6. **Autonomy.** Increasing awareness of one's own Whiteness, reduced feelings of guilt, acceptance of one's own role in perpetuating racism, [and] renewed determination to abandon White entitlement leads to an autonomy status. The person is knowledgeable about racial, ethnic, and cultural differences, values the diversity, and is no longer fearful, intimidated, or uncomfortable with the experiential reality of race. Development of a nonracist White identity becomes increasingly strong.

Source: "Helms's Stages of White Identity Development," in *Multicultural Counseling Competencies: Individual and Organizational Development,* pp. 52–53, by Derald Wing Sue, Robert T. Carter, J. Manuel Casas, Nadya A. Fouad, Allen E. Ivey, Margaret Jensen, Teresa LaFromboise, Jeanne E. Manese, Joseph G. Ponterotto, and Ena Vazquez-Nutall, 1998, Thousand Oaks, CA: Sage.

It is not at all surprising to me that the incorporation of Whiteness Studies in the K–12 curriculum is frowned on in many states; and books that specifically address or allude to the existence of a White racial culture or a White identity, or that challenge White-dominated perspectives on historic events, have been banned from classrooms across the land. Clearly, in a nation that socially, and sometimes politically and economically, sanctions people who engage in courageous conversations about race, Helms's in-depth research and public analysis of Whiteness and White identity is controversial. Yet, understanding and recognizing where our White colleagues (and White students) fall within the continuum of Helms's Stages of White Identity Development is an essential step in moving Courageous Conversations from theory to practice. In this consciousness-illuminating part of our work, racial equity leaders can uncover and examine the harmful ways White people have been programmed to think about race and how such habits of mind and work affect Whites' (and others') teaching and learning.

In the classroom or boardroom, normalizing Whiteness shows up as the conscious or unconscious, intentional or unintentional assignment of higher value to cultural traits and characteristics such as those previously identified by Katz. Because courageous conversations about race are often limited or nonexistent in White homes, unless current events make it virtually impossible not to discuss racial matters, White educators will tend not to realize their predisposition or biases toward White experiences, behaviors, and beliefs.

CLOSING THE "KNOWING-DOING" GAP

Although the Courageous Conversations Protocol theoretically is not overly complex, educators of all positions and races, even the most passionate racial equity leaders, struggle to internalize and apply it consistently. Many face challenges bridging the gap between knowing how to engage in courageous conversations about race and consistently and authentically doing so! Even I, the architect of the Courageous Conversations Protocol and a leader in this type of educational work for the past two decades, have experienced a lapse or two in which I failed to use the Protocol to correct or make sense of my own and other's racial perspectives and experiences.

I recall one such time when applying the Protocol could have assisted me greatly, yet due to my inexperience negotiating the new and specifically challenging subject matter it entailed, which had to do with a conflict between two men whom I admire and respect, I failed to activate my own knowledge. I was having dinner with Matais, a good friend of mine, who is African American and a fellow professor of education, when I felt compelled to ask him what he thought of the evolving conflict between President Obama and Cornel West, the esteemed (or vilified) African American scholar of religious, historical, and social issues. Earlier that week, I had sent out a heart-wrenching e-mail to the six African American men on my staff, inviting each of them to dialogue with me about this unprecedented conversation, but Matais was the first person with whom I actually engaged in a face-to-face courageous conversation about West's increasing public criticism and chastising of Obama in the White mainstream media.

Some readers may not be familiar with the scholarship of Cornel West, who, aside from being a Princeton University professor of African American Studies and religion, has authored numerous articles and books on race. West's best-selling book, *Race Matters*, greatly influenced my thinking. I quoted widely from it in the *Courageous Conversations* field guide. On both personal and professional levels, West serves as an inspiration to me and a source of knowledge, understanding, and truth. I recognize him as a brilliant scholar, so much so that I supported his selection as the national advisory board chair of the Foundation for a College Education, a nonprofit organization that I founded in 1996 to support African American and Latino students' transitions between secondary and higher education.

As reported by the media, West, "encouraged by the populist rhetoric of the Obama campaign," helped to organize and spoke at 65 campaign events for the candidate, believing—as I still do—in Obama's potential to effect great change in the nation. By the end of Obama's first year in office, however, West "like many others who placed their faith in Obama," was bitterly nursing "the anguish of the deceived, manipulated, and betrayed"—this according to Chris Hedges in the website, truthdig.com. West is quoted as describing

Obama as "a black mascot of Wall Street oligarchs and a black puppet of corporate plutocrats."[6]

From the outset, I must interject here my own feelings of conflict and confusion with respect to how President Obama has faced, or seemingly not faced, many race-related issues in this country. Those issues include the advisers he has selected and the government policies, programs, and practices on which he has chosen to focus. Having said this, I am also clear about the highly racialized context in which this president peculiarly operates and the position-threatening, if not life-threatening reactions that could occur from his White opponents, as well as his supporters, if one racially charged Oval Office decision rubs them the wrong way. His leadership quandary as a well-known racially conscious Black man is not enviable.

West, who often sought out the mainstream media with his strident criticisms of Obama, offered this assessment to Hedges:

> I think my dear brother Barack Obama has a certain fear of free black men. It's understandable. As a young brother who grows up in a white context, brilliant African father, he's always had to fear being a white man with black skin. All he has known culturally is white. He is just as human as I am, but that is his cultural formation. When he meets an independent black brother it is frightening. And that's true for a white brother. When you get a white brother who meets a free, independent black man they got to be mature to really embrace fully what the brother is saying to them. It's a tension, given the history. It can be overcome. Obama, coming out of Kansas influence, white, loving grandparents, coming out of Hawaii and Indonesia, when he meets these independent black folk who have a history of slavery, Jim Crow, Jane Crow and so on, he is very apprehensive. He has a certain rootlessness, a deracination. It is understandable.[7]

Given my high regard for both men, West and Obama, I was definitely not prepared to witness one of my most significant contemporary heroes initiate an age-old racial conflict and on such a public stage: that of questioning another's Blackness—that is, Obama's racial authenticity and loyalty. A heated conversation on West's criticisms of the president ensued between my friend Matais and me. On one hand, I felt forced to defend West's right to free expression while simultaneously compelled to protect Obama from the devastating "racial litmus testing" that has destroyed so many of our most successful champions for racial justice. The history texts show that even such monumental figures as Frederick Douglass, W.E.B. Du Bois, Booker T. Washington, Marcus Garvey, and Martin Luther King Jr., were not immune to the race-loyalty question and judgments of others of their own race. Matais's assertion, on the other hand, that Cornel West might be forcing his own, perhaps outdated, racial beliefs onto the President was hard for me to hear, especially because deep down, I shared some of West's milder views about the President. I, too, had hoped for greater recognition and representation by Obama and his administration of the special plight of Black Americans and other people of color during a time of threatening national economic conditions and a heightened assault on social policy and programming. At the same time, Matais's assertion that, in the wake of this unprecedented level of national unrest in our lifetime, Obama was doing a satisfactory job for all Americans, including Black Americans, was also an unshakeable belief to which I clung.

Looking back on that conversation, I credit myself for recognizing that I should not (and did not) begin this conversation by commenting first on what I perceived to be the overwhelming Whiteness that defines and determines this president's public persona and behaviors as well as the public's reactions and responses to him. To my discredit, however, I failed to pay close enough attention to the fact that my entire perspective on the conflict between Obama and West was derived from mainstream media reports, thus resulting in my limited—and perhaps White— understanding of the events that unfolded on a very prominent stage. I wish as well that I could have been more mindful in the way that I engaged with Matais. My resulting disengagement with the Protocol, my defensiveness over my own point of view, albeit a conflicted one, and my dismissal of Matais's perspectives often got in the way of my really listening to his construction of knowledge. Indeed, the Courageous Conversations Protocol recommends that all parties in courageous conversations engage in a continuous cycle of analysis, starting with the personal, local, and immediate and advancing through to an examination of the presence and role of Whiteness. My analysis in this situation, because it did not follow the Protocol, wound up being incomplete and completely unsatisfying.

A tool that might have helped me to "stay in Protocol" with Matais is one that my colleagues and I developed for our advanced seminar, Beyond Diversity II. Modeled after Benjamin Bloom's taxonomy, introduced in 1956 to help educators classify learning objectives for students, the Courageous Conversations Developmental Scale similarly helps leaders for racial equity progress to advance from a rudimentary intellectual understanding of the Protocol to an ability to engage it as a way of interrupting systemic racism. Figure 3.2 provides an illustration of six levels, all components in what Bloom defined as the cognitive domain, for processing the Courageous Conversations Protocol. While the complete taxonomy offered two additional domains—affective and psychomotor, which, respectively, define one's emotional and behavioral learning development—at this time, our team has focused only on adapting the cognitive domain, which is primarily, if not exclusively, embraced and understood by many educators.

Figure 3.2 Adapting Bloom's Taxonomy to the Development of Proficiency in Understanding, Internalizing, and Applying the Courageous Conversations Protocol

- **Knowledge:** Defines, Describes, Recites, Recalls, Recognizes, Identifies, States, Outlines

- **Comprehension:** Comprehends, Converts, Defends, Distinguishes, Generalizes, Gives Examples, Infers, Interprets, Understands

- **Application:** Applies, Changes, Computes, Constructs, Demonstrates, Discovers, Solves, Uses

- **Analysis:** Breaks Down, Compares, Contrasts, Diagrams, Deconstructs, Discriminates, Identifies, Illustrates, Infers

- **Synthesis:** Categorizes, Combines, Compiles, Composes, Creates, Devises, Designs, Modifies, Organizes, Plans, Summarizes

- **Interruption:** Addresses, Eliminates, Eradicates

Figure 3.3 provides a description of how each aspect of the Courageous Conversations Protocol's three components, the Four Agreements, Six Conditions, and Compass, would appear at each developmental level. Embedded is our assumption that leaders for racial equity advance from a place of understanding the Protocol, through internalization toward application—that is we move from knowing to doing or from engaging with Courageous Conversations theory to deepening our antiracist leadership practice.

In retrospect, had Matais and I, early in our courageous conversation, simply announced and affirmed to each other what we both understood to be true about how race was operating or "working" in the situation involving West and Obama, I believe we each would have experienced more profound personal development around the issue. Similarly, by engaging any of the tenets of critical race theory referenced earlier in this chapter, we could have organized our thoughts and comments around some shared racial meaning as well as researched theory.

For the very first time since developing the Courageous Conversations Protocol, this conversation called on me to test the ways in which the Four Agreements, Six Conditions, and Compass lead participants into a spirited dialogue that reveals deeper meaning than otherwise possible. Although I completely understood the value of the Courageous Conversations Protocol in theory, I struggled to apply it in practice in my conversation with Matais. Instead, I camped out primarily in the feeling/emotional quadrant of the Compass and failed to get centered. I allowed my feelings about the widening distance between West and Obama to call up a painful question that has nagged me and literally stopped me in my tracks since middle school: Am I, Glenn Singleton, Black enough?

■ ■ ■

As I was writing this section of this book, I worried that I would worsen an already bad situation by bringing renewed attention to West and Obama's unfortunate public dispute. I still hold a fear that people of color will experience further injury in a racist society when any two powerful Black men (or men of color, for that matter) are observed in racial conflict. By leveling such race-based accusations at Obama, West offers White liberals and conservatives of color permission to attack the president similarly. West's act, in this instance, is racially damaging and dangerous to the president and our society; his is also a highly subjective accusation fortified by the very prominence and power White liberals have bestowed on him. In a sense, is West not guilty of the same racial crime with which he has charged President Obama? So, what does that mean?

Over the past two decades, I have seen courageous conversations between educators of color and White educators come to a screeching halt as they were forced to confront the possibility that one or all might be racial "imposters"—that is, not truly authentic in their racial identity (and subsequently in naming and enacting their personal racial equity purpose or PREP), nor truly racially fit to address issues relating to race in their schools, districts, and communities. In short, why is it that many of us refuse to take antiracist action in the realm of possibility where we already know exactly what we must do and how to do it? To this day, what remains most disturbing to me is how, despite my highest-level engagement with the Protocol, I neglected to move from theory to practice in this

(Text continued on page 63)

Figure 3.3 The Courageous Conversations Protocol Developmental Scale (Beyond Diversity II)

	Knowledge	Comprehension	Application	Analysis	Synthesis	Interruption
Stay Engaged	I know that I must agree to stay engaged.	I understand that staying engaged is essential for advancing the conversation and involves full participation of my mind, body, and spirit.	I demonstrate engagement by actively listening, inquiring and responding to racialized situations or circumstances.	I identify my levels of engagement as well as what triggers my defenses, disconnection, and/or search for detours.	I devise a method for recognizing a pathway through possible detours toward heightened engagement.	I engage at the personal, professional, and organizational levels as a way of addressing and eliminating racism.
Speak Your Truth	I know that I must agree to speak my truth.	I understand that speaking my truth is essential for advancing courageous conversations about race and that it involves getting to know myself as a racial being.	I demonstrate speaking my truth by sharing my racial perspective and asking questions of others about their racial perspective.	I identify my personal truth about my racial experience and deconstruct limiting beliefs I have about speaking authentically about race.	I create space for myself and others to speak truth as a way to raise racial consciousness.	I consistently speak my truth as a way of deepening the conversation and addressing and eliminating institutional racism.
Experience Discomfort	I know that I must agree to experience discomfort.	I understand that experiencing discomfort is essential for advancing courageous conversations about race.	I demonstrate my acceptance of discomfort by my continued participation in courageous conversations about race, even though it is difficult.	I identify my discomfort and am willing to look closely at it to understand better what my obstacles are in courageous conversations about race.	I devise a method for addressing the discomfort that allows me to continue to participate fully in courageous conversations about race.	I seek to experience discomfort in my conversations about race as a way of addressing and eliminating racism.

(Continued)

(Continued)

	Knowledge	Comprehension	Application	Analysis	Synthesis	Interruption
Expect/ Accept Nonclosure	I know that I must expect and accept nonclosure.	I understand that expecting and accepting nonclosure is essential for advancing courageous conversations about race and that this involves an ongoing dialogue with ever-changing solutions.	I demonstrate nonclosure by participating in an ongoing racial discourse where there is no "quick fix," rather the solution is revealed in the process of dialogue itself.	I identify my ways of dealing with racial challenges and my trained desire to find solutions and closure.	I create a method for recognizing a pathway from solutions-thinking to sustaining dialogue on race, recognizing that the more I talk, the more I learn, and the more I learn, the more promising the intervention.	I expect and accept non-closure at the personal, professional, and organizational level as a way of addressing and eliminating racism.
Personal Local Immediate	I know that I must begin with exploring my own personal, local, and immediate experiences about race.	I understand that my own experiences provide a foundation for me to make meaning about race and racism.	I demonstrate my personal explorations of race through my evolving racial autobiography.	I identify the aspects of my personal experience that are affected by race, and I am conscious of that impact.	I create opportunities to discuss the racial aspects of situations that I am immediately involved in.	I address systemic racism when I encounter it in my personal, local, and immediate interactions with others.
Isolate Race	I know that I must isolate race while never failing to recognize that other aspects and forms of diversity continue to affect the racialized scenario.	I understand that by isolating race, I am better able to keep it "on the table" and not allow for other aspects and forms of diversity to supplant racial meaning and significance.	I demonstrate my understanding of race when I can determine its presence, impact, meaning, and/or significance in life situations that others may fail to see.	I identify when to isolate race as a way of holding the space for investigation and understanding of the way in which race affects my own and others' lives.	I combine my deepest analysis of race with an understanding of how other aspects and forms of diversity may be contributing to the process and/or result of a racialized situation.	I address the perpetuation of individual and/or systemic racism by isolating race and insisting that other forms of diversity not be positioned as proxies for race.

	Knowledge	Comprehension	Application	Analysis	Synthesis	Interruption
Multiple Racial Perspective	I recognize that race is a social construct and know that there are multiple racial perspectives.	I understand how race is socially constructed and understand the need to have multiple racial perspectives.	I use multiple racial perspectives to interpret social constructs that have been normalized.	I identify the social constructs that I have normalized about race and compare them to other perspectives.	I combine multiple racial perspectives to modify my own and to reach a critical perspective.	I develop and utilize a critical perspective to interrupt social constructs normalized in Whiteness.
The Compass	I know that there is a Compass; I recognize its components and I can define its purpose in advancing the conversation.	I understand the Compass holistically as well as its components and how they work independently and in relationship to each other.	I use the Compass to sustain courageous conversations about race by locating my response, getting centered, and discovering the location of others' responses.	I identify when to use the Compass holistically as a part of the Courageous Conversations Protocol in order to sustain the conversation.	I combine the components of the Compass into a single tool to center myself and others so that we can together deepen our courageous conversations about race.	I use the Compass as a tool to interrupt the silence about race and racism and to progress into deeper and more courageous conversations about race.

(Continued)

(Continued)

	Knowledge	Comprehension	Application	Analysis	Synthesis	Interruption
Working Definition For Race	I know that I must have a working definition of race in order to engage in courageous conversations about it.	I understand that race is different from ethnicity and culture and that parties involved in courageous conversations about race must agree on a working definition of race.	I use an agreed-upon working definition of race when having a courageous conversation about it.	I identify the nuances that distinguish race from other ethnic and/or cultural characteristics and place race into a social context.	I compile the social indicators of racial classification to capture the ways in which race is operating when I am engaged in a courageous conversation about race.	I use a working definition of race to eliminate detours and thus keep the conversation focused on race.
Examining Whiteness	I know that Whiteness is a condition and understand its aspect and levels as well as the purpose of recognizing it in courageous conversations about race.	I understand that Whiteness is always operating when I engage in any courageous conversation about race.	I use my awareness of Whiteness to demonstrate its impact on any conversation about race.	I can deconstruct the presence and role of Whiteness in my life and can identify the ways that I challenge my own Whiteness.	I can organize my understanding of Whiteness in terms of color, culture, and consciousness in order to capture the ways in which Whiteness is operating when I am engaged in a conversation about race.	I interrupt the perpetuation of White supremacy by recognizing the role and presence of Whiteness and how it affects the critical thinking, beliefs, emotions, and actions of Whites and non-Whites.

(Continued)

critical instance. This only goes to show that we all—educators and racial equity leaders of varying positions, degrees of commitment, and understanding, myself included—sometimes find ourselves incapacitated by the prospect and practice of engaging in courageous conversations about race. Once I recognized my own failure to launch, I chose not to let myself off the hook. Rather, as I continued to develop in "doing" the Courageous Conversations Protocol, I must recommit to staying engaged, speaking my truth, experiencing discomfort, and expecting and accepting nonclosure. As for Dr. West, perhaps a part of his frustration with the president stems from his own personal, local, and immediate place of racial inauthenticity. How much safer and easier it initially feels to ask another to step up or out in a way that we have yet to do ourselves. Sometimes, however, when we ask another to do our own personal heavy lifting, we only create a more substantial racial challenge for ourselves and everyone else in our community.

ESSENTIAL QUESTIONS

Recall an actual situation in which you believe you successfully confronted racism in your work, and answer these questions:

1. According to the Courageous Conversations Protocol Developmental Scale (Figure 3.3), what level of proficiency in each component did you demonstrate in this situation?

2. Which aspects of the Protocol evidenced your lowest-level proficiency development in that situation?

3. What do you believe challenges you to attain a higher level of proficiency in these aspects?

4. How might you hold yourself accountable to advancing toward a higher developmental level on each component of the Courageous Conversations Protocol?

5. How might this situation's outcomes have changed, had you more effectively applied the Protocol?

Voices From the Inside: Devon Alexander

I was born and raised in the suburban Chicagoland area of Chicago, Illinois. Given my lived experience of race within American society and the American educational system, it is fitting that I grew up in an area immortalized in John Hughes's films, like *Ferris Bueller's Day Off, The Breakfast Club,* and *Sixteen Candles.* I grew up as a young male of color immersed in an environment that did not reflect my lived experiences of race. In school, I became increasingly conscious of the disparity between my developing racial consciousness and the people with whom I inhabited these predominantly White spaces. My ability to navigate Whiteness afforded me opportunities and privileges not experienced by my family and friends of color.

I pursued an undergraduate course of study that prepared me to become a secondary school English teacher. I worked with the hope of re-entering the American educational system as someone who could interrupt the systemic racial educational disparities that ravaged the lives within them, especially those of people of color. Despite my lived experience of race and my academic study of the impact of race in American literature and educational institutions, I was ill-prepared to engage in conversations about race at the most personal level: with my family.

Witnessing the devastating impact of racial dysconsciousness—a constructed view of race that is unmatched by racial reality—in the lives of my family, friends, and school community members, I became convinced of the need to ensure that I minimized the traumatic impact of racism in the lives of my children. Conceiving biracial children within my interracial marriage created the real conditions that compelled me to stand steadfast in these convictions. Prior to the birth of my sons, I nearly completely avoided engaging my White family in conversations about the continued social significance and impact of race, racism, and Whiteness within our personal and social lives. I did not want my racial perspective to disrupt my wife's family dynamic. My personal experiences of engaging in interracial dialogue about race convinced me of the impossibility of such discourse ending in anything other than combat. I struggled with these interracial racial discussions, typically being the only person of color in them and often being the only person in the conversation who disrupted the personal views and worldviews of others. The birth of my sons more closely bound me to my wife's White family in ways that I otherwise would have avoided. Their birth, and my convictions about protecting them from the trauma of racism, also required me to learn how to engage more effectively in conversations about race with our White family.

How would I navigate White racial consciousness that was blinded by a color-blind ideology in which race was minimized as a shaping force in these developing familial interracial relationships? How would I protect my sons and myself while protecting my White family from the possible destructive outcomes of interracial race talk? Before I could find answers to the questions that engulfed me during my interactions with my White family, our collective tension within a newly formed interracial family began to weigh on these relationships. In my efforts to clarify the reasons why it was a necessity to talk about race as an interracial family with young children, our interracial conversations about race imploded with racial misunderstanding before they ever really began. All of the deep psychological, emotional, and physical trauma of American society's unhealed racial wounds were triggered within our family.

My efforts to clarify my racial understanding, experiences, and familial position were not the correct tools I needed to redirect this conversation in healthy ways for any of us. The collateral damage of the adults' inability to navigate this conversation would inevitably involve my sons. I was looking into the heart of my deep hurt as the father of sons who would defy the delusion of American social constructions and realities of race. In the midst of this hurt and lack of understanding, I stumbled upon the text, *Courageous Conversations About Race.*

The Courageous Conversations Protocol—with its Compass, Four Agreements, and Six Conditions—provides those engaging in interracial dialogue about race with new tools to have these conversations in new ways and in the hopes of reaching new outcomes. My old tools had me desiring to become uncaring and wanting to launch race as a grenade into this dysfunctional interracial family.

White denial rejected the necessity to develop a critical understanding of race. In my newly formed interracial family, White racial knowledge was used to reject my academic knowledge and lived experience of race. My unique voice of color—speaking out of concern about what the lived experience of race, racism, and Whiteness had shown me was the devastating result of developing this interracial family on the dysfunctional racial foundation of American society—was combatively rejected. Hurt and anger fueled raged within me.

This internal trauma gave rise to a disastrous willingness to unleash my hurt, anger, and rage on White racial dysconsciousness. I desired to destroy my interracial family in my efforts to protect my sons from the hurt and pain of race, racism, and Whiteness. The folly of this paradox, however, was illuminated for me through the Protocol. The Compass provided me with the space to be hurt and angry while creating space for my White family to enter the conversation from their racial perspectives. It called for me to walk my way around the Compass in order to get centered in the conversation. This move on my part enabled me to model this movement for the rest of the family.

The Four Agreements required us to have our interracial conversation about race according to specific parameters that were unlike anything we had been socialized to use in these conversations. We realized that our conversations did not have to end because we were ravaged by American social discomfort about race, racism, and Whiteness. We could use the Four Agreements to walk our way through the discomfort, work out our racial misunderstandings, and find the voice to talk it through, for each other and for my sons.

The Six Conditions focused our talks about race. The Conditions distilled the historic and contemporary realities of race, racism, and Whiteness into content that we could manage. They guided me and those with whom I dialogued toward deepened racial understanding, beliefs, and perspectives.

As I opened myself up to these new tools and new way of having conversations about race with my interracial family, I began to see the possibility of new outcomes. This insight guided me in the process of studying, working out my understanding, and applying the Protocol in these conversations about race. Through this process, I came to internalize the Protocol. I began to see the distinction between ineffective and effective conversations about race, and I could see how the Protocol could be used to achieve outcomes in these conversations that are uncommon within mainstream racial discourse. This internalization has created numerous opportunities for me to bring theory and practice together within professional educational racial discourse regarding the intersection of race, racism, whiteness, and education.

Mainstream American racial discourse is delusional, dysfunctional, and teeming with racial dysconsciousness. This racial dysconsciousness suffocates efforts to address the systemic racial educational disparities that can be traced back to the disingenuous moves to dismantle systemic and institutionalized educational White supremacy in the mid-20th century. The racial discourse of education is drowning in a dysconsciousness that perpetuates systemic and institutionalized racism within schools. These dysconscious educational environments contribute to the systemic racial educational disparities that abandon students of color in their academic and life development. Educational racial discourse is embedded within every educator's consciousness before he or she ever enters professional development activities claiming to be about addressing the intersection of race and education. The Courageous Conversations Protocol can be an effective tool for establishing authentic and honest educational racial discourse. Facilitating educational conversations about race is about guiding educators to understand the existence and manifestations of race within themselves and their practice.

The Compass offers educators the space to be wherever they are personally and professionally concerning the issue of the intersection of race and education within American society and individuals. It creates the pathways we need to hear, inquire, and respond to where we are as educators in an effort to realize the foundations on which we work. As our ability to hear ourselves and others grows, we can work our way to the center of the Compass to effectively investigate our racial consciousness, practice, and educational institutions. The Four Agreements direct us to function in conversations about race in ways that are more effective than what we learned in mainstream American society. Our socialized silence and denial fall away, and we become positioned to give voice to the intersection of our racial beliefs and actions in an effort to develop more effective professional practices for the sake of students. The Six Conditions direct our conversation in the difficult process of unpacking the legacy of the dehumanizing social construction of race within American society and lives. The Conditions represent the process of healing from the wounds of our collective racial mis-education. Working through the Conditions enables educators to develop a racial lens that reveals the personal and social impact of race, racism, and whiteness within educational institutions.

The process of doing this work with educators is about positioning educators to do the work of decentering themselves in their consciousness, classrooms, and schools. The Protocol facilitates this liberation, which gives rise to educators and students in whom transformative racial experiences enrich life development within educational institutions.

Devon Alexander is an English teacher and Beyond Diversity facilitator at Oak Park and River Forest High School in Oak Park, Illinois, a suburb of Chicago and a PEG partnering district. He is a Black American.

FOUR

Seven Years Later

What's Different and What's the Same?

You've pulled something from your storehouse that the creator made just for you!

—Maya Angelou

In 2010, when I sat down to begin writing this book, a fact that was most evident to me was that the United States of America had undergone many remarkable changes—changes such as I had never anticipated in 2003, the year I began writing the *Courageous Conversations* field guide. The geopolitical and socioeconomic landscape of this country in 2010 did not, in many ways, some better and others worse, even remotely resemble what it was 7 years earlier.

Conversely, the overall challenges facing our systems of education during that span of time remained remarkably similar. In 2003, cuts to federal, state, and local budgets had already begun to rob our children of the high-quality schooling experiences they would need to prepare them to face the domestic and global dilemmas of the 21st century. Across wealthy, middle-income, and poor neighborhoods, increasing racial disparities in achievement were already highlighting the nation's persistent inability to face the vestiges of its unfortunate history of racial extermination and enslavement, along with various other forms of racial injustice.

Already experiencing a downward trajectory of the country's education ranking among industrialized nations, U.S. schools in 2003 were continuing to see increasing enrollments of students of color. In 2010, some states, such as California, declared a majority "non-White" school-age population for the first time. Several states simultaneously reached an all-time low in the number of students demonstrating proficiency on state and federal tests.

Of course, a variety of devastating economic forces continue to be at play in our nation and world, all of which are causing schools countrywide to scramble for limited resources. Given so much change, the educational outcomes for under-served students of color in the United States increasingly mirror those of children in developing nations around the world. It is certainly intriguing to realize that school quality and the national commitment to provide a world-class education to all students have been dissipating at a rate inversely proportionate to the escalating rate of children of color entering our preK–12 and higher education systems. Thus, I believe it is essential to offer a simple bottom-line statement. Yes, as my late grandmother, "Nana" Helen Singleton, often said: "The more things change, the more they stay the same!"

The election of the nation's first president of color clearly has had a significant impact on the national conversation, or nonconversation, about race and racism. I have already referenced a few of the negative implications of this extraordinary milestone in this volume's previous three chapters. In this chapter, I will refrain from further commentary about Obama's election, even though President Obama, the First Family, and his administration's policies, appointments, and staffing clearly represent or are somehow responsible for the most dramatic racial shifts of my lifetime, let alone of the last 7 years. I must point out, however, that although this change at the highest level of government is monumental, school leaders may see more significance in the expanding pockets of resistance to transforming our nation's schools into socially just and racially equitable institutions. Specifically, national polls indicate that, compared to 2008, significantly more Americans today would not vote for President Obama simply because he is Black. It is not unreasonable to consider that their racial views may be reflected in the budgetary decisions of government officials regarding programs that would benefit students of color.

Seven years after the publication of the *Courageous Conversations* field guide, when we as a nation measure our progress by student achievement statistics, we find that we are not in a better place. True, the community of racial equity leaders is much larger now and more intricately connected through technology, but so is the army of resisters, who focus on maintaining the racial status quo and intensifying the social norms that exclude, segregate, or relegate children of color to second-rate, poorly resourced schools. Seven years later, systemic racism continues to prompt increasing racial disparities, and school and government officials continue to offer economic excuses for their failure to confront the often-devastating inequities systemic racism creates within and throughout our nation's education system.

In 1949, W.E.B. Du Bois wrote the following:

> Of all the civil rights for which the world has struggled and fought for five thousand years, the right to learn is undoubtedly the most fundamental. . . . The freedom to learn . . . has been bought by bitter sacrifice. And whatever we may think of the curtailment of other civil rights, we should fight to the last ditch to keep open the right to learn, the right to have examined in our schools not only what we believe, but what we do not believe; not only what our leaders say, but what the leaders of other groups and nations, and the leaders of other centuries have said. We must insist upon this to give our children the fairness of a start which will equip them with such an array of facts and such an attitude toward truth that they have a real chance to judge what the world is and what its greater minds have thought it might be.[1]

Du Bois's words serve both as a reminder and as a call to attention and action. If the nation's children continue to be deprived of their basic civil right to a quality education, and if we as educators and racial equity leaders fail to give them true freedom to learn, our hopes of becoming an even greater nation will fade—that is, unless we mount an all-out war on systemic racism and mobilize educators to work relentlessly for educational racial equity.

EMBRACING EQUITY AND NAMING THE "IT": SYSTEMIC RACISM

Many school systems have contacted my firm, Pacific Educational Group (PEG), Inc., to learn more about its racial equity leadership development and programming support for educators. Some never follow through with an agreement to partner with PEG because of its insistence that they specifically identify and name the proverbial elephant in the room—systemic racism—and commit to crafting an explicit policy to address it, its root causes, and its present-day manifestations. Others balk at PEG's insistence that its clients agree in advance to develop and implement a systemic transformation framework that is unapologetically equity-focused and antiracist. The details of this requisite equity policy and systemic framework are discussed in depth in Chapter 7, but partnering with PEG essentially means that school system personnel at all levels must address their underlying fears and/or their disbeliefs about the existence and effects of systemic racism in their midst and courageously commit to implementing equity programming as the solution for meeting the needs of all the children in their schools.

Other districts are reluctant to partner with PEG out of fear that explicitly naming racism as a core issue will upset White teachers, parents, and others in the school community. It is difficult, without a doubt, to get educators to examine and address their internalized, often unconscious, racist beliefs. It is also challenging to ask them to dismantle the racist barriers they often do not see. This covert racism drains individuals and school systems of human and other resources simply because it prevents them from having the freedom to have courageous conversations about, interact with, and act on issues relating to race and racism. However, at PEG, we strive to give school systems and personnel the language they will need to engage in these conversations in ways that are relevant and precise. We help them to reduce and eliminate the cultural insensitivities of the system and its staff and to garner recognition from the racially conscious educators and community activists whose support school systems so desperately need to surmount this challenge.

In 1998, I was asked, for the second consecutive year, to give the keynote address before the curriculum supervisors of the state of California at the Asilomar Conference Center. My focus this time was on educational equity, of course, but as it related specifically to education standards. I titled my address, "Standards: An Opportunity to Learn About Equity!"

My goals were twofold: First, I wanted to lay out a simple definition of equity that my audience of school leaders could easily apply to their important work on behalf of students of color. Second, I wanted to leave them with the understanding that race matters and that the responsibility for investigating the way race influences curriculum and instruction and, in this specific case, the crafting and adoption of new standards was theirs to take.

Having lived in California for only about 8 years at that time, and having only a couple of years under my belt facilitating my Beyond Diversity workshops, I recognized my need to tread lightly with this esteemed audience of seasoned California educators, most of whom were deputy superintendents and chief instruction officers. In retrospect, if I were to give that address again today, recognizing as I do even more now the need to be explicit and to avoid tiptoeing around "taboo" issues, I would have charged that audience to develop a more sophisticated understanding of systemic racism—that is, to discover how it permeates the systems in which they work and how it leads increasingly to disparities in student engagement, participation, and achievement. I would have also stated explicitly that the definition of equity in this country must name systemic racism as being at the core of the issue.

Perhaps my hopes of being invited to return to Asilomar a third time (which, by the way, never happened) prevented me from mustering the courage to speak my own truths about racism to that audience. And the bottom line of my understanding is that while racism is not the only factor contributing to the diminished engagement and performance of under-served students of color, it is indeed *the missing factor* in our education reform efforts. It is also the most devastating to our children, their families, and our society in general.

Today, I have an even clearer realization that our school systems are designed to resist equity and that educational leaders need a more fortified sense of Personal Racial Equity Purpose (PREP) to address that inequity. Too often, racially conscious educators remain silent on these issues as they witness students of color being failed in schools while the students and their families are blamed for this failure. Yet, whether those educators are explicitly purposeful or covert and silent, resistance inside and outside the schools, reinforced with feelings of distrust, eventually occurs—and racial equity leaders *must* have an answer for that.

That is why the definition of equity that we offer to educators, parents, students, and communities must be one that is understandable, irrefutable, and actionable. Predictably, some educators will confuse *equity* with *equality*. This common misunderstanding must be dealt with head on, and as part of my discussion on liberalism in the following chapter, I will unpack the equity/equal ideology and explore the cultural dilemmas resulting from this confusion of terms.

For now, it is critical that educators recognize that if we continue providing "equal" support to students achieving at different academic levels, we will continue to experience and even perpetuate performance disparities. In focusing on equity, educators must confront *all* gaps in student performance—be they racial, linguistic, economic, or gender. Racial equity leaders thus address the student achievement challenges that are hardest to talk about as well as those that are the most difficult to solve.

■ ■ ■

Many of PEG's prospective partner districts cannot envision a way of embracing, and announcing to their school communities, the following equity goal:

EQUITY IS...
Raising the achievement of all students,
while narrowing the gaps between the highest
and lowest performing students,
and eliminating the racial predictability
and disproportionality of which student groups occupy
the highest and lowest achievement categories.

The late African American educator and former Washington, D.C., school district superintendent, Barbara Sizemore, often suggested that in order for schools to become places in which *all* children can learn, the causes or reasons that prevent this from happening must be identified and addressed. Even in relatively affluent suburban school districts like Montgomery County, Maryland (just north of the nation's capital), which has previously received praise for "putting race on the table," naming racism is often beyond the school leaders' consciousness and courage:

> While sharing their differentiation strategy and the results it had produced with colleagues from other districts, [the Montgomery County school leaders] began to think seriously about what challenges remained to achieving excellence and equity across the entire system. As a team, they committed to working intensely on this question when they returned to Montgomery County. In the early weeks following the retreat, senior administrators debated the appropriate language to use when discussing race issues within the district. While some preferred the description *removing institutional barriers,* others favored the term *institutionalized racism* because they believed that it most accurately described the real issue. A few administrators expressed concerns that using the word *racism* could potentially spark fear in some administrators and teachers who would misinterpret it to mean they were racist. [Then-Superintendent Jerry] Weast distinguished between the two phrases explaining that "institutional racism is the failure to act on removing institutional barriers that hold students of a particular race back." The team decided to explicitly define *institutional barriers* as those policies, procedures, and practices that do not serve all children equitably.[2]

Sizemore's teachings are especially instructive to me because they point out the lengths to which educators go to avoid explicitly naming racism as one of the causes of academic achievement disparities and the systemic educational failure of children of color across this nation. Rather than embracing the leadership challenge of developing educators who understand what the terms *institutional racism* and *racist* mean, the educators in the case above expended time, energy, and emotion discovering a way to avoid addressing these factors and instead arrived at various disconnected and sometimes irrelevant solutions and implementation processes.

Why? Because they feared how the least racially conscious and courageous educators and community members among them would react to their honest discovery and assertions. They did not consider that their failure to name the "it"—the causal factor—behind racial disparities in educational achievement would diminish the trust of those school leaders who were ready and eager to face our nation's, and their own, racist demons and deinstitutionalize racism.

Defining racism must not be left up to those educators who possess the least amount of the racial consciousness and courage to do so. Such people will never offer a racial truth that mobilizes practitioners or that moves Courageous Conversations from theory to practice. Instead, they will search for a causal factor that enables them and other, likewise racially unconscious educators to continue feeling relative comfort while holding on to their debilitating racial beliefs and behaviors—beliefs and behaviors that ultimately get in the way of our students' freedom to learn. And as long as racial equity leaders allow them to continue operating from an ill-constructed, invalid, and uninformed definition of racism—and subsequently allow them to conveniently reject the existence of racism in their personal, professional, or organizational interactions—we will never ensure that under-served children of color can exercise their inalienable right to a free and appropriate education.

In crafting my own definition of racism, I was greatly inspired by the thinking of Camara Phyllis Jones, a Baltimore physician and public health researcher and practitioner. Her seminal essay, titled "Levels of Racism: A Theoretical Framework and a Gardener's Tale," attempts to introduce a social rather than biological or medical description of race to people in the health professions.[3] Employing the metaphor of a flower, Jones defines three levels of racism: personally mediated, internalized, and institutional. She offers this description as a means of helping medical investigators explore the potential effects of racism on race-associated differences in health outcomes. Her hypotheses supporting the investigation into the ways racism triggers racial disparities in health conditions are congruent with the ideas I illuminate in Chapter 5 regarding neuroscience and the physiological impact of racism on students' ability to achieve in school.

Over time, I have adapted Jones's theory to my own work, applying it to what I witness nearly every day in schools across the country. I should point out here, however, that although I focus on the ways racism affects students, I realize that the racial experience of the adult educators and other staff members who inhabit the schools, as well as students' family members at home, are also subject to these same racial forces and experiences. The larger idea is that until a working definition of racism has been established, uncovering, examining, or addressing its impact on learning and teaching cannot be achieved.

Personally mediated racism refers to conscious or unconscious, intentional or unintentional transactions between White people and people of color in which the latter generally feel or actually are violated. According to Jones:

> *Personally mediated racism* ... includes acts of commission as well as acts of omission. It manifests as lack of respect (poor or no service, failure to communicate options), suspicion (shopkeepers' vigilance; everyday avoidance, including street crossing, purse clutching, and standing when there are empty seats on public transportation), devaluation (surprise at competence, stifling of aspirations), [and] scapegoating.[4]

Although people of color speak often about the pain and suffering they have suffered as a result of personally mediated racism, internalized racism, or the developed and practiced belief in one's own racial inferiority, can be just as detrimental. Jones offers the following definition:

> *Internalized racism* is defined as acceptance by members of the stigmatized races of negative messages about their own abilities and intrinsic worth. It is characterized by their not believing in others who look like them, and not believing in themselves. It involves accepting limitations to one's own full humanity, including one's spectrum of dreams, one's right to self-determination, and one's range of allowable self-expression. It manifests as an embracing of "whiteness" (use of hair straighteners and bleaching creams, stratification by skin tone within communities of color, and "the white man's ice is colder" syndrome); self-devaluation (racial slurs as nicknames, rejection of ancestral culture, and fratricide); and resignation, helplessness, and hopelessness (dropping out of school, failing to vote, and engaging in risky health practices).[5]

Certainly, when teachers and administrators have low expectations of students of color, diminished student achievement outcomes typically are the result. But when those children of color do not have a personal sense of efficacy, and when their parents also suffer from low self-worth due to their own experiences of racial insult and degradation, the toll on the children's psyches can be devastating. The famed Kenneth and Mamie Clark doll experiments of the 1940s, which later became the deciding evidence to end school desegregation in the 1954 *Brown v. Board of Education* case, revealed how internalized racism destroys the confidence and diminishes the achievement of children of color. Alternatively, when students possess high-level personal belief in their cultural value and academic potential, as illustrated in the "We Believe" creed at the largely African American Urban Prep Academy in Chicago, Illinois, school success rates are greatly improved.

The third level of racism, according to Jones, is that of institutional racism, which, from a school perspective, can center on everything from governing policies and behavior codes to classroom rules and attendance regulations—all of which may serve to limit or eliminate access, opportunity, and participation for students of color while potentially, but not necessarily, providing advantages to White students. The following is Jones' definition:

> *Institutionalized racism* manifests itself both in material conditions and in access to power. With regard to material conditions, examples include differential access to quality education, sound housing, gainful employment, appropriate medical facilities, and a clean environment. With regard to access to power, examples include differential access to information (including one's own history), resources (including wealth and organizational infrastructure), and voice (including voting rights, representation in government, and control of the media). It is important to note that the association between socioeconomic status and race in the United States has its origins in discrete historical events but persists because of contemporary structural factors that perpetuate those historical injustices. In other words, it is because of institutionalized racism that there is an association between socioeconomic status and race in this country.[6]

Whereas Jones's examination of racism ends with the three levels discussed above, I am inclined to offer a fourth level—one that I believe to be the most far-reaching and formidable of all: systemic racism. Systemic racism is the most devastating factor contributing to the diminished capacity of all children—especially Black, Brown, and American Indian children—to achieve at the highest levels. It contributes to the fracturing of the communities that nurture and support children of color in and outside of school, making it more difficult for educators to meet racially targeted students' school-based needs.

My definition of systemic racism incorporates and overlaps with the three levels introduced by Jones, and it also takes into account the residual effects of the history of racial injustice people of color have suffered in the United States. It further considers the contemporary manifestations of structural and environmental racism in a nation that has yet to find a solution to the insidious problem of its enduring racial caste system. It acknowledges, for example, that historically students of color have been tasked to achieve academically in schools they were once legally barred from attending.

Moreover, given that the vast majority of these students only rarely see themselves reflected in either the curricula of the schools or the White instructors and administrators who predominate in those schools, students of color often struggle to establish their relevance in these settings. They are often culturally "othered," or made to feel different or deviant, by these White school leaders. Should they muster the courage to speak to their feelings of racial marginalization that result from their subordination, their claims are often dismissed and denied. Sometimes students of color are reprimanded or punished when they even assert the existence of racism. In disproportionate numbers, they are removed from traditional classroom settings and relegated to special or alternative education programs, where, after dropping or failing out, many determine themselves to be unintelligent and unable to learn.

For those educators who believe that they are doing everything they can to eliminate systemic racism in their schools and to reduce the racial disparities in student achievement, the essential question remains: "What more can I do?" Seven years later, that answer too remains the same: Begin by having courageous conversations about race with those whom you previously have refused to confront.

THE DATA

Some theorists believe the best way to convince educators that they must address issues of race and systemic racism is to launch into deep and meaningful inquiry around student achievement data. Although I certainly agree that racial equity leaders must have a complete and irrefutable set of data to make the case for their antiracism efforts, I also recognize that whatever beliefs educators bring to school, they also bring to their data. That is, educators' damaging racial beliefs and behaviors yield extraordinarily predictable, and likewise damaging, results.

The data on the racial disparities in student achievement in the United States can be disconcerting for teachers and administrators. Given the increasing numbers of underserved children of color populating our nation's schools, the picture of our public education system, in most places, is an ugly one. It is even uglier when we measure school success by the growth in achievement of students of color compared to their White peers, as depicted by standardized test score data and (more recently) in terms of core standards mastery. Without a clear way of describing, through data, how race affects schooling, it will be impossible to address how broadly and deeply systemic racism influences, if not determines, achievement. But analysis of the data alone cannot equip educators with the requisite will, skill, knowledge, and capacity to take an honest look at how race influences their personal, professional, and organization beliefs and perspective with regard to student ability and learning. Nor can data reveal how educators' problematic and unchecked racial beliefs, perspective, and attitudes, particularly those about under-served student-of-color populations, determine the behaviors of those educators inside and outside the classroom.

About six weeks after the *Courageous Conversations* field guide debuted in 2005, I began to receive criticism about a data sample I used in that book to debunk the claim that poverty, not race, was the leading causality factor behind the so-called achievement gap between Whites and Blacks in the United States. Interesting enough, the attack on those data, which detailed SAT scores reported by The College Board, was focused not on their validity or reliability but rather on their datedness. According to those critics, the data I used, which were compiled in 1998 (see Figure 4.1), indicated trends in the nineties. My book was published in 2006; thus, they claimed, my data were outdated. I feel it is important here to first restate and then perhaps to clarify my analysis of that earlier data set. SAT data from 2011 and other complementary data sets that are even more recent support my assertion that achievement not only has not improved, but predictably is getting worse. As I stated in the *Courageous Conversations* field guide:

> Income does impact achievement: The scores of all races improve as their family income increases. However, wealth or poverty alone fails to fully explain the racial achievement gap, which persists irrespective of income level. In most studies and reports, achievement gaps are addressed in terms of economic differences with little or no connection made to race. The University of California 1998 SAT data, which shows intersectionality of race and income, reveals important subtleties about racial achievement gaps. First, at every income level, Black and Brown students are outperformed by White students. Specifically, Black students are predictably the lowest performing group at every level. Second, such data help us to see the astonishing achievement disparity existing between Black and White students who are equally poor. Third, we see that poorer White students actually outperform middle-income Black and Brown students. Consequently, even if we were to project the data to students in families with incomes of $200,000—clearly a greatly diminished pool of Black and Brown families—the racial gap would most likely persist. To suggest that the achievement gaps evidenced in the University of California study of SAT scores has nothing to do with race or racism stands in the way of a complete explanation of the disparity within and between income levels.[7]

As Figure 4.2 shows, identical patterns emerge from the most recent 2011 SAT data. In analyzing data such as these, some educators get stuck in the intellectual

Figure 4.1 Average SAT Scores by Parental Income and Race/Ethnicity

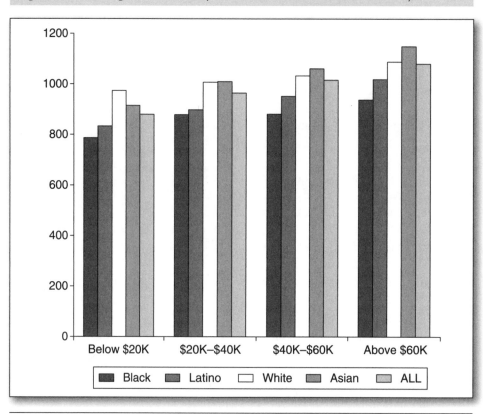

Source: National Center for Education Statistics, U.S. Department of Education, 1998. A similar version of this chart appears as Figure 3.1 in *Courageous Conversations About Race: A Field Guide for Achieving Equity in Schools* (p. 30), by Glenn Singleton and Curtis Linton, 2006, Thousand Oaks, CA: Corwin.

quadrant of the Courageous Conversations Compass. They focus their questions about the data on the relative size of the population or they seek deeper understanding of statistics and methodology instead of addressing the central issue of why the Black, Brown, and American Indian children are categorically outperformed by their White and Asian American counterparts. Although some of these questions may be provocative and even enlightening, educators should not be allowed to escape the plain and obvious truth: that the darkest children are at the bottom of the achievement scale, no matter how one cuts, dices, or slices the data. Indeed, I am fairly certain that if the positioning of White and Black children were interchanged in the data table, specific questions about the White students' experiences in school would be raised and discussed—in fact, viewing the situation this way may help move educators from the intellectual to the emotional quadrant. In addition, I am certain that we would not require reams of data to inform us if our Black, Brown, and American Indian children, in proportionality, were outperforming their White counterparts . . . we would be able to feel this difference in our school culture and climate. That feeling would be equity, achieved!

Figure 4.2 2011 Average SAT Scores by Parental Income and Race/Ethnicity

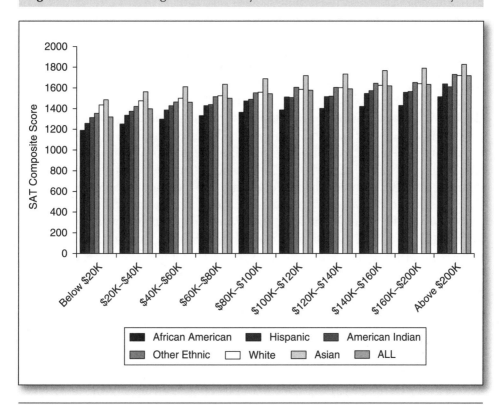

Source: Data derived from "College-Bound Seniors 2010 and 2011, Total Group Profile Report—ETHNICITY (Table 11)," Copyright © 2010–2011 The College Board, retrieved from www.collegeboard .org.

One of my biggest worries is that the time allowed for educators to pontificate on new and different presentations of the same or similar types and amounts of data is not time spent transforming the beliefs and behaviors that yield differential institutional policies and instructional practices for White children and children of color. Until these latter areas are addressed, the gap in student achievement will continue to widen. Educators' continued failure to view the lack of improvement in the academic achievement of students of color as a systemic issue, and thus their failure to do what they are *paid* to do—which is, presumably, to educate *all* children—will result in the continued academic failure of children of color by day and the continued disparagement of the families and communities they travel home to by night.

I offer the following set of questions as a more logical and focused starting point for educators to begin their analysis of racially disaggregated testing data:

1. What do these data tell you about student performance?

2. Do you notice any gaps in performance?

3. How do you define/describe these gaps?

4. How do these data compare with data in the school system in which you work and/or live?

5. What do you believe to be the cause of such gaps?

To move Courageous Conversations from theory to practice, racial equity leaders must be able to offer concise and irrefutable data highlighting the racial achievement disparities in their schools and districts. Given that a frequent response to such data is skepticism, if not dismissal, it is critical that the sample used depicts a correlation between three variables: race, income/wealth, and achievement. Data that identify only income and achievement variables invite plausible objection to the notion that race matters. To fully explain the saliency of race, one cannot dispute the devastating achievement disparities that exist between children of poverty and their most wealthy counterparts, regardless of race. But we also must illuminate the racial gaps that exist among student cohorts within the same income level. Finally we must examine why is it that higher income students of color continue to be outperformed by their lower income White counterparts. Again, this is not to say that race is the *only* factor that determines educational inequities; rather, it is too often the missing aspect of analysis—the one aspect that we in American society typically bend over backward to avoid and overlook when we attempt to understand why predictable groups of children of color do not succeed in our schools.

MINDING THE GAPS

The phrase *achievement gap* can be found on more than 50 pages of the *Courageous Conversations* field guide. Why? Because under the official mandates of the No Child Left Behind (NCLB) legislation, it became common practice to define and measure this gap using standardized test scores to determine which subgroups were not proficient in mathematics and English language arts. Soon after the *Courageous Conversations* field guide was published in 2006, I experienced an epiphany that, to this day, I have been desperate to share in print with educators who, like me, quest for "racist-free" schools. I realized then that the language I had adopted to describe the disparities in achievement between White students and a majority of students of color was in fact reinforcing the very Whiteness and White norms I was seeking through my work to "right-size."

I will expound on this a bit later in this section, but for now it will suffice to say that, at the time, I thought the NCLB requirement that districts and schools measure their effectiveness in terms of disaggregated student test score data was a definite move forward in terms of achieving racial equity. For the very first time, I believed, educators, parents, and concerned citizens alike would have at their fingertips data on how historically lower-achieving groups of students were performing.

In the years before and since, of course, some educators have criticized NCLB for its emphasis on standardized testing data, claiming that it leads school districts and personnel to overemphasize testing above broader aspects of learning. Some organizations even argue that NCLB's mandated focus on testing has led untold numbers of educators across the country—perhaps close to 200 teachers and administrators in the Atlanta Public Schools alone—to engage in unethical and unprofessional behaviors such as cheating.

Listen to Bob Schaeffer, public education director of FairTest, an organization that challenges standardized tests:

> The cheating spike is the predictable fallout from the pervasive misuse of standardized tests in public schools. When test results are all that matter in evaluating students, teachers, and schools, educators feel pressured to boost scores by hook or by crook. Just as in other professions, some will cross the ethical line.
>
> Cheating is not the only negative consequence from test misuse. Many schools have turned classrooms into drill-and-kill test-prep centers, reduced the difficulty of exams and narrowed curriculum. Some even encouraged students to drop out in order to boost scores. Basing teacher evaluations on students' test scores, as some propose, is guaranteed to ratchet up the pressure and further distort schooling.[8]

I do not buy such claims, although some criticisms of testing may be valid. To its credit, NCLB enables racial equity advocates to gain a deeper understanding of and insight into how various groups in the nation's public schools are performing. It also opened the door for some very positive equity developments and discussions. At the same time, however, the testing and test preparation frenzy that accompanied NCLB often overshadowed or took the place of opportunities for quality teaching and learning in many of our most challenged schools. Nevertheless, the destructive ramifications of the alleged cheating scandals cannot negate NCLB's impact on fortifying the language of the so-called achievement gap.

Even so, every time I hear or read the phrase *achievement gap* today, a feeling of dishonesty overtakes me. As I realize more and more that we as educators seem more intent on measuring only the achievement of *our students,* and not each other, I am saddened. Even though it is widely recognized that low performance, especially by under-served students of color, is the result, not the cause, of systemic dysfunction, I cannot shake the feeling that something is decidedly wrong.

Perhaps we should be referring to the current crisis in public education as an *instruction gap* or as an *educational opportunity and access gap.* Both terms better characterize the state of racial inequity in U.S. public schools. Perhaps since the term *gap* suggests a comparison of one group to another, and thus *racial achievement gap* suggests that the performance results of students of color should be referenced to White students, we should consider a change of course. Establishing White achievement as the norm or normal reifies the foundational principle of racism or White supremacy. It also inappropriately suggests that the achievement of students of color should be benchmarked against White students' performance. Given that White students are often not the highest achieving racial group in the United States any longer (in many cases, Asian American students are) and that White student performance has been in decline for well over a decade, setting White student achievement as the standard for children of color is both an artificial measure and an undemanding expectation.

An appropriate alternative as well as an antiracist measurement of student achievement would be one that references all groups of students to a common set of content standards and skills criteria. With this done, our gap discussions would focus on criteria rather than White normative references. Having said this, I must make an important distinction: using criteria-referenced gap language is essential for defining educational outcomes such as student achievement and graduation rates, while the continued use of White racial-norming language is essential for measuring and signaling disparities in educational inputs such as human and fiscal resource allocation, access to highly qualified teachers and rigorous curricula, and placement in gifted versus special education programming. The latter is especially important in terms of the input that is decidedly the hardest to measure: high expectations for student success. The heart and soul of Courageous Conversations lies in examining and addressing this input. Indeed, I will be referencing high expectations repeatedly throughout this text whenever racial gaps or disparities are mentioned.

When I look at the achievement data of any medium-size, racially diverse school district (those enrolling from 10,000 to 25,000 students), what I often notice first is the existence of multiple student achievement gaps. Rather than a single gap, I see achievement disparities between students in various economic, gender, language, and racial categories. When I dive deeper into these output-related data, I typically discern important information about the gaps in educational inputs, such as which student populations are gaining access to advanced curricula and various postsecondary prerequisites (i.e., college entrance and placement examinations). Yet, when politicians, educators, and community organizers reference *the achievement gap,* with regard to similar data I often find myself wondering which of the gaps in the data they are looking at. More important, which ones *should* they be examining—the results data relating to the student, or the input data relating to instruction and resources?

For some, these questions may seem insignificant, but in a society that continuously looks for a variety of ways to talk about race without really engaging in courageous conversations about it, racial equity leaders must be all the more specific about and accurate with the language they use to promote an emphasis on racial equity. To move Courageous Conversations from theory to practice, racial equity leaders must insist that our educator peers make a clear distinction between the two types of achievement data—inputs and results. We must also demand that the focus be on the former more often than the latter.

Why Are We Still Norming White Student Achievement?

Establishing and holding all students and school systems accountable for achieving White norms or standards is one of the most basic characteristics of racism. Given that Asian American students are more often the highest-performing racial group in the U.S. data sample, why do we not compare all American students to their Asian American peers? Furthermore, when we notice that Asian American students outperform White students, why do we not interrogate White students and their families in the way other racial groups have been challenged when White-normative references are the standards?

In my former experience as a college admissions director, I often observed a practice by which Asian American students were penalized for outperforming White students. Somehow, instead of increasing the likelihood that Asian American students would be accepted into college, their higher test scores and grades signaled to the majority-White university officials (and influential, largely White alumni base) a lack of dimension and interests beyond academics. Regardless of whether these students had mastered playing musical instruments at a high level or had served as leaders of organizations in their communities, they were not seen as being as "well-rounded" as their White (and other) counterparts and subsequently denied entry. What was considered the normative reference for "well-roundedness," and thus admissibility, was White students. An article titled "No Longer Separate, Not Yet Equal: Race and Class in Elite College Admission" provided important insights into this matter:

> The negative coefficient associated with students from Asian heritage raises the question of whether there are "discriminatory admissions policies against Asian American applicants to elite colleges and universities."... The two-year review of Harvard's admission policies conducted by the U.S. Department of Education's Office for Civil Rights concluded that "[o]ver the last ten years Asian American applicants have been admitted at a significantly lower rate than white applicants; however ... this disparity is not the result of discriminatory policies or procedures ... We determined that the primary cause of the disparity was the preference given to children of alumni and recruited athletes."... The Office for Civil Rights also found that Asian applicants were typically stronger than white applicants on most standardized tests and other measures of academic performance (with the exception of the SAT verbal test) and that white applicants were rated higher on such nonacademic indicators as athletics and personal qualifications.... It is likely that incorporating in our models an even fuller range of academic performance measures as well as these other nonacademic factors would cast the effect of coming from an Asian background in a different light. With the information at hand, however, we are not able to settle the question of whether Asian applicants experience discrimination in elite college admissions.[9]

Before college-entry criteria were adjusted to advantage White students over Asian American students, the latter were being admitted into the most prestigious universities at rates much higher than their demographic proportions in this country. This trend apparently caused a great deal of unease among White Americans, who previously had bought into the White norming ideology and practice and who assumed that adherence to those norms would maintain the White-dominated status quo on college campuses across the land. As private higher education institutions, Harvard University among the most notable of these, began to discriminate in the admissions process against Asian American students by shifting emphasis away from those students' highest achievement and academic success, public systems such as the University of California also began to make claims that Asian students were overrepresented on their most competitive campuses and thus subject to harsher and more subjective scrutiny in the admission process. As a number of critical race theorists maintained, White students were never deemed overrepresented in college admissions or any other aspect of American life, for that matter. Indeed, they noted, the nation's affirmative action policies were never aimed at reducing White overrepresentation in higher education, but rather at increasing the underrepresentation of students of color.

Ironically, as admissions policies and practices began to shift toward re-establishing the strength of White normative references, the same groups that had spoken out consistently against admissions targets that increased Black and Brown student enrollment applauded efforts to place a ceiling or quota on Asian American student enrollment. The unfortunate de facto result, however, has been that decreasing Asian student enrollment while not increasing Black, Brown, and American Indian student enrollment has effectively created more spaces for White students to attend competitive universities all across the country. At the K–12 level, similar practices of White normative referencing have succeeded in curtailing Asian American student placements and minimizing Black and Hispanic placements in gifted and talented education (GATE), advanced placement (AP) courses, and international baccalaureate (IB) enrollment.

To identify closing the achievement gap as one of the greatest challenges facing U.S. public education when our sole focus previously has been on limited measures of student achievement indicates that we as a nation believe that failure to master our educational standards is the fault of our students. However, as evidenced by our national insistence on White norming processes as well as by the many vestiges of a more than 100-year-old tradition of racism in U.S. public schooling (which, as I have noted previously, was never designed to educate children of color effectively), student failure is due largely to educators' lack of will and to the failure of our society to provide quality education to *all* its children, not just the White-skinned, privileged majority.

Later in this book, I will highlight the stark contrast in results that occur when educators and school systems muster the courage and develop the knowledge, skills, and capacities to meet the needs of all children. But highlighting those systems that have shown remarkable improvement begs another question: Why aren't all or most systems improving? As the late Ron Edmonds said:

> It seems to me, therefore, that what is left of this discussion are three declarative statements: (a) We can, whenever and wherever we choose, successfully teach all children whose schooling is of interest to us; (b) We already know more than we need to do that; and (c) Whether or not we do it must finally depend on how we feel about the fact that we haven't so far.[10]

The Opportunity Gap

Keeping constant watch on racially disaggregated student achievement data to determine academic progress is essential to our efforts to move Courageous Conversations from theory to practice. This process also requires that we establish reliable ways to measure, report, and address the disparities that exist for students of various racial groups in terms of opportunities, access, expectations, and quality of instruction. At PEG, we employ the innovative tactic of Equity Walks to show racially conscious school leaders in our partner districts the extraordinary differences in the way equity-focused education is delivered by teacher, by classroom, and by building. By periodically organizing racial equity leaders from across a district or within a school to walk through corridors, classrooms, and offices, noticing how students of color are learning and how teachers are teaching, we learn a great deal about what we "must see" and what "can't continue" in order that we achieve educational equity. We add to these insights recognition that the quality of education greatly differs from district to district within a state, as well as from state to state across the nation to help our partners understand why the nation is facing a broad educational crisis. We also emphasize that eliminating racial achievement disparities nationally begins with addressing the degree to which local districts and individual teachers consistently deliver quality education to children of color in every classroom, in every building, every day.

In her groundbreaking work, *The Right to Learn,* teacher educator and researcher Linda Darling-Hammond[11] speaks to the many ways schools fail to provide opportunities for children of color to achieve high standards. Her focus on schools' "opportunity-to-learn" standards precisely pinpoints whether children are provided the essential personnel, program of study, cocurricular activities, supplies, and facilities to achieve at their highest level. She posits that when schools or teachers fail to make these resources available to all children, whether for budgetary or other reasons, they fail to award all children the free and appropriate opportunities to learn that are mandated by law. The result is what I call *the opportunity gap.*

Racial equity leaders not only measure and assess how such opportunities are made available and awarded in their classrooms and districts, they also work to ensure that best practices in one part of a district are replicated and scaled up throughout their entire school system. They achieve this through conversation with, observation of, and support to school leaders and by monitoring and addressing disparities observed in the following four areas of opportunity:

Access for all. Racial equity leaders ask the following questions about access: Do *all* children in their classrooms, schools, and district have access to rigorous coursework and high academic standards? That is, do their schools and district provide enough academic and co-curricular offerings to accommodate the entire population of students? And when reductions must be made in the number of opportunities that can be made available, what formula is used to calculate which schools and students will or will not experience the most dramatic cuts?

High expectations for all. Racial equity leaders ask the following questions about expectations: Are *all* children in their classrooms, schools, and district consistently held to the highest expectations in terms of their participation, engagement, and accomplishment in rigorous academic and co-curricular opportunities? If not, what changes should be made in the policies, practices, attitudes, and behaviors of classroom teachers, school administrators, and district officials to ensure that such high expectations are in place every day, in every classroom, for every child?

High-quality instruction for all. Racial equity leaders ask the following questions about instruction: Are *all* children in their classrooms, schools, and district exposed to the highest quality of instruction available? Where teachers lack specific competencies to effectively meet these needs, do their schools and districts have in place an effective professional development process that can help teachers and administrators develop those proficiencies in an accelerated period of time? What process determines which students are assigned to the best teachers, and is that process one that ensures racial equity?

Support and advocacy for all. Racial equity leaders ask the following questions about support and advocacy: Do *all* students in their classrooms, schools, and district have in-school support systems for students and families, complete with advocates who not only understand the needs of those students and families but are also effective in translating those needs to teachers and to school and district officials? Are these advocates provided opportunities to interact with the schools' teachers, counselors, coaches, and other adult resources so that networks of support can be formed around students and families, thus minimizing students' chances of failure or institutional disenfranchisement?

CAN WE REALLY AFFORD EQUITY?

On my very first day of kindergarten, my Nana reluctantly boarded me on Mr. Sims's red Volkswagen bus. I was crying, begging my grandmother not to leave me in this stranger's hands. Yet, as soon as I arrived at the school and was ushered into Mrs. Porter's "learning oasis," I was at peace. Never again did I cry about attending school. In fact, I truly began to look forward to what would unfold each day at school, and not only in Mrs. Porter's classroom but also in the theater, at the gymnasium, and on the playground. In 1969, Hilton Elementary School #21 in Baltimore City, in my mind, offered everything a school could and should offer. I was busy learning the basics from start to finish, and I always felt that I was under the watchful eye of dedicated, caring, culturally proficient, and highly qualified teachers. Back then, my family members referred to the faculty at PS #21 as simply "good teachers."

Although I did not qualify for free or reduced-price lunches, my transportation on the public buses was covered by the school system. I was a "latchkey kid," as the adults in my working-class family had a very precise formula for making ends meet that required them to work well into the late evening hours. Never did I feel like the elementary education I received was inferior in terms of fiscal resources or otherwise—that is, not until I entered The Park School.

The Park School is a private, predominantly Jewish day school in suburban Baltimore. I attended it from seventh to twelfth grade. At Park, it immediately became clear to me that the suburban Baltimore students had been provided with many opportunities to learn that I lacked coming from the underfunded Baltimore City Public Schools. However, the strong literacy and numeracy foundation I had received from those schools, coupled with the confidence they had instilled in me as a learner, enabled me to stay focused in my studies and believe in my own ability to achieve at a high level. Although Park's academic program was accelerated and its instruction was consistently elevated, failure was never an option for me because it had never been a part of my previous schooling experience. I believe this confidence was instilled in me at Hilton. It carried me through Park School and also enabled me to face systemic racism within my profession while authoring a litany of articles and two books on the topic.

So much has changed in our society since my graduation from high school in 1976, the year of this nation's bicentennial. Technology, for example, has opened up many doors, enabling students to explore worlds of people and phenomena far beyond our neighborhoods, cities, and shores. This same technology, however, has confronted us with the challenge to discover ways to ensure that we do not exacerbate the inequities already present prior to the birth of the Internet.

So often, these technology inequities, like most other measured gaps, are attributed immediately to resource disparity. With regard to education, for example, we as a society are quick to define and explain systemic inequities as being the result of funding differentials. I do not want to suggest that money does not factor greatly into the equation of racial achievement disparities in our nation's schools. However, I do believe that the continued underfunding of the schools that serve the highest concentrations of students of color and poor students has been used as an excuse for our not having the "real" conversation about what children of color need most in schools: highly qualified teachers.

I have often heard it said that no teacher goes into the teaching profession to get rich. Similarly, no public school system that serves primarily children of color operates with the belief that it will ever be overfunded, or even adequately funded. What is essential, both for teachers and for such school systems, is the desire to serve, or the uncompromising *will* to provide the best possible education for the children who come to their schools. I know now that my teachers at PS #21 personally supplemented their classroom supply budgets due to the systemic shortfalls; they simply took it on themselves to do what it took to get the job done. How they did this remains a mystery to me because they themselves were not highly paid. Those teachers who could not abide or afford this sacrifice—well, they apparently moved on to other occupations, free from judgment by those who remained and were successful. What was unacceptable to the educators at my inner-city elementary public school, however, was a teacher who refused to go that extra mile to educate Baltimore City's children, who chose instead to stick around and complain about the challenging conditions.

Perhaps the fact that so many of my teachers then also entrusted their own sons' and daughters' learning to their colleagues each day was the reason why they created a culture of efficacy and accountability. Because they too lived in the neighborhoods where their students attended school, perhaps, they also expected all teachers to live up to the highest standard of the profession. Whatever the reasons, the overriding emphasis was not on the deficits and deficiencies of the school budget. Rather, Hilton teachers worked hard at overcoming the deficits and deficiencies in opportunities to learn that, if not mitigated, would negatively impact the achievement of their students.

The greatest barrier to our efforts to move Courageous Conversations from theory to practice is our focus on externalities such as economics and funding—areas over which the everyday practitioner has limited or no control. The recent global economic downturn has served to exacerbate the national preoccupation with drawing funds away from the social services that poor families and children of color disproportionately depend on for survival. In this scenario, educators are often the frontline soldiers, charged with buffering the children of these families from the harmful impacts of poverty. Racial equity leaders must take the lead in this charge and devote time and attention toward discovering ways to mitigate societal inequities and other factors that diminish the educational experiences of children of color so that these children too can experience freedom to learn while in school.

Overfunded Prisons and Underfunded Schools

In her groundbreaking book, *The New Jim Crow: Mass Incarceration in the Age of Colorblindness,* Michelle Alexander[12] painstakingly documents what she concludes has amounted to the "criminalization" of Black men in the United States. Contrasting the alarming rise in the incarceration rates of these men over the past 30 years with the decreasing rates of violent crimes committed by this same group, she reaches a conclusion that may seem alarming to some but obvious to others: Our country has a predilection for incarcerating Black and Brown men. In essence, Alexander concludes that the nation derives more economic value from imprisoning these men, often for misdemeanor offenses such as drug possession, than it gains from educating them.

As a result, in prisons across the land, men of color with no record of violent crime are consigned to complete low-skilled tasks obediently as they await release. Their lack of education, socialization, and ability to land work or housing due to their conviction is evidence of systemic racism and assures that many of them will return to prison after their release. Even if they wanted to use the civil process to voice their consciousness of and complaint about this "natural order" of things, the fact of their incarceration strips them of the right to vote, thus rendering them politically impotent in our so-called democracy.

Alexander's research further shows that the penitentiaries that citizen groups often fight to keep out of their neighborhoods are now, in many states, the soundest source of economic recovery or development for the same communities. She cites numerous studies demonstrating that city, county, and state government planners can accurately predict the future prison occupancy in their locales based on the third-grade reading levels of the African American and Latino students in their school districts. Such data, which reveal the nature and extent of racial inequity in our nation's schools, are also used to determine the best date for construction of new prisons or expansion of existing ones as well as the size of prison or prisons needed to maximize the efficiency of the incarceration process.

How Much Does It Really Cost to Talk About Race?

It never fails. Whenever someone from the press contacts one of PEG's partnering districts to inquire about the "controversial" equity work, specifically Courageous Conversations, in which the schools are about to engage, one of the top questions is how much the district will be paying Glenn Singleton. Sometimes, but only rarely, do they inquire specifically about the compensation to be paid to PEG as an entity. I find this line of inquiry not only fascinating but fraught with the very racism my firm and I are contracted to address.

What first strikes me is that this type of public scrutiny generally does not surround the hundreds of curricular reform packages that school districts have purchased—often to the tune of millions, if not billions, of dollars—over the past two decades or so. The media also conveniently overlook the fact that districts across the country have paid consultant teams headed by White education professionals millions of dollars annually, just to have them speak to their educators on generic topics such as leadership or professional learning. Apparently, those expenditures are deemed not only sensible but also above scrutiny by the White-controlled media, White parents, and White boards and community action groups.

Then there are those critics who agree that the kind of work we at PEG do in schools should be done, but they believe it should be done out of charity, not as a formal business enterprise. Others conclude that, especially in times like the past decade, when school districts have experienced extreme budgetary shortfalls, investing in PEG's equity leadership training is somehow a "luxury" that districts cannot afford. I argue that nothing is further from the truth. I wonder what price these critics believe is worth paying to deinstitutionalize racism in a school system and thus improve the likelihood that authentic and meaningful opportunities to learn for *all* children can be provided. I wonder also if they have ever attempted to calculate the value to taxpayers of ensuring that their communities' children are highly educated and then gainfully employed rather than committing sustenance crimes and draining municipal social services or wasting away due to incarceration?

How courageous it would be for those who neither understand the importance of racial equity programming nor support its implementation simply to admit their lack of knowledge about what that programming entails. Ironically, the financial cost of engaging, sustaining, and deepening interracial conversations about race, when compared to large-scale program improvement or facilities renovation, is relatively small. Discovering that a school district is paying "Glenn Singleton" $200 or $200,000 fosters no real understanding of what we at PEG are being contracted to do within a new partnering district or what we have accomplished elsewhere. But make no mistake about it, providing brand new school buildings or purchasing an adequate number of up-to-date multicultural textbooks for all the children in that school is no proxy for a cadre of Courageous Conversation-trained, racially conscious teachers who have the passion to serve traditionally under-served students of color, the persistence to implement practices that can reach those children, and the subject-matter proficiency to teach them effectively. As one equity-focused superintendent of a large urban district recently declared,

> I am choosing to invest in racial equity professional development rather than retaining personnel in many cases, because having a lower student-to-teacher ratio when that larger number of teachers cannot effectively reach all students is not preferred to having fewer culturally proficient teachers who are experiencing success with our growing number of under-served students of color.

True, there are real costs involved in contracting with PEG to implement the Courageous Conversations program, but those costs are less financial than they are emotional, moral, intellectual, and relational. Sometimes these costs are derived from continuing to operate in the zone of productive disequilibrium brought on by the failure to recognize, own, and confront the school district's responsibility for the needs of all the children entrusted to it by a community. In other instances, Courageous Conversations training enables educators to discover how they actually participate in the funding of failure for students of color, thus effecting change through awareness.

Just as Michelle Alexander has concluded that our nation is invested, morally and economically, in maintaining racial disparities in its incarceration rates, I maintain that we are similarly invested in failing children of color and perpetuating White privilege in our classrooms, schools, and school districts nationwide. My conclusions, derived from two-and-a-half decades of qualitative work I have done in schools across the country, complement Alexander's exhaustive quantitative analysis. I have talked to literally thousands of educators, students, and parents and examined numerous school policies, programs, and practices. But given my lengthy history of close-up engagement with school stakeholders and nearly 20 years of my own formal education, I, like many others who choose to remain racially conscious and do not fear living in a racially just society, feel qualified to offer my personal commentary on race and education.

The failure of our nation's education system to invest in systemic racial equity transformation generally and to engage in courageous conversations about race specifically, despite the relative low financial cost and high economic value of both, often causes me to wonder what it is, exactly, that we, as a nation are investing in, education-wise. Why do school districts with financial means fail to use their resources to implement well-researched, proven strategies that have been shown to improve the academic participation and performance of students of color? Why do districts that depend on categorical and perhaps integration funds not focus those resources on addressing what the vast majority of people of color, either those who have been or felt trapped by the education system or those who have negotiated it more successfully, point to as the major impediment to their collective success: systemic racism?

In my chosen line of work, I hear a lot of *rhetoric* from school leaders about the importance of achieving equity and the necessity to focus on what is good for all children. It is, however, the obvious "disconnect" of this espoused ideology from congruent practices that challenges me most in my efforts to mobilize educators to move Courageous Conversations from theory to practice. Seven years ago, when I wrote my first book on Courageous Conversations, my hope was that educators would learn to use the Courageous Conversations Protocol to bring about meaningful transformation in learning outcomes, especially for under-served students of color. Today, many educators have done just that. The qualitative and quantitative successes they have achieved in their classrooms, schools, and even districts are promising, and they serve as a great encouragement to me and my colleagues at PEG to continue applying our will, skill, knowledge, and capacity to understanding, exploring, and dismantling racism.

As I write this second book on the topic, I no longer have any doubts about the effectiveness of the Courageous Conversations Protocol when it is implemented properly. What I have found is what worked before—in terms of uncovering, examining, and addressing systemic racism—works even better after 7 years of additional learning and growing with the PEG team and our Courageous Conversations partnering districts. What has not changed is my firm belief that achieving racial equity in schools is still about passion, practice, and persistence!

In a recent book published by Harvard Press, titled *Leading for Equity*, administrators from one of the nation's largest and most diverse school systems, Montgomery County Public Schools (MCPS), indicate that addressing race head-on, in partnership with PEG, and using the Courageous Conversations Protocol, were key to that district's systemic equity transformation:

> In an early-fall meeting, [we] had a breakthrough. Glenn Singleton, whose work on Courageous Conversations had long been part of the diversity training, had agreed to consult directly with MCPS on its efforts to explicitly address race and achievement. During a meeting, he noticed frameworks, process diagrams, and data maps that adorned the conference room walls, and asked why it was that

they had not developed an equity framework for the district. Such a tool could be adapted to help every employee in the district understand what equitable practices would look like in their work and how those might ultimately connect to student learning. The question sparked a renewed intensity to break the links between race and student outcomes.[13]

In Chapter 11 of this book, I present a case study of Eden Prairie (Minnesota) Schools. Written by current and former administrators in that district, it quite powerfully gives credit to Courageous Conversations as a cornerstone to unprecedented achievement gains for Black and Brown students—and steadily improving results for already high-performing White students. The following snapshots from a couple of PEG's other partnering districts also capture some of the significant and symbolic improvements being experienced by these school systems, which are deeply engaged in systemic equity transformation guided by the PEG Systemic Racial Equity Framework.

Saint Paul Public Schools (Minnesota) is a diverse urban school district serving more than 37,000 students from preschool through high school. Seventy-six percent are students of color; 36% are emerging bilingual students. The district's commitment to excellence in equity is the foundation for its Strong Schools, Strong Communities Strategic Plan, which seeks to transform schools and classrooms, thereby transforming students' lives, families, and neighborhoods— touching the whole community.

Racial equity leadership through Courageous Conversations About Race is at the heart of the district's racial equity work. Beginning with the superintendent, school board, district administrators, and school principals, the work is growing to include more than 60 school sites. A learning community of seven Beacon Schools is leading the way through the development of school-based equity leadership teams (E-teams), where principals and staff are deeply engaged in developing their personal, professional, and organizational capacity to identify and address beliefs, practices, and systems that contribute to racial educational disparities.

The early impact of Saint Paul's equity work can be seen in assessments from principals and district leaders. They describe a heightened awareness of systemic racial inequities, an appreciation of the tools shared that encourage self-reflection and discussion, and increased courage and ability to have difficult conversations about race.

- 100% are aware of the need to address issues of race and equity in SPPS, a 26% increase over prior assessments.
- 92% of leaders believe that the district's racial equity work will increase achievement for all SPPS students.
- With each training experience, more leaders identified that they have the tools and resources to address issues of race in their school or department.

(Continued)

(Continued)

In the words of one Beacon principal, "This (work) is very valuable and is changing the culture of the buildings, our expectations, our leadership. This is speaking the truth."

The district's school board members are also actively engaged in thinking about their governance role through the lens of racial equity. Reflecting on their personal equity learning experiences over the first 18 months, Board members noted that in order for (equity work) to be effective, it must go deep, and to go deep, it takes time to build knowledge and trust. "This is school reform and involves personal behavior and beliefs; it takes time and effort to implement."

Portland Public Schools (Oregon) is the largest school district in Oregon, serving more than 47,000 students from pre-kindergarten through high school. The district is focused on raising achievement and graduation rates for all students. Utilizing a Milestones Framework, the district measures student success at key transition points in Grades K–12, setting clear targets for reducing racial student achievement disparities. For Portland Public Schools, the early impact of this work is clear:

- Third-grade reading scores improved for all students by 5 percentage points, while simultaneously, racial achievement disparities were reduced by 5 percentage points (largest disparity—African American/White students)
- Reading readiness in high school improved for all students by 10 percentage points, while simultaneously, racial achievement disparities were reduced by 4 percentage points (largest disparity—African American/White students)
- The number of ninth-grade students on track to graduate high school improved by 5 percentage points, while simultaneously, racial achievement disparities were reduced by 5 percentage points (largest disparity—African American/White students).
- District graduation rates for all students improved by 7 percentage points with Latino students showing a 14 percentage point gain and Black, American Indian, and Asian students all showing gains of between 7 and 8 percentage points.

At the district level, training is helping leaders address systemic inequities, resulting in changes in policy, practices, and procedures. In June 2011, the district passed its Racial Educational Equity Policy, which outlines the district's intentionality in addressing inequities in the system. In addition, practices such as administrator and teacher hiring, district contracting of services, and budgeting practices are being analyzed and restructured with the use of a district-developed Equity Lens Tool. The district's Equity Department provides an infrastructure to support equity progress in all areas of the district, instructional and operational, building capacity and sustainability for racial equity transformation.

APPLYING NEW TECHNOLOGY
TO RACIAL EQUITY WORK

Much new technology has evolved since the field guide was published 7 years ago. While I must admit, I still have my own phobias when it comes to experimenting with some of the newest electronic communications platforms. I also worry about educators' ability to have a virtual courageous conversation if we have never successfully had such a talk in person. But in recent years, launching PEG's online courses (including Beyond Diversity) and virtual coaching support for leaders and racial equity social networks has made me a believer, and thousands are already participating around the world. Now, I believe that effective use of technology can truly accelerate the movement of Courageous Conversations from theory to practice in at least five, very specific ways:

1. Using social media websites such as Facebook, LinkedIn, Twitter, and Ning to create a national and/or international platform for racial equity leaders to network, share tools, and discuss strategies for eliminating systemic racial achievement disparities

2. Using various virtual conferencing sites such as WebEx to provide computer-based professional development through distance learning, thereby saving time and money for trainers and trainees alike (PEG makes frequent use of such platforms to address client needs and provide customized trainings)

3. Using "cloud-based" applications, such as Google-Drive to increase the amounts of data, research, and literature that racial equity leaders safely can store and share with each other electronically

4. Using computers and interactive whiteboards in classrooms as part of everyday instruction to forge connections and activate increased engagement using the Internet and World Wide Web, between and among students from different parts of the city, country, and world

5. Using platforms for online learning, such as Moodle, to enrich or augment traditional face-to-face instruction and offer students and teachers opportunities to engage with each other during nontraditional hours and locations when and where more significant teachable moments may be occurring

In applying new technology to our racial equity work, we must be mindful of yet another gap: the gap between what Marc Prensky[14] calls "digital natives"—that is, our young people, the students of today, who have basically grown up on the electronic technology that literally virtually dominates our world—and their "digital immigrant" teachers, who have yet to plug completely into technology applications like social media and other computer-based applications. Although computers are almost ubiquitous components of the modern American classroom, there are still classrooms where technology is not available widely to students nor well integrated into their routine learning activities. Some educators have had difficulty transitioning from what is now "ancient" technology such as overhead projectors to the new wave of electronic equipment such as interactive whiteboards. Some teachers use the state-of-the-art equipment in their classrooms in much the same manner as they used the older technology. The result: increased distance between educators and students.

It is essential for racial equity leaders to accelerate their understanding and use of technology as a key strategy for moving Courageous Conversations from theory to practice. The Obama 2008 presidential campaign was probably the best evidence and example of technology making a difference in outcomes. From virtual town meetings, to regular status updates on Obama's Facebook page, to the candidate's Twitter "tweets" from his smartphone, the president used technology to link to and get to know a whole population of young voters who, in previous elections, typically failed to register, much less get out and vote. Elections in this country will never be the same. Similarly, racial equity leaders can and should use technology to interact with and relate more meaningfully to their students, by appealing to youth through their native communication systems.

ESSENTIAL QUESTIONS

Now might be a good time to consider the development of your own Personal Racial Equity Purpose (PREP) as discussed in Chapter 2 and answer these questions:

1. What motivates you to engage in Courageous Conversations work in your personal and professional spheres of influence?

2. What accomplishment defines your Courageous Conversations work thus far?

3. Under what circumstances have you allowed your Courageous Conversations work to be compromised?

4. What will motivate you to rise above your fears and persist in your quest for racial equity in the future, especially when you are confronted with those same and different circumstances that challenge your purpose?

Voices From the Inside: Donna Hart-Tervalon

I live and work in Madison, Wisconsin. Madison is the capital of Wisconsin and is well known for its frequent ranking as one of the best places to live in America. It is also well known for its four beautiful lakes, scenic bike paths, clean streets, stellar university, and healthy lifestyle.

In Wisconsin, particularly in Madison, we take great pride in our liberal thinking and liberal politics. Even our prevalent racism has been rationalized, sanitized, and liberalized so that it appears to be subtle, infrequent, and far less insidious or pervasive than it actually is. We live in an environment that far too often accepts, condones, and in some instances promotes what I call "Wisconsized liberalized racism."

For the past 10 years, I have worked both as a consultant and as an assistant director of special education for the Wisconsin Department of Public Instruction (WDPI). In the 2002–2003 school year, the WDPI's Special Education Team formed (and I was invited to join) a Disproportionality Workgroup to address the overrepresentation of students of color. Specifically, our workgroup was developed to review data and identify factors contributing to students of color being inappropriately referred, identified, and placed in special education programs.

I served as the first chairperson and currently serve as cochair of this incredible Workgroup, initially comprised of 14 WDPI staff (12 White, 1 African American, and 1 American Indian). When our group was formed, we all agreed that we had limited knowledge, limited skills, and were lacking capacity, as either a Workgroup or as an agency, to address this challenge on even a small scale, much less to tackle statewide issues of disproportionality. However, we all had the will. What we lacked in racial diversity we were able to compensate for with our diversity of ideas, background experience, personalities, strong opinions, and voices. Our collective will was the key ingredient to making our workgroup a powerful, resourceful, actively engaged, and sustainable force for change.

My leadership role with this group has been extremely challenging, but it has afforded me an opportunity to learn on the job, not only to learn more about the mechanics of leadership but also how to customize my leadership style without compromising my personal values and beliefs. I have learned the importance and value of multiple perspectives and shared leadership. I have learned to facilitate contentious discussions by allowing space for dissension and reflection without losing sight of group goals and timelines. I have learned to develop streamlined, focused agendas. I have learned how to strategize and work with agency administrators to ensure that our workgroup goals are aligned with agency goals before developing agendas and action plans. I have also learned that collaborative leadership is the only style of leadership I am comfortable with. I have learned to lead effectively without being dictatorial or aggressively directive in either my intent or style of delivery.

Over the span of 10 years, I have had the privilege of working with two different co-chairs, both White women allies whom I have come to respect, trust, and love. While we have not always agreed, we have always been able to compromise and focus on whatever was necessary to advance our shared vision and shared work. I believe racial equity work is often best done by a team consisting of a person of color and a White ally. There have been times when my co-chairs and I needed to strategize using a tag-team approach to reach certain audiences and advance certain initiatives. We always present a unified front and model for others: the racially balanced, collaborative leadership approach that we have embraced.

I've also learned that, as a Black woman, having a co-chair who is a White woman forced me to practice what I was preaching. I had to be open, vulnerable, trusting, and accountable in ways that were challenging on both a professional and personal level. This model allowed each of us to respectively identify other allies of color and White allies within our agency and our school districts who were willing to commit themselves fully, engage in our activities, and "recruit" others who were willing and able to do the same. The end result was well worth the effort, and the payoff, evidenced by what we accomplished through this collaborative leadership model, is ongoing.

The role of allies within our agency has been critical. They are key players within our organization and have been extremely valuable in supporting, enhancing, sustaining, and advancing statewide systemic antiracist transformation. My immediate supervisor, the state director of special education, is a White woman ally whom I respect, trust, and love. Our Disproportionality Workgroup and everything that followed was the result of a series of conversations between the two of us, held in her office prior to the formation of our workgroup. Beyond encouraging me to think outside of the box, she has often identified ways to support ideas and projects I only dreamed of. Her early and consistent support has allowed me to stretch myself beyond self-imposed limits and dream big.

The head of our division, the assistant state superintendent of learning support for equity and advocacy, is a Black woman ally. In addition to being my supervisor, she is a personal friend, mentor, role model, and my all-around "shero." The highest-ranking person of color in our agency of about 600 employees, she is respected for her leadership, admired for her intelligence, and envied for her ability to manage and lead with conviction, passion, and compassion. I have learned more from her than is possible to convey in this narrative, so I've chosen to highlight one extremely significant lesson learned.

It is critical to understand the politics, policies, policy agendas, and platforms that are fundamental to an agency or organization. Knowing this, really getting it, and applying it allowed me to lead our workgroup in aligning our racial equity goals and to work with other agency-sanctioned, successful, and supported initiatives. Having this knowledge and focus also allowed me to lead our workgroup in acquiring approval and ultimately funding for racial equity projects and initiatives with a solid rationale and clear connections to our state agency's strategic plan. The impact and influence of an agency's politics are powerful. For racial equity leaders in particular, underestimating their significance can be a fatal mistake. I never really considered myself politically aware or savvy until I learned this lesson. Thankfully, due to phenomenal mentoring and opportunities to observe and practice the timing, aligning, streamlining, modifying, and stratifying of racial equity goals with agency politics, I have avoided many pitfalls that could have blurred our vision and compromised our work.

Our state superintendent of education is a White male ally. Before he was elected, he served as deputy state superintendent, and in this capacity and during this timeframe, I had opportunities to interact with him directly and observe firsthand his interest in, support of, and commitment to racial equity, not only verbally but actively with recommendations for funding. As state superintendent, he has continued supporting and engaging in our work, and he also has increased our annual budget, which is now just under $1 million.

Frequently, I become frustrated by the challenges and barriers that constantly emerge and by the attempts of others to derail our racial equity work and the credibility we have established. I question how effective my leadership has been and whether or not my collaborative leadership style has contributed to any evidence of success. I am especially proud of several accomplishments. These include establishing our

Disproportionality Workgroup; securing support and funding for major initiatives such as our minigrants, demonstration and project grants, and the tools developed as a result of these grants; the establishment of the Wisconsin Consortium on Racial Equity in PreK–12 Education (a partnership with PEG that is now in its fourth year); and our CREATE (Culturally Responsive Education for All: Training and Enhancement) Wisconsin Initiative, which is our largest and most comprehensive initiative to date.

CREATE is a statewide system-change initiative designed to eradicate the achievement gap among diverse student populations and eliminate race as a predicting factor of participation in special education. I am also proud to have played a part in the establishment of our State Equity Leadership Team, which consists of 28 members representing every division and every team in our agency. I take great pride in these accomplishments, and I acknowledge that my role as a racial equity leader has been significant.

As a Black woman educator with more than 35 years of experience, I have gradually, incrementally, and progressively either identified or created opportunities to advance and support racial equity in education, both professionally and personally. In recent years, I have framed, renamed, and claimed my approach as one that has daily personal, local, and immediate goals over which I have some control and longer term equity and advocacy goals that must be aligned carefully and strategically with agency agendas and priorities. Realizing that there are no part-time racial equity leaders (as Glenn frequently points out) has been a difficult pill to swallow. There have been times when I have wanted and needed a "time-out" from this challenging and emotionally draining work, but my black skin does not allow for this personally; and my passion and commitment to creating more equitable educational opportunities for all students of color does not allow for a professional opt-out.

I continually find myself facing and confronting the "usual suspects" and barriers to implementing and sustaining a focus on race and racial issues. The usual suspects include the belief of many well-meaning White educators that a "color-blind" approach is the best way to level the racial playing field, insistence that poverty trumps race whenever race becomes the focus of attention and resource allocation enters the equation, and denials or dismissals of the prevalence and impact of White privilege.

The greater challenge for me has been confronting the Wisconsinized form of liberal racism and those who come cloaked in ally garb but speak and act in ways that are divisive. I also confront those who are unable to experience discomfort personally without ensuring that everyone else is made to feel uncomfortable, a subtle but profound difference; and those who can only accept multiple perspectives if their perspective is the first one heard and the last one standing after they have failed to adhere to the conditions and agreements of engaging in courageous conversations. I believe these potentially lethal challenges can be successfully deflated if the highest level of agency administration has sanctioned the work and supports racial equity leaders when both internal and external forces attempt to undermine the focus, momentum, and trajectory of racial equity work and related initiatives.

For the past 10 years, I have experienced opportunities and challenges that have allowed me to acknowledge, grow into, and finally (most recently) to claim and embrace my role as a racial equity leader. Over the years, I believe I have acquired the knowledge, will, and skills to facilitate courageous conversations that allow for open, respectful discussions of race, racism, and related topics—conversations that include multiple perspectives and that are structured to provide an environment that is safe, where time for reflection is part of the agenda and not an afterthought. I know that this work cannot be done effectively and consistently without putting oneself on the line and fully accepting both the mantle and the challenges that come with the role.

I used to believe that to be a true racial equity leader, you needed to be fearless. I now believe that you must allow yourself to act and advocate even in the face of fear, even when you may be risking a high professional and personal cost. So I now have a different attitude and an accompanying mantra: as Joyce Meyer[15] maintains in her book, I "do it afraid." And I encourage others to do the same.

Donna Hart-Tervalon serves as assistant director for special education for the Wisconsin Department of Public Instruction, where she chaired the department's Disproportionality Workgroup. That workgroup focused on improving the academic performance of the state's Black, Brown, and American Indian students. She is a Black American.

FIVE

Why Are We Still Talking About Race?

The task for me is to not only comprehend the world, but to change the world. I would like to see a world where America lives up to its ideals, and resolves the contradiction between reality and principles.

—Ron Takaki

BEYOND A MORAL IMPERATIVE: NEUROSCIENCE AND THE PHYSIOLOGICAL IMPACT OF RACISM

When I was a young boy, once a week, and sometimes daily, depending on the time of year, I would arrive home from middle school with a story to share with my mother about how my being one of three Black students in my entire class had played out in some embarrassing or otherwise disturbing way. Now, my mother was very upfront about racism, and her response was pretty much always the same: that if I was ever going to amount to anything, I simply could not let White folks' racism bother me so much. Often during these conversations, she would remind me of what ultimately became my adult work ethic. In this unfair life, she told me, I would have to work twice as hard as the White kids to get half as far.

I guess it was at a very young age that I became committed to not allowing racism to kill me—or even to stand in the way of my life's chances and opportunities for success. Certainly, my conjectures at that time about the impact of my classmates' racist actions were a bit hyperbolic, given that Black men were no longer being lynched for interacting with White women, as was the tragic situation for my grandfather's brother in the early

1950s. Rarely were cross burnings reported in Maryland in the 1980s, even in known Ku Klux Klan stronghold communities like Catonsville and Prince Georges County, as had been the case when my mother was growing up. What I saw around me on a regular basis, however, were my otherwise happy family members and friends, each of whom, to varying degrees of severity, had been deeply affected, physically and emotionally, by their interactions with powerful and privileged White people at work and in leisure. "The Man," which is how many of the men in my family referenced White America, seemed to take a toll on my loved ones in ways that clearly diminished their potential and lessened their pride, confidence, and self-esteem. And my mother was commanding me to ignore or rise above all of that! It was a huge demand to make of a child, but so typical for many of the Black boys and girls of my era who achieved success in the still-turbulent decades of racial and social change that followed.

From a longitudinal perspective, the enslavement, slaughter, and colonization of Africans in America not only brought physical abuse to them and their other brethren and sisters of color, it also exacted a psychological toll on the oppressed. Black psychologists, such as Na'im Akbar and Wade Nobles, have long argued that a posttraumatic slave syndrome of sorts psychologically and physiologically affects those of African descent even today. Certainly, the historic dispossession of land and language experienced by American Indians as well as Latinos in the Americas continues to re-traumatize their descendants today. The Jim Crow years, also known as the Nadir Era or the years from the end of Reconstruction through the early 20th century, are widely recognized as the most violent of our nation's racial past. During those decades, people of color were terrorized, mainly through acts of extraordinarily depraved physical violence, including lynching, burning, and dismemberment. In the modern era, racism seems almost exclusively to weaken, confound, or kill its victims from the inside out. The impacts of contemporary racism and its vestiges on people of color seem to cause greater psychological and internal physiological damage, and our society overwhelmingly fails and refuses to recognize the prevalence of racial injustices and the way in which racism affects human outcomes, even today.

I recognized then, by age 12, that I needed to find a different solution to growing up in a multiracial society in which White people clearly controlled many of the pathways to my economic success. I also needed a way to combat their unique ability to inflict, often unconsciously, this weighty psychological damage—which I now recognize as *racial trauma*—on my psyche. At such an early age, the actions of my White school peers and teachers made it perfectly clear to me that I would need to engage effectively with Whiteness, not only to acquire my own opportunities but also to live an emancipated existence free from racism's scarring effects.

My initial strategy for surviving racism, which I deployed for nearly 20 years, was deeply rooted in assimilation. Specifically, I would do whatever the White students in school did, however they did it, and whenever it was appropriate to do. Almost overnight, my diet, dress, likes and dislikes, mannerisms, expressions, and desires changed. While engaging in this personal transformation, I felt embraced by my White peers and faculty at Park School but increasingly marginalized and often outright ridiculed by some family members and neighborhood friends, who accused me of "acting White." As my transformation deepened, it seemed to me that racial struggle and racism were quickly vanishing as well.

I now recognize that I was becoming callous or perhaps blind to racism—my adopted coping strategy for getting through school and later work—and I see that it clearly exacted an emotional toll on me, despite my best efforts to ignore and deny its presence. For the most part, however, I was the one who became desensitized to race, not my teachers or peers. I can recount hundreds of racist episodes at Park, the University of Pennsylvania, and my first places of employment after college. Only on rare occasions would an uncharacteristically vehement racial slight shake me out of my denial into a place of unfamiliar anger and frustration.

As a Stanford University graduate student living in the largely White, liberal Palo Alto, California, community, I realized that assimilation into Whiteness was no longer an effective or affirming way for me to navigate the racist society in which I lived. Allowing White faculty members, classmates, friends, and even city officials to remain ignorant of their unconscious racist beliefs and unintentional racist behaviors while I remained silent or internalized racism was becoming just too much for me to bear. My long-held strategy of silently enduring racism was aging me beyond my years, I felt. It was even causing my physical systems to deteriorate. I could no longer view this strategy as physically sustainable or socially progressive.

Many of the people of color in my highly educated, highly successful circle of friends continued to placate racially disrespectful White peers and colleagues as a way of avoiding racial friction, struggle, or strife. Yet, during the rare times when we could create a buffer from our White-dominated world or plan an outing in racial affinity, so often our conversations resembled a collective vomiting of all the racial hatred we had ingested over the years of our lives. For example, when convening informally as a circle of friends, one person of color might offer a short narrative that highlighted his or her recent brush with racism in the workplace. As if on cue, other members of the circle usually chimed in with stories of related encounters in which White friends and/or colleagues said or did something racist that caused them personal stress. Next thing you know, a relaxed and jovial gathering among friends had devolved into a tense and unhealthy exchange. This too, I came to see, was an indication of the psychological trauma we were each experiencing and an example of the harmful, physical effects. Recognizing the fatalistic nature of this adopted lifestyle of coping with and acquiescing to racism was my primary calling to develop the Courageous Conversations Protocol.

■   ■   ■

Back when I decided as a seventh grader not to allow racism to kill me, little did I know that medical research would eventually suggest that growing up in Baltimore City as a Black male had already reduced my total life expectancy by 10 years. Today, collaborating physicians, epidemiologists, psychologists, and sociologists are beginning to discover a link between the cumulative effects of racism and the onslaught of life-threatening diseases such as diabetes, hypertension, and obesity. They are finding now that after controlling for personal life choices like diet, exercise, and alcohol and tobacco consumption, otherwise healthy, middle-class Black, Brown, and American Indian people develop these diseases at rates two and three times that of their lower income, less educated White counterparts.

A 2008 film series produced by California Newsreel, titled *Unnatural Causes: Is Inequality Making Us Sick?*[1] uncovers and examines this perplexing dilemma. It cites how, for example, the damming of the Colorado River in the early 1900s to redirect the water toward the developing White suburbs of Arizona, New Mexico, and Colorado created a water shortage for American Indian farmers. That shortage led to drought in their farm areas, damaging their subsistence economy and agricultural systems. No longer able to harvest healthy crops or care for their livestock, many of these farmers and their families were forced to turn to government food subsidies for survival, and those rations consisted primarily of refined flour and lard. The resulting staple food of the government-rations diet, fry bread, soon became just one of many unhealthy substitutes for what was once the healthy staple diet enjoyed by many American Indians. I do not doubt that the combination of an unhealthy diet, coupled with the stresses stemming from hundreds of years of dispossession, is a significant factor behind America's southwestern tribes having the highest rate of diabetes in the entire world.[2]

Similar studies indicate tremendous gaps between poor White Americans and middle-class Latinos diagnosed with hypertension and between upper-middle-class Black Americans and poor Whites in terms of premature births. Again, despite having proper medical care and making good personal health decisions as far as diet, exercise, and drug/alcohol consumption, people of color continue to fare badly compared to White counterparts, even those of lesser means.

Just as society tends to blame under-served students of color and their families when they fail to demonstrate proficiency in or connect with the school environment, medical doctors and health researchers have long believed that the behaviors and attitudes of adults of color led to the young people's disproportionately poor health outcomes. Ironically, like educators, health professionals were once quick to deny the saliency of race or the permanence of racism in our society when uncovering racial disparities in health outcomes. They, too, would point to various groups of people of color as having pathological cultural deficiencies; yet when these same scientists began to investigate the impact of racism on the functioning of the mind and body, different meanings arose.

I can provide a very basic summary of the relevant neuroscience research findings and analyses, along with my own interpretations about the impact of this research on the schooling of Black, Brown, and American Indian students. And here it is: according to the research, when a person experiences stress, be it from war, neighborhood violence, or the perceived insensitive or unfair treatment of a racially unconscious teacher, that person's body produces and secretes a hormone called cortisol into the bloodstream. Cortisol is known as the "stress hormone" because it is secreted at higher levels during the body's "fight-or-flight" response to stress. Cortisol levels must be balanced to ensure proper glucose metabolism, blood pressure regulation, insulin release for blood sugar maintenance, immune system functioning, and inflammatory response. Whereas small increases in cortisol have positive health effects, large, prolonged, or constant secretions can cause fatigue, memory lapse, immunity deficiencies, heightened sensitivity to pain, and overall imbalance and dysfunction of bodily systems.

The omnipresence of racism in our society, and in our schools specifically, disproportionately inflicts stress on students, families, and educators of color. Not only does that stress have detrimental emotional and/or psychological effects, it also has potentially harmful physical effects due to the prolonged presence of higher levels of cortisol. These effects, which can present as impaired cognitive and emotional functioning and poor academic performance, are exacerbated by an education system that denies the presence of racial inequity. Thus, acknowledging and addressing racism in schools would not only improve academic performance but also support better health among students of color.

Increasing numbers of students of color who live in high-poverty and high-crime, neighborhoods, according to the research findings, will be found to have high levels of cortisol in their bloodstreams. For these students, it seems even more critical that school be a place where they can experience physical calming so that their cortisol levels can return to normal and they can ready themselves to learn. Too often, however, just the opposite occurs: Students of color are raised in a society that persists in denying the presence of racism, only to enter institutions (schools) that blame them for their inability to cope effectively in that society or to function adequately in school. For these children, the systemic denial of the plausibility of racism stimulates the release of epinephrine, also known as adrenalin, into their bloodstreams, which has impacts similar to cortisol. It is very difficult for children traumatized in this way to sit quietly and follow the directions of an adult who looks like their oppressor and who, in all likelihood, *is* the very person who triggered their stress reaction in the first place.

In her 2011 book, *The Pedagogy of Confidence,* literacy expert Yvette Jackson supports the aforementioned scientific research and offers some concrete classroom examples that support the conclusions of that research:

> Stress associated with prejudice, degradation, stereotype threat, reactions to abuse, feelings of failure, inability to succeed, positional or marginalizing language, and feelings of low self-esteem not only causes production of cortisol—which inhibits comprehension, resulting in low achievement—but stress can also rewire the brain to predispose an individual to keep doing the same thing over and over again ... The negative repercussions of stress are compounded for school-dependent students when they are confined to prescribed remedial programs that supersede the enrichment needed to stimulate interests and develop strengths ... It is critical to consider some other impairing effects of stress on learning and achievement so that practices and structures can be sought to mitigate these factors and stem the tide of low achievement. These effects include impediment of creativity, explicit memory and the ability to sort relevant from irrelevant information ...; barriers that disable input from reaching those parts of the brain responsible for language acquisition, restricting how meaning is constructed ...; reduction of blood flow in the top frontal lobe area that activates on-your-feet thinking ...; and the impairment of immune functioning.[3]

Although many educators recognize their responsibility or the moral imperative to educate all children, this recognition often comes with conditions such as, "the student must want to learn" or "the family must be involved." Some very basic understandings in neuroscience can help educators interpret why, at times, students of color are not physically able to learn in school and why, in those instances, educators must take the necessary steps to ensure that the school environment reduces the students' stress levels and thus supports their highest social, emotional, and intellectual functioning. To truly embrace this responsibility, racial equity leaders, in particular, must further explore the emerging body of research connecting neuroscience and race, paying careful attention to how it intersects with the learning and teaching of under-served students of color.

■ ■ ■

As a prerequisite for embarking on the next phase of our journey toward achieving racial equity in our schools, I challenge you to inquire about and discover whether you have truly located your purpose in this work. As you advance through the remainder of this book, you should return on occasion to your responses to these earliest chapters' "Essential Questions" to clarify and fortify your Personal Racial Equity Purpose or PREP as well as test your development toward proficiency in applying the Courageous Conversations Protocol. That evolved sense of purpose and mastery of the Agreements, Conditions, and Compass, coupled with the new leadership insights, language, and illustrations you will gain from this book, will help you determine your course of action—your roadmap—for moving Courageous Conversations from theory to practice.

A CRITIQUE OF LIBERALISM

While facilitating one of the earliest Beyond Diversity trainings in San Francisco, my co-trainer and friend Pam Noli, who is White, shared a surprisingly salient comment with the workshop participants. "We White liberals," she said, "are the most dangerous people in this work because we care, we think we know and understand about the plight of people of color . . . but it is we White liberals who *don't know what we don't know* . . . and that is why we are so dangerous!"

I gasped when I heard that statement coming out of Pam's mouth, not because I disagreed with what she was saying or because I was particularly worried about the audience's reaction to her assertion. No, I gasped because I was unprepared to hear such an important and powerful truth uttered by a White person, even one whose commitment to and understanding of racial equity work I believed to be genuine. (Incidentally, a great deal of predictable volatility did set in immediately.)

I was caught completely off guard. Over years and years of dealing with issues of race and racism, personally and professionally, I had taught myself to avoid articulating the words my colleague spoke so clearly and forcefully that day. I had avoided saying what she said to even my closest White allies for fear that such words would be debilitating to those allies and threaten their antiracist purpose and desire. Yet, in that moment, Pam's action of "calling out" that group of San Francisco liberals made perfect sense to me.

What was especially shocking to me was her use of the word *we*. That simple inclusive pronoun instilled in me such a profound understanding of what racial equity work is all about. I knew, then and there, that if racial equity and justice are to be achieved, the specific form of racism exhibited and practiced by the vast majority of White people, including those who are racial equity leaders and my good friends, had to be confronted.

In Chapter 4, I offered a definition of systemic racism and invited you to view the three distinct, yet potentially overlapping, levels at which racism operates in our schools and society. As I carefully explained, the thoughts and actions that perpetuate systemic racism can be conscious or unconscious, intentional or unintentional, overt or covert. It is critical that each of us discovers—and be willing to uncover, examine, and address—the ways in which we contribute to the current existence and manifestations of racism in our lives and the lives of others. For those of us on the front lines, who fight for racial equity on a daily basis, it is sometimes quite difficult to see our own "racial blind spots" or those lapses that make us less effective or sometimes even destructive to the very cause we are championing.

Hardly a day goes by when I am not confronted with educators, especially White educators, who fail to notice the ways in which their ingrained self-concept of goodness and slightly elevated racial consciousness has been a prompting factor for greater rather than lesser racial unrest in their classrooms, schools, or district offices. "I don't see color," these educators proclaim, "I treat *all* my students the same in my classes," or "This has more to do with (*fill in the other diversity category*) than race." These are just a sampling of the debilitating expressions that spring from the unexamined, often unconscious racist belief systems of White liberal educators. Challenging and correcting these ingrained perspectives calls for both an understanding of some basic theoretical foundations about race and a recognition of how the concept of race interfaces with some of the normative ideals commonly embraced by White liberals. Let me first briefly address the latter, the great American ideal of liberalism, and then offer an interpretation of how this construct can affect the beliefs, behaviors, and results of racial equity leaders negatively.

As early as I can remember, the concept of liberty as innately connected to the founding philosophies of the United States was a staple part of my schooling diet. From the Pledge of Allegiance to discussions about what justified America's engagement in war, the impetus to defend our individual freedoms to express and govern ourselves seemed foundational. As a racially isolated Black student in an elite, predominantly White middle school, I could already detect that the ideals of liberty and justice might be a bit more elusive for me than they were for my White peers on both an individual and racial group level, but I proudly believed, even as my critical understandings of history and contemporary politics developed, that those ideals were attainable and defensible.

Foundational to the American definition of liberty is the philosophy of 19th-century British political economist John Stuart Mills, who argued that individual freedoms should always have voice and power over the will of government, as long as the exercise of those freedoms did no harm to others. He was outspoken as an opponent of slavery and a fervent advocate of equal rights for women. To some degree, Mills's ideas very much align with the thinking of many of us who work for racial equity in the contemporary era, specifically as he speaks to the inherent immorality of enslavement. However, it is important to note that some of Mills's philosophy, as I understand it, particularly his notion that collective and representative government should guard against human beings' natural motivation to act in a self-interested way, was in strong contrast to the prevailing 16th-century ideas of Thomas Hobbes as well as those of other contemporary thinkers. These philosophical foundations—which, without exception, place individual will over the power of collective government—are also at odds with the beliefs of many of us who champion racial equity. Dissecting this history and evolution of thought might lead us to a clearer understanding of why, in Chapter 7, I underscore that systemic equity transformation, as a vision and strategy for improving student achievement, must necessarily and unapologetically be a top-down initiative.

More directly, however, I mention this to point out how these opposing constructs of liberty may contribute to the delayed, gradual, and sometimes nonexistent response that aptly characterizes our contemporary efforts to eradicate racism in our schools. In short, regardless of what Mills, Locke, Rousseau, and other early White political philosophers and economists believed about the American concept of liberty, today's educators continue to struggle with and must challenge their own debilitating ideas and beliefs about racial equity, race neutrality, the velocity of change, and color blindness. Having a vision and a framework for systemic racial equity transformation must include a theory of action for identifying, addressing, and eliminating racial achievement disparities in districts and schools, which I will share with you in Chapter 7. Integral to this process of transformation is the development of a deeper understanding of some basic theories about race.

Although any number of conceptual models could have been chosen for our analysis of race, for reasons I will explore later, critical race theory emerges as my framework of choice. Scholars of critical race theory offer a unique and unsurprisingly controversial critique of four basic notions that have been embraced by liberal legal ideology: color blindness, neutrality of the law, differentiation of equality and equity, and incremental change. As Jessica De Cuir and Adrienne Dixon (2004) maintain:

> At face-value, all appear to be desirable goals to pursue to the extent that in the abstract, colorblindness and neutrality allow for equal opportunity for all; however, given the history of racism in the U.S. whereby rights and opportunities were both conferred and withheld based almost exclusively on race, the idea that the law is indeed colorblind and neutral is insufficient (and many would argue disingenuous) to redress its deleterious effects. Furthermore, the notion of colorblindness fails to take into consideration the persistence and permanence of racism and the construction of people of color as Other.... In other words, arguing that society should be colorblind ignores the fact that inequity, inopportunity, and oppression are historical artifacts that will not easily be remedied by ignoring race in the contemporary society. Moreover, adopting a colorblind ideology does not eliminate the possibility that racism and racist acts will persist. Under the notion of incremental change, gains for marginalized groups must come at a slow pace that is palatable for those in power. In this discourse, equality, rather than equity is sought. In seeking equality rather than equity, the processes, structures, and ideologies that justify inequity are not addressed and dismantled. Remedies based on equality assume that citizens have the same opportunities and experiences. Race and experiences based on race are not equal, thus, the experiences that people of color have with respect to race and racism create an unequal situation. Equity, however, recognizes that the playing field is unequal and attempts to address the inequality. Hence, incremental change appears to benefit those who are not directly adversely affected by social, economic, and educational inequity that come as a result of racism and racist practices.[4]

It is important to unpack or define each of these racial components emerging from the concept of liberalism and to offer specific language and references for how they occur in the so-called antiracist work of racial equity leaders. (I will attend later to the use of the term *antiracist* and the accompanying ideals of those who march under this banner as they address racism at the personal, professional, and organizational levels.) In any event, I am less concerned with how we racial equity leaders name ourselves than I am with how we fail to address the racial blind spots overlooked by so many of the well-intentioned, well-meaning White educators who enter this work. What troubles me even more about this is that we often do not even recognize these blind spots as forms of racism.

Additionally troubling is the finding that much of the research on the topic of racial color blindness is written by White sociologists who seek to position themselves as racially neutral. In his paper titled "The Dangers of *NOT* Speaking About Race," psychologist Phillip Mazzocco (2006) writes:

> Social psychological research done in the 1980s and early 1990s generally supported the view that drawing attention to race in any way would automatically result in stereotyping and that such stereotyping would invariably lead to prejudice and discrimination. Many social psychologists therefore concluded that it would be best to divert attention away from race and toward individual characteristics or higher-level categories such as humanity (two kinds of color-blind approaches). However, subsequent work revealed that racial categorization occurs automatically and that efforts to minimize attention to race do not consistently reduce prejudice or discrimination.... Not only are we insistently color-conscious with respect to others, but the self-esteem benefits we derive from our racial group memberships mean that we are equally color-conscious with respect to our own identities ... Diverting attention away from race, it seems, is simply not possible.[5]

Based on Mazzocco's findings, one can easily extrapolate that the color-blind approach to achieving equity allows White educators to ignore policies, practices, and programs that diminish students of color while advantaging White students:

> If one believes that there are no racial disparities, or that existing disparities are the "fault" of people of color, or are natural phenomena, then there is no need for policies intended to reduce those disparities. Moreover, any race-targeted program can be seen as superficially inconsistent with the principles of equal opportunity and meritocracy.[6]

In her 1992 book, *A Race is a Nice Thing to Have: A Guide to Being a White Person or Understanding the White Persons in Your Life,*[7] Janet Helms offers that a belief in the existence of race neutrality and an adherence to the prosocial goal of color blindness are two critical aspects of White identity development. Although the two notions can be viewed as distinct ideas, they overlap in a way that demands examination. Throughout their lives and right into and through their credentialing programs, many White educators have been encouraged to believe, sometimes by mere omission of the topic, that their being White is benign and has no meaning. This idea typically is coupled with the notion that it is somehow virtuous for White teachers not to "see" the color of their students. It is also linked to the belief that racial meaning is a false and debilitating construct formed in the minds of people of color—thus, the oft-heard question from the mouths of so-called liberal White people: "Why can't you people just *get over it* (meaning race)?" When teachers render meaningless any of their students' visible characteristics (including race, sex, age, or physical disability), they give themselves permission not to notice how student characteristics affect student engagement and learning. Ironically, in my observations and experiences as a racial equity leader, it seems that White educators, students, and community members are the ones who, more often than not, cannot *get over* seeing race, as manifested in their use of deficit language to define people of color and their fight to maintain racial distance and separation as a way of reifying unearned White privilege, thus assuring their continued White advantage.

White theologian Andrew M. Manis answers the question raised and directed at his White readership by the title of his article, "When Are WE Going to Get Over It?" and offers several additional queries:

> How long before we white people realize we can't make our nation, much less the whole world, look like us? How long until we white people can—once and for all—get over this hell-conceived preoccupation with skin color? How long until we white people get over the demonic conviction that white skin makes us superior? How long before we white people get over our bitter resentments about being demoted to the status of equality with non-whites? How long before we get over our expectations that we should be at the head of the line merely because of our white skin? How long until we white people end our silence and call out our peers when they share the latest racist jokes in the privacy of our white-only conversations?
>
> . . . How long until we white people start making racist loudmouths as socially uncomfortable as we do flag burners? How long until we white people will stop insisting that blacks exercise personal responsibility, build strong families, educate themselves enough to edit the *Harvard Law Review*, and work hard enough to become President of the United States, only to threaten to assassinate them when they do? How long before we start "living out the true meaning" of our creeds, both civil and religious, that all men and women are created equal and that "red and yellow, black and white" all are precious in God's sight?[8]

Defining race or racial impact as "neutral" gives White people the opportunity to not notice how White racial power and privilege are playing out in any given situation or circumstance. In the same way that we might expect American Indian educators to process a problem with cultural biases relevant to their experiences, White American educators are certainly as or more likely to operate from a place of White American bias rather than a racially neutral one. Similarly, district policies, programs, and practices created by all-White work groups carry with them an unexamined White bias. Outcomes such as standards mastery and graduation rates, derived from these perceived race-neutral protocols, further institutionalize advantages for Whites.

In advocating for open and honest investigations into race and specifically for a color-conscious rather than a color-blind approach to achieving racial equity, I am aware of the societal disengagement and divisiveness such advocacy can create. The negative out-comes can be mitigated, if not eliminated, however, if White leaders for racial equity, in particular, develop the will, skill, knowledge, and capacity to have effective courageous conversations about race. Of course, some may wonder why I feel the need to engage in a conversation about color blindness in the first place. After all, any White educator who is focused on moving Courageous Conversations from theory to practice must already be beyond Helms's first level of racial identity development, and people of color cannot be color-blind, right?

On the contrary, as my colleague Pam Noli suggested in her comments to the Beyond Diversity group, quoted at the beginning of this chapter, it is precisely race-conscious

White educators and educators of color who, like me, have been trained not to point out racial differences, who slip into a color-blind posture at the least opportune times. Our liberal silence can be deafening, speaking louder than the conservative voices that flood the nation's corporate boardrooms, newspaper columns, and talk radio and television shows, advocating for the defunding of our equity work.

Color-blind racism goes far beyond the simplistic "I don't see color" to include a multiplicity of ways individuals contribute to the diminishing of the power and importance of engaging multiracial perspectives and experiences. Referencing the work of Eduardo Bonilla-Silva,[9] Mazzocco identifies four distinct frames of mind that, when not recognized and acknowledged, lead to exacerbated racial disparities and their corresponding structural impact on marginalized racial groups:

> The first frame involves a minimization of the existence of ongoing racial disparities. To the extent that disparities are acknowledged at all, the second frame blames them on pathological non-White cultures, rather than on structural constraints or White privilege. The third frame justifies racial phenomena as natural (e.g., racial segregation as a natural result of our preference to interact with others like ourselves). Finally, the fourth frame upholds ideals such as equality and meritocracy, but either fails to take into account important preconditions such as a balanced playing field or assumes a balanced playing field based on the first frame.[10]

Mazzocco provides empirical data suggesting that a color-conscious rather than a color-blind approach better supports the goals of racial equity work. From his research examining the attitudes and behaviors of White college students, we can extrapolate how White educators who profess to be politically liberal are just as likely as their conservative counterparts to opt for the color-blind approach *when a situation or circumstance has greater personal implications.* In his investigations with White college students who also self-identified as either liberal or conservative, Mazzocco found that the two groups held distinctly different views on the presence of racial injustice but surprisingly similar views on and support for race-based remedies to foster greater equality. Specifically, the liberal students were more likely than their conservative counterparts to recognize racial injustices and to be sympathetic to the plight of marginalized minorities when listening to historical narratives that explained such inequalities. When it came to demanding and supporting equity policies such as affirmative action college-admission programs, however, both groups' responses were statistically indistinguishable.

Mazzocco included roughly 170 White college students in his sample. He asked a control group of liberal and conservative students simply to offer their views on race-based equity remedies such as affirmative action (e.g., To what degree do you support race-based affirmative action?). He asked the students in Group A the same questions, but only after providing them with messages about contemporary racial disparities in American society (A). He did the same with Group A + B but also provided them with messages about the related structural impacts of such disparities (B). Last, he provided Group A + B + C with all of the other groups' questions and messages but also exposed them to messages that challenged the blind application of concepts such as meritocracy and equality (C). Figure 5.1 illustrates Mazzocco's findings.

Figure 5.1 White Support for Progressive Racial Policies

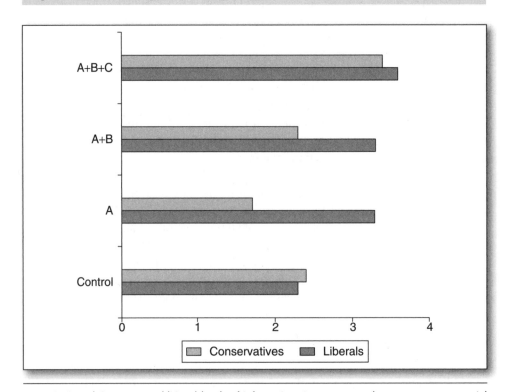

Note: A, B, and C represent additional levels of information. A = messages about contemporary racial disparities; B = messages about the related structural impacts of the disparities; C = messages that challenge the blind application of concepts such as meritocracy and equality.

Source: Adapted from *The Dangers of NOT Speaking About Race* (p. 6), by Phillip Mazzocco, 2006, Columbus: The Ohio State University, Kirwan Institute for the Study of Race and Ethnicity. Adapted with permission.

Not surprising is the fact that the self-described liberals in all of the experimental groups demonstrated greater acceptance of racial equity policies such as affirmative action. What is most illuminating to our work as racial equity leaders is Mazzocco's finding that the liberal and conservative students who were not exposed to any messaging about racial disparities (the control group) expressed *similarly low levels* of commitment to racial equity and that those who received complete messaging (Group A + B + C)—that is, exposure to a comprehensive race-conscious approach—*expressed statistically similar higher levels* of support for equity. The self-described conservatives, in fact, showed greater marginal growth in their commitment to such policies after they were exposed to messaging about racial disparities and the structural impacts of those disparities. In other words, the deeper the messaging about racial inequalities the conservatives received, the more likely they were to embrace race-based equity remedies. On the other hand, the racial equity views of the self-proclaimed liberals were less influenced by changes in the level of messaging. Whether no messaging (Control Group) or deep messaging (Group A + B + C) was offered, liberals and conservatives responded quite similarly to racial equity policies such as affirmative action. Significant disparities between the liberals and conservatives response to equity policies only appeared when a low level or incomplete explanation of racial injustice, as a phenomenon, was offered.

One can safely deduce from these findings that, for educators—regardless of their political leanings and particularly for White educators—an intense socialization focusing on the concepts of individualism, meritocracy, and effort/reward paradigms (all characteristics of Whiteness) will lead to an internalized resistance to equity. For those White people who define themselves as liberals, this ingrained resistance can be especially problematic because it rarely leads them to challenge their fundamental mindsets. This is the basis of Pam Noli's assertion that White (politically leaning) liberals, compounded by the fact that they live in a so-called liberal society, are "the most dangerous people in this work."

■ ■ ■

To help readers understand better how the "go-slow" notion of gradualism and incremental change impedes racial equity, I will share the following experience. Recently, close to 20 school leaders, policymakers, and postsecondary educators, I among them, came together in Minneapolis to discuss the state of school integration in the United States. Organized by One Nation Indivisible, an important and timely project of the Poverty and Race Research Action Council and the Charles Hamilton Houston Institute for Race and Justice at Harvard Law School, the conference was convened to examine and mount a response to the aggressive attacks made against racial integration efforts in Minnesota's Eden Prairie Schools and various other districts across the nation.

Early on in the meeting, several participants of color—again, me among them—found ourselves dumbfounded by the realization that the discussions at this 2011 conference sounded remarkably similar to those we had heard our elders talk about having when *they* were sitting in our chairs decades ago. Indeed, our conversations, focused as they were on achieving racial balance in schools, ending racial segregation, and promoting equitable learning opportunities for children of color, could easily have been lifted directly from the casebooks leading up to the landmark 1954 *Brown v. Board of Education* decision. In my own moment of realization, I was overwhelmed by a deep sense of sadness as I forced myself to recognize how little things had changed, despite the mighty examples of racial progress evident in the accomplishments of Barack Obama, Sonia Sotomayor, Colin Powell, and Condoleezza Rice. With regard to our nation's system of education, however—the system that offers the only real assurance that the advances of people of color in politics and government will be structural and permanent rather than random and episodic, I felt as if time was standing still. I also felt intense anger and frustration stemming from how academic and cavalier many in my generation of people of color seemed to be, while attending to these circumstances.

Out in the hinterlands of my Courageous Conversations Compass-based emotional quadrant, I felt my cortisol production surge, followed immediately by a kick of adrenalin. I was paralyzed by my own silence and sorrow and remained so for much of that day. Alone, in my self-induced solitude, I immersed myself in an online search to locate some gem of wisdom, some jewel of knowledge and experience that could help me surmount what Lisa Delpit calls the barriers that restrict how meaning is constructed. Delpit's words were edifying:

> When I consider the origins of my views, I realize that my personal history, by necessity, contributes considerably to my current belief systems. I write from a life lived in many margins, usually while struggling to approach the center of whichever page of my life is unfolding at the moment. It has been that struggle to understand and adapt to various contexts that has led me on the personal journey of discovering other realities.[11]

Then certain to find a solution to my prolonged silent anguish in the words of W.E.B. Du Bois, I "googled" *The Souls of Black Folk* and came upon the following:

> To the real question, how does it feel to be the problem?
> I answer, seldom a word.[12]

In that moment, it became powerfully clear to me how people of color, and children of color especially, are still viewed by White society as a "problem." This is a belief that those of us who profess to be racial equity leaders must challenge and overcome every day, from Du Bois's time to the present and very likely well into the future. Then and there, I was reminded that turning this belief upside down, to point the finger of blame at systemic racism and those afflicted with that disease—and thus to single those elements out as needing care and attention—was our best choice as a solution.

In that moment, too, I realized why the efforts of my generation to address systemic racism seemed not to have had the significant impact of our parents' and grandparents' movements: White people in America have yet to collectively champion racial equity in public education. Whether Black, Brown, Yellow, and Red children receive a free and appropriate public education in the United States is determined largely by the desires of White voters, school board members, and local government officials. Particularly in the nation's urban centers but elsewhere as well, the masses of children of color will never experience high-quality educational instruction, learning facilities, or other academic resources until the largely White teaching workforce, their supervising administrators, and policymakers determine that it is time to embrace the principle of racial equity. The reality is that these children's future opportunities are dependent on our ability, as the racial equity leaders of today, to convince an albeit-shrinking White majority of the value of ensuring those opportunities. This is a deplorable (not to mention morally reprehensible) fact.

Although it is appropriate to lay sizeable blame for failure to correct this troubling reality on White people, the people of color of my generation have also contributed in significant ways to the slowed pace (and sometimes reverse trajectory) of racial equity progress. We have embraced some of the damaging beliefs characteristic of Whiteness—that is, individualism and color blindness—and we have failed to help our children resist developing post-racialism beliefs and avoid succumbing to the delusion that racial equity has already been achieved. For many children of color, such debilitating beliefs and lack of awareness challenge their ability to be resilient and persevere in the face of the myriad overt and covert forms of racism that persist to this day. How can we, the forebears of this generation of children of color expect them to work, as my mother instructed me, "twice as hard to get half as far" as their White counterparts when we do not provide them with any explanation for why such increased effort is necessary? More important than simply telling them about the need to acknowledge, confront, and surmount racism in both its interpersonal and institutional forms, we need to model for children of color the effective behaviors they should exhibit to succeed in a society still grappling with its racist legacy.

■ ■ ■

I emerged from my solitude (and online research) and sought to authentically connect with my colleagues at the One Nation Indivisible conference. Thanks to Du Bois, I saw clearly, once again, the importance of staying engaged and speaking my truth in the midst of my personal discomfort and momentary doubts about the future of racial equity progress. Bolstering me to renew this quest was the truth I found in his words:

> After the Egyptian and Indian, the Greek and Roman, the Teuton and Mongolian, the Negro is a sort of seventh son, born with a veil, and gifted with second-sight in this American world—a world which yields him no true self-consciousness, but only lets him see himself through the revelation of the other world. It is a peculiar sensation, this double-consciousness, this sense of always looking at one's self through the eyes of others, of measuring one's soul by the tape of a world that looks on in amused contempt and pity. One ever feels his two-ness—an American, a Negro; two souls, two thoughts, two unreconciled strivings; two warring ideals in one dark body, whose dogged strength alone keeps it from being torn asunder.[13]

With Du Bois's sage invocation fresh in my mind, I was able to refocus and rejoin the conference. After lunch, I was scheduled to give a short presentation to the assembly on my organization's work in Eden Prairie Schools. In my truncated remarks, due to conference time limitations, I simply challenged the attendees to be bold in reconsidering whether their present-day notions of post-racialism and gradualism, and even their deep-rooted attachment to the construct of integration, may in fact be harmful to today's children of color. I urged them to invoke a sense of urgency in countering the efforts of those who believe we should "go slow" on racial equity progress, to lose patience with teachers' unions and school boards that often collude in ways detrimental to that progress, and to demand accountability for the educational success of children of color from those charged with (and paid for) instructing them. In closing, I pointed the group toward self-examination and underscored that each attendee must develop an authentic sense of purpose around racial equity work that would not allow them to falter, even when their personal or professional circumstances were being threatened.

With that, it seemed that the group was ready to engage in courageous conversations about racial segregation, desegregation, and integration in public education. I wonder what might have happened that day if I had engaged the Courageous Conversations Protocol *before* lunch was served!

■ ■ ■

Earlier, I mentioned that I am challenged by White educators' use of the term *antiracist* to define their work and perhaps an important contemporary movement in education. I do not take issue with the notion of White educators challenging racism. Indeed, I wholeheartedly support much of the excellent classroom-, school-, and district-level interventions and strategies in which many of these educators engage. Yet, to me, *antiracist* connotes a defined way of being, regardless of situation or circumstance, that I have yet to see exhibited by my White colleagues. The mere fact that White educators continue to evoke skin-color privilege in many areas of their personal lives, even while challenging racism in many of their professional spheres of influence, makes it impossible for them to be truly and holistically antiracist.

My fear is that categorizing educators by their antiracist propensities will create unnecessary hierarchy and competition among those fighting for the same cause. Furthermore, some White educators would view themselves as "getting it" or reaching a "there" as far as their racial consciousness, while others "don't get it" or "are not quite there, yet." Such phrases have sprung up as defining and divisive markers in some of our partnering districts, independent schools, and institutions of higher education. At what level of will, skill, knowledge, and capacity does one earn the distinction of being called an *antiracist*? More important, what acts of unconscious or unintentional personally mediated racism would demand the forfeit of such a distinction? And how would people of color, whose mere physical appearance can serve as a confrontation with racism, fit into the definition of antiracist? Spending time answering these and a variety of other antiracist certification-type questions can distract otherwise effective White leaders from accelerating their meaningful racial equity transformation in their personal and professional lives.

No doubt about it, to focus on antiracism or to embrace strategies that are antiracist makes a great deal of sense to me. But if you, like me, feel put off by the antiracist label and are searching for a new way of describing yourself and your work, particularly one that will not cause others to challenge your commitment to resisting racism or prevent you from challenging theirs, I suggest *racial equity leader*.

ARE BLACK MALES BEYOND LOVE?

In his critical race theory ethnography, titled *Beyond Love: A Critical Race Ethnography of the Schooling of Black Males*,[14] Garrett Duncan offers a compelling and almost linear description of how schools relegate Black males to marginalized circumstances, such as special and alternative education, leading to their academic, social, and emotional demise. For me, a transition similar to what Duncan describes occurred sometime around seventh grade. No longer did I feel the world viewed me as a cute little Black boy. At times, I felt I was being treated as if I had done something horribly wrong to random strangers on the street. Perhaps growing up in a loving Black community and attending an all-Black elementary school buffered me from the criminalization that I began to experience immediately on entering the larger, Whiter society, but when the parents of one of my elite middle school classmates chose not to invite only the three Black boys in their daughter's class to her Bat Mitzvah, I knew something had definitely changed.

I lost my racial innocence and, from that moment on, I became increasingly conscious, and thus guarded and defensive, believing that I would constantly be the target of racism. I cloaked my spirit in an invisible suit of protective armor to shield me from racial slights and injustices. I have worn that protective armor every day since seventh grade, just in case I am denied access to the freedoms I see those around me enjoying without care or concern of rejection. I wear it in case someone "not-of-color" decides to exercise his or her White skin privilege without regard for my feelings or circumstances. My armor helps me not take this differential or denigrating treatment personally. Often, it prevents me from violently lashing out against society's injustices on my own behalf and that of others like me, a reaction that could land me in prison or potentially lead to my demise.

For many Black males, the onset of experiences such as those I have revealed in my personal racial autobiography occurs as early as kindergarten. In her book titled *Bad Boys: Public Schools in the Making of Black Masculinity,* Ann Ferguson (2001) refers to these criminalizing experiences as moments of *adultification.* Thus, she notes, by seventh grade, Black male students "can no longer bear the weight of their own experience and begin to retaliate against the system or attempt to assimilate and maneuver in school and society without their much-needed protective armor."[15] Both these options, she maintains, "clearly lead to dangerous ends." For me personally, it was not an *either or,* but rather a *both and,* which is to say that by seventh grade I had already succumbed to institutional pressure to assimilate while sharpening my retaliation skills necessary to fight against racism at Park School.

The irony of this adultification and criminalization is clearly evident in a nation that can elect a Black man president when Black men are concurrently the most scrutinized, distrusted, marginalized, sexualized, vilified, and criminalized population in our country, if not the world. Then again, if the White U.S. majority could collectively lower its racial defenses and raise its racial consciousness for just one day, they could all see how President Obama and his family have been racially mistreated from the time he announced his candidacy. As for me, I anticipated the racialized backlash against Obama's candidacy and his presidency because many White Americans have never had a substantive conversation with a Black man, let alone accepted leadership from one. The "Obama effect" is yet another manifestation of the nation's inability to recognize and act on the continued deplorable racial experiences of the internal population that poses the greatest threat to White male supremacy and dominance in the United States.

As the age-old rules of the game change for this president in terms of how he is judged to be effective, whether on issues of moral character or statesmanship, even the White liberal population struggles to offer President Obama the respect and credit he is due. And, once again, silence in the presence of racial injustice is the most lethal form of racism. President Obama took office at one of the worst times in this nation's history, during a period of multiple wars and economic downturn. Arguably, however, many White Americans fail to see the extraordinary significance of Obama's color-barrier breaking election, insisting that he still "prove himself" by becoming some sort of "superman," absent, of course, of cheering fans or thankful citizens.

Thus, one very critical national courageous conversation would center around the following questions: Why have there been more threats against President Obama's life than that of any other sitting president? Why are senators and governors allowed to openly disrespect him, even in the very halls of Congress? Why can't President Obama and his family continue to worship in a Black church? Why can't he and First Lady Michelle Obama redecorate the East and West wings, which have never previously been inhabited by a Black family, free of public scrutiny?

And then there is perhaps the largest question of all: Why can't we, as a nation, simply have a courageous conversation about our thoughts, feelings, and beliefs surrounding this monumental and historic transition of executive branch power from White to Black? In asking this question, I am compelled to break my silence on this matter and venture a response on behalf of America's Black males, many of whom realize that one racial transgression by President Obama could not only cost *him* the presidency but also have a detrimental effect on Americans' view and treatment of Black males in particular and our race as a whole, thus further limiting our children's prospects for the future in general. Within the latter group, the future of the schooling conditions in which Black male children will find themselves is particularly dependent on a successful Obama presidency.

As Pedro Noguera writes in his article, "The Trouble with Black Boys: The Role and Influence of Environmental and Cultural Factors on the Academic Performance of African American Males":

> Rather than serving as a source of hope and opportunity, schools are sites where Black males are marginalized and stigmatized. Consistently, schools that serve Black males fail to nurture, support, or protect them. In school, Black males are more likely to be labeled as behavior problems and less intelligent even while they are still very young. Black males are also more likely to be punished with severity, even for minor offenses, for violating school rules; often without regard for their welfare. They are more likely to be excluded from rigorous classes and prevented from accessing educational opportunities that might otherwise support and encourage them.[16]

According to *Yes We Can: The 2010 Schott 50 State Report on Public Education and Black Males*,[17] an exhaustive study executed by the Schott Foundation for Public Education, stacks of research reports have indicated for years that Black male students are not given the same opportunities to participate in classes offering enriched educational offerings. More frequently and inappropriately, Black boys in schools are removed from the general education classroom and placed in special education due to misclassifications wrought by existing policies and practices. On average, more than twice as many White male students are afforded the extra resources of gifted-and-talented programs than are Black male students. Advanced Placement (AP) classes enroll only token numbers of Black male students, despite The College Board's urging that schools open these classes to all who may benefit. In districts with selective college-preparatory high schools, it is not uncommon to find virtually no Black male students in those schools. In addition, the national percentage of Black male students enrolled at each stage of schooling declines from middle school through graduate degree programs.

The great variation in these factors among districts and states indicates that the driver is not the individual student, but rather the adults who are responsible for the implementation of racially biased and discriminatory educational policies and practices.

What this says to me is that the time has come for us all to recognize such schooling for what it is: a pipeline to prison for Black males. To redirect this conduit and rectify this educational atrocity, we must exercise our moral courage and professional responsibility.

It has taken me well over a decade to name and address the role and impact of race in the education of Black males, but Barack Obama's successful candidacy for and election to the highest office in the land within that decade has emboldened me in my quest. He has recharged my will to address the needs of the lowest-performing, most under-served demographic group in our nation's entire educational system: Black males. Coincidentally, that is the group to which I feel most connected and about which I feel most knowledgeable. Previously, however, I feared that focusing on this group and entering into such discussions would be equivalent to committing professional suicide. I also feared that I would not have the physical fortitude and healthy disposition needed to advocate, personally, for an experience so close to my heart. In addition, I supposed that I would not be able to maintain the professional decorum necessary when discussing the issue, and thus I would be further marginalized from my chosen profession. Once I overcame those fears and, again, emboldened by Obama's victory, I understood and fully accepted the risks I was taking by tackling the issue of race in the United States as a Black man and, even more specifically, addressing the peculiarly devastating racial reality of Black males in our society.

Racial equity in U.S. public schools cannot be achieved until Black males are no longer predicted to be the lowest-performing population in that system. Changing this phenomenon will require educators with abundant amounts of passion, scores of effective practices, and unyielding persistence. It will also require educators to muster the courage to ask if their own levels of care and concern for these most under-served students is sufficient to address the cultural and structural barriers that line these boys' pathways to success.

Why have so many of us positioned ourselves as bystanders to the systemic demise of Black males in schools and society? In discovering what has prevented us from acting in the past, we must uncover what will compel us to respond differently now and in the future. Not unlike other issues I address in this book, I attribute much of this challenge—namely, that of educating Black males effectively—to our collective lack of purpose, not to a lack of knowledge, skills, or capacity to get the job done.

It is likewise important to do whatever it takes to bring adult Black males and students "to the table"—that is, to bring Black men back into the schools—to discuss the problem and participate in the designing of meaningful solutions. Too often, the voices of Black men—be they educators, parents, or students themselves—are excluded from such conversations. This leads to their lack of awareness about the critical conditions facing Black males in schools and their lack of involvement in the educational solutions to those conditions. Only by inviting Black men into specific processes that empower their young counterparts can they help to guard Black boys against engaging in self-destructive behaviors in school environments.

Every teacher, administrator, parent, and student in the United States today must commit (or recommit, as the case may be) to being a part of the solution—that is, to help create, for the first time in our nation's history, an *intentionally* positive educational environment and experience for Black male students. To do anything less would be an act of educational malpractice, not to mention acquiescence to the continuation of status-quo racism.

DEFINING RESISTANCE AND
TRANSFORMING "RESISTERS"

In my trainings years ago, I would attempt to combat educators' disbelief in the power of meaningful and authentic conversations about race by sharing my thoughts on the early U.S. space program. I would begin by telling them how amazed I was by the fact that human beings were able to travel thousands of miles away from Earth's atmosphere to explore our solar system. I would then point out how prior to our astronauts' journey to the moon, scientists gathered in many locations across the country to build the spacecraft that could endure an atmosphere no human had yet to experience. Technologists worked for decades on the communication devices that would allow a team of mechanics and physicians on Earth to monitor the expedition and remain in direct conversation with the space travelers. Nutritionists and fitness experts devised plans to ensure that Alan Shepard, the first American in space, would stay healthy and remain as comfortable as possible during his explorations. Thousands gathered at the Cape Canaveral, Florida, launch pad to see the Freedom 7 spaceship take off, and millions gathered around televisions nationwide to witness the capsule touchdown in the Atlantic Ocean after the mission.

I noted also that shortly after the National Aeronautics and Space Administration was founded in 1959, space exploration became not only commonplace for this country, but a priority and a measure of our prowess in comparison to the Soviet Union and other nations. In effect, we had the national will to discover frontiers beyond our own planet because we recognized the political, economic, military, and intellectual benefits to be gained from it. Although my recollections probably failed to capture many of the salient milestones in the history of the U.S. space program and perhaps strayed from technical validity in many ways, the point of my reflections was that the American space program blossomed during the 1960s and 1970s, even though many believed it could not.

Similarly, I noted, many people do not believe that racism can be challenged and ultimately eradicated. However, if the United States can put men and women on the moon, I argued, it should be able to greatly reduce racism in its schools, even though racism is as foundational to the American way of life as its citizens' aspirations for freedom. Sadly, the country has not rallied around deinstitutionalizing racism in the same way that we supported our expeditions to other worlds. For many, African slavery, Asian internment, and American Indian genocide are only horrific memories from the American past, yet they continue to present residual effects for the descendents of the victims of those injustices. These vestiges are especially evident in the school experiences of Black, Brown, and American Indian children. As a result, moving Courageous Conversations from theory to practice will require racial equity leaders to promote belief in the possibility of achieving a racially just system of education while effectively confronting, managing, and surmounting the resistance that often slows and occasionally blocks that progress.

■ ■ ■

When I first started my racial equity training work, I was quick to label whole groups of educators as resistant to this cause, especially when they, in my opinion, questioned the presence of racism in American society and schools or when they challenged my assertion that talking about race could lead to deep and meaningful transformation in educational outcomes. These resisters, as I called them, seemed continuously to construct roadblocks to my leadership program, and they opted for detours to rather than head-on confrontations with the complexity and discomfort that characterizes racial equity leadership development. I realize now that dismissing so many folks from this work served only to release them from their personal responsibility and professional obligation to serve all children fully, leaving only a paltry few to bear the enormous weight of achieving systemic racial equity.

Since then, I have come to view educators' resistance to the idea of racial equity less as a permanent and defining quality and, at least for the majority of educators, more as a stage in their development. I have explored several theories and have arrived at one that documents what my colleagues and I experience in training others for this work and provides a model that helps us build and expand the ranks of racial equity leaders rather than deplete the rolls and tear down the spirit and confidence of potential allies. My theory draws heavily on the ideas Anthony Muhammad shares in his book, *Transforming School Culture: How to Overcome Staff Division.*[18] Muhammad contends that there are four types of educators (Believers, Tweeners, Survivors, and Fundamentalists), each of which brings a slightly different personality and purpose to the school environment that ultimately affects the way racial equity efforts are designed, delivered, and experienced.[19]

According to Muhammad, Believers support the notion that success for every student academically, socially, and emotionally is not only possible but also plausible. They tend to go about their racial equity work quietly and consistently, as opposed to resisters, who often seek power and recognition in their building and central office departments. Believers are not content, nor do they feel successful, until every child within their influence maximizes his or her potential. Except in extreme cases, however, Believers tend to be passive about and permissive of colleagues who perpetuate inequity, hold low expectations for students of color, and construct roadblocks to school equity reform, and thus Believers often become bystanders to acts of racism.

Tweeners, Muhammad maintains, generally are new to the education system. In most cases, these educators refrain from offering perspective or sharing strategies for improving the racial culture and climate in their schools or central office departments. They also often feel that they lack the essential knowledge, supportive relationships, and important political power to make a difference due to their limited time in the environment. Championing controversial causes such as equity tends to threaten Tweeners' sense of safety. Given that many school districts' diversity recruitment efforts stem from relatively new policies, educators of color often fall into the Tweener category. (Ironically, educators of color often struggle to express their own cultural perspectives and share culturally relevant teaching strategies with their colleagues. Of course, this defeats much of the purpose districts had when they set out to diversify their workforces in the first place.) Like Believers, however, Tweeners fortify the so-called resisters by their lack of engagement and tacit observance of inequitable practices.

Survivors are educators who have given up, for the most part, on practicing effectiveness in their work and instead are focused on a single mission: survival until the end of the school year, or perhaps sometimes, until the end of the school day. The path of least effort and intellect is Survivors' option of choice, thus they cannot be counted on to lead in any type of school transformation or reform. And, as resistance mounts to any given innovation, Survivors, like Believers and Tweeners, will most likely not offer any challenge to their colleagues who construct roadblocks to equity or who diminish children of color and their families. Instead, Survivors determine which strategic directions will require the least of them in terms of physical, intellectual, and emotional energy.

Fundamentalists are usually experienced educators who believe that the traditional model of schooling offers the only pure, practical, and undisputable way to educate children. They are, as a result, often the most strident resisters to racial equity transformation. Fundamentalists are vanguards of tradition, protectors of the status quo, and purveyors of power. Given their personality traits as well as their veteran status, Fundamentalists often are forces to be reckoned with in a school district if the leadership truly hopes to achieve racial equity, as social justice principles are not considered traditional. Not only must Fundamentalists be challenged when racial equity efforts are undertaken, but their very fundamentalism must be eliminated. This is because fundamentalism limits educational access and opportunities for children of color, especially those who are impoverished, who are English language learners, or who have academic, physical, or emotional special needs. Fundamentalists rarely view themselves as such and believe that the fundamentalist principles they advocate are right.

It is worth emphasizing that the lack of racial equity leadership demonstrated by Believers, Tweeners, and Survivors is as detrimental as other resisters' outright assault on racial equity work. Too often, outstanding racial equity work is compromised, even in partnering districts of the Pacific Educational Group (PEG), not because of opposition to those efforts but rather because supporters of racial equity choose to remain silent or passive and thus become our most dangerous and powerful resisters. If we do not capture their hearts, minds, and energies, the Fundamentalists certainly will. When it comes to deinstitutionalizing racism, there is no neutral ground on which educators can rest. Every action taken in our nation's schools either challenges or perpetuates racism. To have no impact or position on racism is to help solidify its place in our education system and society.

To maximize our progress, racial equity leaders must carefully determine those colleagues, parents, or community members who are opposed to and will attempt to block our efforts to meet the needs of all children. Equally important, we must recognize those who simply need additional information, greater support, or a different pathway into understanding their role and responsibility in this work. Defining resistance and transforming resisters enables us to develop and nurture the mightiest racial equity leadership force we can, while keeping careful watch over those who seek to maintain the status quo and distract or deter us from our efforts to achieve racially equitable schooling. This too is a critical strategy for moving Courageous Conversations from theory to practice.

WHAT SHOULD BE "SPECIAL" ABOUT SPECIAL EDUCATION?

Like clockwork, at the same time on Tuesdays and Thursdays, Marco, a student in my third-grade class at Hilton Elementary in Baltimore, always got up from his desk located somewhere near the door of Mrs. Sandifer's classroom and walked out. Initially, his classmates, myself included, believed that this was just another one of Marco's innocent acts of defiance. In retrospect, however, given Mrs. Sandifer's general strictness, this excuse did not hold much water. Wherever Marco was going, we were all certain that in just a short time, he would rejoin the class and be up to his usual tricks.

One day, as our class marched in double-file lines, one for boys and one for girls, to the music classroom, I noticed Marco sitting inside a very small room engaged in an activity with an adult who was not familiar to me. Whatever this person had Marco doing, it certainly seemed to calm and captivate him. By the time I returned from 40 minutes of singing, clapping, and swaying to Mrs. Buckskin's engaging melodic selection, asking Marco about what he was doing in the little room with the stranger had completely slipped my mind. Only much later did I find out that he was being "pulled out" for what the adults called "special instruction."

Although Marco was prone to disrupt class occasionally with an inappropriate remark or gesture, he remained one of the teacher's pets and was a good friend to many of us kids. To the best of my recollection, he was the only student I remember who had to be pulled out in that manner, but never did any of us kids view him as differently abled, and we certainly never believed he was not intelligent or capable of advancing with our class to the next level of learning.

Only in 1992, when I began my graduate fieldwork as a counselor at suburban Menlo Atherton High School in Northern California, did I discover the "label" for Marco: He was, I learned, a special education student. Whether or not there were other Marcos in my class who escaped my third-grader's recognition is not the point, however. Things had changed dramatically in public education in 20 years. Schools had become so densely populated with Marcos that large staffs of special education teachers, in big rooms—and in some districts, even whole schools—were necessary to accommodate an educational experience once barely noticeable.

Since my time at Menlo Atherton, my work has taken me into thousands of elementary and secondary schools in which Black, Brown, and American Indian children are grossly overrepresented in special education programs. In 2009, my appointment to the California State Board of Education's Committee on African American Achievement exposed me to a special education narrative and statistics that sounded my personal alarm. It also prompted my resolve to bring greater attention and remedy to this quiet and costly illustration of systemic racism.

The committee found that White male students in California are more than twice as likely to be placed in gifted/talented programs as are Black male students. The latter, however, are more than twice as likely to be classified as mentally retarded as White male students, despite research demonstrating that the percentages of students from all racial/ethnic groups are approximately the same at each intelligence level. The persistent overclassification of Black male students as mentally retarded reflected, at best, a lack of professional development in that area for teachers and other staff.

The committee also learned that, even though the College Board recommends encouraging enrollment in advanced placement (AP) classes for all students, more than four times as many White male students take AP mathematics and science classes as Black male students. Furthermore, more than twice as many Black male students as White male students receive out-of-school suspensions, and three times as many Black male students as White male students are expelled from school for disciplinary infractions. Out-of-school suspensions, in many cases, lead to students' ending their school careers before graduation, thus possibly accounting for a significant portion of the Black male student population in the state who did not graduate with their cohort.

Many years prior to my appointment to this committee, I met Deborah McKnight one Sunday morning in church. At the time, I had no idea that she was the mind and muscle behind the San Francisco Unified School District's (SFUSD) aggressive and prominent efforts to stem the tide of runaway placements of students of color in special education. When I met her, she had been the SFUSD's director of special education for 10 years. Deborah is a quiet yet determined woman, and as I got to know her, I quickly discovered that she had dedicated her life to being a "special educator" and that she saw transforming special education as a moral and economic imperative. Often, I would listen to her tell stories of inappropriately labeled students, misinformed parents, "malpracticed" educators, opportunistic lawyers, and unethical doctors. Despite the demand on her attention (and pilfering from her dwindling budget) by this callous cast of characters, Deborah could still boast of pacesetting achievement gains for students in SFUSD's special education program.

Special education is a systemic racial equity leverage point precisely because Black, Brown, and American Indian children are disproportionately labeled as special needs students. More than most aspects of schooling, a district's special education program's design, functioning, staffing, and achievement data reveal the system's overall commitment to equity and excellence. The percentage and demographic breakdown of students receiving special services speaks to a district's traditional education philosophy as much as it tells a story of each school district's compliance under federal special education law, as mandated by the Individuals with Disabilities Education Act or IDEA.

With respect to special education programming, those of us who are racial equity leaders can take a variety of concrete steps that help to move Courageous Conversations from theory to practice. First, we must develop a thorough understanding of the purpose of special education as well as the law governing it, which mandates certain types of programming. We must also pay particular attention to Section 504 of the IDEA, which explains when and why students should be referred for special services, the categories of special needs, and students' and parents' rights and responsibilities. Armed with such knowledge, we can dramatically decrease the number of misplacements of students of color in special education. This careful stewarding will keep children of color out of inappropriate learning environments and enable special educators to attend to children who require their expertise. Given that the federal mandate to provide special education services to all "qualified" students is grossly underfunded, fewer placements will result in school districts saving valuable resources that can be used elsewhere. One can only hope, however, that these savings will translate into support for other critical equity programming.

We racial equity leaders must also recognize the importance of integrating special education professionals into every dimension of our equity work at the school site and central office levels. Too often, equity leadership teams do not include special education teachers, psychologists, counselors, or paraprofessionals, all of whom work closely with special needs students. But these are experienced and knowledgeable voices that must be heard if we are to address racial disparities in schools in meaningful ways. Integrating these personnel will require effort to break down the walls that have been constructed between traditional and special needs educational programming. School principals will be instrumental in guiding and supporting the development of this integrated professional learning community. Superintendents and district directors of special education will have to assist in bringing traditional and special education curricular leaders into partnership at the central office level. Special education personnel at school sites will need to receive the same intensive racial equity training as traditional classroom personnel. Most important, they will need opportunities to develop their Courageous Conversations knowledge, skills, and capacity.

Only through such multilevel collaboration will the root causes of the disproportionate designation and placement of under-served students of color in special education programming be uncovered, examined, and addressed. Working together, they can eliminate racial disproportionality in special education program referrals and placement and share the burden of federal compliance monitoring. Such collaboration will also free teachers of special needs students to focus on instruction and transition their students to the least restrictive environment possible.

■ ■ ■

Given what we currently understand about the physiological impacts of racism, we know that our efforts to move Courageous Conversations from theory to practice have both moral and economic implications. Supporting all educators in recognizing and dismantling racial barriers that serve to traumatize students of color and trigger their behavioral disturbances will lead to fewer referrals of these students to special education placements and ultimately to a decrease in the amount of funding needed to educate them in more costly classroom environments. Providing *all* children with a schooling environment that is free of racism will give them the freedom to learn and the opportunity to discover their truest capabilities and achieve all that is truly possible in life.

ESSENTIAL QUESTIONS

Chapter 5 outlines several key issues that beckon educators into *MORE Courageous Conversations About Race:*

1. Which of these key issues are most pronounced in your system and what data supports your assertion?

2. Which of these key issues will you take on in a more purposeful, courageous way?

3. Who will join you in your new level of leadership for racial equity and what will your fortified and innovative practice entail?

Voices From the Inside: Charles L. Hopson

In my former role as superintendent of the Pulaski County Special School District (PCSSD) in Little Rock, Arkansas, the challenges for me actually differed very little from those I experienced growing up in that state during the desegregation of schools in the early 1960s. I was warned that "you can never really return home again," but for me, it became a moral imperative—an unavoidable obligation to sacrifice all and return to my native roots to lead the Pulaski County district in comprehensive reform aimed at providing equity of academic access to every student. The South I returned to was one in which so many were imprisoned in psychological jailhouses of fear and complacency. As I would often ask patrons in the district later: Why do you settle for so little? Why don't you demand more of people like me?

I recall the raging anger I felt as I walked through a low-achieving school serving students predominantly of African descent where the restrooms were so filthy, many students would hold bodily functions until they went home. I immediately contracted a crew to clean and repaint that school, working around the clock until it was in accept-able condition. I bristled as the workers shared with me that they had to scrape inches of dried urine off the floors to get to the surface to paint. Yet, I could drive 15 miles to a wealthier, predominantly European American part of the district and witness the con-struction of a multimillion-dollar, glitzy, state-of-the-art facility. I pondered how in 2010, desegregation efforts had failed so miserably in this district, state, and country. The conditions and degree of disparity were worse than what I remembered of the segre-gated schools of my youth. I vowed that race and poverty should not be a determiner of the quality of facilities that students attend—in any district. It was separate-but-unequal at its worst, yet the federal court had diverted billions to the district over the past 22 years to address such inequities.

The segregated schools I attended in my youth may have not been the quality of the schools the White students attended, but they were exceptionally clean, and the expectations for learning were extremely high. Nonetheless, I talked to students and faculty at the aforementioned district high school, who had not experienced either. My moral imperative as superintendent was affirmed then and there. My obligation to serve was unavoidable. There was no turning back.

In theory, the intent of desegregation efforts all across this country was to address systemic educational inequities in public schools. In practice, I question whether this country was ever really committed to the true purpose of desegregation. This is espe-cially the case when I witness many of the gross systemic inequities that still exist in my current and past school districts and in districts all across this country.

Have we simply been giving lip service through desegregation efforts since *Brown v. Board of Education* to truly eliminate racial academic disparity and systemic inequities in our public schools across this country? Do we really have the will and courage as a country to confront the core cause of racial inequities in our schools, or do we wish simply to con-tinue to languish in the comfort and rewards of "business as usual" and live in an illusion of perpetual denial that claims it does not see race? This paradox has provided the greatest frustration and challenge for me as a racial equity leader during my tenure and career in moving Courageous Conversations About Race from theory to practice.

■ ■ ■

I recall that during my early experiences as a student at McRae Elementary School, my parents enrolled me in the segregated school system of the South that existed in

Prescott, Arkansas, at the time. My father was a Marine, and I spent my kindergarten year on a base in Quantico, Virginia, with integrated classrooms, prior to our move back to Arkansas. As I think back now, attending the segregated school in my home state was the initial building block to my establishing the powerful, systemic counternarrative that drives my passion as a racial equity leader today.

Even though I initially had attended the integrated military base kindergarten class, where my race was essentially invisible or nonexistent to me, I entered a world at McRae Elementary where everyone around me had my skin color. I recall looking out the window at McRae during the afternoons, feeling awe and pride as I listened to the school's band, all dressed in majestic purple and gold, swaying and dancing in formation as they played a popular tune of the time (which I now know as "The Horse"). Many of my classmates and I daydreamed as we watched the high school students about one day being a part of what we witnessed outside our elementary classroom windows.

Inside the classroom, however, the recurring pedagogical message that provided the thrust for my current counternarrative paradigm as a racial equity leader was that we Blacks had to be "twice as good" and had to study "twice as hard" as White students. This theme was common from every teacher at McRae Elementary, in both their overt and covert actions.

At that time in my life, I did not have the intellectual capacity to understand that the faculty and staff at McRae were creating a powerful counternarrative within each of us that would be transformational in my future as I matured as a racial equity leader. The one thing teachers in segregated schools had in common with us as students was that they had experienced firsthand the ugly and deadly stings of institutional racism, the racialized norms of inferiority, and the lies of systemic inequity we children saw and would see around us.

I have come to understand, in my maturity, that the illusion or lie around racial achievement disparity, or the so-called achievement gap, has focused on addressing false assumptions of deficiency aimed at "fixing" the students so that they fit the cognitive or psychological model of middle-class White male students. As a racial equity leader, my anger becomes a rage as I see school districts across this country treat the widening academic disparity between students of African descent and others, as well as their failure in public schools, as a product of intellectual deficiency. This is a lie from the pits of Hell!

■ ■ ■

The greatest single challenge I face as a racial equity leader in moving Courageous Conversations from theory to practice is the dueling tension of creating the counternarrative that once existed in the classrooms of McRae Elementary and challenging the powerful, systemic constructs of a dominant White narrative in our public schools. The dominant narrative is so entrenched and institutionalized by the status quo or "business as usual" that it presents a constant threat to educators' career security. If you challenge it by work or action, you are open to scrutiny and attack. This is why the most difficult thing for me to witness has been the fear evidenced by some educators of African descent who have embraced the dominance of the majority narrative through acculturation or assimilation for the rewards it offers. Those educators shy away from providing their students with the culturally affirming counternarrative because of the risk of the punishment that the dominant narrative can administer through the power of systemic control.

The systemic control of the dominant narrative exerts the forces of both covert and overt institutional racism to counter my efforts as a racial equity leader. Thus, I have come to accept my place as an educational leader to be one of alienation and isolation. As a racial equity leader, I find that I often am viewed as radical or different and that some are guarded in their association with me or with the practices I attempt to move from theory into practice as a transformational leader.

I remember so vividly that as a high school principal leading this work in a Portland, Oregon, high school, I was constantly reminded about the tremendous risk or danger to my career if I fell from this tightrope of transformation without a "safety net" from the system. I have come to understand the fear that is created by the dominance of the majority narrative as part of my battle in "walking the talk" of racial equity work. Although I have overcome the fear that once paralyzed and stifled me as a racial equity leader, I now have to be constantly sensitive to the fear created within both the context of the dominant narrative and the new counternarrative by courageous transformational equity leadership. I know now that the dominant context fears what it does not fully know or understand, while the new counternarrative that we seek to create as racial equity leaders is fearful of retribution or lack of acceptance from the majority status quo.

This work is not for the faint of heart. It requires a passion, conviction, and courage to be comfortable with not fitting in or with having others around you not always feel comfortable because you never shy away from constantly keeping that uncomfortable topic of race front and center. I think one has always to remember that, as a racial equity leader, there are going to be times when your moral imperative or unavoidable obligation in this work will result in significant personal and professional sacrifice.

I often refer to my appointment as superintendent of the Pulaski County Special School District as my own biblical Jonah experience. The Bible says that Jonah was a reluctant servant who did not want to accept God's word to arise and go to Nineveh and to cry out against the city for its wickedness. Jonah chose instead to flee to Tarshish, away from the presence of God and the charge to speak out against the wrongs in Nineveh. He had no desire for that city to be his destination or charge. Yet, Jonah was thrown overboard from the ship to Tarshish during a terrible storm because of his disobedience to God and was swallowed by a great fish. Only after being in the belly of the great fish for 3 days and nights and after being vomited from its belly did Jonah obediently go to Nineveh, according to the word of God.

Having grown up in Arkansas, my strong foundations were shaped by powerful family and church influences. However, I had no desire ever to return to my native state to lead a school district. Arkansas represented a "racial Nineveh" of sorts for me with regard to my experiences as a youth with racism, segregation, and lack of opportunity. Although these experiences made me stronger as a person, I could never see myself working in the state, even though I did see myself returning at some point to a nearby state.

When I was asked to apply for superintendent of the Pulaski County Special School District, I did so initially with great reservation and hesitation. I pondered the decision until close to the deadline and ultimately submitted my application thinking surely it would go nowhere and my conscience would be clear. I recall the interview process and the visits with the various community groups. I was shocked at how much the district had regressed since I had left the state more than 21 years earlier. I remember asking the human resource director to explain the gross inequities of the facilities, and she had no response. I felt a knot in the pit in my stomach as I observed a new multi-million-dollar high school being constructed in the most affluent region of the district while also visiting schools in the predominantly African American and impoverished parts of the district that should have been condemned.

Although I initially had no desire to return to the racial Nineveh of my past, it was clear to me, based on what I had witnessed during my visit of the schools, that leading the Pulaski County district was going to be my unavoidable obligation. Was it career suicide to return to my home state? Could I adjust, or better yet, could the district adjust to whom I had become, 21 years removed?

I continued my Jonah experience with ongoing attempts to sail to Tarshish in an attempt to avoid my racial Nineveh, and I pursued other superintendent searches after visiting Little Rock. The Pulaski school board met after my first interview and removed me as a finalist. I shrugged it off and said to myself, "See there, Lord? I knew I was not supposed to return South." I chalked the decision up to a board and a state that could not embrace who I had become as a nationally recognized systemic equity leader and as an affirmation that Arkansas was not my destination.

■   ■   ■

Weeks later, I flew home after a grueling 2-day superintendent interview process in Lincoln, Nebraska. After several close finishes in a number of Midwestern urban super-intendent searches, I was exhausted and decided that I would remain in Portland for another year as a deputy superintendent. My cell phone rang a few days later, and I could see that it was a consultant from the search firm representing the Pulaski County district. I declined to answer the phone. Then the phone in my residence rang. My wife answered it and said, "Charles, there is someone calling you about the super-intendent position in Pulaski County." I asked my wife to take a message.

For several moments, I pondered what the call was about. I had already been informed that I had been eliminated as a finalist. I reluctantly called back and the consultant answered. She said, "Dr. Hopson, the board made a terrible mistake and now they have lost all their candidates, including you. The students of the district need you. Will you reconsider?"

My first response was to say "Hell no," but before I could get the words out of my mouth, the consultant said, "I believe you are a spiritual person, but you do not want to accept your calling. Why would you desire to go everywhere else in the country as a superintendent and give of your talent to those students, yet not give the same to students in your native state?"

I responded, "You don't understand, returning to my native state is to confront a 'racial Nineveh' that I left behind two decades ago. A racial Nineveh in which I heard my grandpa referred to as 'uncle' by White patrons as I would ride with him while he went to the back entrances of segregated restaurants to pick up slop to feed his hogs. We could not enter the front or eat in the restaurant. The cooks would give us something to eat from the rear of the establishment. It was a racial Nineveh in which I experienced segregation for the first time in my life in schools that were separate yet unequal in facilities and resources."

I continued: "My father was in the military, and my prior experiences in military schools had been in integrated settings. Arkansas is the racial Nineveh that my father taught me was a lie. He enrolled me in the segregated White schools as a counter-narrative to the lies of Jim Crow. I recall the tears and humiliation I shed as I was often called 'Little Black Sambo' by the older White students, and I recall the adult who came up to me while I waited on my mother to pick me up from school and stated, 'Why don't you go back to your own school where you belong? You are not wanted here. There is a school across town that is for you.'"

And I went on: "I did not like who I was when I attended the predominantly White school, and I internalized my feelings about my African features, including my dark skin, as ugly. I became painfully withdrawn and shy as a result of the low self-concept I developed, defined as it was by White standards of beauty."

I finished with: "Hell no, Lord! I do NOT want to return to Nineveh!" The search consultant listened patiently to what I said and responded deliberately: "Dr. Hopson, I have heard all you said, but those are all the reasons you should return and lead this district! The students need you!"

I realized at that point that, within the context of my Jonah experience, I was in the belly of the fish. By attempting to escape this unavoidable obligation, I had been thrown overboard from my ship to Tarshish and would not be vomited from its belly until I confronted the demons of my racial Nineveh by accepting the leadership of the Pulaski district.

Thus, I accepted a second invitation to visit the district and was soon back en route to Little Rock. When the plane touched down in Phoenix for the transfer flight, I noticed several voicemails on my phone. It seems that there was considerable confusion among the Pulaski board about the scheduling of my interview, and as I listened to the messages from several of the board members expressing their concerns about this conflict, I decided that if my candidacy could not unite the board on that logistical matter, I sure was not going to contribute to its further divisiveness. So I called the board president and told him that I was returning to Portland.

When I boarded the plane back to Portland, I felt as if I had escaped from the fish's belly once again. I thought, "Surely, Lord, this has got to be an affirmation that I am not to return to Nineveh. How much clearer can it be?"

I landed in Portland relieved but feeling very much as if I was still a captive in the belly of the fish. I was still attempting to elude my racial Nineveh.

■ ■ ■

When I was chosen as superintendent of the Pulaski district during academic year 2010–2011, the pushback from the status quo and business was fierce as usual, both within the district and from political forces within the state government. Still, I stayed anchored to the moral imperatives for systemic equity that were affirmed within my own "belly-of-the-fish" experience. As superintendent, I knew that we had to push the district beyond its comfort zones to provide first-class facilities for all students, to eliminate racial disparities through comprehensive professional development, and to provide equity of access and academic opportunity for every student.

The night I was hired—unanimously—by the Pulaski school board, I presented each of the board members with a copy of the professional learning plan blueprint I had developed for addressing the widespread racial inequities in the district. I stressed the urgency of my plan, due to the lack of progress that had been made there during the past 20-plus years under federal court supervision. The majority of the board members remained committed to supporting equity under my leadership, but the discomfort of the work was a concern shared by a high-ranking member of my executive cabinet, through feedback from two recently elected board members. I actually was pleased at the interest and questions of the two new board members and invited the entire board to take part in the districtwide equity transformation coaching I had arranged for members of the district's executive leadership team.

Tensions within my cabinet resulted in questions and doubts among the board members about the discomfort of courageously confronting racial disparity. Allegations that White district administrators felt belittled or "beat up on" by the pace of change were rampant during two of the board's meetings that first year. I often had to remind board members that achieving true systemic equity in a district is not easy and that it requires productive dissonance to move all parties past thinking within the box of business as usual. I also by then clearly understood that it was the forces of the status quo and business as usual within the district, those forces that had controlled previous administrations, that were raising their ugly heads to preserve the comfort of not having to look in the equity mirror.

The biggest barrier to my leadership during my first year was the fear factor that was so deeply imbedded in the district. It was almost like a plantation mentality from the old colonial South. During my visit to the various school communities, for example, so many citizens would share concerns about whether my tenure as a superintendent could survive the culture I was working within to move the district forward. One parent said to me during a visit that she was hopeful about me as a superintendent but fearful if, in my future tenure, I would see any fulfillment of the goals I articulated. Specifically, she said, "We do not want to get our hopes up too high and be disappointed like we have in past years because the superintendent is not here long enough to deliver on anything." I often found myself leaving these forums with a sinking feeling in my stomach because I could offer no assurances about my future. All I could do was just hope that things can and will get better.

I have found fear, whether real or imagined, to be the single most debilitating threat to empowering liberating change in an institution or organization. As I have moved up the ranks throughout my career, I witnessed many colleagues who were controlled, paralyzed, and eventually compromised by fear. Fear causes us to procrastinate, think only of ourselves, and become puppets to all of the "what-ifs" or worst-case scenarios of life. I refuse to be fear's puppet. In fact, I would go so far to say that I am most rebellious when it comes to facing fear. I will admit that there were times in my career where succumbing to fear may have been the path of least resistance and created less turbulence, but it has been confronting fear that has shaped me as a leader and superintendent.

During my tenure as Pulaski County superintendent, I spent an inordinate amount of time assuring principals that it was OK not to fear. It seemed so many of them had learned to just stay silent in fear for their job and to avoid retribution. I will never forget a young principal that I asked to meet with regarding concerns parents had shared with me about inappropriate sexual activities at the middle school where she was assigned. This particular middle school's students and teachers were predominantly of African descent, and the school itself was created as a result of political power brokering by a prior school board member, void of any best practices modeling in its organizational and instructional structures. In short, the school was a disaster waiting to happen. Although I had deep concerns about what had happened at the school, I was also aware that the principal and a few others in the school community were being wounded by the "friendly fire" of a district-created problem.

When the young principal stepped into my office with the deputy superintendent, I noticed she was shaking uncontrollably and on the verge of tears. I listened to the tremor in her voice as she informed me of the circumstances at her school. I sensed that her entire experience in the district had been shaped by fear. As the meeting ended, I addressed her fear through a question. I told her that she appeared to me to be afraid and that a large part of turning things around at her school would be to confront the fears that prohibit that from happening. When I asked her to identify what those fears were, she asserted that it was "the district itself." The past practices in the district, she said, had created a culture around race where compliance and control were gained through fear.

Although it was hard to hear this from an otherwise talented and promising administrator of African descent, I realized then more than ever that my leadership around systemic equity had to model an assurance and confidence that would empower leaders—at the building level—to confront their fear of the status quo. I decided that afternoon that I would start by building a "fire of confidence" around this young principal to help her confront her institutional fear. I would begin by empowering her to take the risk of challenging her fear by providing her with support from the institution she feared the most: the district.

■ ■ ■

In the end, when the state commissioner marched into my office accompanied by state troopers to inform me that my board was dissolved and that I was dismissed as its employee, I had a high sense of satisfaction despite the disappointment of the moment. I and others had been obedient to the moral imperatives of thousands of students in the Pulaski district. Personally, I had confronted my biggest fear, which was returning to a district that was not my destination of choice. I had confronted the demons of my personal racial Nineveh head on. I no longer was a captive in the belly of the fish. Collectively, our cause was right.

Escorted by state officials, I left my office that day for the final time as the superintendent of the Pulaski County Special School District without a single regret. Why? Because I clearly understood my purpose. And I was alright with that.

Charles L. Hopson is former superintendent of the Pulaski County Special School District, where he attended school as a boy. He is a Black American.

SIX

Moving Courageous Conversations Beyond Black and White

Because I, a mestizo, continually walk out of one culture and into another, because I am in all cultures at the same time, alma entres dos mundos, tres, cuatro, me zumba la cabeza con lo contradictorio, estoy norteado por todas las voces que me hablan simultaneamente.

–Gloria Anzaldúa[1]

EMPOWERING ALL PEOPLE OF COLOR

Despite my earnest efforts to be and appear inclusive, a number of White educators (and some non-Black educators of color) who have attended my workshops and training sessions have told me that they believe I am concerned only about Black people or about addressing only the Black-White racial conflicts arising in schools. This assertion has always caused me to pause—if only for a moment—before mobilizing to push back in objection. The people who have made such claims often point to what they perceive as my overemphasis on my Blackness and my personal racial narrative and experiences as an African American. What some may fail to realize, however, is that, according to the Courageous Conversations Protocol, acknowledgment of these attributes must serve as a necessary starting point for all Courageous Conversation exercises. It troubles me when White educators in particular grow irritated or frustrated by the mere mention or acknowledgment of identification with a specific racial group—other than the White one, of course. I view this as a covert way for some White educators to avoid having to face how children of color suffer at their hands. At the same time, however, I am also hypersensitive to the use of *Black* and *Blackness* as one-size-fits-all code words for all groups of color. This emphasis, I believe, typically causes educators to overlook, or even sometimes to negate, the important racial nuances that exist among diverse populations of color.

Invalidating others' perspectives, regardless of how personally demeaning or off-putting they may be, is a way of silencing them, which ensures that dialogue will not advance to its deepest point. Thus, it is important for me to address these concerns about going beyond the Black and White racial binary. Also, moving Courageous Conversations from theory to practice entails creating a culture and climate in which multiple racial perspectives, derived from the unique lived racial experiences of all groups, can be expressed and honored. If White people and other people of color who are not Black sometimes struggle to hear the inclusiveness I attempt to convey when I express my philosophies and beliefs through my Black image and perspective, then it is important for me to understand how I must be and what I must do to foster greater validation of their perspectives and achieve the level of inclusivity that is so critical for racial equity leadership work to advance.

No matter how difficult it may be for me to seek out, listen to, and comprehend the distinctive perspectives of racial others, doing so aligns both with my personal values and professional responsibility. I see this as an especially challenging yet necessary process for White racial equity leaders, as I believe it will help them to improve their effectiveness in working with people of color of all groups. Knowing the complexities of that challenge, however, I have developed over the years a greater sense of empathy for White racial equity leaders' unique and difficult plight.

Necessarily then, this chapter will read quite differently from previous ones. It will reveal, for example, my admission that I, Glenn Singleton, believe I am in the relative infancy of my lifelong journey toward understanding, much less capturing in writing, what it means to move Courageous Conversations from theory to practice. This is especially the case when it comes to uncovering, examining, and addressing how systemic racism affects White people and other groups of color. Initially, I thought I might include sections offering insights and analyses for each of the various non-Black groups of color in the United States, sections that empathetically conveyed the voices and that authentically captured the experiences of the peoples of those diverse groups. I quickly realized, however, that I had not yet crossed the critical and provocative junctures of knowledge and understanding prerequisite to comprehending each group's realities, thus such narratives would seem impersonal, shallow, and forced. A few of my (and the Pacific Educational Group's [PEG's]) new learning partners, however, have expressed willingness to be my teachers and mentors in that regard, and they have begun to share their wisdom, knowledge, and experiences with me in ways that support the level and depth of development I need and desire.

As much as I would like to say that it was a sense of altruism that caused me to write this chapter on the topic of inclusiveness, it was actually two very specific and recent life experiences that led me to recognize how listening more closely to the voices, histories, perspectives, and nuances of White people and non-Black people of color serves my interest in promoting and achieving racial equity for *all*. I will share those experiences in the following sections and discuss the resulting growth, development, and discovery related to my journey-in-progress toward greater racial consciousness.

I do not believe that people can experience transformation, in the truest sense of the word, until they have had an experience that causes them to desire and seek change. Such experiences help us to unearth personal value for what we can become. They also help us to develop a personal intolerance for what we currently are. I hope that my acknowledgment of where I am in my own personal interracial learning and understanding process will inspire you, my readers, and other racial equity leaders to consider being more transparent about your own place of authentic understanding about other groups, be they White or Black or other people of color.

MAKING THE INVISIBLE VISIBLE: A COURAGEOUS CONVERSATION ABOUT AMERICAN INDIANS AND SCHOOLING

One little, two little, three little Indians; four little five little six little Indians; seven little eight little nine little Indians; ten little Indian boys!

—Traditional American nursery rhyme

In kindergarten, singing this song with all the energy and excitement my teacher, Mrs. Porter, taught her students to provide, I received my first formal introduction to the original custodians of the land we call the Americas. Complete with feathers in our hair and whooping, hand-to-mouth chants, my fellow students and I had already learned that the indigenous inhabitants of this land were a savage, uncivilized population of red-skinned people who were neither successful at maintaining their claim on the continent nor capable of caring for themselves. Through a seemingly innocent nursery rhyme, Mrs. Porter began the process of formulating for me a belief system about an entire group of people—people who were quickly constructed and then just as quickly deconstructed to the point of invisibility.

In retrospect, I can see now how teaching this version of the story of the American Indian to school-age U.S. children would cause me and my classmates to develop both indifference to and a lack of respect for these nearly exterminated people and their culture. I am certain too that our textbooks and classroom conversations from kindergarten on referred to American Indians in less than positive ways. These negative stereotypes and perceptions stuck with me throughout most of my school years, in large part because that foundational understanding had already made obsolete the Native people and their circumstances.

To be completely honest, my relative disregard for and disconnect from the American Indian narrative was evident until just several months prior to writing this section of the book you are holding in your hands today. Unlike other topics in which I provide readers with racial counternarratives mined from my work and that of PEG with districts across the nation and abroad for nearly two decades, regarding the plight of the American Indian, my re-education is just beginning. This realization often makes me feel as if I need to start over in my personal, local, and immediate processes of organizing and applying conventional wisdom about the impact of race and racism in my life. For how can one truly understand the traditional origins and contemporary essence of racial disparity in this country, or in any country for that matter, without first uncovering, examining, acknowledging, and addressing the history of its original inhabitants? Absent such a foundation, American students of all races are programmed to overlook the presence and role of Native people and subsequently to misunderstand some of the important realities of colonization, as well as, in the case of the United States of America, genocide, land dispossession, and cultural appropriation.

With all humility, I write this section now not only because I believe it is the right and significant thing to do to extend the practice and impact of courageous conversations about race but also because it challenges my belief that eventually we as a nation will arrive at a place of consciousness where we no longer serve as our own most destructive racial force. Moving Courageous Conversations from theory to practice demands that each of us must act on what Joyce E. King calls our own *dysconscious racism*—or "a form of racism that tacitly accepts White norms and privileges"[2]—in transparent and urgent ways. And even though we may not offer the most significant truth, guidance, or meaning, we can still highlight the place in which we exist, explain how we got there, and discuss our intentions and strategies for transforming our habits of mind and work.

So here's how my personal transformations happened.

■ ■ ■

About a year ago, the Portland (Oregon) Public Schools' chief of staff, Zeke Smith, an American Indian and a descendant of the Osage and Oneida people, confided to me that he was struggling to find his place in the broad and expansive equity work unfolding in his district. He gave me a well-constructed explanation for why he was having a hard time continuing to hide behind his (relatively) White skin rather than more overtly answering the call to make himself more visible in this important work as an advocate for his people and their racial struggles in school and society. Like many light-complexioned people of color, Zeke was caught in a quandary. Although he wanted the privileges associated with Whiteness, he was also feeling the inner turmoil and self-loathing associated with purposeful and intentional "passing" for White. Nearly in tears, Zeke told me about his desire to have his children embrace their Native heritage and his fears that they, too, would have to assimilate into the dominant White culture if they wanted to excel and succeed in school and elsewhere.

As I listened to Zeke's racial autobiography, I found myself caught up, not only in wanting to simplistically name his racial quandary as typical but also in not understanding the unique racial invisibility that accompanies being an American Indian. Like many other racial equity leaders, I arrived at my "race place" with an intellectual understanding that America's Native peoples are people of color and that they collectively suffer from racial oppression just like other non-White groups. What I did not understand until my recent conversation with Zeke was just how alienating—and even disrespectful—the very language, racial narratives, theories, and strategies that we non-American Indians use to address racism can be to American Indians, who are, after all, the very first group to have been racially defined and marginalized in and by the United States. Only then did I really understand that I had been participating in, and sometimes initiating, the process of making the traditional custodians of our land invisible. Worse, I had been helping to create and substantiate the oppressive conditions that contribute to their invisibility.

Zeke's narrative reminded me of a courageous conversation I had in 1998 with an American Indian who approached me at the conclusion of one of my Beyond Diversity workshops. The man first graciously thanked me for a wonderful professional development experience, then asked me to consider an idea that he believed would make my training more inclusive of the views and needs of Native people. His request was simple: "Show *us* in your SAT data." He was referring to the data from The College Board in Figure 6.1, which I had presented during the workshop—data that did not include Native Americans:

Figure 6.1   Average SAT Scores by Parental Income and Race/Ethnicity

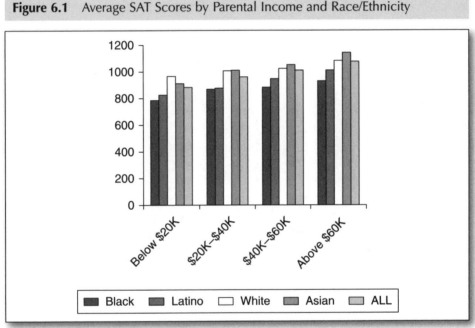

Source: National Center for Education Statistics, U.S. Department of Education, 1998. A similar version of this chart appears as Figure 3.1 in *Courageous Conversations About Race: A Field Guide for Achieving Equity in Schools* (p. 30), by Glenn Singleton and Curtis Linton, 2006, Thousand Oaks, CA: Corwin.

I must admit that my first response to this American Indian's request came from a place of embarrassment deep in the emotional quadrant of my Courageous Conversations Compass rather than from a place of belief. I had not realized the omission, nor had I thought much about the data when I included it in my training materials. (What was even more troubling to me was the fact that a variation of these data was published in the 2006 *Courageous Conversations* field guide, which came out almost 10 years after I began facilitating the Beyond Diversity workshops.) Yet, if there is to be enlightenment, there must first be provocation.

Shortly after this glaring mistake was brought to my attention, I was on the phone with The College Board, passing my moment of shame on to whomever I could reach there, for I erroneously perceived the source of the data to be the source of the problem. I demanded to know why the Board's SAT data failed to represent American Indian performance along with that of other groups. I had to make repeated requests to get the information; my calls went unanswered. I must also admit, however, that I did not try very hard to get at the core beliefs, both those of The College Board and my own, from which the exclusionary data emerged. For the moment, I simply felt satisfied by making sure that all of my data presentations going forward, like that in Figure 6.2, included American Indian students:

Figure 6.2 Average SAT Reasoning Test, Critical Reading Scores by Parental Income and Race/Ethnicity in U.S. College-Bound Seniors, 2011

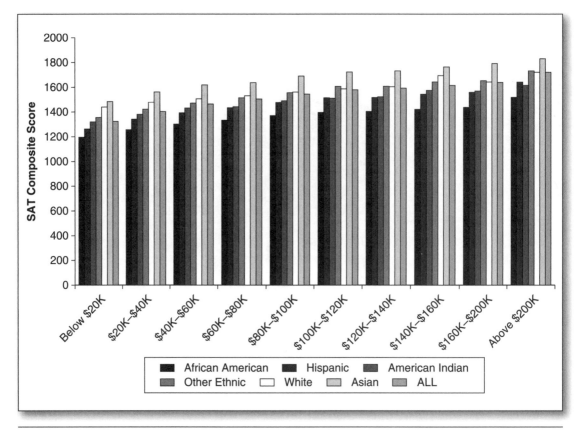

Source: Data derived from "College-Bound Seniors 2010 and 2011, Total Group Profile Report—ETHNICITY (Table 11)," Copyright © 2010–2011 The College Board, retrieved from www.collegeboard.org.

Although this is good and important information, the SAT data revealing that Native American children outperform Black and Latino children at all income levels simply is not corroborated by other standardized testing data coming out of the states and nation. That is, despite what a relatively small population of self-identified American Indian students taking the SAT suggests in terms of achievement, this population continues to greatly underachieve because they are severely under-served in our education system.

At the very least, racial equity leaders must question the racial/ethnic disparities in college entrance testing data to determine the underlying causes for these patterns. More, we should avoid being overly optimistic about Native students' relatively higher performance on college entrance exams, given that those students experience neither high levels of participation in higher education nor success on other elementary and secondary school scholastic indicators. These data must serve as our call both to action and to ask the deeper and more essential questions about the racial experiences of indigenous children in American schools.

Sadly, merely updating academic achievement and other pertinent data to include American Indian students does not bring us much closer to understanding how our processes of schooling and our strategies for achieving racial equity may exacerbate the continued invisibility of those students. What the inclusive data do reveal is that American Indian students typically are aggregated, to their disadvantage, into a single, homogenous group regardless of their specific tribal affiliations or blood composition or even the type of schools they attend (that is, traditional public, parochial independent, or reservation schools). Each of these distinctions is quite important to our understanding of the educational status and achievement of American Indian students, and the treatment of Native children varies greatly based on each of these characteristics.

For example, reservation schooling for American Indian children is necessarily supplemented with critical cultural experiences that are not found in nonreservation contexts. This supplemental curriculum, if you will, often both empowers and challenges American Indian children as they approach the stage at which they must make decisions about their postsecondary or continuing education. It influences whether or not they choose to attend college and which institutions they consider. It further affects their capacity to negotiate the various barriers to gaining admission to higher education opportunities and ultimately matriculating and graduating from college.

College entrance examinations do not assess American Indian students' proficiency in their indigenous cultures, but such learning is essential for the preservation of those cultures. Issues of racial bias in admissions tests and college application procedures serve to misappropriate American Indian culture and render native people invisible. These factors can challenge the performance and perseverance of the most academically prepared American Indian students.

Conversely, American Indian children who attend traditional public and parochial schools often learn to mask their indigenous identities. These students rarely find themselves in the kinds of supportive environments that can help them develop deeper understandings of their native cultures. Whereas other students of color, such as African American students, often are invited to establish student unions and clubs or are called on to offer their unique cultural perspectives to relevant (or irrelevant) racial issues, American Indian children more often are consigned to silence, isolation, or invisibility. Throw in a battle over a racially insulting school mascot or a racially insensitive school slogan, and it is not hard to see how the plight of American Indian students in private, public, or parochial schools can often silently injure the psyche and destroy the spirit of those children and youth. Then, as the deadline for college applications approaches, American Indian students attending these schools often are ill equipped to designate themselves appropriately because of the lack of emphasis on cultural or racial affiliation in those contexts, whether for the purpose of ensuring the child's emotional and perhaps physical safety or for the sake of acculturation and assimilation. One must ask, how do the testing data reflect these and so many other racial nuances that are, for the most part, invisible to non-American Indian people?

At one time, we racial equity leaders believed that we needed lots of hard and fast data if we were to have any hope of proving to others that racial disparities not only existed but were also brought on by racism. I have since learned that even with mounds of irrefutable data, many still struggle to embrace the notion that schools, and the educators who inhabit them, serve as the primary perpetuators of racial inequity in our society. For example, for some, data revealing that American Indians exist at or near the bottom of many achievement scales, regardless of family income, simply confirms their beliefs that these students and their families just are not as capable as their White counterparts.

Merely requesting inclusive data from The College Board and ACT was only the beginning of my challenge. To get to the heart of the matter—that is, the belief system that made rendering native students invisible the norm—I first had to admit that I did not include American Indians in my initial and deepest thinking when I spoke of underserved students of color. And that admission meant I had to acknowledge that until recently—even as late as last year when I first set out to write this book—I had not begun to really understand, and thus to consider, either the history or the contemporary experiences and plight of indigenous students. Thus, although I cannot offer a comprehensive understanding of the specific circumstances of these students' schooling, what I can offer is a true and transparent narrative that invites you, my readers, to understand the place of continuous improvement that we all share in this racial equity leadership work. The following section details my journey to greater consciousness and enlightenment.

■　■　■

In fall 2011, I was invited to Perth, Australia, to work with a consortium of universities that were in the process of adopting the Courageous Conversations Protocol as a part of a systemwide approach to surmounting the challenges arising from the increasing racial diversity in its member institutions. I had been to eastern Australia many times before, visiting Sydney and Melbourne as a tourist on leisure/exploration trips, but never to Perth, the largest city in the Australian West. As I unfortunately have come to anticipate, overt racism reared its ugly head long before the details for this trip were finalized. Even before the contract was awarded, some White Australian educators protested the fees that PEG had quoted to cover the costs of this difficult and exhausting work—work that can take years off the lives of those of us who lead it, if we are not purposeful and precise. I responded to the cost concerns by noting that only rarely are critics of racial equity work aware of the very racism inherent in such a line of questioning. I also pointed out that the same critics only rarely challenge, with similar interest or intensity, the costs associated with other, non-race-related reform work or programs. I knew that embedded in these protests was an unfounded lack of support for racial equity work, no matter the cost, coupled with the belief that such work should be offered free of charge. To these questions, I responded with several of my own: What is deinstitutionalizing the racism in your system worth? What are you willing to pay? What constitutes too high a fee and how is that determined?

Others of my Australian critics questioned my professional qualifications and competence, not merely to conduct the specific training requested but also even to work in higher education. They did so despite my certifiable advanced degrees, my higher education-focused graduate studies, and my years of teaching and administration experience at the university level. I dismissed these protests with the realization that they were but petty manifestations of avoidance and fear and by referring those concerned to the readily available documentation of my credentials.

Still another critic raised a more perplexing question: "As a Black American," he asked, "what can you, Glenn Singleton, possibly know about race issues in a country like Australia, which has so few Black people?" On the surface, this particular voice of resistance probably believed that he was asking about my understandings of Australia's Aboriginal people—which would have been a valid question. What I believed this voice of resistance was actually suggesting was that, as a Black person from the United States, my insights about race were limited to my individual perspectives and experiences. The illogic of such criticisms continues to create challenges for me in my racial equity work, both at home and abroad.

Rather than inserting personal meaning to these criticisms, I reminded myself that my previous visits to Australia did not equip me well with specific details about the state of Aboriginal education or about that group's particular social, cultural, political, or economic issues. However, those visits had exposed me firsthand to the ongoing social marginalization and cultural extermination being experienced by Australia's first people. I also realized although the voices of hatred being directed by some White Australians toward the Asian people (and, more recently, Middle Easterners, post-9/11) in their midst were lethal and loud, the abusive treatment of Australia's Aboriginals was insidious and often so harsh that it simply could not escape my consciousness.

Fortunately, my (and PEG's) advocate in Perth, Malcolm Fialho, an Australian of East Indian heritage, responded to this person's concerns on our behalf. He stressed that my initial work with the consortium's faculty and administrators was not going to be focused so much on my own understandings of Aboriginal culture but rather on my ability to assist those educators in developing the will, skill, knowledge, and capacity to have courageous conversations about race and racism on personal, professional, and institutional levels. Malcolm assured his colleague that he and his other Australian colleagues of color at the consortium would be better suited to describe and define the presence and role of Whiteness in Australian higher education and the larger, interconnected society. They—not me, an outsider—would assume that responsibility during the workshops.

With that, all of the critics were quieted. PEG's contract with the University of Western Australia and Curtin University was approved, and I was off to Western Australia.

■ ■ ■

Moments before beginning my Beyond Diversity workshop at Perth's Curtin University, Malcolm reminded me to thank a number of people who had worked on my and PEG's behalf to make my visit possible. He also suggested that I should express my gratitude to the original custodians of the land. Malcolm's latter request caused me to pause a bit in my momentum to start the workshop. It also initiated what was for me a significant process of personal transformation that continues to this day.

Not being one who is comfortable expressing words that do not have direct, personal meaning for me, I questioned Malcolm about what he meant by thanking the original inhabitants of the land. He explained that when assembling a group of people in western Australia, it is traditional practice to honor those who came before the White man. He then provided me with instruction in performing a ritual of words and actions to that effect, and for the first time in my career as a professional development consultant, I expressed sincere gratitude to the original custodians of the land on which the group had assembled for important learning. As I paid tribute to the Aboriginals, I wondered why such a ritual, thanking the American Indian ancestors, was not a part of U.S. custom. From that moment on and into the first 15 minutes of my Beyond Diversity training, despite my close familiarity with the curriculum, I felt well above my personal limit of tolerance—that is, I had ventured beyond what Ronald Heifetz and his colleagues refer to as the zone of productive disequilibrium.[3] I wondered how much more of my training might be in violation of indigenous ritual and cultural beliefs. Since then, my recognition of the greater magnificence of such rituals has increased and expanded. I sometimes feel moved to offer similar invocations in the trainings and workshops I lead in the United States.

Being in a room where the vast majority of participants were White was nothing new to me, but the ways in which that first training group of White Australian educators demonstrated their connection to race was totally and literally foreign to me. The group was unusually quiet during the first moments of training, showing no overt signs of connection to or satisfaction with what I was saying. In those initial and telling moments, I realized that there were no other African or even Latino people in the room to provide me with a subliminal "gauge" of how this group was experiencing the content, processes, or pace of the workshop. I also realized that all the ways I was accustomed to "taking the temperature" of the room during my trainings were absent and that the success of my Beyond Diversity training in the Perth setting would depend on me learning perhaps an entirely different way of listening, inquiring, and responding.

So, after making a brief personal introduction, I uncustomarily invited the group to consider what they believed to be some important distinctions between race and racism in Australia and in the United States of America. One gentleman suggested that the people in the United States had "more racial baggage"; another posited that Americans "talked about race far more." But it was Dawn, one of only three identifiably Aboriginal women in the group, whose response provided me with the means of understanding my training audience and a way to determine the pacing for my remaining 3 days of work in Australia.

Dawn noted first of all that it was quite unusual and perhaps culturally inappropriate for her to speak out in a forum such as the workshop. Not only was talking about race uncommon in Australia, she said, but also speaking out in such a foreign format was a cultural challenge for her. Nonetheless, she felt that it was critical for her voice to be heard in this particular setting. She then provided the participants and me with a personal narrative—her own unique racial autobiography—that included some pretty amazing and especially candid insights into her experiences as an educator at Curtin University and as an Aboriginal woman in Australia.

We all listened intently, recognizing that Dawn was sharing important personal knowledge about how racial oppression in western Australia had affected the lives of Aboriginal people and continued to do so. I soon realized that, in Dawn, I had found the conduit through which I could effectively connect to the others in the room. I decided that I would monitor her participation closely throughout the 2 days of the workshop and, more important, observe carefully how the other participants interacted with her as a way of guiding my facilitation.

At the end of Day 1, all of the participants had found their way to the Color Line—a group exercise that I created after reading Peggy McIntosh's article, "Unpacking the

Invisible Knapsack,"[4] which illuminates W.E.B. Du Bois's 1903 conjecture about the significance of the racial color line and the impact of White privilege on the lives of people of color. Standing next to me, on one side, was Dawn; but on the opposite side, with the lowest score on the Color Line exercise (indicating that she had the least amount of White privilege) and a much darker complexion than either Dawn or me, was Marion, another Aboriginal woman in the group.

The concluding exercise of the day was one I call the Walk of Privilege. I chose Marion to engage in the Walk of Privilege with me as I shared my personal story about being a school-age child and having to leave each day a racially segregated and isolated place—that is, my urban Baltimore community—to attend a suburban, elite private school where most of my classmates had—and exercised—unearned, unacknowledged White privilege. As Marion and I figuratively traveled from our scores in the low teens around the room to interact with her White colleagues, many of whom scored as many as 130 White privilege points, I could not help but see the striking color line differences, the distance between the darkest and lightest participants in the room, and sense their feelings of shock and perplexity at the rigidity of their racial stratification.

As we walked, I explained how students of color in the United States and Canada ride buses from their own communities to attend schools in communities bursting with the accoutrements of White privilege, and how they are expected to reach the same standards as their White counterparts without access to all the advantages afforded White students. Marion expressed familiarity with my descriptions of how the long-standing and deeply entrenched racial inequities and the resulting achievement gaps in U.S. society are exacerbated by those who embrace a color-blind ideology. She acknowledged that this ideology protects White people from examining the specific entitlements their own White privilege grants them. Then she shared her own racial autobiography with the group and me.

Many of the seminar participants, including those who knew Marion's story, were shocked to hear how similar Marion's and my own educational experiences had been. Some even believed that I had prescreened and preselected her to participate in the exercise. To be truthful, I had sensed earlier that her narrative might be quite similar to mine simply because she was a very dark-skinned, well-educated woman and a highly functioning person of color at a predominantly White institution.

To my relief, at the end of the exercise, both Dawn and Marion graciously thanked me for what they said was a wonderful experience. What most impressed them, they said, was my ability to engage the entire group of participants in learning and conversations about the genuine racial issues and challenges that afflicted them. Many White participants also expressed gratitude for the awakenings they had received and told me that they were looking forward to continuing their learning the following day.

Before the start of the next day's training, Marion asked me to join her for lunch. She also told me that she had a gift for me. Now, when I do my work well, receiving a gift or two is not uncommon because racial equity training, done right, is for some an extremely liberating and uplifting experience for which they are particularly grateful. During our lunch, however, Marion, who had just recently completed her doctoral studies, informed me that she had postponed an appointment to present her adviser with a copy of her completed dissertation so that she could participate in the Beyond Diversity training. And instead of presenting him with the first copy of her dissertation, titled "An Examination of How Culturally Appropriate Definitions of Resilience Affect the Physical and Mental Health of Aboriginal People," she offered that copy to me with the following personal inscription: "To Glenn, Please enjoy. I hope this, my story, is a learning experience, M. G. Kickett." I was truly moved.

That night, I skimmed Marion's paper, cover to cover, before I went to bed. In her gripping research, I found that she offered as much personal racial autobiography as exposition on the conflicting definitions and philosophies of resilience and the implications of these theories for the education and broader development of Australia's native people. Marion's dissertation helped me to understand immediately why the U.S.-embraced notion of resilience that I had alluded to in the first day of training, if viewed according to Reich, Zautra, and Hall's definition[5]—that is, as an outcome of successful adaptation to adversity and one that often is viewed as a skill when it is developed by under-served children of color—was not supportive of the success of Aboriginal children in Australian schools. Embedded in this definition of resilience, Marion asserted, was the belief that the ascribed adversity exists in these children's homes and communities and that unless Aboriginal students assimilate or at least effectively adapt to White culture, they cannot transcend the problems imposed on them by their supposedly dysfunctional families and communities.

To counter this notion, Marion offered an Aboriginal Resiliency Framework in her dissertation. This framework is grounded in key concepts such as healing, forgiveness, and letting go. It also offered a decidedly different definition of resilience:

> [Resiliency is] the ability to have a connection and belonging to one's land, family, and culture: therefore an identity. Resilience allows the pain and suffering caused from adversities to heal. It is having a dreaming, where the past is brought to the present and the present and the past are taken to the future. Resilience is a strong spirit that confronts and conquers racism and oppression strengthening the spirit. It is the ability to not just survive, but to thrive in today's dominant culture.[6]

Marion's active engagement in the Perth Beyond Diversity training, along with Dawn's nurturing and thoughtful guidance, set my own personal transformation in motion. I discovered that I needed to acknowledge having, and then let go of, my distinctively American, Black and White racial paradigm. Indeed, Dawn, Marion, and other Aboriginal acquaintances I met during my stay in Perth showed me a different approach to racism. I saw in them an unmatched racial consciousness coupled with an inner peace derived from what I believe to be an intentional process of healing through forgiveness. Their remarkable magnanimity got me to thinking: What if I could learn to fortify the feeling quadrant of my own Courageous Conversations Compass with a belief in fully letting go of my distrust of White people and instead offering them greater compassion, as opposed to maintaining the distrusting beliefs that fueled ever-increasing anger and frustration? Might not this heightened trust, compassion, and forgiveness, extended especially to those racially unconscious White people who offend me, lessen the physiologically destructive impact of racism in my own life as well as enable me to foster the development of a more inclusive, larger, and more nurturing community of racial equity leaders?

During my remaining days in Australia, I embraced my personal need to understand the racial experiences and perspectives of indigenous peoples without comparing them to those of my people—or any other people of color, for that matter. And I have attempted to do so ever since, especially after returning home to the United States.

The invitation to conduct a workshop in Australia certainly challenged me to broaden my perspectives about how race, and especially Whiteness, affects educational outcomes. Perhaps the best way to capture the impact of this work on my thinking about indigenous people is to say that I now have an experiential reference and thus a more authentic understanding and greater appreciation for what is meant by a phrase I often use in my Beyond Diversity workshops: "You don't know what you don't know!"

■ ■ ■

It turned out that the first visit I made to one of PEG's partnering districts following my journey to Australia landed me in Portland, Oregon, where Superintendent Carole Smith wanted me to meet her newest board member, Matt Morton. Matt was the deputy executive director of the Native American Youth and Family Center (NAYA) in Portland. Since I do not believe in coincidences, I jumped at the opportunity to continue expanding on the new understandings I had gained in Australia about indigenous peoples. I asked Carole right away if Matt could give me a tour of NAYA the evening I arrived. To my delight, Matt obliged and indicated that he would do his best to introduce me to other American Indian leaders who were instrumental in the center's success.

So, for roughly an hour, I toured NAYA's facilities, which included a school and recreation center as well as a variety of gathering and meeting spaces for traditional American Indian worship, celebrations, and community leadership development. I saw native students studying with tutors and playing basketball while other youth and elders met together in a council to discuss important issues and determine solutions for American Indian people. Every part of NAYA—the walls, display cabinets, the books in the library— spoke to a culture of people who had been invisible to me prior to entering its doors.

Years of going to Powwow celebrations[7] at Stanford University, where I attended graduate school, did not come close to conveying what it meant to me to see American Indian youth and adults at NAYA proudly and unapologetically instilling within each other their indigenous cultural identities and resilience. NAYA's success with American Indian youth speaks volumes to the findings that these young people generally do better in schools and society when they are firmly grounded in their racial and cultural identities.

I learned that the center's unique form of resilience training begins with the intake process, which, like that of the Aboriginal people (as described by Marion in her dissertation), is less clinical and more conversational in nature than mainstream practices and steeped in the American Indian's traditional focus on family and relationships. The intake conversation invites affiliation with one's tribe and understanding of one's family circumstances (including intergenerational trauma due to racism) as well as of one's financial, health, and emotional stability and one's educational/professional history and desires for the future. Programming is aimed at supporting American Indian cultural identification as a way of ensuring self- and collective preservation. It also addresses issues such as the invisibility of native people within and across a range of activities, from the U.S. government Census to outright discrimination and marginalization; the need for improved academic participation and performance; and increased home ownership and economic viability.

As a proud partner and educational arm of Portland Public Schools, NAYA was a place where the tensions inherent in balancing multiculturalism and inclusion in a White-dominated American society collide with a self-preservation-focused brand of ethnocentrism. Nowhere were these tensions more apparent than in the relative academic success many NAYA students experience over their non-NAYA affiliated, public school counterparts. Although the traditional indigenous philosophy and teachings emphasize honoring and respecting the culture of others, when the pervasive Whiteness of the public school environment impedes rather than supports the healing of American Indian children and their families, the staff and leadership of NAYA advocate that separation from such environments is in the best interest of American Indian self-preservation.

As my university students often tell me: keep it personal, local, and immediate. And that is how I will conclude this section about my own personal introduction to Native American culture and thought. Prior to declaring my own space of cultural blindness, however, I want to acknowledge that I now clearly see the ways in which I contributed to rendering native people invisible in my racial equity work. I know now that I simply *did not know what I did not know.* On an intellectual level, I recognized that American Indians, as people of color in U.S. society, were targeted and have suffered extensively as a community from systemic racism. But I truly did not feel personally connected to their struggle, nor did I believe that understanding and engaging in that struggle would serve as a way to understand better my own racial struggles and perhaps other opportunities and challenges that I face as a Black man on a daily basis.

On committing myself to deeper and more courageous conversations about race, I have focused on uncovering, examining, and addressing the ways in which race and racism influence the schooling of American Indian students. I have already learned some very important lessons from Dawn, Marion, Zeke, Kehaulani, Karen, Elona and others that strengthen my work as a racial equity leader. More important, I feel as if I am a more effective person because I have arrived at the quintessential understanding that my life previously lacked richness because Native people and their unique perspectives and experiences "lived" in my racial blind spot, or rather, in only the intellectual quadrant of my CCAR Compass.

Establishing my Personal Racial Equity Purpose (PREP) around American Indian education circumstances required that I see benefit for me in such development, in the same way that I have insisted that White educators must view transforming their racial beliefs as self-empowering rather than something they do for other people's children of color. At this early stage of my journey, I have already experienced improvements in my facilitation allowing me to lead educators in Portland, Oregon, and Perth, Western Australia, effectively. Seizing on the opportunities to interact with the very first people to experience racism, and arguably, understanding their culture, which has been destroyed more completely than any other by White supremacy, my racial insight has broadened. I now arrive at all locations, both at home and abroad, as a healthier man in mind, body, and spirit because the indigenous perspectives are transforming the ways I work, live, learn, and show appreciation for the Earth that nourishes *all* people, especially the traditional custodians of this land.

BROWN SPACE

Prior to my indigenous awakening, my first collision with my personal racial blind spot occurred in 1990 when I relocated from Philadelphia to Los Angeles. For the first time in my life, I was living in an area in which Black people were not the "majority minority." And although I had studied Spanish in high school and college and had a close friend who was Puerto Rican, nothing could prepare me for the unique cultural immersion experience I would soon undergo.

Initially, my efforts to connect with the varied national, linguistic, and ethnic groups within the Latino community—I soon learned that was the preferred way to refer to the largely Mexican American residents of the area—acquainted me more with stereotypes and derogatory expressions. In these earliest moments of my Latino socialization, I learned how diverse and polarized the perspectives within this group were, particularly with regard to skin color, which, among this group, ranges from palest white to darkest brown.

For a variety of reasons, most of the Latinos I met in Los Angeles worked in the professional and recreational arenas. Many were Mexican American educators who seemed to understand my expressions of racial identity and solidarity and who often adapted their own theories about race, racism, and racial experiences to the narratives on these topics that I was beginning to share more and more publicly. Their general acceptance of my ideas seemed to me, at least in this predevelopment stage of my Courageous Conversations theory, to signal that I was really on to something. When Latinos and other people of color seemed unable to assimilate their racial experiences and perspectives into my own, I thought (wrongly) that they just did not "get it."

However, as my work and social interactions with Latinos in California increased, I realized that the compliance of Latino audiences only contributed to my developing an increasingly large blind spot in my theories about race and racism. Those experiences totally transformed the ways I relate, then and now, to Latino people in the United States. But that transformation was only at a personal level. I now am also beginning to recognize my professional role, responsibility, need, and desire as one of engaging *with* Latinos as a way of actualizing my mission of achieving racial equity in schools, rather than of channeling them down a path predetermined by my own racial experiences. I also now understand that before I can lead the process of racial equity leadership change for others, I must first understand the perspectives, traditions, history, and objectives of all the diverse groups involved in that change. That transformation—as challenging, ego-crushing, and eye-opening as it may be—has to begin within.

A workshop I was asked to facilitate at the 2007 La Consecha Two-Way/Dual-Language Conference, held in Albuquerque, New Mexico, was my first invitation to present the Courageous Conversations Protocol and concept to an exclusively Latino audience. In this instance and in several other keynote and workshop invitations that followed, including the Two-Way CABE (California Association of Bilingual Educators) conference in 2008 and 2009, I recognized the need for this particular audience to layer skillful discussion about race over their more focused concerns and interests around English language skills development, bilingualism, and biliteracy. Although I sensed that my Latino audiences very much wanted to embrace Courageous Conversations, I continued to feel as if a chasm existed between the Protocol and its examples and the interwoven racial perspectives and linguistic concerns of Latino people. I was determined, however, to bridge that divide, and the 2010 Summit for Courageous Conversations, which was to be held in San Francisco, seemed the perfect opportunity for me to showcase how differently I had come to understand the challenges facing Latinos at the intersection of race and schooling.

At the core of those new understandings was my belief that, as a Black man, I could not authentically shape the courageous conversations about race that must be had by Latinos. What I could do, however, was offer an established platform for those deliberations and ask that the participants consider the issues that have challenged the progress of PEG's and my own racial equity work relating to the Latino community. So, rather than craft the session content for my 2010 Summit Latino audience, I intended instead to simply create a physical space in which some influential and credible Latino racial equity leaders could design and determine the flow and outcomes of the discussion.

I crafted the following call to action for the workshop, which I provocatively titled "Brown Space":

> Race is a topic that creates extraordinary divisiveness for Latinos in the United States. There are divergent ideologies not only about its existence, but also [about] the importance of race, how "race" is defined, and the impact and implications of race in the Latino community.
>
> Racial identity among Latinos, the largest and fastest-growing group of color in this country, is complicated by the intensely political intersections of language (Spanish, English, and bilingualism) and race (indigenous, African, and European racial ancestry), all of which have a significant impact on how Brown children are educated in this country. White, Black, and Brown-skinned Latinos and all others across the broad spectrum of the Latin American community have a choice: To unite as leaders for racial equity, continue to engage in intragroup conflict, or join the White American majority in its "color-blind" stand. The choices made today will determine how race is dealt with for generations to come.
>
> …"Brown Space" is a structured, facilitated place for Latinos to safely come together in racial affinity to engage, sustain, and deepen their understanding of the impact of race on the schooling of Brown children. Here, educators will share multiple racial perspectives and explore the layers of language and immigration politics, together crafting a powerful voice and position on antiracist educational leadership.

Unfortunately, a labor strike affecting a large number of Latino hotel employees in the San Francisco Bay Area caused the 2010 Summit to be postponed for a year. Given my interest in bridging the Latino racial divide with respect to Courageous Conversations, I also canceled the summit because I believed Brown Space could not be launched successfully in an environment considered hostile by many Latino hotel employees. The next year, however, close to 50 Latino educators, students, and community members, representing 10 states, gathered in San Francisco at the 2010 Summit, and the Brown

Space workshop ultimately came to pass. At last, the silence around the racial issues unique to Latinos in U.S. schools and society could be broken.

A second part of my strategy to broaden PEG's appeal to and support of Brown people was to hire Luis Versalles. Luis is an accomplished bilingual, biliterate, and bicultural Cuban American educator, and my collaborations with him have helped me to understand better the racial underpinnings of the language debate as it affects Latinos in the United States. I asked Luis to lead PEG's efforts at Brown Space and beyond.

Given that I could not be a participant in the inaugural Brown Space workshop because the experience was deliberately designed for Latino educators exclusively, my insights about the work accomplished at Summit '11 were derived from my later conversations with Luis. He shared some of the themes captured and explored during the workshop, including the following:

- the complexity of Latinos as a racialized group that spans the racial divide to include White, Black, Brown, mestizo (or mixed-race), and indigenous groups
- the social creation of Brownness, Blackness, and Whiteness in Latin America, as viewed from an historical perspective
- the "colonization" of the Latino mind as a result of unexamined Whiteness; the critical role of cultural, linguistic, and racial identity development for Latino students (particularly the need for more K–12 bilingual/language immersion programs that leverage the linguistic assets of Latino students and provide a pathway not only to bilingualism and biliteracy but also to cultural and racial pride as well as stronger academic outcomes)
- the need for constant vigilance to address the allure of Whiteness and the abandonment of Latino cultural affinity as Latinos rapidly attain numerical dominance in the United States and potentially gain access to societal leadership and its privileges
- the cultivating and equipping of Latino students such that they have the requisite will, skill, knowledge, and capacity to combat institutional inertia and lead for racial equity
- the need for practical tools for educators' use in re-engaging Latino students through dialogic strategies
- the importance of drawing, as a nation, on the strength of our Latino ancestors as we move forward in a societal (and eventually international) dialogue about racial equity for Latinos and other people of color

Moving forward, at future summits as well as other established meeting and conferencing spaces, PEG and the Brown Space movement seek to nurture an ongoing national intra- and interracial dialogue about the Latino educational experience. The vision, mission, and purpose of achieving racial equity for this particular student demographic, which is so critical to the present and future sustainability of our nation's domestic affairs and international competitiveness, makes cultivating and expanding Brown Space an extremely viable and essential option. Advocacy for racial, cultural, and linguistic equity for Latino students has since been at the forefront of PEG's work to transform K–12 and higher education in the United States.

THE POLITICS OF ENGLISH-LANGUAGE ACQUISITION: SKIN COLOR, IMMIGRATION STATUS, AND OTHER BARRIERS

Although conversations about English-language acquisition and mastery for non-native speakers in the United States have implications for much broader audiences than solely the nation's Latino population, those conversations are interconnected and integral to a number of other issues associated with the engagement of Latinos as racial equity leaders. Faced with having to guard simultaneously against discrimination due to Spanish language, skin color, and immigration status, such debates have often divided Brown people. Discussions and research on the language barriers facing Latino students typically are presented as disconnected from race and immigration status. Similarly, work on race is distanced from a focus on immigration. Likewise separated are issues relating immigration status and English-language acquisition.

I have long been fascinated by how my non-native English-speaking friends and colleagues around the world have gained mastery of a variety of foreign languages, especially given that many of us who are native English speakers, hailing from countries such as the United States, most of Canada, Australia, and the United Kingdom, often seem to lack either the will or skill to master a second language. What is even more egregious is that many of us in these countries tend to grow up with a perspective that those in the rest of the world should address us solely in our native language if they wish to engage with us or learn from us. In my own case (and admittedly to my personal embarrassment), despite years of Spanish language classes, I too simply have not made it a priority to be multilingual or develop spoken or written literacy outside of English.

Some powerful ironies surface in this society's lack of second-language appreciation, and they are coupled with an all-out assault on Spanish in particular. On the one hand, opportunities for native-English-speaking White children to enroll in introductory to advanced placement second-language courses are abundant and embraced as an entitlement. Moreover, the expectation that secondary schools will offer Romance languages, including Spanish, along with a variety of Asian and perhaps Slavic languages, is grounded in the belief that U.S. high schools should do so to enhance students' chances for admission into competitive universities where foreign language study, but not mastery, is preferred. Subsequently, advanced placement and honors-level Spanish study is reserved primarily for non-Brown children, some merely seeking to improve their odds in the college admissions process.

On the other hand, those for whom Spanish is their native language experience a peculiarly harsh treatment in many U.S. school systems. For Latino students, the stigma associated with their home language and, in some schools, the outright punishment that comes when these students attempt to converse in their native tongue, prompts resentment or embarrassment, both of which serve as reasons for Brown children in the United States to disconnect from their schooling. Latino children who are English language learners (ELL students) typically are disparaged, chastised, or made to feel embarrassed for practicing or developing their Spanish language skills and speaking Spanish. For them and their parents, this can lead to feelings of Spanish language inferiority and English language supremacy. Then, for many, the opportunity to become bilingual is diminished by a system that defines their native language in deficit terms and constructs structural and emotional barriers to accessing improved Spanish language skills. Furthermore, native-Spanish-speaking students are rarely present in the advanced language courses; nor are native Spanish speakers from Mexico, Puerto Rico, Cuba, and various parts of Central America typically hired to teach advanced courses, even though much of our nation's student population has roots in those countries.

This lopsided cultural backdrop defines the landscape on which most non-English-speaking immigrants experience the United States and, I suspect, our nation's Anglo allies around the world. Thus, in one part of the K–12 experience, Brown students are experiencing alienation from their native tongues, while in another part White students are being taught to demonstrate Spanish (or Chinese) mastery on a written examination to earn advanced or higher standing. In elementary schools, rather than serving as the research-based best practice for *ELL* students to develop in both their native and second languages, two-way immersion programs have become another curricular option for *White* students to gain additional academic and cultural advantage in public education. Typically, these highly sought-after programs are situated in suburban schools predominated by White students, and they are presented in such a way that learning Spanish for non-native speakers is prioritized over English language development for the Brown children from Spanish-speaking homes. When school programming is not focused on the development of the latter group, Latino children can emerge lacking proficiency in both Spanish and English.

What appears fairly obvious to me is that the way in which Spanish language development is viewed differently and, in most instances, "deficitly" in the United States represents a disservice to Brown students. Beyond the occasional phrase or two in a Ricky Martin or Jennifer Lopez song that rises to anthem proportion—and not to mention the state, city, and street names in three of our nation's most populous states and a few smaller states and territories as well—Spanish seems to be the taboo language in U.S. society and particularly U.S. schools. Indeed, anyone speaking a language other than English is subject to a kind of scrutiny and marginalization in the post-9/11 United States, but in places such as California, Arizona, New Mexico, Texas, and even Florida—ironically, those areas where Spanish is so much a part of the origin and development of the local cultures—penalizing those who embrace Spanish is also a way of maintaining power, through language.

For educators who champion "English only" interactions, race enters the discussion in a quiet way that is sometimes not apparent even to those who are being oppressed. To many Latinos, defending their right to speak and learn the Spanish language is disconnected from a racial assault on Brown people. I have witnessed rigid and divisive lines being drawn between and within ethnic groups of Latinos on this issue, and those lines tend to be marked by three factors: immigration status, nationalism, and skin color.

The immigration issue is complicated because of generational distinctions—that is, when and where one's family immigrated to the United States—and by how one is defined in terms of being a legal or documented versus an illegal or undocumented immigrant. From the generational standpoint, John Ogbu's work[8] around voluntary and involuntary immigration status helps us understand why some Latinos would be more likely to sacrifice their home language of Spanish to fit into the English-only societal norm. Ogbu's theory suggests that those who see themselves as involuntary immigrants—they were caught up in the U.S. annexation of Mexican territories—tend to have been in this country for several generations, and they have seen Brown people experience oppression whether or not they speak English fluently and without a Spanish accent. In contrast, voluntary immigrants came seeking success in this country through assimilation and adaptation. They often compare the schooling opportunities available to them and their children in the United States to those in their native Mexico or respective Central American country. As a result, they are more willing to adopt the culture, language, and beliefs about themselves and other immigrants from the perspective of the dominant White American group.

The latter Brown parents embrace a belief that Spanish-language skills and dialect serve to impede one's progress in developing English fluency and becoming a "true" American, and thus they prohibit their children from speaking Spanish. Those who define themselves as involuntary immigrants do not seek to relinquish their language or other proudly held primary cultural traditions. They further demand that conceding their language and culture to mainstream America should not be the price of acceptance and opportunities for success and a better life for their families.

Still other Latinos seem to be focused more on their challenges with other Brown people than on the dominant White majority's assault on their shared language. Rather than unite in their support for dual language immersion programs for their children in schools, they struggle to interact with each other in the divisive ways introduced to them and their forebears by their Spanish colonization, which instilled beliefs about racial and skin color supremacy and inferiority. Although the Latino racial pecking order is real, the peculiar brand of racism widely practiced in the United States more often than not positions Brown people as a collective race rather than as a diverse array of people with distinct ethnic, racial, and national origins. Some Latinos fight this collective grouping by marginalizing other groups of Latinos or by affiliating with organizations that foster and promote a divisive agenda such as the English-only (read: anti-Spanish) viewpoint.

Racism further complicates the quest for multilingualism and, specifically, dual Spanish and English language development for Brown children. Given that Latinos represent a broad spectrum of skin color identities—that is, they can be White, Black, and all gradations of Brown in between—their ranges of racial perspective and experience are quite varied. Not surprisingly, some fair-skinned Latinos experience far less, if any, racial oppression because they often, purposely or not, "pass" for White and adopt a color-blind perspective comparable to the earliest stage of White identity formation (as defined by Janet Helms and explained in Chapter 3). When these Latinos speak Spanish, they are likely to experience linguistic discrimination in many parts of the United States but not overt racial discrimination. Other, darker hued Latinos experience racism and discrimination on a frequent basis and often are assumed to be non-English-speaking even before they open their mouths to speak.

Immigration status, English-language skills, and race collectively also seem to determine how much protection Brown people, particularly Brown children, receive under the law in the United States. Sordid reports tell of Brown children of undocumented families being emotionally, physically, and sexually abused by adults in schools and other institutions because they do not have proper legal advocacy, care, and protection. For example, at a Los Angeles-area elementary school, several such children recently were the victims of sexual abuse. Two White teachers and a Latino teachers' aide were arrested for child molestation and child pornography in that case, which allegedly involved other school personnel and scores of children. Virtually all the students came from what were described as "poor Latino homes, a majority from immigrant families where English isn't spoken at home, and some with parents lacking legal immigrant status."[9] Their community was dubbed as a "voiceless" one, "where fear is ingrained—fear of authority, fear of the police, fear of immigration enforcement, fear of retribution . . . just the kind of place where an adult with bad intentions could take advantage of a child, knowing there was little chance a victimized family would report the acts. Or if they did, little chance they would be believed."[10]

The reporters covering this story interviewed Lisa Aronson Fontes, a psychology professor at the University of Massachusetts and author of *Child Abuse and Culture: Working with Diverse Families.*[11] Fontes attempts to explain the increasing cases of predators targeting the children of Spanish-speaking immigrants, noting that these children and their families face a culture of silence, disbelief, disempowerment, and denial at most schools. She reports, "Families who feel disempowered in a variety of ways are going to have trouble challenging authorities like a teacher. If they are first-generation immigrants, if their English skills are limited, if they are low-income, they're going to have an even harder time challenging authority."[12]

The only factor missing from Aronson's analysis, predictably, is race. Does being Brown have anything to do with the failure to educate these children, much less to keep them safe from harm? Educators throughout the United States are required to offer basic human protection to Latino children who, by law, are guaranteed a free and appropriate education, regardless of their parents' immigration status or English language proficiency. At the center of the battle for multilingualism in this country are Brown people, who stand to benefit significantly and advance more rapidly should our nation's best understandings and designs for dual-language immersion become the proposed and endorsed pedagogy for all U.S. students. Ironically, to equip all students with dual language skills and proficiencies would also serve as one of the best strategies for achieving racial equity in schools. Embracing the interconnection between language and race offers a more substantial way of understanding and expressing one's support for multilingualism as it places this issue in the larger and broader context of racial equity leadership.

In addition, as mentioned in a previous chapter, special education has become a dumping ground for children of color in U.S. schools, and this is especially the case for ELL students. Too often, rather than addressing the deficit-oriented thinking and beliefs about Brown and other students of color for whom English is not their home language, these students are designated as special needs children and relegated to restrictive educational environments. For many of these students and their families, their home language skills—and not their teachers' problematic approaches to English language development—are blamed for their inability to acquire and learn in the English language. Consequently, many of these children develop neither proficiency in English nor in the language they speak at home. In many schools, special education placement also ensures that ELL students experience de facto racial segregation in school and rarely have opportunities to learn and engage with students of other racial groups. The virtually unexplored intersection of special education (SPED) and English language learners (ELL), or SPELL, where an increasing number of Brown families are finding their children being located in schools, merits greater and immediate attention. This is one of the important and strategic directions of our work at PEG, which we believe will provide fertile ground for accelerating movement of Courageous Conversations from theory to practice.

Finally, Brown students (and other students of color) rarely seem to receive the intended benefits of language immersion programs. Spanish immersion programs in schools, for example, often serve as the carrot that lures middle-class White families into districts that are diversifying racially. Such programs and schools often employ fair-skinned Latino educators from Spain and strategic parts of Latin America to offer accelerated studies in language alongside the other basic disciplines, thus offering White families assurances that their children will continue to be advantaged and perhaps not integrated. Brown parents from Mexico, Puerto Rico, and many Central American countries—many of whom are struggling to gain naturalization, English language fluency, and ethnic appreciation in these same districts—do not fail to observe how these programs and schools work to exclude their deserving children. What they sometimes lack, however, is a cultural understanding or the English language skills to describe how systemic racism manifests in the United States, therefore they struggle to name these and other injustices. Some turn their frustration inward and blame themselves, leading to feelings of guilt and shame. Others blame their children for not having the necessary high levels of achievement to gain entry into these coveted programs and schools, likewise fostering feelings of inferiority on generations into the future.

■ ■ ■

The Essential Questions at the end of the chapter emanate from a personal challenge I made to myself as well as one I offered my staff at PEG and my students at San José State University. The racial equity leadership challenge presented to us and to you, my readers, is to engage authentically in making the invisible visible in our practices. For these questions, I offer my deepest gratitude to Nanette, Jude, Zeke, Shawnee, Elona, Kehaulani, Marion, Dawn, Debby, Matt, Nichole, and several others. Each has graciously assisted me in better understanding what I could not or refused to see for decades.

The Voices From the Inside narratives included in this chapter are from two of my valued journey partners and equity coaches. I have turned to Luis Versalles and Elona Street-Stewart on numerous occasions, with humiliation and sometimes unadulterated shame, to seek meaning about Brown and Native peoples, respectively, because they know, understand, and experience authentically. Through their wisdom, I recognize my own infancy of consciousness. I also embrace my responsibility as a racial equity leader to share their wisdom in ways that help to uplift the many children and families who are marginalized, abused, and neglected in our nation's systems of education.

ESSENTIAL QUESTIONS

These questions will help you begin appraising the circumstances surrounding American Indian and Latino students in your school or district.

1. What is the status and condition of American Indian and Latino students and their families in your system?

2. How does your system currently address the intersection of race, language, and culture as described in this chapter?

3. To what degree have special educators and English language development staff been involved in your personal and your system's equity-focused programming?

4. What changes will you suggest that will serve to diminish invisibility and increase empowerment of the American Indian and/or Latino communities?

5. How are Latino and American Indian children and their families identified and designated in your educational system? What is their current proportion in your district or school, and what are their growth projections over the next 5 to 10 years?

Voices From the Inside: Luis Versalles

My racial equity journey with the Courageous Conversations About Race Protocol began in fall 2004, when I first came to the Richfield Public School district. This experience profoundly changed me, both personally and professionally. Richfield, a first-ring suburb of Minneapolis, is frequently referred to as a small suburb with an urban demographic. As many others have found, in the 21st century, *urban* has become synonymous with a demographic of color, and this is what excited me about coming to work in Richfield. This narrative will recount my experiences as the founding principal of Richfield Dual Language School (RDLS), the first suburban two-way elementary school in the history of Minnesota.

In so-called dual-immersion or two-way immersion programs, a student population consisting of a relative balance of both native-English-speaking and native speakers of another language (most frequently Spanish in the United States) are integrated for instruction in grade-level subject matter in both languages of study. The program goals are fostering bilingualism, biliteracy, and cultural competence. My involvement with the development of the Richfield program from its inception in fall 2007 provided me with the opportunity to work in partnership with the dedicated staff and families of RDLS, who are committed to the principles of educational equity and excellence for our students.

As a second-generation Cuban American reared in a bilingual, bicultural home, I have always been intrigued by the juxtaposition of race, culture, and language that has framed my life experience. For this reason, the core ideology of cultural, linguistic, and educational equity that characterizes two-way immersion programs energizes me and fuels my passions as an administrator. Being able to start a school from the ground up is truly the dream of any administrator.

In our initial planning phases, my staff and I engaged community members, prospective parents in the school, and district staff members in a process of visioning of what the school would become. After a lengthy process, the following vision statement emerged:

> In partnership with our families and the community, the vision of the Richfield Dual Language School is to prepare all students to become lifelong learners and leaders in their local and global communities who successfully meet or exceed grade-level expectations in English and Spanish through an education built on the foundations of bilingualism, strength of diversity, academic rigor, critical-thinking, and mutual respect.

From the beginning, our philosophical orientation was that bilingualism, for most of the world, is not an exception but rather the natural state of human existence. Therefore, we advocated for widespread and equitable access to our school. Children of all racial backgrounds and all socioeconomic classes the world over are bilingual—only in the United States, with our historically deep problematic relationship with linguistic diversity, could the notion be widely accepted that the mental capacity of our students will only accommodate a monolingual schooling experience and that only the exceptional few are fit to be schooled bilingually. (Sadly, the rhetoric of No Child Left Behind, with its overemphasis on English-only outcomes, reinforces this belief.) Subsequently, many language immersion programs historically have been elitist—in deed or in perception—putting forth the idea that such programs are appropriate only for a certain profile of student. Too often, this has translated into immersion programs perpetuating the critical race theory tenet of Whiteness as property, specifically the "right to absolute exclusion" for students of color.

As principal, I was continually amazed to see entire classrooms of students become bilingual—that is, literate and academically successful in two languages. As this process unfolded, however, I was sadly equally amazed by and reminded of the permanence of racism in our society. Although the state of Minnesota, dating back to the early 1980s, had established a long legacy of foreign language immersion programs that provide native-English-speaking students with opportunities to develop academically in English and an additional language, the type of programming we had created in Richfield was much more rare. Only a handful of such programs existed in the cities of Minneapolis and St. Paul, but none in the suburbs.

Particularly at the outset of the program, letters to the editor in the local newspaper alleged that dual immersion was robbing our Latino students of the opportunity to "tough it out" as many previous immigrant groups had done in our nation's history. Some went even a step further, indicating that it made no sense to teach our Latino students in Spanish or the language that they "already know." I wondered how these same cynics rationalized the fact that the majority of our schools teach mostly native-English-speaking students almost exclusively in English every day in schools across the country, yet they make no claim that English-speaking students are wasting their time with content they have already mastered!

Furthermore, critics tended not to mention that in our school, although it is true that we have an increased focus on Spanish academic vocabulary and literacy development in the early grades, our students are instructed in both languages every year.

The recurring theme of the hypervisibility of our Latino students and the dysconsciousness around their bilingualism was heard not only in the year leading up to the founding of RDLS; it has continued during the past 5 years of the school's existence.

Among the many fascinating aspects of the two-way immersion model, from my perspective, is the dichotomy of race and bilingualism for our White students and their Latino counterparts. It is also among the most fascinating and unsettling aspects, all at once. To the untrained eye, this educational model represents a simple exercise in supporting two primary linguistic groups that are both moving toward bilingualism, only from two different starting points. Although, at the surface level, this conceptually may be the case, the way that these two groups are perceived externally—and the assumptions, conclusions, and resulting beliefs formed about them as they go about this process—could not be more disparate. Even worse, I have heard immersion educators at regional and national conferences, caught in their unexamined racism, openly question the appropriateness of language immersion programs for students of color, particularly for our poor students of color. This logic flies in the face of immersion research, which indicates clearly that immersion students of all racial backgrounds perform at least as well as and, in many cases, outperform their nonimmersion peers.

In my journey, as I have come to understand another critical race theory tenet—the permanence of racism—I am reminded how, through the frequently unexamined and unconscious psychological residue of the centuries of racialized American history (with its clear racial designations of superiority and inferiority), this rhetoric is revisited. I am also reminded that if we are not engaged in a continual process of examining our consciousness about these deep-seated notions of social dominance based on race, these frequently unconscious beliefs surface in the policies and procedures we put forth as administrators.

As is the case in most two-way programs, about half of our students were Latinos, with about three fourths of this group speaking Spanish as their dominant language when they entered the program. Although many of the attractive features of the program were the same for our White families and our Latino families, the significance of the program goes much deeper for the latter. Not only is command of Spanish an instrument for future success for our Latino families, it is also a birthright and a conduit to their cultural heritage. From the perspective of the parent, it represents a passing of the torch of the mother tongue to that of the larger American culture, whose track record is mired by systematic eradication of native languages; by a particularly heightened sense of xenophobia toward what Leo Chavez of the University of California at Irvine has termed "the Latino Threat"; and by a rhetoric of mainstream American fear, distrust, and, at its worst, contempt for the Latino experience.[13]

As for their language proficiency in the languages of study, our Latino students frequently face differential pressures and expectations about appropriate proficiency gains in English, beginning even in kindergarten, compared to the higher expectations placed on their White counterparts for acquiring Spanish. How can such a discrepant interpretation of what is essentially the same process, only occurring in two different directions (starting from English monolingualism and moving toward bilingualism, or starting from Spanish monolingualism and moving toward bilingualism) be explained? Clearly, it has always been apparent that the very presence of a language in any society is an exercise in politics.

Language, it could be argued, is nothing more than a linguistic representation of whose values, ways of thinking, believing, and acting and whose sheer power over other groups has come to bear. The history of our country is one of a relentless pursuit of English monolingualism, beginning at the expense of a multitude of indigenous American Indians and their native tongues and extending clearly to the perceived threat of the Spanish language (and Hispanics or Latinos), which predates the formation of the nation. Because of this historical context, English and English speakers in U.S. society have gained what linguists call "language-majority status" by virtue of speaking English as a dominant or native language. Conversely, native speakers of any language other than English exist in "language-minority status." These research-based constructs are incredibly important in understanding how it is that these two linguistic groups of students move toward bilingualism and biliteracy. They also help frame a more critical understanding of how race and language are layered and lived differently based on racial designations.

An understanding of the linguistic dynamics of RDLS students' backgrounds affirmed what I knew for a long time to be a tragic aspect of our educational system: that it fails to capitalize on the potential of our Latino students, who, by virtue of their status as language-minority students, possess a tremendous linguistic and cultural asset and hold tremendous potential to become the bilingual, multicultural leaders our country desperately needs and will continue to need. Indeed, our system is figuratively beating the bilingualism out of our Latino students at a time when we can least afford it. Previous generations of Latinos physically endured reminders that their language and culture had no place in our educational system. This is a clear example of the Whiteness as property tenet. It also typifies the exclusion of whatever doesn't align with an ethnocentric notion of English monolingualism as being synonymous with appropriate schooling. Worse, our Latino students experience the betrayal of seeing many of their White counterparts being lauded for their attempts at second language acquisition and being provided access to a myriad of programming options to develop their bilingual skills (albeit with varying degrees of success).[14]

I believe that two-way immersion represents a program model that holds tremendous promise in advancing the conversation of racial equity, particularly for Latino students. At its core, racial equity work is the process of matching our espoused beliefs regarding what all students can achieve to structural support systems that mirror those beliefs. In two-way immersion, the program structure communicates to all students that they can achieve at a high level in two languages, and the students respond appropriately. Despite the structural orientation toward linguistic and cultural equity represented in the programs, however, administrators must lead thoughtfully and courageously for racial equity to deliver on the mission of two-way immersion. In fact, absent such adaptive leadership, the opportunity for inequality to emerge is great.

Whether or not schools are implementing two-way immersion, the linguistic assets that all of our language learners bring to our schools ought to be nurtured and leveraged to unleash their potential as bilinguals, not problematized as has been the case for too long in the American educational legacy of subtractive bilingualism. Nelson

Mandela once said, "If you talk to a man in a language he understands, that goes to his head. If you talk to him in his language, that goes to his heart." Multilingualism is a goal to which all American students should aspire, and we do our students a great disservice by not honoring the linguistic arrows they carry in their quiver of knowledge, culture, and identity.

In summer 2011, I was offered the opportunity to join Pacific Educational Group (PEG) as an associate director of district programming. As I have told many friends, family, and colleagues since I made the decision to embrace this new phase of my career, this position and the work that we do at PEG represents one of the few positions I could have imagined taking me away from the principalship at RDLS. Although this was an extremely difficult decision in some ways, in other ways it was quite simple. The experience and opportunities that I feel the staff at RDLS has created in partnership with the families at the school are extraordinary, and I would love to see many more students, families, and educators experience this throughout the country. My current role affords me the ability to promote this as I partner with the districts PEG serves. Furthermore, much like the two-way immersion principle itself, the nature of our work at PEG seems to attract a certain caliber of visionary leadership that is invigorating to be around. I experience this invigoration through the partnerships we form with school leaders, educators, students, and families across the country in our work.

Luis Versalles, an educator for more than 10 years, is the founding principal of the Richfield Dual Language School, an innovative public school in Richfield, Minnesota. In 2011, Luis joined PEG, where he currently serves as the director of leadership and focuses especially on developing and supporting Latinos and other English language learners to engage in racial equity transformation in their local school systems. He is a Cuban American.

Voices From the Inside: Elona Street-Stewart

"All my relatives." This is a common greeting for many American Indian people. Growing up, my father always introduced himself by describing a long string of family relationships between the person we were meeting and ourselves. He did that so we would remember how we came to be. That is when we were among people like us. It made sense to them. To other people, we were known as Delaware's forgotten folk, the Nanticoke.

But we have not forgotten. People remember stories and carry information from the past into the future. As an American Indian, I learned that racial identity and historical reality are intricately interwoven. Our family history is the story of how racial identity and discrimination evolved in America. Our original name meant the Tidewater People, living around the mid-Atlantic bay areas. While sailing the Chesapeake Bay, Captain John Smith recorded contact with the Nanticoke in 1608. As more Europeans continued to arrive, our Delaware (Lenape) villages experienced devastating upheaval along the shore areas and into territories now known as Pennsylvania, Delaware, Maryland, and Virginia. Chapters of American history typically begin with the War for Independence, but our memory is that 100 years prior, the Dutch kidnapped Delaware children to force land concessions; the English, French, and Swedes falsely bartered tribal alliances for land acquisition; and new diseases wiped out up to two thirds of the Algonquin-speaking villages. Harassment, murder, fur trade conflicts, and land furor escalated. In 1656, the Virginia Assembly made it legal to kill any Indian construed as trespassing on a colonist's land. Nanticoke and other tribal chiefs were lured to peace meetings and assassinated by foreign military.

After Jamestown, a colonial practice of officially listing Indians as slaves resulted in thousands being sold into slavery. These three patterns of exploiting the native population—(1) removing children from families; (2) making dishonest land claims and treaty alliances; and (3) redefining and misrepresenting tribal identity—formed the basis of future race laws for the emerging nation.

Black and White race laws in Pennsylvania, Delaware, Maryland, and Virginia were applied to American Indians and defined who we were; what we were; and where we could live, shop, farm, swim, eat, talk, and learn. It started back with my great-great-great grandparents, but even I faced the same. Colonial experiences are still painful today. Over the centuries, most of the Delaware were forcibly moved north to Iroquois nations or northwest into Ohio and then Oklahoma, but our remnants remained along the tidewater. My people survived by hiding in plain sight, not disappearing.

I tell you now that it is hard to measure the trauma of being denied one's true identity, but the high rate of suicide in our communities is a valid reflection. We had to prove what we were not, just as much as we had to prove who we were. No one else's identity in the United States is legally subjected to these contemptible alterations. To be American Indian is where race and judicial reality are fused.

How could our ancestors ever imagine that despite their courageous sacrifice, our blood, our eyes, our residence, our language, our worship, would all be whitewashed over centuries? Subjected a thousand times to "What are you, really?" I can sense the question, however rude, inappropriate, or out of context, emerging from someone's mouth. I am not who people think I am or should be.

Residing in multiple places in the United States and Canada, [my people's] identity is defined by authorities outside of the community. Still, we persistently refuse to separate descendants from the Nanticoke tribe. Like other genocide survivors, my people have already faced being the last one on Earth.

Traditionally, Indian children were taught the responsibilities of kinship because the highest honor one could achieve was to be a good relative. My parents led us to look for relatives wherever we went. That is the Nanticoke story. Native people always look around to see familial connections with land and events. We know that geography, historical institutions, and public law are permanently infused with Indian relations. America's history is the American Indian story.

We are proud, beautiful, intelligent people. When I see how we have been treated, it feels like if we didn't die, we are supposed to be hidden away in a museum drawer or reservation. But the attempts to bind us to a forgotten past always fail because we still survive in the present. I see this when I look at pictures of native people with real names that will not be forgotten. I have a yellowed photo of a Nez Perce family, circa 1930s, all dressed up in buckskin and feather headdress, sitting and smiling in a long open touring chassis. Captured in that snapshot is their spirit of survival. Moccasin feet on the gas pedal, enjoying native pride inseparable from the adaptive culture of ancestors who learned how to ride a horse, sew shell buttons on cloth, and cook in iron pots.

Moving forward since contact, we had no idea we were being caught up in a massive reorganization of the world, from Old to New. How could the Delaware, or Dakota, or Dine have known that the newcomers would walk over our lives and reduce us to landscape? Efforts to conquer and eradicate tribal nations grew into a tyranny of assimilation. Religious conversion and sale of land as property were employed since early colonial times. Decades later, after treaties confined tribes to reservations, the best tool to civilize American Indians and effectively bar them from their native self was education. Children were separated from their families, prohibited to use their language, stripped of tribal practices, and forced to reside at religious missions and boarding schools. Education was institutionalized to replace Indian culture with White values. Building on colonial practices, Congress authorized the Office of Commissioner of Indian Affairs in 1832 to provide education to Indian children and convert them into farmers and traders. We will never forget that the purpose was to rid us of our native culture and not to support our academic achievement.

Recently, while reading *The Word Carrier,* a historic Dakota newspaper, I came across an article written by Bertha Wilkins in 1900 during the boarding school era. I think the words of this early social scientist are profound. She noted, "When children droop and pine away with homesickness at boarding school, they can usually be saved by sending them home. This is often done in time to save them; more often they come home to die. It is awkward for the superintendent to report death. Dying is not the curriculum."

Even more shocking are the following words. In 1928, the federal Meriam Report concluded that American Indians were the victims of grossly inadequate health and abusive education services. U.S. Indian Commissioner Thomas Morgan said it was "cheaper to educate Indians than to kill them." A predecessor, Carl Schurz, calculated in 1882 that it cost nearly $1 million to kill an Indian in battle, but $1,200 for 8 years of schooling.

Attentively, native people still wait for the United States to discover these forgotten experiences. We still see racism camouflaged in law and cultural conquest through education. After being mistreated and stereotyped, I know we will continue to voice traditional truth, develop cultural resilience, and claim our identity. We are still here.

Elona Street-Stewart currently serves as a member of the board of education for Saint Paul Public Schools in Minnesota. She was the 2011 recipient of the Summit for Courageous Conversation Community Empowerment Award. Elona is an American Indian.

SEVEN

A Vision and a Framework for Achieving Racial Equity in Education

A very great vision is needed and the man who has it must follow it as the eagle seeks the deepest blue of the sky.

—Crazy Horse/Tashunkewitko, Oglala[1]

In a keynote address presented several years ago to the National Staff Development Council on "Why School Reforms Do Not Work," Professor Linda Darling-Hammond[2] maintained that too often educators do not give reforms ample time to affect the systems to which they are applied. That is, she said, school districts often change direction way too soon, abandoning innovations long before they can be implemented effectively or any of their positive results realized. Darling-Hammond's point especially resonated with me at the time because I was beginning to notice a growing impatience among some of the school leaders in the Pacific Educational Group's (PEG's) partnering districts.

Critics of our programs were beginning to clamor for an end to our work in school districts, citing slow progress toward racial understanding and equity and only minimal improvements in student performance. Ironically, the most impatient of these critical voices were often the very same ones who argued early and loudly that our consultants needed to slow down and lessen the intensity of their racial equity activities—PEG's trainings in particular—and show more consideration for "overburdened" and "weary" educators whose efforts—and results, in PEG's view—were advancing too slowly. The most vocal critics were those who wanted their districts to abandon PEG's seminars and programs prematurely for no other reason than that they disagreed with our objectives or simply felt too uncomfortable with our insistence on school leaders engaging in deep self-examination and systemic indictment. Others were anchored in the conflict of wanting to achieve equity and excellence quickly but not wanting to make the unpopular decisions or take the potentially job-threatening actions doing so might entail.

At PEG, we have long realized that effective pacing and sequencing are essential when it comes to moving Courageous Conversations from theory to practice. Even more important is discerning the pulse of the school systems we work in, learning how those entities "think," and determining what exactly are their internalized beliefs and behaviors related to race and equity. That is why we steadfastly explain to our partners—at the outset—that it could take anywhere from 3 to 5 years before they can begin to see and feel tangible school-, district-, or systemwide changes in culture, climate, and achievement as a result of their systematic implementations of the Courageous Conversations Protocol and the PEG Systemic Racial Equity Framework, or PEG Framework, for short.

Why does this pulse-taking, "belief-reading," and soul-searching take so much time? Well, at the heart of PEG's efforts to uncover, examine, and address racism is the search for indicators. That is, before proceeding with our work in any district, we are careful to determine that our partners are poised and ready to fully embrace the Courageous Conversations objectives—and to do so as a personal, professional, and organizational transformative *process* as opposed to merely authorizing a few random, albeit provocative, trainings or seminars about race. We do not partner with districts that seek to gain a quick fix to their racial equity problems and thus counter the release of some embarrassing data, complaints from communities of color, court orders or injunctions, or simply to pacify the prevailing consciousness of liberal-minded educators who yearn to do or say "the right thing." No, my team and I take pride in the fact that we demand and practice partnership in the truest sense of the word. Not only do we commit to working closely with our partnering districts and institutions of higher education, independent schools, and community organizations—and then recommit annually thereafter to continuing the work until the desired results are achieved—but we expect and set high standards for our partners to work with us. If, at any time in our collaborations, we feel that a partner is not operating in good faith nor demonstrating a sustained commitment to achieving racial equity, as evidenced by measureable results, we opt for disassociation.

It is, of course, imperative that our partnering districts see improved achievement results. That is essential. But it is also important that the leaders of those districts, universities, independent schools, and organizations not act in ways that intensify or increase racial disparities within their systems while stating publicly that they are committed to achieving racial equity. Such hypocrisy can be highly detrimental and perhaps even damaging to the spirit and psyche of those educators, students, and parents who are authentically and earnestly engaged in the racial equity transformation process.

Not only do systems fail to achieve racial equity because, as Dr. Darling-Hammond suggested, they do not stick with the effort long enough. I have found that many districts lack the full engagement and commitment of their executive leaders in that effort. For teachers to feel supported and comfortable with being held accountable for meeting the needs of under-served student of color populations, school principals must also feel as if they have a deep understanding of the racial equity transformation process. Principals also need the unwavering support of the central office to develop and hold those teachers accountable. Thus, when principals confront a resistant or poorly performing educator, they must feel confident that they have the authority and support to sanction that teacher. Those who supervise principals must be able to support these key administrators, understanding the complexities of the equity reform process at the site level. In addition, they must gain the support of the superintendent to deal appropriately with any principals who resist, are challenged by, or are not suited for leading equity efforts in their schools.

Thus, from the teacher to the principal to the directors and cabinet or executive team, when anyone in the chain of leadership and authority is allowed to opt out of, resist, or fail to master the basic principles or specific details of racial equity work, under-served children of color—indeed, *all* children—will remain under-served. However, the district superintendent, independent school head, or university president operating under a racial equity board policy is the only person who can insist on and thereby ensure that equity transformational work is consistent, coherent, and practiced with fidelity. On stating a commitment to achieve racial equity, all eyes within the system and throughout the larger community should necessarily remain fixed on the leaders at the highest level to determine if their statements of commitment to this goal are authentic or simply rhetorical. This is because equity reform is unlike many other critical system reforms to which a superintendent or head of school or organizational leader can appropriately delegate authority to a subordinate to get the job done. Achieving equity requires that the system leader be the visible "lead learner" and lead practitioner. Only by talking the racial equity transformation talk, walking the racial equity transformation walk, and thus moving Courageous Conversations from theory to practice can these leaders generate commitment rather than compliance or resistance to the goal of equity. Only then can they foster environments that develop, support, and hold every educator accountable to improving the achievement of *all* students.

Before launching into a detailed description of PEG's Framework, I want to pause and invite you, the reader, to address the following prompt as a way of determining your own system's readiness for transformation:

PROMPT

Has your system engaged in any form of Courageous Conversations training or racial equity leadership professional development? If not, what do you think has prevented it from engaging in this type of work? If so, what has been the focus and scope of that work?

Based on what you have read so far in this book and the *Courageous Conversations* field guide, would you view your system's Courageous Conversations or other racial equity effort(s) to be systemic? If so, what is the next logical step for deepening the impact of your work? If not, what is missing from your overall efforts in terms of equity programming consistency, coherence, and fidelity?

■ ■ ■

As part of my research in writing this book, I carefully reviewed PEG's client roster from the past decade. On one hand, I wanted to see if I could arrive at any conclusions about the types of school systems and communities that are more likely to embrace our belief that systemic racism is the most devastating factor contributing to the diminished achievement of all children and especially children of color. I asked myself: Do those school districts, systems, or locales share any characteristics in common (e.g., geographic location, size, racial demographics, achievement results, etc.)? I hoped to determine if any one or several characteristics were critical, not only for engaging in racial equity work but also for sustaining and deepening Courageous Conversations as a strategy for driving systemic racial equity transformation.

If the resulting typical district profile indicated rural location as a characteristic (which it did not), my inquiry would center then on what does being rural have to do with engaging in courageous conversations about race and how does being rural ultimately support districts' abilities to "go the distance" with this kind of work or to take a different direction over time. I also wanted to determine where our partnering districts were currently in terms of their efforts to move Courageous Conversations from theory into practice. Which factors or characteristics tend to prompt persistence in this kind of work? Which were associated with its abandonment?

For the purposes of that assessment and this discussion, I considered only those districts that entered into a multiyear partnership with PEG to engage in our formalized Systemic Racial Equity Framework programming, the details of which were introduced in the *Courageous Conversations* field guide and will be expounded on in this and subsequent chapters of this book. I did not consider the many systems that have organized such efforts on their own, without directly contracting PEG, by way of purchasing and screening our *Closing the Achievement Gap* video series, organizing study groups focused on the *Courageous Conversations* field guide, or creating their own racial equity leadership programs or initiatives with little or no engagement from PEG. Similarly, I did not factor in those districts that had been visited by me or a member of the PEG team to offer what we refer to as "one-shot" encounters such as single-day workshops or keynote presentations. I excluded these districts because we at PEG have long maintained—and the research on professional learning supports this—that although such equity events may have significant short-term impact on individuals, they do little to transform cultures, climates, belief systems, and behaviors at the classroom, school, or system level over time. Thus, I focused only on those systems that have partnered with PEG in the fullest sense to gauge where and how our programs have had the most impact—and why.

I discovered that the vast majority of districts that partner with PEG and adopt our Framework are suburban school districts that are or have engaged in formal or de facto racial integration relationships with their larger neighboring urban school districts. These include the school districts surrounding Minneapolis and St. Paul (Minnesota), Portland (Oregon), Detroit (Michigan), Washington, D.C., Baltimore (Maryland), Chicago (Illinois), Milwaukee (Wisconsin), Wilmington (Delaware), San José (California), Denver (Colorado), and Philadelphia (Pennsylvania). Another large segment of PEG's partnering district population can be defined as school systems located in smaller, progressive (at least perceptually so) communities surrounding major universities. These districts include Chapel Hill (North Carolina), Lawrence (Kansas), Ann Arbor (Michigan), and

Evanston (Illinois). Included in this latter category are some of the nation's historically high-performing school systems, which have struggled to maintain the same high-level achievement for their growing student of color populations as they have for their White students. Other PEG partners include suburban districts that were once all or predominantly White. Rapidly shifting demographics due to "color flight" have caused these systems to search out solutions to address their fallen achievement indicators. This category includes the school districts of Plymouth-Canton (Michigan), Talbott and Montgomery counties (Maryland), and St. Cloud (Minnesota).

The most striking finding in my process of reviewing PEG's partnering district list was the virtual absence of systems in the nation's four most populous states: California, Florida, New York, and Texas. These states contain some of the country's largest school districts, and they educate the largest populations of Black and Brown students. Some states that educate large numbers of American Indian students, like Wisconsin and Minnesota, are represented on our list, but several of the most populous states for American Indian children—states like California, Arizona, Oklahoma, New Mexico, Alaska, and the Plains States of Wyoming, Montana, and North and South Dakota are also noticeably absent. What is it about an explicit investigation into race as part of a systemic strategy for addressing racial achievement disparities that might prohibit districts in these states from engaging with PEG to achieve racial equity in education?

PROMPT

Consider the demographics of PEG's partnering districts described above. Beyond those mentioned, what other characteristics, if any, do you think prevail among them?

What, if any, meaning can you draw from these characteristics as it relates to engaging, sustaining, and/or deepening the Courageous Conversations racial equity work?

What does that meaning suggest to you about why some systems, particularly those in large states that are highly populated with students of color, are categorically absent from partnering with PEG?

A guiding principal of our work at PEG has been to build capacity in our partnering systems so that, eventually, they can carry on with their racial equity work without outside intervention. We sincerely believe that one of the truest markers of our success is when we have worked ourselves *out* of a job. When one of our partnering school districts is able to hold itself accountable for recognizing, examining, addressing, and dismantling systemic racism in their philosophies, policies, programs, and practices at the district, school, and classroom levels, PEG is pleased to see them graduate from service. The better we are in supporting our partners to achieve their racial equity goals, the more successful we view those partnerships.

In every successful PEG/district partnership, critical performance indicators such as suspension and expulsion rates and the number of D and F grades awarded have shown dramatic decline. Attendance and graduation rates, on the other hand, dramatically improve. And when this happens, standardized testing data, which traditionally has been used to measure racial gaps, typically show marked improvements for *all* children. More important, these districts demonstrate more significant improvements for under-served student of color populations—which we define as racial equity.

Chapter 11 is dedicated to describing the journey of one such district. The narrative of Eden Prairie (Minnesota) Schools not only depicts successful transformation at the system level, it also presents a tribute to the many districts around this country that have demonstrated the deep and sustained-levels of purpose, passion, practice, and persistence necessary to achieve what public education was never designed to achieve: racial equity.

"JUST SAY NO!" . . . TO RANDOM ACTS OF EQUITY

Achieving racial equity transformation in education is an unapologetically top-down process. It demands that superintendents, independent school heads, or college presidents in their communities take the lead in the design, development, implementation, and evaluation of transformation processes that are systemic, adaptive, and, most of all, courageous. Anything short of this, my experience has shown me, leads to "random acts of equity" that result in pockets of excellence rather than systemic and systemwide transformation.

Best practices for racial equity can only be amplified or replicated in distressed parts of a system of education when a culture of excellence has been established through a systemwide vision for equity. All or most of a district's school-building and administrative personnel must embrace and strive for that vision of high-quality professional learning.

PEG's Framework offers leaders an overarching structure within which their unique institutional equity plans and processes can take shape. Although many systems struggle with identical racial equity challenges, each is somewhat distinctive due to its unique history, setting, leadership structure, composition, and temperament. For this reason, systems must not simply adapt PEG's Framework or one shaped by another district to their own circumstances. Rather, they should craft—through a process of leadership learning, growth, and development—their own unique vision and structure for achieving racial equity.

The PEG Framework illustrated in Figure 7.1 evolved out of the Courageous Conversations Protocol. Both are based on the premise that racial equity transformation in classrooms, schools, districts, and higher education systems cannot occur until the very nature and dimensions of the conversations about race and racism that are (or are not) taking place are examined and addressed. The Courageous Conversations idea thus surrounds or creates the container, if you will, in which the racial equity transformation process begins.

At the center of this conceptual model are six hands representing disaggregated racial groupings of students. These hands symbolize the American Indian, Asian American, Black, Brown, multiracial, and White children of our nation and serve to remind us what all of our work is truly about: improving the schooling experience of *all* children. They are located at the center of the diagram because too often efforts to transform schools are aligned more with the interests of adults in the system than the needs of children. Practice in addressing the question, "How is what we're doing good for *all* students and especially our under-served students of color?" is an excellent way to keep system leaders focused on what matters most when it comes to crafting policies, allocating resources, and launching new programming in the name of racial equity.

Figure 7.1 The Pacific Educational Group (PEG) Systemic Racial Equity Framework

The guiding principles of the PEG Framework, or those elements that support racial equity transformation, are depicted as the inner circular wall that provides support to the Framework. The first of these, the principle of *Antiracism,* speaks to PEG's recognition that the U.S. system of education suffers from historic and contemporary vestiges of racism that must be uncovered, acknowledged, examined, and addressed before any substantive improvements in the performance of *all* students can be realized. The *Equity* principle speaks to the system's mandate to provide what is needed for each child and demographic group of children so that they may experience success in school and life. Differentiation of instructional inputs is a hallmark of the Equity principle and represents a set of educator beliefs and behaviors that define antiracism. Conversely, the provision of standardized instruction to all groups of children or refusal to pay attention to different racial/cultural needs ensures continued and perpetual disparities across race as well as other diversity categories. The act of engaging those whose voices and experiences traditionally have been marginalized or silenced by the system is a first step toward realizing the principle of *Empowerment.* Too often, however, leaders fail to go beyond simply enlisting the perspectives of under-served educators, students, parents, and community members of color to actually acting on their requests. Empowerment is derived from exercising voice *and* inspiring change. As each of these three key principles is translated into practices that become habitual among individuals and sustainable throughout a system, the principle of *Equality* becomes a tangible reality.

When the Courageous Conversations Protocol becomes the primary tool for achieving excellence and is applied together with the four principles of *Antiracism, Equity, Empowerment,* and *Equality,* transformational leaders can engage in a cycle of improvement that yields achievement gains for *all* students. The resulting improvements will be seen in three distinct, yet overlapping domains: *Community, Leadership,* and *Learning and Teaching.* The following three chapters (8, 9, and 10) provide a full explanation and description of how transforming beliefs and behaviors in each of these domains, individually and collectively, focuses and fortifies systemwide responses to systemic inequity.

Also shown in Figure 7.1, PEG's Framework offers a theory of transformation defined by four content and process realms that racial equity leaders must understand and in which they must take action to realize systemic, sustainable change. The first of these realms is the Courageous Conversations Protocol, which essentially requires educators to develop the requisite will, skill, knowledge, and capacity to move Courageous Conversations from theory to practice. Indeed, advancing such conversations is the most fundamental and foundational aspect of the PEG Framework's theory of transformation. Armed with continuously improving skills to engage, sustain, and deepen interracial dialogues about race, educators have a way of understanding and organizing racial meaning that is theoretical as well as practical. Brain researchers often speak about our need to establish schemas for processing complex and voluminous information.

A second realm is critical race theory, which can assist educators in making sense of and discovering truths about the complexities of race and racism where it intersects schooling. In their article, "'So When It Comes Out, They Aren't That Surprised That It Is There': Using Critical Race Theory as a Tool of Analysis of Race and Racism in Education," Jessica De Cuir and Adrienne Dixon offer five overlapping prisms through which race can be examined and understood:

- Counterstorytelling—The perspectives and narratives of educators, students, parents, and community members of color and their White allies tend to be absent in conversations, problem-solving, and strategic planning sessions—that is, their "stories" are not included among the viewpoints of record when decisions are made about resource allocation, program development and outreach, and other critical education matters. When these missing voices are sought out and those who have new and different perspectives are empowered to speak, radically different outcomes typically result.
- The Permanence of Racism—When educators view racism as intractable and a foundational aspect of our nation's education system, they can understand more fully the need for mental fortitude and emotional courage to effectively deinstitutionalize race. When racial equity educators enter their analyses of this issue seeking to determine "how" rather than "if" race affects the learning and teaching of all students, they can discover the blind spots in the prevailing color-blind ideology that has allowed or forced society to overlook those impacts.

- Whiteness as Property—As discussed in Chapter 3, Whiteness is manifested in many ways by all people, even those of color, in various ways and forms. The idea of Whiteness as property, or the pervasive sense of entitlement that White people carry with them due to their racial socialization, goes beyond the legal posturing that accompanies land and material ownership to issues relating to school integration, affirmative action, and assumptions that the best schools and schooling are somehow naturally and exclusively the province of White people.
- Interest Convergence—Determinations of limited resources have forced many into a belief that only *some* rather than *all* children can benefit from a quality education. This shortage mindset leads to the sorting and selecting of students for success or failure rather than to an emphasis on educating all students to make unique and meaningful contributions to their communities and the larger society. Changing this mindset is critical to eradicating systemic racial biases and barriers and creating a culture that promotes learning for *all*.
- A Critique of Liberalism—Educators must be challenged to understand and examine four tightly held liberal mythologies associated with race that ultimately cause efforts to address systemic racism more difficult. You may recall these from your reading in Chapter 5 as: adopting a color-blind stance; confusing the meanings of equity and equality; insisting on gradual and incremental rather than radical change; and positioning oneself and the laws devised in a racist society as racially neutral. Each of these perspectives challenges racial equity leaders' attempts to surface racial inequities in schools and to hold educators accountable for deinstitutionalizing racist policies, programs, and practices.[3]

Examining education systems through these distinctions can help educators not only address racial issues in schools but also explain and perhaps predict how, why, and when such issues arise. Together, these five tenets constitute a new system or schema for organizing racial information. They further offer racial equity leaders a deeper understanding of how to engage in the equity transformation process with enhanced will, skill, knowledge, and capacity. Moreover, for leaders of color, who, like me, sometimes struggle to move outside of the feeling quadrant when addressing issues of race, critical race theory offers a modern, multidisciplinary, activist-oriented framework for determining racial meaning and intelligence that validates our emotions and elevates our insights.

■ ■ ■

Systems thinking is the third realm of the PEG Framework's theory of transformation. As Peter Senge maintains in his groundbreaking text, *The Fifth Discipline*,[4] complex systems must be viewed in their entirety, rather than in parts or components. He also posits that to achieve lasting, systemwide change in an institution experiencing dysfunction, one must view all parts of the system as contributing to that condition and thus as critical elements in any formula for achieving overall or systemic transformation.

Senge further maintains that systems are rarely if ever broken. Rather, on closer examination, one clearly sees that they are doing exactly what they were designed to do and achieving exactly the results they were intended to achieve. Take the U.S. education system, for example. Given that it was designed originally to offer instruction exclusively to White American males, one must conclude that it continues to work reasonably well and in accordance with its original plan.

Senge suggests that the beliefs of an organization, especially the ones that exist below the surface and that, as Roland Barth[5] maintains, are often "non-discussable" are usually the driving forces behind the organizational behaviors that, in turn, determine the goals, objectives, and results of that system. This explains why many of the adults who work in our nation's education system truly do not believe that moving Courageous Conversations from theory to practice is a useful strategy for improving student achievement. It also explains why many do not believe that the Courageous Conversations Protocol will assist educators in examining and resolving racial conflicts in the schools, and why some seem to struggle to memorize the Four Agreements, Six Conditions, and components of the Compass, much less practice using them. In addition, it explains why educators generally fail as well to readily identify or address racial issues as they surface and choose instead to blame externalities and technicalities for their own failures to internalize and apply the Protocol, rather than admit that they simply did not, and could not, buy into the Courageous Conversations approach. Why? Such beliefs run counter to the prevailing and unspoken organizational beliefs. They call into question the core foundational and organizational beliefs of the system.

According to Senge,[6] true professional learning communities are those whose members continually expand their capacity to create the results they truly desire, where new and expansive patterns of thinking are nurtured, where collective aspirations are set free, and where people are continually learning to see the whole together. Central to this idea is Senge's emphasis on establishing conditions for effective learning so that real beliefs and values of the organization can be surfaced, examined, and transformed. He further argues that only those organizations that are able to adapt quickly and effectively will be able to excel in their field or market over time, and that they do so by emphasizing core learning capabilities: aspiration, reflective conversation, and understanding complexity.

Senge also maintains that learning organizations manifest two conditions at all times. The first is the ability to design the organization to match the intended or desired outcomes; the second is the ability to recognize when the initial direction of the organization runs counter to the desired outcome and to take the necessary steps to correct this mismatch. He also identifies four challenges to initiating systemwide change. First, there must be a compelling case for change. There also must be time to change and help during the change process. Last, as the perceived barriers to change are removed, it is important that new problems not considered important before or perhaps not even recognized previously do not become a critical barrier.

For systemic transformation to take place in education, educators must experience conditions that will enable them to surface, examine, and transform those systemic beliefs and attitudes that run counter to the changes they wish to see. They must become invested in the change process as well as the envisioned future possibilities. Lasting change cannot be forced; it must be embraced willingly and willfully. At best, educators who are forced to change in light of new racial equity directives passed down from their supervisors will comply with those directives only to keep their jobs. At worst, they will resist and resent change and cause greater disruption to student learning.[7]

To support educators in surfacing, examining, and transforming harmful racist beliefs about the educability of the students they serve, Senge offers two tools: the Ladder of Inference and the Iceberg.[8] Both are extremely helpful and merit further explanation and discussion. The Ladder of Inference (see Figure 7.2) invites us to recognize how our beliefs can cause us to focus on certain factors and their contributions to devastating schooling outcomes—say, for example, the effects of family involvement or poverty on the achievement of African American males—while perhaps overlooking other, more salient factors such as race in determining the same or similar results for this population of students. The Ladder of Inference guides us to identify which data are observable and to determine which aspects of those data we are unable to, or choose not to, analyze. Senge contends that we educators often select certain data to guide our analyses upward while leaving other critical information "on the floor."

Referring back to the SAT data discussed in Chapter 4, for example, you may have noticed that the students from families with incomes of more than $200,000 scored among

Figure 7.2 Senge's Systems-Thinking Tools: The Ladder of Inference

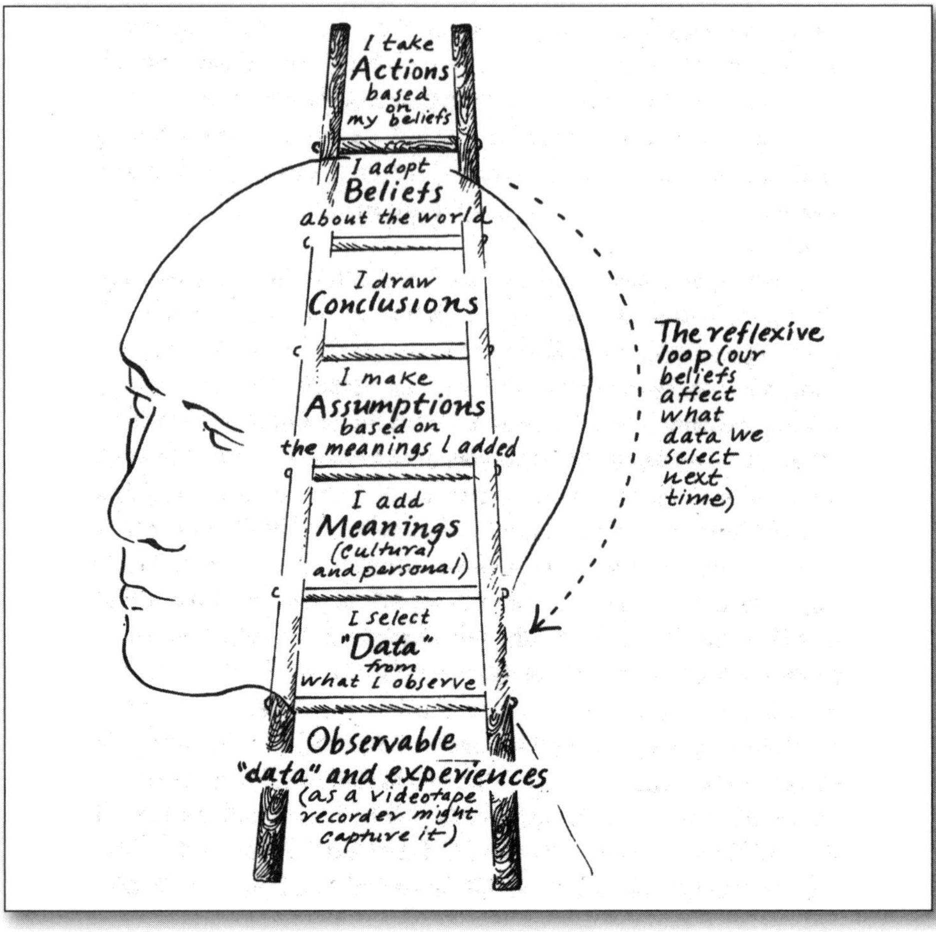

Source: From *The Fifth Discipline* by Peter M. Senge, copyright © 1990, 2006 by Peter M. Senge. Used with permission of Doubleday, a division of Random House, Inc.

the highest on the SAT while those students with family incomes of less than $20,000 scored quite low. In selecting such information, you could then construct meaning, make assumptions, draw conclusions, and formulate, or more likely reaffirm, the belief that poor children cannot perform well on the SAT. Although such an analysis and determination might be accurate and even useful, what Senge and his Ladder of Inference systems-thinking tool help us to do—and this is essential—is to question why some might choose *not* to consider the fact that Black students, or even Black and Brown students, are the lowest-scoring groups, regardless of their family income levels. Indeed, how might your meaning, assumptions, conclusions, and beliefs have been different had you chosen to pick that observable data up off the floor for your analysis and subsequent problem solving? Using the Ladder of Inference can help racial equity leaders to recognize how educators continually seek out the very same information about lower-achieving students of color, as well as about their White counterparts, to confirm or affirm existing beliefs about these students' educability.

Figure 7.3 presents a second systems-thinking tool that supports educators in better understanding how their beliefs, as professional adults in schools, drive their behaviors and subsequently determine student results. At the top or the tip of the Iceberg diagram,

Figure 7.3   Senge's Systems-Thinking Tools: The Iceberg

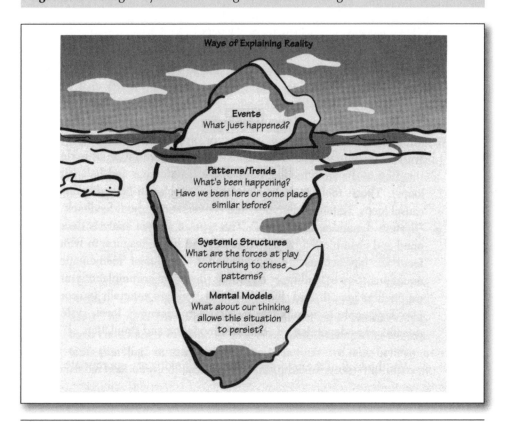

Source: From *Schools That Learn: A Fifth Discipline Fieldbook for Educators, Parents, and Everyone Who Cares About Education* by Peter Senge, Nelda Cambron-McCabe, Timothy Lucas, Bryan Smith, Janis Dutton, and Art Kleiner, copyright © 2000 by Peter Senge, Nelda Cambron-McCabe, Timothy Lucas, Bryan Smith, Janis Dutton, and Art Kleiner. Used with permission of Doubleday, a division of Random House, Inc.

Senge invites school leaders to name the problematic circumstance or situation that is occurring in their system. Referring again to the SAT data discussed in Chapter 4, this would mean that high school educators would need to recognize that Black students, as a group, are the absolute lowest-scoring group of students and thus begin the process of questioning their beliefs that surface as a result of this circumstance. Using the Iceberg, educators can discover the poor testing patterns of Black students evident in their own schools and determine how they, as racial equity leaders, might behave to mitigate or correct this outcome.

Working your way down the Iceberg, you see that you next would determine what other patterns and trends could be surfaced for analysis that might contribute to the testing results of Black students. You might question, for example, whether Black students are being exposed to rigorous curricula or if these students are being encouraged to take (or discouraged from taking) the PSAT in their sophomore and junior years as preparation for the SAT. Then, you might also examine what structures in your school or district might support the perpetuation of such patterns and trends. For example, do Black students in your school or district have genuine access to counselors who can guide them effectively through the course- and college-selection processes or provide them with academic tutoring, should they struggle with the more rigorous curricula needed to prepare for college? Are a sufficient number of advanced placement (AP) courses offered and accessible to Black students in your school? At the base of the Iceberg, Senge guides all school personnel—be they superintendents, principals, teachers, or support staff—to ask which of their "mental models" or beliefs cause structures, patterns, and trends such as poor testing performance to persist, thereby causing systemic and even national problems, in this example, for Black male students in particular.

When used consistently and with fidelity, the Ladder of Inference and the Iceberg will enable racial equity leaders to uncover, examine, and address harmful beliefs—beliefs that we may not even recognize we hold—about our under-served students of color and how they experience schooling. Until the majority of educators truly believe in the educability of Black, Brown, and American Indian students, our education system will continue failing to provide the rigorous and relevant educational opportunities these students need to learn and thrive. Educators of all races must be equipped with the tools they will need to make meaning of race and dialogue interracially. They will also need to experience the conditions that can inspire them to examine their own racial beliefs and practices to determine if they are congruent with original intentions of the education system or with their aspirations for *all* children's cognitive, emotional, and social development in schools.

■　■　■

Adaptive Leadership principles comprise a fourth and final realm of the PEG Framework's theory of transformation. This realm encompasses what is known and unknown about the nature of efforts to lead education organizations through the process of systemic racial equity transformation. I'm certain that most of my readers are aware that the creation of schools in which *all* children—regardless of their race, everywhere, and every day—can have access to and take advantage of meaningful opportunities to learn has been a hard-fought battle waged by generations of great minds with no end in sight. To achieve our vision of racial equity, we must follow a radically different course than that of our predecessors. Finding this path will not be easy, nor will it necessarily be a safe course to take, personally or professionally. That is why the key word defining this realm is leadership because changing the course of schools so that they serve *all* children requires first and foremost that those who have the authority actually take the lead in racial equity efforts. But it also requires those leaders to inspire the other educators in their systems to take ownership of their parts of the challenge and participate with the leader in finding solutions.

Ronald Heifetz's[9] concept of Adaptive Leadership represents the cornerstone theory supporting this realm. Many elements of his theory are congruent with the way racial equity transformation leadership plays out in K–12 and higher education systems. Heifetz, of course, has written many books and articles on his theory. The foundational ideas include the distinctions he makes between technical problems and adaptive challenges, leadership and authority, productive disequilibrium and intolerant stress, predictable resistance and dangerous defeat. What is important to note, however, is that, like most theorists whose ideas I incorporate into my own, Heifetz does not consider specifically what happens when one is confronted with systemic racism, arguably the most difficult issue facing societies around the world. Thus, I have provided in Figure 7.4 a graphic adaption of Heifetz's Adaptive Leadership model as it applies to the challenge of achieving racial equity in education.

Figure 7.4 Adaptive Leadership: A Safe "Holding Space" for Courageous Conversations

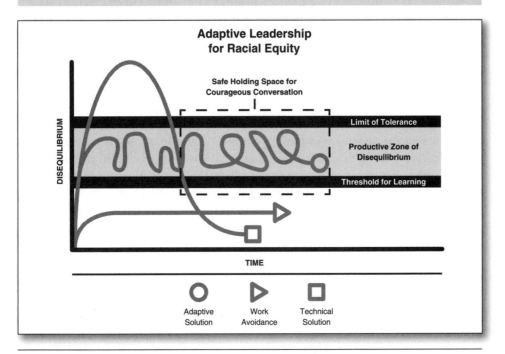

Source: Adapted from *Leadership on the Line: Staying Alive Through the Dangers of Leading,* by Ronald A. Heifetz and Martin Linsky, 2002, Cambridge, MA: Harvard Business Review Press.

Looking at the vertical and horizontal axes, our model of adaptive leadership suggests that for racial equity transformation to occur systemwide—be it in school districts, independent schools, or institutions of higher education—the system's educators must experience a level of sustained stress, or disequilibrium, over a protracted period of time. You have, no doubt, heard the adage: "No pain, no gain"? Well, this is precisely the prevailing belief regarding the objective of creating racially equitable schooling environments for all. To discover meaningful, sustainable solutions to age-old racial challenges, we must avoid looking for quick fixes and cease investing in outdated, often-the-same-but-renamed programming. Instead, we must resource a community of educators, family members, and community leaders as well as students to learn and work together using actual racial problems of practice to discover innovative strategies and processes for implementation.

Racial equity leaders must be able to distinguish between and disentangle two radically different types of obstacles they most likely will encounter in their work. Heifetz[10] calls these impediments *adaptive challenges* and *technical problems,* and he notes that discovering or creating solutions for each requires very different leadership approaches. Cambridge Leadership Associates, an organization focused on training people to be adaptive leaders, offers the following differentiation between adaptive and technical leadership:

> The most common leadership mistake is treating Adaptive Challenges as if they were technical problems. Technical problems can be solved by an authority or expert. They have a known solution. Adaptive Challenges are quite different. They have no known solution—the skills and answers are outside your repertoire. Adaptive Challenges are those you have to grow into solving and require mobilizing people's hearts and minds to operate differently. Luckily, these skills can be learned regardless of position or function. Leading effectively requires recognizing both the adaptive and technical aspects of a situation and tailoring your efforts accordingly.[11]

Heifetz also contends that issues facing organizations generally come "bundled"— that is, they present as both types of problems simultaneously. Given PEG's decade of success in supporting school districts to post higher achievement gains for *all* children, important improvements like establishing an equity policy, implementing a uniform discipline code, or creating district- or site-based equity teams are technical problems. That is, they can be addressed using known solutions that yield tangible, realizable outcomes. What is adaptive about these same types of improvements, however, is their impact on efforts to redefine educators' beliefs and behaviors so that such innovative policies and codes can be crafted and enacted or teams can be formed and begin to properly function in otherwise unchanged institutions. If a system is already at a crisis stage—as many are, insofar as educating Black males is concerned, for example—only adaptive leadership will be effective. This is not to say that some parts of the solution to an educational challenge are not technical in nature, like hiring more racially conscious, Black male educators for U.S. schools. But how most of our nation's current teachers (that is, White females) learn to modify their beliefs and behaviors so that they can learn effectively with and from their colleagues of color is a far more challenging prospect compared to the difficulty of locating, recruiting, and employing exemplary Black male teachers, who are, I admit, rare individuals—at least, they are rare in the American system of education.

Beyond not having known solutions, what truly differentiates adaptive challenges from technical problems is that they require us to look beneath the surface of the issue at hand and uncover what are often the hidden beliefs and values that cause that issue to be persistent or recurring in the first place. In such instances, exercising an adaptive style of leadership is much more compatible and consistent with systems thinking and clearly an appropriate theory to support practices that challenge racism and promote racial equity.

After committing to engaging in an adaptive process to address this issue, racial equity leaders must determine, usually through practice, their system's limit of tolerance and its organizational threshold for learning. For example, at some critical points, systems fail to be productive in their quest to discover adaptive solutions for achieving racial equity because either they are too complacent, and thus not learning and growing as they should, or they are too stressed to function in effective, professional ways. Between these two debilitating points is what Heifetz refers to as the Productive Zone of Disequilibrium. As illustrated graphically in Figure 7.4, this zone is the place where systems are seen as living entities that cycle through triumphs and tragedies, meaning and confusion, acceleration and decline, progress and setback. Outside this zone, they tend to approach problems in mechanical, technical ways, which often are linear, neat, and predictable from start to finish. Given that most educators generally demonstrate a preference for the latter habits of mind and being, racial equity leaders must exercise whatever authority they have gained to keep their systems in disequilibrium until adaptive solutions can be discovered and implemented. Cambridge Leadership Associates offers the following advice:

> Every organization faces two competing demands: it must execute its current activities and adapt those same activities to face future opportunities and challenges. These two tasks of managing for efficiency or effectiveness and leading the organization through change correspond to the two functions of Authority and Leadership. Few organizations or individuals can do both well.
>
> Since the bottleneck to growth for most organizations is the depth and breadth of leadership, leadership pathways often need to be created for those with and without formal authority. By separating the functions of leadership and authority, you can more easily build integrated competencies across an organization, which is critical to create new and sustained value.[12]

How systems adjust to stress, or disequilibrium, over time is defined by their leaders' ability—and *courage*—to discover solutions to the underlying adaptive challenges those systems face rather than their skill in locating quick fixes to unrelated technical problems that have already been addressed. Stress is a natural and normal function of adaptive transformation. Not only do adaptive challenges such as achieving systemwide racial equity in education lack a known solution, most often the adaptive processes employed to resolve them also usher in situations and interactions that are difficult for the educators within such systems to navigate. Sometimes, however, the potential danger involved in discovering greater meaning and solution to important issues prevents system leaders from embarking on the adaptive course. Although many school leaders theoretically embrace the importance of achieving racial equity, and even recognize their own moral and positional responsibility to assure racially bias-free environments for *all* students, they often fail to exercise their courage, leadership, and authority in ways that authentically address systemic racism.

In addition to understanding important distinctions between adaptive challenges and technical problems, leadership and authority, and productive versus unproductive stress, adaptive leaders recognize that they must lead like there is no tomorrow. Indeed, a critical part of their formula for success involves discomforting the comfortable and further stressing those who are already stressed. Adaptive leaders call this "turning up the heat"!

Interesting enough, in their groundbreaking work, *Leadership on the Line*, Heifetz and his coauthor, Marty Linsky, devote an entire chapter to what they call "The Faces of Danger." That chapter speaks directly to leaders' challenges stemming from trying to focus a community on issues such as racism that prompt dissonance and discomfort. Heifetz and Linsky suggest that danger is present for school leaders when they are successful in holding their staff in the Zone of Productive Disequilibrium. As Heifetz and Linsky write:

> The dangers of leadership take many forms. Although each organization and culture has its preferred ways to restore equilibrium when someone upsets the balance, we've noticed four basic forms . . . When exercising leadership, you risk getting marginalized, diverted, attacked, or seduced.[13]

They continue with this discussion, noting the following:

> Seduction, marginalization, diversion, and attack all serve a function. They reduce the disequilibrium that would be generated were people to address the issues that are taken off the table. They serve to maintain the familiar, restore order, and protect people from the pains of adaptive work. It would be wonderful if adaptive work did not involve hard transitions, adjustments, and loss in people's lives. Because it does, it usually produces resistance. Being aware of the likelihood of receiving opposition in some form is critical to managing it when it arrives. Leadership, then, requires not only reverence for the pains of change and recognition of the manifestations of danger, but also the skill to respond.[14]

Over the past two decades, I have witnessed numerous school leaders' responses to the faces of danger as they focused their systems on sustained racial equity transformation. Unfortunately, knowing and understanding these dangers has probably caused many school leaders to avoid working on the leading edges of the racial equity struggle.

You might ask then: Why should I lead like there is no tomorrow and engage in racial equity work when I could risk losing my credibility or even my job? My response is always the same: Keep your focus on the PEG Framework, in which *students are always at the center.* Embrace the moral imperative, work to achieve equity, and develop as adaptive racial equity leaders. Be mindful as well of Heifetz and Linsky's general guidelines throughout their book, which I paraphrase here:

- Find partners
- Keep your opposition close
- Accept responsibility for your piece of the mess you're in
- Acknowledge your opponents' losses
- Model the behaviors you want to see
- Accept the fact that there will be casualties[15]

In short, racial equity leaders must understand that the work we have begun cannot be done alone or by a mighty few. Achieving racial equity demands a broad and deep base of advocates and champions who understand the perspectives and know the whereabouts of their detractors and resisters as well as they know their own inner voices. It requires courageous, adaptive leaders who recognize that they too are part of the problem and that transformation requires letting go of beliefs and behaviors that may make them and others comfortable or feel capable to achieve success.

As Malcolm X once said: "You can't teach what you don't know, and you can't lead where you won't go." Achieving racial equity calls for true leaders to step out front. It also calls for some, or perhaps all, of those who currently occupy positions of power and authority to step back or step out of the system altogether—that is, if they cannot muster the courage and develop the will, skill, knowledge, and capacity to advance the vision of equity and excellence.

For me, the most relevant and important aspect of Adaptive Leadership for racial equity leaders is its focus on building capacity within systems to solve internal problems. Adaptive challenges exist within classrooms, schools, and districts because educators typically desire quick fixes to persistent challenges and because most either resist or resent the need to search deep within to identify those beliefs and behaviors that exacerbate, if not cause, the very problems they are attempting to solve. As long as those of us who are parents, community members, school officials, educational policymakers, voters, and, yes, racial equity leaders continue to encourage and reward those who offer technical solutions to adaptive problems, we will continue to be disappointed by the lack of systemic transformation and, thus, the lack of improved academic performance and outcomes for under-served students of color. We must answer the call to hold each other, and each and every educator, accountable for changing our education system in such a way that we are no longer the problem but a collective manifestation of the adaptive solution.

■ ■ ■

The PEG Framework and its theory of transformation—through the focused philosophy, clear vision, four core principles, three overlapping domains, and four innovative realms of development they offer—guide racial equity leaders in transforming themselves and redesigning their systems to achieve enhanced participation and performance for *all* students. School districts such as Minnesota's Eden Prairie Schools have proved that when this framework is clearly understood, consistently adhered to, and practiced with fidelity, students experience what many believe to be impossible: school systems in which *all* students experience what W.E.B. Du Bois called for so boldly in 1929—the *freedom to learn!*

UNMASKING COURAGEOUS CONVERSATIONS ABOUT RACIAL DISPARITIES IN INDEPENDENT SCHOOLS

One Saturday morning during the final editing phase for this book, I received an e-mail from Scott Sellman, a longtime friend and the only fellow student from Park School with whom I have maintained contact since seventh grade. Scott wrote, "Hey buddy . . . how are you?" As usual, I responded with a brief list of things going on in my life and then shared with him that my 87-year-old grandfather's illness was causing me to feel far away from my family in Baltimore and homesick. I ended my e-mail to Scott with the following: "I am running now (what's new!), but I will be home to Baltimore soon and I will check-in with you, Scotty Waddy Do Da Day!"

Indeed, Scotty Waddy Do Da Day, a name I fondly branded him with while we were in upper school, was one of only a handful of independent school chums to ever visit my home or who actually knew members of my family. Similarly, I spent a great deal of time with "Waddy's" parents, Jerry and Mickie, and his sister, Beth, and came to understand and positively define and embrace aspects of Whiteness as an adopted member of the Sellman family. We're still in touch occasionally, too.

Along with Jimmy Smith, my friend since age 6, who traveled with me each day from our predominately African American neighborhood to Park School from Grade 7 through 9, Scott was part of hundreds of wonderful moments we shared there. We visited each other while in college, he at Emory and me at Penn, and I even dressed a frazzled adult Scotty Waddy on his wedding day because he was too nervous to button his shirt.

This is all to say that I have many treasured Park School memories and one beautiful and everlasting Park School friendship that still means the world to me. Sadly, this glorious reality will always sit alongside the many conscious and unconscious racial struggles that lined the way of my middle and high school experience. Altogether, my time at Park School had two very different sides, and that reality has followed into my adult years.

In 1995, just a few years after I had become a racial equity consultant (known then as a diversity consultant), a woman by the name of Evelyn McClain telephoned my office. She wanted to speak with me about working with the students and faculty at my alma mater. Although I had begun my consulting practice working exclusively with independent (or private) schools, at the time of McClain's call, I was already shifting my attention to addressing racial inequities in public education. I had also begun to grow disillusioned with what I believed was a lack of sincerity on the part of the independent school leadership generally to address the persistent culture and climate issues, stemming from unacknowledged systemic racism, that affect students of color.

McClain told me she had learned about my Expressing Our Differences seminars, the precursor training that later became Beyond Diversity, through her associates in the national network of independent schools, and she believed that I would be uniquely qualified to work with Park's educators, students, and families. I was both shocked and curious that McClain, who is African American, had been hired as the middle school principal of The Park School. In the 6 years I attended Park, where I received rigorous academic and social preparation for postsecondary education, only once did I have a teacher of color. That was Mr. Moreno, who taught me Spanish, but I never recognized him as a man of color partly because my racial reality at the time was positioned in a Black and White dichotomy. Aside from Leon the custodian, Linwood the bus driver, and Coretha the cafeteria worker, the adult population of the Park School I attended was entirely White.

Was the school finally, in 1995, sincere about addressing the racial diversity crisis its students and parents of color had complained about for decades, I wondered? McClain's invitation for me to return to the school as a consultant came with several parameters.

First, she could only assure engagement and acceptance within the middle school—that is, she was acting on the issue only within her own sphere of influence. She admitted that she had not experienced much success in elevating the conversation about racial disparities in learning opportunities and outcomes to the system level. This meant that, at the time of her invitation, neither the school's head nor the lower- or upper-school principals had chosen to engage my services or even welcome this conversation. McClain also informed me that she could not afford my normal fee without enlisting the support of the other divisions and that this might stall, if not block, her ability to contract with me. In fact, she said she could not guarantee me more than a day's work.

Compelled by a force I could not explain, but certain that it was not self-interest (since McClain had told me she was not sure how much or when I would be paid), I began mentally packing my bags for Baltimore as soon as I hung up the phone.

■ ■ ■

Days before leaving San Francisco for my hometown, my former Park School adviser and English teacher, Rachel Johnson-Work, telephoned me and asked if I would be willing to engage in an informal dialogue with the upper-school faculty at Park at the end of my day working with the middle school. She assured me that this would be an invaluable and quite timely experience for the increased number of students of color in the upper grades. Of course, I consented to her request. I was really looking forward to having an adult-to-adult conversation with Park faculty members about my own experience and that of so many other students of color in an environment known for its progressive open-mindedness. Neither Rachel nor I had any real idea what would ultimately transpire in that 90-minute interaction. As it turned out, we would both be in for a rude awakening.

The leadership at The Park School, like that at many other independent schools with whom I had worked in the first 3 years after I created PEG, insisted that diversifying their faculty with qualified teachers and administrators of color was virtually impossible. They claimed then that such educators simply did not exist. This belief was never challenged in practice, at least not until Evelyn McClain arrived at Park's middle school. She arrived, however, to find an all-White faculty; thus, within a year, she began an effective campaign of hiring talented teachers of color.

You have to understand my surprise when I returned to the school almost 20 years after I first entered it. It was almost surreal. I found myself conversing at my formerly all-White alma mater with several Black teachers and a Black principal! The middle school felt so alive to me. Its diverse faculty seemed poised to confront the challenges of going beyond the numbers and investigating what changes were necessary to make Park a place where people of color could thrive without totally, and often unknowingly, assimilating into White culture and consciousness.

A highlight of my day was working with a multiracial group of middle school students who clearly were more open to engaging in conversations about race with me and with each other than were my classmates when I attended Park. I attributed this evolution to the fact that for the current students, such topics were routinely validated and discussed by the school's educators of color. The members of the middle school faculty were also open and engaging as they examined the racial dynamics of the school with me. They identified some areas of progress as well as some key remaining challenges. At the end of the day, several middle school educators who had joint appointments in the upper school made a point of wishing me luck in my conversations on this topic with their colleagues "upstairs."

My experiences during my youth had convinced me that conversations about race were essentially off-limits in Park's upper school, but I never expected that opening such a dialogue several years later as an adult would be cause for incivility. After all, many of the teachers with whom I was to meet had taught me personally. I thought they were liberal educators who believed in social justice and who proudly advocated for what is best for their students. I suspected that revealing aspects of the secondary years via my racial autobiography might be quite emotional for me and somewhat discomforting for them, but I was certain that most, being my former teachers, would understand and even comfort me.

Those 90 minutes, it turns out, still rank as among the most difficult of my entire career. The dominant voices in the exchange were those of White male faculty members, including my former history teacher, varsity basketball coach, and adviser. A couple of revered educators callously invalidated my narrative and requested that such conversations cease immediately. When I spoke about a virtual absence of images of Black people in everything from the curriculum to the performing arts, token examples were hurled my way as if they might change what the faculty members viewed as *my* obvious lack of knowledge about non-White perspectives and cultures. When I criticized the fact that my counselors never recommended that I explore enrollment in a historically Black college or university, they deemed me ungrateful, pointing out that the school had "elevated" me by supporting my successful admission to more than one Ivy League institution. They further accused me of attempting to shame them or to make them feel guilty. To my shock and surprise, when the session was over, many defiantly insisted that my work with The Park School was also over! As a result, despite 7 wonderful hours of work in the middle school, the all-White upper school faculty and administration effectively and totally silenced a courageous conversation about race at The Park School.

That experience, although personally hurtful, provided me with an important sign, and that sign directed me to locate the real emphasis of my work elsewhere in education. It became abundantly clear to me that the independent school directors I had encountered at Park and elsewhere were preeminently opposed to talking about race in a personal, local, and immediate way. They favored discussions that surfaced "naturally" in literature or history classes or preferred to deal with race only if it arose in individual White students' banter, jokes, or struggles to make personal sense of diversity. Thus, for the 5 years following that experience, my work and that of PEG focused exclusively on public school education and educators, who were often just as if not more resistant to discussing race or racism than their independent school counterparts, but who did not seem to hide behind a veneer of academic freedom and individual liberty to the same extent.

To this day, it strikes me as ironic that despite their abundant resources, prestige, purportedly progressive ideologies, and—most critically—their control over the student selection process, independent schools, for the most part, have not closed performance gaps in a way that their highest and lowest achievement levels cease to be predictable by race. Although I decided to steer clear of the independent school environment professionally, I continued to recognize the moral importance of holding private schools to a higher standard with respect to achieving racial equity. It remains critically important, in my view, for these institutions to embrace opportunities for and possibilities of eradicating racial disparities in educational outcomes and to recognize their role in perpetuating these inequities.

In cities and suburbs across the United States in the early 1960s through the late 1970s, many independent schools first opened their doors to students of color. A new level of prominence with regard to integration and diversity occurred precisely because White families wished to buffer their children from "forced" or legally mandated school desegregation efforts while still benefitting from a manageable level of racial diversity. During the 1980s and 1990s, private schools continued "mining" public school systems for talented scholars and athletes of color so that they could diversify their school environments and bring attention and success to their sports programs, primarily in football and basketball. Today, although many families of color do not depend on financial aid or diversity recruitment incentives to support their children's independent school education, the Black, Brown, and American Indian students at these institutions are still experienced as "visitors" to the White-dominated private school "preserve."

To be certain, on integration, independent schools provided White students and their families with the carefully crafted, monitored, and controlled racially diverse environments that they desired or felt required to create. However, these same private schools have also represented a major source of challenge to the nation's public schools in the quest to ensure a quality education to *all* students. For students like me in my day and many other students of color since, these independent institutions offered unmatched opportunities for academic success. Yet, as my Nana Singleton would often say to me regarding my own independent school and Ivy League education: "To those whom much is given, much is expected!" As she also used to say, however, "Freedom ain't free."

In addition to the benefits that stem from attending a school whose facilities, teacher quality, and curriculum rigor is beyond reproach, communities of color pay a definite price when their most prepared and promising children are removed from local schools and invited to attend elite independent schools, typically located far, far away from those communities, physically and otherwise. First, a student of color's chances of experiencing high achievement in such settings is predicated on his or her ability to adopt, adapt to, and openly and authentically celebrate the elite school's White cultural traditions in education and other areas. The markers of this educational process typically include the student's ability to embrace and espouse a racial color blindness that is grounded in the illusions of social meritocracy. In other words, the "Whiter" the student of color becomes in his or her worldview, the greater acceptance he or she will find in the independent school community. An additional cost to students of color who attend independent schools and those students' communities is the distancing of those students from their families and their primary cultures, which is induced by a pedagogy steeped in Whiteness and the often unconscious beliefs and unintentional behaviors of White students, educators, and parents, who (also often unconsciously but sometimes overtly) promote White supremacy and color inferiority.

Second, when students of color at independent schools even momentarily or circumstantially opt to examine, challenge, or worse, reject Whiteness, their continued success in the elite education environment is hard won, if not impossible. The large cultural price that I personally paid to experience academic success in an independent school continues to haunt me today. From not being made aware of the historic and contemporary contributions of Black leaders and icons throughout the world or even in my hometown of

Baltimore, to having been blinded to the opportunity of being educated in an environment steeped in the legacy of literary, scientific, and artistic American voices of color, I feel even today that I have missed out on so much that is the Black cultural heritage of Baltimore, the nation, and the world. As an adult and as an advocate and leader for racial equity, I do not believe that one must abandon one's primary racial culture and consciousness to attain academic excellence. Indeed, I am convinced that independent school students can emerge as effectively bicultural and biliterate with respect to race when their educators properly and thoroughly uncover, examine, and address issues of systemic racism in tightly embraced and rigorously implemented policies, programs, and practices.

After 5 years of disengagement from independent schools, I have gradually reconnected with these institutions because of my renewed belief that they can face the tough racial equity questions and emerge as true leaders in this arena. My interactions with some incredibly courageous independent school educators, such as those at Marin Academy located in California's Bay Area and New York City's Spence School, substantiate this renewed belief and fuel my evolving passion to discover more effective ways of meeting the educational needs of *all* children.

Paradoxically, independent schools today compare themselves to each other by the statistical level of racial diversity they achieve. Still, meaningful conversations about race unfortunately rarely advance beyond the numbers, even in the Obama era. In fact, it is rare that contemporary independent school educators are required to grapple with their own attitudes and beliefs about race, the importance of racial diversity in their schools, or, more specifically, the value these schools obtain from and reasons they are so intent on enrolling students of color. For a variety of reasons, the conversation about racial disparities is more difficult to commence in independent schools than in public school. This is not to say that public school educators are instantaneously receptive either, but because public schools have been framed as the entity in which the so-called racial achievement gap is situated and perpetuated, public school educators collectively feel greater pressure to recognize the issue as one that must be confronted. Independent school educators, more often than not, tend to frame racial issues as a student life matter rather than as something that pertains to the province of teaching and learning. Under the broader rubric of diversity in the independent school community, race is connected to achieving admission targets and providing limited time for celebrating perceived differences.

Like public school educators, independent school administrators and teachers hold tightly to the belief that racial disparities are based on economic status or social class rather than race. Although SAT data are helpful in dismantling this belief, one of the greatest challenges I've experienced in working with independent school educators is helping them to understand socioeconomic status as a phenomenon that exacerbates racial disparity, not as the root cause of it. For independent and public school educators alike, acknowledging and addressing systemic racism comes with time, patience, and very careful cultural, social, and intellectual maneuvering.

Specifically, so much about independent schooling revolves around money and lots of it. In some of these institutions, families pay upwards of $50,000 per year to ensure that their children receive the best social treatment and schooling, as well as enhanced opportunities to attend the more prestigious universities in the country or world. Although racial equity work is not focused on interrupting White children's progression to prestigious universities, it is, at its core, aimed at creating circumstances that enable traditionally under-served students of color to partake as well of these same abundant opportunities. One might argue, however, that when more children are academically and socially effective, competition for college and work will be more intense. But when competition among a rich diversity of students becomes the norm, the result will be increased productivity and thus greater effectiveness for *all* students and greater social and economic prosperity.

Educators often arrive at the reform table believing that they are already equipped with a sufficiently high level of consciousness and competence to address whatever issues are presented. Thus, as specific challenges emerge from the Courageous Conversations process, a wonderful sense of efficacy, as it relates to finding and implementing meaningful solutions, also rises. A look at the many independent schools such as Deerfield Academy in Massachusetts, which have transformed from elite, all-male, and very exclusive environments into coeducational institutions is an indication of the power of independent school leaders to act when the cause suits them. Still, given the depth and seeming permanence of the racial equity dilemma in independent schools, there is still much reason for concern. For example, I sometimes worry that basic yet difficult questions continue to go unaddressed as a way of preserving this culture of perceived educator competence and success while simultaneously camouflaging the reality that many of these school leaders, as well as the families to which they have historically catered, do not truly value or prioritize racial equity.

Thus, to shift independent school leaders deeper into the mindset and practice of unmasking, understanding, and addressing racism, I suggest that racial equity leaders engage them intellectually around a series of essential questions including but not limited to the following:

- What meaning do you bring to the phrase *racial equity,* and how is your meaning illustrated, or not, in the policies, program selections, and practices at your school?
- What would it look and feel like to achieve racial equity in your school? That is, what would be different in terms of curriculum and instruction, admissions, alumni relations, development, governance, and student activities? What would remain the same?
- To what degree does what one's family pays determine how one is treated in your school? What would result if wealth did not determine reward as significantly as it does currently?
- Why is it important that your school attract, matriculate, and graduate students of color? What role do students of color play in establishing the culture and climate of your school? Are they and their families made aware of their importance and role in the school prior to attending?
- Can you honestly say that the voices and viewpoints of students of color, as those aspects relate to their racial experience in your school, have been thoroughly mined? What, if any, changes in policy, program, or practice have been implemented in direct response to these students' narratives?

■   ■   ■

Returning full circle to my earlier reflections, I recently received an announcement from The Park School that identified the newly appointed head of school as an openly gay (White) man who is partnered and raising school-age children. I could not help but recognize how significant a stride this was, even for a school that prides itself on representing the pillars and cornerstones of progressive education. I felt a deep sense of pride in my alma mater and saw this advance as one that would make many children at Park who are struggling with their own sexual orientation feel safer, perhaps. Another part of me, however, returned to the unanswered question of whatever happened to Park's African American principal Evelyn McClain and the band of educators of color that she brought to that institution's middle school in the early 1990s. I wondered if the Park community would continue to overlook the same value that children of color would gain from seeing themselves in the leadership, faculty, curriculum, and instruction.

Two years ago, a racial equity leader from Park's development office invited me back to the school to consult with a schoolwide faculty study group that had been charged with addressing the age-old racial diversity issue there. The administrator had recently discovered and read my first book (the *Courageous Conversations* field guide), but she was completely unaware of my previous unpleasant experience with the upper-school faculty. I courageously accepted her invitation, and by the end of the day, I was both relieved and impressed with the group of caring educators I became acquainted with during that meeting. They were enlightened individuals who felt a deep sense of responsibility to stand for change in the face of their colleagues', students', and parents' embrace of the harmful and entrenched doctrines of color blindness and meritocracy.

I engaged the members of the study group in discussions centering around the types of essential questions presented in this book, confident that their answers could move my alma mater beyond mere satisfaction with statistical diversity toward the more authentic and noteworthy goal of achieving racial equity. Although I am not yet convinced that The Park School community has mustered the collective will, skill, knowledge, and capacity to address and resolve these questions, I believe a time will come when my former school will challenge its pervasive and perceived racial dysconsciousness and replace it with elevated consciousness, confidence, and cultural competence. Until such a time, current and future generations of racially conscious students of color will continue to complain to seemingly sympathetic educators about their inequitable schooling experience at Park and their feelings of racial marginalization at the school—or worse, those students will shut down and suffer their private school years in deafening and debilitating silence or inwardly focused rage.

■ ■ ■

I met Bodie Brizendine many years ago when she was head of the Bryn Mawr School in Baltimore. Immediately, I was struck by how integral issues of racial equity were to her ideas about and practices for effectively leading an independent school. Later, as Brizendine was preparing for her journey west and the head job at Marin Academy, an exclusive, private school nestled in the hills of the most affluent (and White) county in California, I sensed that our work might intersect in increasingly meaningful ways. Never did I realize that she and I were on the verge of what I believe to be some of the most exciting and courageous racial equity work occurring in independent schools today.

Like most of the educators I encounter, Brizendine easily convinced me of her sincere concern for the well-being of her students of color. She was also quite clear that her prospective institution (Marin Academy), predictably, was not working as well for its Black, Brown, and American Indian students as it was for its White students. And although Brizendine was determined to address this negative trend, one that she had observed elsewhere throughout her career, she was not yet equipped with the tools she would need to allow her to complete three subsequent tasks. Those tasks, I told her, would be essential to the success of her efforts to address racial disparities in her new school.

First of all, she—as the leader of her school in a position similar to that of a superintendent in a public school district or the president of a university or college—needed to articulate the racial equity challenge publicly to her entire school community and then commit, likewise publicly, to addressing it. Second, she needed to begin developing a vision for achieving racial equity at her school. That development would require her to gain a deeper understanding of and a language for talking about race with her core leadership team. Only then, I explained, could those leaders take on the third task or closely examine the racial challenges at Marin Academy and begin to surface and address the root causes for these issues and circumstances, many of which had persisted for decades. Immediately, I was able to help Brizendine with these first two tasks, but the third would require me to engage in more intensive, ongoing collaboration with her and with Marin Academy's leadership as well as provide training and development with the entire school community.

After identifying a number of leaders in her new cabinet who would be receptive to engaging with her in this controversial, high-stakes adaptive work, Brizendine boldly stated, as I had advised her to, that her courageous mandate for racial equity transformation was not a directive in the typical head-of-school fashion but rather a vision in which she hoped to enlist others in realizing. She convincingly explained that her bold vision was based on the Marin Academy community's obvious collective belief that such transformation was not only the right thing to do but also highly do-able.

With her school leadership "bought in" and committed to engaging in professional training and development around the issue, the final task for all of us—Brizendine, her leadership team, faculty, staff, students, parents, the board of trustees, PEG, and me—was to design an effective method and strategy for taking the racial equity conversation schoolwide. So I asked Brizendine's team: "Why do you believe children of color should attend Marin Academy?" It did not surprise me that so many of their initial responses signaled a type of *narcissistic altruism,* a phrase used by social worker Kim Anderson to describe the condescending belief held by some in the helping professions (e.g., teachers, doctors, social workers, etc.) that they and their actions alone are solely responsible for the rescue or salvation of others who, in their view, lack the agency to help themselves—in this case, poor children of color at exclusive, independent schools. As Anderson notes:

> Helping others is a good thing, but when our professional identity is built solely upon our good works and our personal identity is dependent upon them, we are at risk of narcissistic altruism. We believe that no one else can help or teach as well as we can: *No one else can understand this student as well as I can ... I have more experience with this type of client or this population ... I can handle this challenge because I'm tough.* The greatest risk of narcissistic altruism is recklessness. When we think we know it all, we are at greatest risk of not knowing what we don't know we don't know.[16]

This finding signaled that I needed to engage the group in conversations that would offer them multiple perspectives on their beliefs and behaviors. Many needed help to understand the price students and their families of color paid to attend their exclusive school and how the presence of students of color helped the White educators, students, and families at Marin Academy feel less exclusive and, perhaps, less racist.

Although Brizendine developed and led a mighty army of leaders for racial equity at her school, when she departed Marin Academy for The Spence School, a private, all-girls K–12 school in New York City, few of her reforms, nor many vestiges of our Courageous Conversations work, would survive the transition at the top. Unfortunately, Brizendine did not empower the Marin leadership to own and insist on the continuance of this essential work when she exited.

These are critical lessons learned that are now very much a part of Brizendine's modified approach at The Spence School. Her narrative at the end of this chapter offers readers keener insights into her thoughts, processes, and compelling outcomes achieved to date.

WHERE IS HIGHER EDUCATION? A CALL FOR SEAMLESS RACIAL EQUITY IN PREK–16 EDUCATION

If there is one question I am asked most often it is, "How did you get into this line of work?" My typical answer: "I have no idea!" In truth, I never envisioned myself starting a company to develop and deliver racial equity leadership training for educators. I never envisioned myself starting a company at all. Soon after I got over my childhood desire to be a veterinarian, I saw myself working in the media—perhaps writing for, producing, or appearing on television news shows.

As a communications major in college, I was intrigued by the workings of electronic media and enjoyed the numerous college-level courses, activities, and internships that exposed me to the inner workings of the television field. My first real job after graduation was as a general assistant in a large New York City advertising agency. There, I learned about corporate hierarchy and cronyism. Very much in denial about racism at the time, I believed that my Ivy League credentials, coupled with my well-honed skills in disarming people of power, would earn me a fast-track journey to an executive-level position.

What I experienced was an undeniable, spirit-dampening bout with racism that sent me back to the University of Pennsylvania, where I had already experienced undergraduate success, to serve as an admissions officer. My plan was to stay in that role for a couple of years or so until I figured out what I really wanted to do with my life. It was already clear to me, however, that my college education was going to have very little to do with the professional path I ultimately would choose to take.

Nonetheless, from my beautiful office in College Hall, I began to truly appreciate higher education administration. Traveling the United States in search of talented prospective students for Penn gave me a picture and understanding of secondary education that challenged my dormant racial consciousness and inner yearnings for social justice. Being educated in an elite private school and then progressing on to attend and graduate from an Ivy League university were cause enough for me to enter into a protracted period of structured blindness—forgetting what I once knew as a sixth grader in the Baltimore City Public Schools, forgetting the "root wisdom" of my beloved Nana Singleton and other members of my extended family and Baltimore neighborhood community and their warnings about life's pitfalls and the need to take personal responsibility for one's actions. Both Park and Penn taught and encouraged me to think of myself as an individual first and to never see the color of my skin as a factor of significance. In fact, I was tacitly rewarded for not aligning with other Black students at Penn. For example, when Black students protested the blatantly racist remarks made by a legal studies professor during my sophomore year, I stayed on the sidelines, refusing to get involved. Having learned to put conversations about race into the off-limits category at Park, coupled with there being only a handful of students of color in the entire school, enabled me to develop and solidify the color-blind ideology that I then believed was a prerequisite to my achieving later academic and career success.

Three years after returning to Penn, I was appointed director of western regional admissions. I also began to hear the voices of color on campus in a new way. A group of Black students made a request to the school's administration for support to launch a Black student newspaper. The administration initially answered with a definitive "No!" and a complete lack of support for the venture. It wanted to keep racial issues swept under the proverbial carpet. This refusal caused me to engage in a closer examination of the acceptable Whiteness of *The Daily Pennsylvanian,* the university-sanctioned student newspaper. It also awakened within me a dormant racial consciousness.

I subsequently became an adviser to *The Vision,* the independently conceived, directed, and supported Black student newspaper at Penn, and reopened my eyes to the pervasiveness and patterns of racial inequity on Penn's campus that had gone unaddressed, at least since (and probably long before) my days as a Penn student. I also reopened my eyes to the realities of racial resegregation in supposedly desegregated secondary education settings—realities I was confronted with firsthand while visiting hundreds of public high schools in California, Washington, Oregon, Arizona, Alaska, and Hawaii in search of talented students. Increasingly, my recruiting experiences made it clear to me that the nation's elementary and secondary education systems were perpetuating, if not creating, pervasive racial disparities in terms of opportunity and access to higher education for students of color.

For the few students of color who, uninvited by a teacher or counselor, made their way to my information sessions about Penn, even fewer had the requisite coursework, testing, and grades to withstand the school's competitive admissions process. I soon decided that my life's work ultimately would center on addressing those inequities, but I was unclear exactly how to go about getting on the path to achieve it.

When I enrolled in the Graduate School of Education at Stanford University, I missed a prime opportunity to supplement my education with a different type of personal and academic enrichment: I chose to engage the familiar, predominantly White institution of higher education rather than exploring the choice of a historically Black college or university—an HBCU. On entering Stanford, I thought I ultimately would become a university president, and that my chosen course of study in administration and policy analysis of higher education would equip me to convert that aspiration into reality. Instead, the lack of racial diversity in my faculty and graduate cohort, as well as my repeated interactions with racially unconscious undergraduate students as a teaching assistant, stirred my intensifying desire to address issues of racial inequity in preK–12 education as the best way of transforming higher education.

Today, I am less didactic in my thinking. Indeed, I am convinced that it is essential to work on both sides of the education equation to achieve the successes racial equity leaders seek. Discussions about whether it is more important to develop students earlier versus later in their formal education, or about which part of the education system is most racially damaging, only hide the fact that preK–12 and higher educators need to work together, from both ends of the system, to realize true racial equity systemwide.

Given that the bulk of my Courageous Conversations theory and practices are molded from my work in preK–12 public school systems, I first simply want to acknowledge that, with the exception of a few classes here and there on race and cultural studies, this segment of education has been noticeably absent from the racial equity dialogue. As in independent schools, substantive conversations about race tend to begin and end in the college or university admissions office or cultural center. This must change!

Alternately, there are three major reasons why higher education leaders cannot afford the luxury of their continued absence from courageous conversations about race and the pursuit of racial equity in preK–12 education. In the United States, for example, our nation not only depends on college graduates to lead in the established professions, it also expects us to represent progress in terms of intellectual curiosity and social consciousness as we embrace and pursue truth, liberty, and justice . . . presumably for *all!* Too often, however, the college or university's role in engaging students around challenges associated with race ends with first-year dorm assignments and optional social affiliations or with the generally relatively sparse offerings of elective coursework on the topic.

For many years as a university administrator, I witnessed students become enmeshed and embroiled in unresolved interracial conflict because the institution failed to offer them a safe, authentic, and meaningful way to dialogue and act cross-racially. Lacking such structures and guidance, students generally cluster themselves into racially segregated groups or refuse to expose themselves to racial beliefs, values, and cultures other than their own. The result is that the vast majority of college/university students end up graduating with racial dispositions remarkably similar to those they held upon matriculation. And beyond enrollment statistics, today's U.S. college campuses fail to reflect the kind of racial progress that will enable our nation to capitalize on its rich diversity and provide leadership for an increasingly multicultural, multiracial world.

The second reason higher education must engage in courageous conversations about race is because it is where the next generation of preK–12 and college/university teachers and administrators are trained. I have taught for the last 8 years in the Urban High School Leadership Program at San José State University. There, my colleagues and I have developed an equity-centered curriculum that functions in a sea of state requirements for administrative credentialing as well as those the university stipulates for the conferring of a master's degree. Students in our program engage in courageous conversations about race, learn the tenets of critical race theory, and practice systems thinking and adaptive leadership while engaging in culturally relevant teaching based on the Collaborative Action Research for Equity (CARE) model, which enables them to develop understanding and mastery of the principles of equity. Unfortunately, very few programs like ours exist elsewhere in California or around this nation. Thus, it is likely that our graduates will find themselves leading in schools where their pedagogical philosophies and practices are seen as foreign and may be dismissed by their peers and supervisors. The growing number of elementary and secondary alternative credentialing programs being created throughout the United States is a direct response to the ineffectiveness of schools and colleges of education when it comes to preparing candidates to be effective in today's racially diverse classrooms.

One such program in one of PEG's partnering districts, Pittsburgh Public Schools, not only offers apprentice teachers an opportunity to shadow effective teachers but begins their training with an introduction to the Courageous Conversations Protocol. The curriculum for this residency program, which was designed by effective Pittsburgh Public Schools educators, addresses precisely what beginning and veteran teachers describe as the key challenges they face in meeting the needs of under-served student of color populations. Although Pittsburgh schools had the foresight to recognize the challenge and mustered the resources to solicit a sizeable grant to fund such an innovative program, the vast majority of school districts continue to rely on higher education to train and prepare teachers and administrators to be effective in tomorrow's schools.

The third reason higher education must be present in courageous conversations about race at the preK–12 level is to help create a seamless transition and elevation of such dialogues for students moving from secondary to postsecondary studies. When high school teachers engage students in culturally relevant ways, changes in curriculum, assessment, and grading practices often are required. Many of these elements do not "line up" with the current forms of college admissions evaluation and course determinations. This lack of alignment could demand a departure from traditional course titles or a switch from advanced-status demarcations, currently determined by number of seat hours (Carnegie units) and letter grades, to performance- or narrative-based assessments. It can also severely alter which students appear on paper as competitive or even college-ready.

Too often, secondary schools feel the weight of traditional college admissions much like an albatross around their neck. This burden often makes it virtually impossible for them to set into action critical reforms. Parents of college-bound students will often demand that school boards not change their schools' curriculum or assessment requirements or grading practices, so as not to jeopardize their children's higher education admission opportunities. Rarely, however, are these politically charged debates about articulation with higher education focused on what is best for student learning. Rather, most are about what "requests from below" the university or college community will or will not accept.

■ ■ ■

Before we racial equity leaders in the United States can even speak about moving Courageous Conversations from theory to practice in our nation's system of higher education, we must first engage in the most basic conversations about the impact of race on postsecondary education. I have initiated this dialogue many times during the span of my career, not gaining to date the level or scope of buy-in necessary to sustain and deepen those conversations, much less prompt, antiracist responses to obviously racist higher education policies, programs, and practices. In my work with administrators and faculty members at both 2- and 4-year colleges as well as graduate and professional schools, I have found that many acknowledge the relevance of the Courageous Conversations paradigm and perhaps the need for a systemic framework for addressing institutional racial biases, but few commit to action on this issue.

In my experience, the primary excuses for not investing in systemic racial equity transformation include concerns over a faculty's loss of academic freedom or about the need to develop personal responsibility within students, as well as budgetary shortfalls and professional development time constraints. Even for institutions whose progress in attracting, retaining, and graduating growing populations of students of color has stalled—or worse, declined—such excuses prevail. For preK–12 systems to institutionalize a culture and climate that embraces racial equity transformation, higher education must be at the table, exercising the kind of leadership that enables and encourages elementary and secondary school teachers, administrators, students, and parents to recognize the importance of such transformation.

To realize this optimum condition, preK–12 leaders can begin by inviting their local college/university leaders to come back into their classrooms—to observe and participate in the work as it unfolds in district offices and school buildings. Teachers who are working with pre-service teachers can help to equip those novices with the will, skill, knowledge, and capacity to be successful in making racial equity a cornerstone of their student teaching and later practice. They can also send those student teachers back to their postsecondary institutions with racial equity questions and resources for the faculty in their schools or colleges of education. Finally, preK–12 counseling staff should interact with visiting university admissions personnel to inform the latter of the important racial equity reforms that are under way in their schools. Additional conversations are necessary between preK–12 counselors and administrators at educational curriculum and assessment organizations such as The College Board and International Baccalaureate. These entities often participate in the stifling of a school system's efforts to depart from racially stratifying programming, and if uninterrupted, they may encourage higher education administrators to maintain and expand their racially biased admissions policies and practices.

ESSENTIAL QUESTIONS

Chapter 7 explores the notion of systemic racial equity transformation, encouraging school leaders to move away from "random acts of equity."

1. How might you assist your school system and your institution of higher education to partner as a way of fostering a more seamless K–16 equity experience for your students?

2. What challenges do you anticipate emerging as you begin initiating such collaboration?

3. What opportunities exist through collaboration for K–12 and higher education, in terms of improving the educational experience and outcomes for underrepresented student of color populations?

4. In what ways might public and independent school educators collaborate to accelerate and fortify racial equity efforts and deepen the impact on student achievement?

Voices From the Inside: Bodie Brizendine

When I was head at Marin Academy, Cornell West came to speak, and he had a phrase he used that captures not only my transformative work with Glenn but also what I take to be perhaps my single most important charge in my work as an educator. Dr. West said that one "should be prepared to enter the conversation and to be prepared to be changed by it." Both at Marin Academy and now at The Spence School, this call—this call to engage and to be changed—captures best the spirit of our work with Courageous Conversations.

Glenn and I have known each other for a very long time, and my professional life has been immeasurably shaped by our work together. As a White woman working exclusively in independent schools, my perspective, far from expansive, remains subject to the confines of the single story, and my White privilege can always be counted on to confuse limitation with success. Before my work with Glenn, diversity work in my schools meant workshops, long-range plan initiatives, statistics, budgets, and diversity directors: all tools that make a difference, indeed, but also all tools that ultimately fall short.

When we began to work with Glenn, we shifted from one-time (or even several) workshops and from directors of diversity to substantial change in the way in which we engage. We began to change not only the conversation, but also the culture. Beginning with the senior leadership team, Glenn worked with us individually over a period of almost 3 years so that every senior administrator increased capacity and skill in conversations about race and ethnicity. As teams composed mostly of White educators, our work set both the example and the expectation that our mostly White schools would engage in the same manner. In other words, we learned how to lead by example, and we moved from not engaging in conversations about race to "being changed by" the ones we helped to lead: big difference.

Our work continues and deepens at The Spence School, and as we get ready to embark on working with all adults at our school, the administrative team and faculty members who have participated in Beyond Diversity training will lead the way. The structures for both faculty and students are in place for ongoing conversations and learning, which stretch far beyond any definition of workshop and far beyond the leadership of any single head of school. And that has made all the difference.

As my personal and professional work with Courageous Conversations continues, I have made several observations about diversity work in independent schools or, at the very least, about those independent schools in which I have been lucky enough to work and lead. Suffice to say that these patterns I list below all hold hands with good intentions made by mostly White independent schools. I've never met a school that didn't want to do the right thing, but stubborn practices and limited perspective continue to hold us hostage.

- There are no romantic rescues in this work. It is not about saving or accommodating the "other;" it is about cultural change. It will get messy; it will get "local"; and it will take time, consistent commitment, and continued resources. There is no quick fix, no single answer, and no check-off closure.
- You have to know why you are doing this work, and you must be able to say, write, and articulate why all the time and in all places. Your narrative has to be spot on.
- When you talk about race, you are not talking about class. As with everything else, there are nexus points that are shared when one begins talking about perspective and being changed by that discussion. But White people in mostly White schools often have a default mode of diverting a focus on race to one about class. When this happens, however, you ultimately don't talk about race.
- This is not about eliminating a school's history or what came before. It is not about removing the august portraits of White founders from the halls or the historic wallpaper depicting joyful Native Americans. It is quite the contrary. Covering up, removing vestiges, and restricting access will not make the right kind of difference. It is about owning, even respecting, those parts of our history collectively and realizing the limitation of the single story for all of our students as we move forward.
- One person, one director, one coordinator cannot do this work in a single school, no matter its size. There are some tremendous educators out there with empowering and legitimate titles who have done some fantastic work in independent schools, but unless the structures, and I mean all of the structures, have this work as part of their responsibility, the work toward diversity will be marginalized or person-dependent. It will not be lasting; it will not be integrated into the normal, every-day life of the school, no matter how much authority is given to a single position.
- This work is for every student and every educator in the school. It is not about "making it OK for students, staff, and faculty of color." It is about educating all of our students for the scholastic life they will continue to lead. It is profoundly about being prepared to be that lifelong learner we talk so much about in independent schools.

Let me close with a salute to Glenn—my friend, my colleague, and my teacher. Thank you, Glenn, for working with us so carefully and so determinedly. When I think of the students leaving our schools better prepared "to enter the conversation and to be changed by it," I think of you and your legacy.

Thank you.

Bodie Brizendine currently serves as the head of the Spence School, located in New York City. She is a White American.

Voices From the Inside: Akemi Matsumoto

I attended [the Beyond Diversity workshop] last year, mainly curious to see for myself what members of President's staff had characterized as "powerful" and "personally transforming." I was unprepared for what I found. We embarked on a thoughtful, compassionate, and unthreatening exploration of racism and the ways—hidden and overt—it is [manifested] in our daily lives. I saw glimpses of a world in which people I care about live that is very different from the world I know and experience on a daily basis. I was able to understand the cumulative impacts of these experiences and how they affect interpersonal communication and student learning. It wasn't just talking and thinking about issues of race; it was experiencing them in a small way. And, yes, it was transformational. (Jean Floten, from the president's invitation for the Beyond Diversity workshop)

Courageous Conversations on Race, Racism, and Whiteness was first created as a safe place for Bellevue Community College[17] employees to dialogue and learn across race. The 5 years of continuous weekly courageous conversations at the college became the bedrock of our Pluralism Initiative and built a network of employees who passionately engaged in the process of transforming Bellevue into an antiracist pluralistic institution with positive results for students and employees.

Bellevue wanted to explore ways to become more pluralistic and inclusive to students and employees of color, inclusion being a core value of the college. Glenn Singleton was engaged to help us increase racial awareness, train Courageous Conversations facilitators, and assess our progress as an institution. The main vehicle Singleton used to engage the community was the Pacific Educational Group's two-day Beyond Diversity workshop. The workshop increased awareness about the depth of racism in our society, communities, and colleges and built a commitment among participants to continue their personal learning after the workshop by attending ongoing, weekly courageous conversations. A testimonial from one participant demonstrates this growth:

I too am a race. Did I achieve what I've achieved because I am hard-working and intelligent or primarily due to my race? I thought that acting "colorblind" was the best answer to racism; now I know that only worked because I was unaware that our social system works for me. I didn't think about race because I don't have to.

A total of 244 employees from every employee group, every department, and every race across the campus participated in the workshops. Seventy-five of the 244 participants (31%) subsequently participated in courageous conversations. In addition to deepening racial relationships, Courageous Conversations generated a foundational network of employees who actively and passionately worked to help the college reach its pluralism goals and objectives. The organizational chart (attached at the end of this article) of the Pluralism Initiative of the college demonstrates the comprehensiveness of our organizational transformation efforts. Before Glenn's interventions, these pluralism efforts were mainly driven by the employees of color with a few White allies. Courageous Conversations broadened the base of this initiative and became the fuel for our Pluralism Initiative.

Since the first Beyond Diversity workshop, 30 Bellevue Community College employees became facilitators. These facilitators then became the employees who volunteered their personal time to co-leading the weekly courageous conversations. Four to eleven ongoing courageous conversations were scheduled each week, every quarter.

To include students in Courageous Conversations, the Human Development Department offered a two-credit course, Race in America, to prepare students for the cross-race dialogue. The courageous conversations for students welcomed any student who had taken a class about race. Students from Interdisciplinary Studies, English, Sociology, Speech, and Ethnic and Cultural Studies courses participated. Students fully engaged; two even became Courageous Conversations facilitators themselves. Students and employees held separate conversations until employees requested permission to attend conversations with students. We also maintained some courageous conversations for employees only.

During the fifth year, the college trained 18 Beyond Diversity workshop trainers to offer an 8-hour workshop for all new employees every quarter. The trainers did additional workshops for college departments or community groups by request.

The Courageous Conversations facilitators and trainers not only worked on the Pluralism Initiative of the college, but also carried their racial justice learning to the broader Bellevue community. They were facilitators at some Bellevue City Dialogues on Race and at the Bellevue Multicultural Fair dialogues on religion. Three of them led a workshop on Courageous Conversations at Odle Middle School for teachers and parents. Others discussed race on the college radio station (KBCC), and still others shared their institutional experiences with Sacramento City College. The trainers also did a Courageous Conversations workshop for the Diversity Committee of St. Martin's College in Lacey, Washington, and the Bellevue Community College experience.

Courageous Conversations has renewed, inspired, and educated a group of Bellevue college employees, and their passion is found in the five pluralism committees on campus: the Community, Student, Employee, and Instructional pluralism committees and the Diversity Caucus. Student government now has a Pluralism Advocate, and our course offerings expanded to include not only racial justice courses, but also courses about sexism, homophobia, classism, and ableism.

As a person of color participating in the Beyond Diversity workshop and more importantly, in the ongoing Courageous Conversations [groups], I found comfort and energy in the support of other people of color and White allies at the college. I saw people of color at the college blossom and reengage with White colleagues. I saw and felt hope for systemic change. We met a lot of resistance and it wasn't easy; but we kept doing the work.

The Bellevue college community learned many lessons on its journey as an institution trying to sustain race as a central topic. Some of these are:

1. High-level sponsorship was essential to sustain the program. In our case, sponsorship was top-down from the president and vice president of human resources as well as bottom-up from the students and employees who were curious and eager to engage deeply with each other about race. This combination of support worked for the college.

2. Agreement on the structure, organization, and accountabilities of the Courageous Conversations program ensured a shared vision of success and how that success would be measured.

3. The Beyond Diversity workshop should have been mandatory for every new employee, to create a common vocabulary and a common ethos of recognizing racial difference as a means to ending institutional racism at the college.

4. A standing committee structure was necessary to support the Beyond Diversity and Courageous Conversation work in order to capture the energy and enthusiasm of staff to reach pluralism goals in three critical areas:
   a. *Students* (measures include diversity of students, teaching them cultural competence, and educational gap closure)
   b. *Employees* (measures include workforce diversity, cultural competence in serving students, and inclusive work environment and opportunity for continuing education)
   c. *Curricula* (measures include availability of multiple courses that address race, racism, pluralism, and cultural competence as well as other barriers to inclusion)

5. Courageous Conversations prompts (discussion topics for each week on a central topic) were necessary to keep the weekly conversations meaningful and focused. This also helped people who attended different conversations to have a central topic to discuss outside of the Courageous Conversations events.

6. Bellevue Community College briefly created a White Allies Courageous Conversations by request of those who felt they had common needs. It was controversial among employees of color because of its exclusiveness. The group stopped meeting after only a few quarters.

7. The separations between faculty, administrators, and staff were bridged in these courageous conversations by establishing the ground rule of leaving work identity behind when one stepped into these events.

8. Since the program dealt with interpersonal trust and deep interaction, safety valves needed to be in place to attend to the interpersonal process, to ensure trustworthy behaviors, and to resolve conflicts constructively. "Safety" included facilitator training and evaluation and established protocols for group dynamics.

9. Dedicated engagement of a full-time employee who has a strong background in counseling and race and culture was essential to provide ongoing direction and guidance for the program. This person also planned Beyond Diversity workshops, scheduled weekly Courageous Conversations events each quarter, and had regular training sessions for the training cadre and the Courageous Conversations facilitators. She also provided skilled conflict management.

10. The most difficult group to recruit for Beyond Diversity workshops was White male faculty members. Recruitment included one-on-one and White-to-White outreach, but these efforts were not very successful. Their participation rates were much lower than any other employee group. At the same time, there were many White male allies in the Pluralism Initiative.

Confronting racism is work of the heart. It pulls out hope and human aspiration for justice. It motivates commitment to change unjust barriers. It is truly courageous work.

Akemi Matsumoto was the Courageous Conversations coordinator and human development faculty member at Bellevue Community College in Bellevue, Washington. She is an Asian American.

EIGHT

Leadership for Racial Equity

From Theory to Practice

> *To act is to be committed, and to be committed is to be in danger.*
>
> —James Baldwin[1]

As a fifth-grader at Hilton Elementary School in Baltimore, I remember the tension I felt deep in the pit of my stomach whenever a friend or I was sent to the principal's office for misbehaving in the classroom or on the playground. Mrs. Emma Bright, the principal, carried herself with a no-nonsense flair. She commanded respect, and a bit of fear, from students and teachers alike. She was our leader, and we all marched to the beat of her drum.

Aside from my Nana, Mrs. Bright was the most powerful and influential person in the world, as I saw it then. It wasn't until later in my professional life that I learned that schools were led by superintendents and governed by boards of education, not by principals. But as a kid in elementary school, I had no idea what all those other district leaders did all day, particularly with a woman like Emma Bright in charge.

Today, I understand quite clearly the enormous roles both superintendents and school boards play. I still believe, however, that the effective principal does the heaviest lifting at the school-building level and is thus the determining factor in whether equity theory is converted into practices that transform teachers, who in turn influence student learning. Like Mrs. Bright, principals—when they are true, on-site (school-building) racial equity leaders—must be able to attract, hire, develop, and support teachers who share their vision for racial equity and commit to achieving it. It is also the principal's job to buffer highly qualified teachers from the district minutiae that are certain to interfere with racial equity work in particular and effective instruction in general. Principals' leadership notwithstanding, achieving equity and excellence in schools requires leaders at *every* level to commit to their own personal transformation before attempting to engage others in the difficult process of uncovering, examining, and eradicating racism at the personal, professional, and organizational levels.

In this chapter, I will revisit one of the most important understandings I have gained and developed over the years about the process of achieving racial equity in schools, and that is the essential role of purposed, passionate, and skillful leadership. In my first book, I talked about an equity-centered principal, Yvette Irving, who not only had the will to eradicate racial disparities at Del Roble Elementary School in San José, California, but also crafted and executed a plan that transported her, her staff, and her students to that vision. You've met other principals in this book. This chapter is focused on providing detail about how other key leaders for racial equity—namely, school board members, superintendents, independent school heads, university presidents, and executive teams—must participate in holding a place and setting the stage for systemwide equity and excellence. Their efforts, in turn, ensure that courageous principals are nurtured, supported, and rewarded for doing all that heavy lifting.

From the outset, I want to be clear in stating that no matter how courageous and skilled a principal may be—or, for that matter, an entire district administrative team of principals—achieving equity is a systemwide matter. It must be envisioned and led, competently and enthusiastically, by the superintendent and his or her executive cabinet. Without this centralized and prioritized leadership from the top down, the "random acts of equity" and pockets of excellence that I described in Chapter 7 will be the result, especially in schools led by equity-focused and -centered principals.

■ ■ ■

I often wonder why all districts with racial achievement disparities do not engage in a robust, prioritized equity and excellence strategy. What is it that gets in the way of superintendents and boards taking the Courageous Conversations approach or, more important, moving Courageous Conversations from theory to practice? One answer might be that talking about race as a behavioral trait runs counter to how many White people are socialized, thus the logic of having courageous conversations about race would seem to run counter to the prevailing beliefs. As I noted in the *Courageous Conversations* field guide, the public school superintendency continues to be the most White- and male-dominated aspect of our entire national education system. Given this race- and gender-lopsided leadership scenario and because leaders typically enjoy working from their existing skills sets and strong suits, it is easy to see that the tools for challenging racism typically would not be a part of the existing superintendents' arsenal of problem-solving skills. Moreover, developing those skills probably is not thought of as an activity that might elevate superintendents' self-efficacy or competence.

Our understandings of adaptive leadership and systems thinking illuminate several reasons why leaders with authority fail to tackle thorny issues like systemic racism. For one, too often the public rewards school leaders for finding quick, technical solutions to education challenges. Rarely do we invite those leaders to invest time and energy in transforming their systems into learning organizations that are capable of examining the problematic beliefs and behaviors that hold change captive. The lack of congruence between our desire for change and our willingness to equip and require leaders to enhance their racial equity will, skill, knowledge, and capacity is also at the heart of this challenge. Simply put, school leaders often do not know enough to care appropriately about why so many children of color are under-served in our various systems of education or they are not encouraged or courageous enough to learn what they need to know—and *do*—to ensure racial equity.

Another reason for the relative lack of commitment to racial equity programming at the highest levels of school system authority is that many district leaders are not familiar with the Courageous Conversations Protocol as a tool for talking about race, nor is the Pacific Educational Group (PEG) Systemic Racial Equity Framework part of their knowledge base. Because *they don't know what they don't know,* they cannot examine the merits of the Framework's theory of transformation or gauge the appropriateness of implementing Courageous Conversations in their systems.

Among the leaders who are familiar with PEG's work, some have chosen to embrace the Courageous Conversations Protocol, and some have not. Those who fall into the latter category most likely are not reading this book. But perhaps you, as one of their subordinates, are. Thus, the enormous job of getting your supervisor to shift his or her beliefs about the importance of confronting race directly falls on your shoulders. To you, I suggest that you encourage your superintendent to engage in one-on-one or, perhaps more broadly, an executive team book study of the *Courageous Conversations* field guide. A nonthreatening, strategic introduction to the Courageous Conversations philosophy and Courageous Conversations Protocol as well as the PEG Framework might unlock some entrenched leadership blocks and barriers.

In the meantime, the understandings you can gain from this second *Courageous Conversations* book can help you personally to develop, support, and maintain whatever random acts of equity and pockets of excellence exist within your school or school system. Simultaneously, because systemic racial equity transformation demands top-down leadership, I encourage you to petition your district leadership for a systemwide vision of and commitment to racial equity. For those of you who work in systems that are currently implementing the Courageous Conversations Protocol and perhaps the PEG Framework, ask yourself these questions: To what degree is my district's engagement truly systemic? Does my superintendent have clear and obvious proficiency in the Courageous Conversations Protocol? Does his or her administrative team, including all site and central office leaders, feel invited and supported in (and are they evaluated for) their own emerging and applied leadership for racial equity? Last, do their efforts to further the envisioned transformation elevate them, personally, professionally, and organizationally?

EQUITY DEVELOPMENT FOR SCHOOL BOARDS

A number of school superintendents have telephoned my office asking for advice on how to get their school boards "on board" with their implementations of the Courageous Conversations Protocol so that together they can begin engaging site and central office leadership in more comprehensive racial equity professional development. As I will discuss later (in Chapter 10), lay boards, in my experience, typically lack the requisite level of understanding about the intersection of race and schooling to make qualified decisions about the importance of districtwide engagement in racial equity programming and development. But because school boards typically approve district expenditures for large-scale improvements, superintendents first must convince board members about the importance of racial equity work before this essential training can take place.

The controversy surrounding this work certainly does not help equity-centered superintendents gain school board members' confidence. The fact that this controversy is almost exclusively generated by White parents, educators, policymakers, and other community stakeholders, most of whom have never personally engaged in racial equity work, presents another significant challenge. The amount of blogging about the issue on the Internet is also considerable, even though most of this chatter, upon closer scrutiny, simply amounts to unsubstantiated personal attacks on the proponents of racial equity work and "fringe" or lunatic expressions.

What does help is the abundance of data, disaggregated by race, that is available to superintendents to illustrate the problem, including data on racial disparities in educational achievement, by district and nationwide. Such data also clearly demonstrate the fact that existing programmatic interventions have proved to be insufficient to address systemic racial disparities in achievement, discipline, special education and gifted/talented placements, and graduation and dropout rates. Racial equity leaders must arm themselves with a constant, current, complete, and irrefutable storehouse of data that clearly and concisely illustrates the racial equity challenge.

Using data and language that board members can understand (like *achievement gap*), a superintendent may be able to obtain board buy-in for racial equity programming with less-than-ideal understanding of the programmatic concepts and ideas involved. Once the board is thus engaged, however, the superintendent should immediately schedule racial equity training for those very board members so that their will, skill, knowledge, and capacity to have courageous conversations about race can be strengthened. Only then can this governing body develop and ratify the essential racial equity policies that must follow to hold the district accountable for achieving its vision of equity and excellence and thereby meeting the needs of *all* students.

DISTRICT EQUITY LEADERSHIP TEAMS (DELT AND DELTA)

The superintendent who is impassioned and purposeful about achieving racial equity must also be effective in transferring his or her vision to the executive leadership teams whose job it is to supervise the execution of racial equity programming and practices throughout the system. According to PEG's Systemic Racial Equity Framework and its theory of transformation, the superintendent—using an unapologetic, top-down approach—guides his or her executive team in determining the depth, breadth, and velocity at which equity programming occurs.

To move Courageous Conversations from theory to practice, district superintendents have five primary roles.

1. They must serve as the primary keepers of and voices for their districts' racial equity vision. They must also be recognized as being highly advanced themselves in executing racial equity practices.

2. They must assist in the professional development of their boards of education, transforming them into bodies that can effectively oversee the ratification and execution of sound racial equity policy.

3. They must spearhead the transformation of their executive team into a District Equity Leadership Team (DELT) charged with developing, monitoring, and assessing the districts' movement toward equity. As a prerequisite, DELT members also must receive professional development to help them uncover, examine, and address the ways in which race influences their own personal, professional, and organizational beliefs and behaviors. An effective DELT engages in its own development and that of key site and central office leaders, and members also craft, execute, monitor, and evaluate their districts' equity transformation framework.

4. Superintendents must lead their DELT to establish a professional learning community ethos for site administrators and central office directors in which all are expected to develop their individual and collective will, skill, knowledge, and capacity to lead their schools and divisions toward embracing a culture and climate of equity and excellence.

5. After the racial equity work is under way at the district level, superintendents must create a multiconstituency team who can offer honest feedback on the nature and impact of the equity work systemwide. This group, known as District Equity Leadership Team Advisory (DELTA), should be made up of people who are uniquely determined and situated to understand and speak to how the equity work is being experienced "on the ground." These constituencies include, but may not be limited to, principals, department managers, teachers, parents, students, and community-based organization leaders. Superintendents must also ensure that the DELTA is well supported and that its members feel empowered to have courageous conversations about race at the system's highest levels.

SITE AND CENTRAL-OFFICE DEPARTMENT LEADERS ENGAGED IN EQUITY/ ANTIRACISM DEVELOPMENT (LEADs)

With superintendents thus focused on achieving systemic equity and excellence, the key leaders at the school sites and in central office departments are challenged to embed the Courageous Conversations principles and Protocol deep into the culture and climate of their schools and departments, and therefore into the beliefs and behaviors of teachers as well as operational and instructional support staff. Genuine reform—reform that is significant and sustainable—occurs only once the vast majority of classroom teachers and other school site personnel challenge their harmful assumptions about the abilities and potential of under-served students of color, those students' families, and their community support systems.

Principals and central office department managers play a huge role in guiding this transformation of beliefs and behaviors. Their task is to create the safe environments in which educators feel encouraged and expected to grow and change. For this difficult work truly to take hold, systems must develop a culture of trust and openness. This is especially important when leaders will be presented, as they most likely will as a result of racial equity efforts, with tough decisions to make about personnel issues, professional challenges, and organizational "non-discussables." If leaders are not accustomed to collaboration, data-based decision-making, or inquiry-based learning and development, addressing systemic racism will prove virtually impossible.

Superintendents must work to empower DELT members to own and actualize their districts' vision of equity and excellence in ways that outlive their leadership. Similarly, principals and directors must infuse their passion for equity into their school-site or department staffs. Given these challenges, racial equity leadership professional development activities must help principals and central-office managers not only to embody a commitment to racial equity and excellence but also to "spread the good news" about racial equity efforts generally and specifically.

Mere compliance will not suffice if achieving racial equity is the ultimate goal, nor will leading by intimidation help to engage school site and central office staff in equity work and practice. At best, it will result in compliant people who will do only what is asked of them and no more. Equity-focused development activities must also provide both leaders and those whom they lead with sufficient practice and feedback on their equity thinking and actions.

The following outline should provide insights into the topics school-site and central office leaders have found useful as they develop their transformative racial equity plans.

PEG (PACIFIC EDUCATIONAL GROUP) EQUITY SEMINAR CURRICULUM SAMPLE TOPICS

- What will it take? A professional development strategy for addressing racial achievement disparity
- Introduction to the Courageous Conversations Protocol
- Mindfulness: Listening, inquiring, and responding
- Understanding critical race theory and schooling
- Systems thinking and organizational learning
- Principles of adaptive leadership for racial equity
- Positive deviance approach: Examining our professional learning community
- Key Factors in the Development of Culturally Relevant Teaching
- Collaborative Action Research for Equity (CARE) Introduction: CARE Team Roles and Responsibilities
- Exploring the Levels of Family Interaction: Involvement, Engagement, Empowerment
- Partnerships for Academically Successful Students (PASS) Introduction: PASS Team Role and Responsibilities; PASS Guiding Principles and Implementation Phases
- Leading the Process of Change
- Characteristics of an Antiracist Leader

EQUITY TEAMS

When principals and central office managers have developed the requisite will, skill, knowledge, and capacity to hold a systemwide vision for racial equity and are able to lead others into understanding and action toward this goal, racial equity efforts can rise to the third level: that of planned and purposeful distribution of leadership and authority. At that level, principals and central-office managers are guided in how to select a team of teachers or operational support staff to help lead, under their supervision, the dissemination of their vision, will, skill, knowledge, and capacity school- or departmentwide.

This is where the Courageous Conversations Equity Team (E-team) comes into play. E-teams truly are the engine of transformation for moving Courageous Conversations from theory to practice, with the school-site principals or central-office managers being the conductors. Given that educators at all levels tend to learn a great deal from those who function in the same or similar roles, E-teams should include a broad sampling of site or central-office department leaders of diverse races, genders, roles, and seniority and disposition levels. Given the system's propensity to marginalize or isolate certain departments such as Special Education and English Language Development, leaders should always strive to put these educators on the E-team. Such teams can facilitate role-alike, job-embedded courageous conversations about race more readily and effectively, in a way that guarantees relevancy and engenders trust and credibility. Once properly selected, however, they must guard against trying to "fix" other school personnel or find "quick-fix" solutions. Instead, they should dedicate their time and attention to internalizing the Courageous Conversations Protocol among themselves and to assessing the key ways in which racism affects each E-team member personally and professionally. By growing collectively in their ability to uncover, examine, and address racism, E-teams can begin planning and executing professional learning and development experiences for themselves and their colleagues that can have a meaningful impact on the larger organization—that is, the school.

Although students' educational improvement and success hang in the balance and the need to demonstrate a sense of urgency in their efforts to advance equity transformation is great, E-teams should also avoid attempting to carry out racial equity actions in a vacuum or prematurely. Their school-site or central-office colleagues might suffer from such incompletely framed actions, and the avoidable blunders of a passionate yet unskilled E-team member might become ammunition to challenge equity work as a whole.

Several factors help explain why the E-teams created in different PEG partnering districts have moved at different speeds and sometimes in different directions. First, principals and central-office managers have tremendous influence over who is selected to serve on each E-team. Quite often, E-team membership is a reflection of these leaders' racial equity will and skill. If a principal or central-office manager is challenged to gain staff confidence and collaboration around nonequity aspects of their school or department vision, this lack of staff support will become even more evident when it comes to leading for racial equity.

Second, educators are themselves quite unique as far as their commitment to racial equity and their skill to lead in racial equity work. Potential team members come with varied levels of will, skill, knowledge, and capacity to uncover, understand, examine, and address issues of race in their own lives and in the lives of others. When members collectively demonstrate a high level of passion for this kind of work, their teams tend to move faster.

A third reason E-teams across PEG's partnering districts struggle to maintain a unifying pace is that school cultures, climates, challenges, and strengths relative to addressing and eliminating racial disparities vary significantly. After a certain level of professional development, the teams are charged with supporting their school or department colleagues in embracing and advancing a vision of equity. This responsibility can be quite challenging, even for skilled E-teams when a high proportion of educators resist or struggle to understand the importance of racial equity. In such cases, PEG's work is slowed. Conversely, when an E-team's work, and the goal of racial equity generally, are embraced universally by that team's colleagues, the pace of its efforts is quicker, and the deeper meaning of equity is realized.

THE BEACON PROJECT

Among the more successful E-teams are those working with principals who are also quite motivated to move Courageous Conversations from theory to practice rapidly. For such schools, PEG designed the Beacon Project as a means of accelerating equity transformation and providing tangible markers and models for other schools in those schools' districts.

Principals self-select their schools into the accelerated Beacon Project process by committing to prioritize racial equity work above all other reform efforts in their schools. Beacon Project E-teams receive intensive equity seminars and immediate, direct coaching support so that each member can begin focusing on realizing his or her personal and professional racial equity leadership transformation. Later in the process, these E-team members are led to create and execute a collectively generated plan for institutional or organizational change. Beacon Project site principals share their racial equity learning and work-in-progress with their fellow principals via administrative team meetings; they also sometimes participate in designing and leading racial equity professional development exercises for other district leaders.

Launching a Beacon Project within the broader framework of school-site and central-office racial equity leadership development is one way of ensuring that systemic progress on this front does not suffer from the predictable gradualism and incremental change that has delayed the arrival of quality education for all children in this country. Beacon Projects also provide opportunities for school systems to develop their internal capacities for leading equity transformation more quickly by offering accelerated schools earlier access to the resources and supports they need to convert racial equity theory into practice and providing mechanisms for sharing the results of those practices with others in their schools and districts in advance of overall system change.

STAFF OF COLOR EQUITY DEVELOPMENT

Even more essential than the need (discussed in Chapter 6) to support school staff and administrators of color in racial equity leadership development is the need to include educators of color in the systemic racial equity transformation process. In most instances, these educators require specialized and supplemental professional development and encouragement to "stay the course" in that process. This is so for several reasons.

First, much of the existing racial equity leadership literature targets and is geared toward White educators and blatantly lacks any focus on the needs and perspectives of educators of color. Why? Because White educators typically hold the vast majority of leadership roles in schools and districts across the country and because they typically have the most work to do to divest themselves of color-blind perspectives and embrace the color consciousness that fosters true racial equity. The process of developing this consciousness, and the courage to act on it, proceeds along distinctively different trajectories for White school leaders and school leaders of color. Thus, while many White educators typically resist or struggle with the process of racial self-discovery and require more time to grasp the concept of color consciousness, many educators of color "get" those processes immediately and are eager to engage in them.

Requiring educators of color to participate in their White colleagues' racial consciousness development can be exhausting for them, can damage their emotional and physical health and well-being, and also wastes time. As Janet Helms[2] contends in her discussions about the six stages of White identity development, many White people experience periods of guilt or shame as they move from color blindness to color consciousness. This reaction often is prompted by the disintegration or shattering of their perceptions of Whiteness as a race-neutral existence. As White educators delve more deeply into how White skin color privilege plays out in their personal lives and in society, and as they learn how that privilege contributes to the oppression of people of color, they are likely to experience anger, consciously or unconsciously, which they may unload or project toward their unsuspecting non-White peers.

Thus, in PEG's Staff of Color Equity Development Training, non-White educators are shown how to recognize and address the racial identity dynamics at work among their White colleagues, even if those efforts seem painful and cause temporary stress. They also come to understand these signs as an indication of growth and progress.

Educators of color also deserve and require specialized support for racial equity leadership development because White staff members often perceive courageous conversations about race as more threatening, and thus less effective, when they are initiated or led by people of color. For example, when I speak my own racial truths as a Black man in my seminars (or even in conversations with my White friends and professional associates)—which I try to do as gently and nonthreateningly as I can—I am often perceived as "attacking" White people in general or as causing them to feel fearful. Apparently, my racial reality (and I suppose that of many other Black people as well) shatters one of the dominant myths of Whiteness: that we Americans exist in a post-racial, color-blind society. Staff of Color Equity Development Training shows educators of color how to navigate these predictable situations without sacrificing their integrity and how to enhance the quality of their own engagement in courageous conversations about race as well as that of their White counterparts.

School districts that partner with PEG must also commit to advancing educators of color to higher levels of positional and decision-making authority, and racial equity work is often a good way to begin that process. Most White Americans live their entire lifetimes in a habit of mind that Joyce E. King[3] calls *racial dysconsciousness* or a skewed, uncritical awareness about race, particularly about their own Whiteness. African Americans, on the other hand, often become conscious of their own and others' racial identities at an early age. According to William Cross's theory of Black identity development,[4] this process, for most Black people, begins within the first 3 years of life. Thus, an educator's depth of experience in addressing racial consciousness issues can serve as a determining factor in identifying who is best suited to lead a school system toward a vision of racial equity.

Racial consciousness alone, however, is an insufficient criterion for leadership in this regard. Educators of color must demonstrate a thorough understanding of how to effectively engage and lead White educators in racial equity work. They must also be equipped with the proper tools and demeanor to challenge and support other educators of color, who often have struggled with their own racial identities and/or have been socialized to adopt the color-blind, race-neutral perspectives of the dominant (White) society in which they live and work.

Intentionally and effectively dedicating resources to develop racial equity-focused educators of color as leaders assures that PEG partnering districts will improve in their ability to attract, maintain, and promote people of color. It also goes a long way toward advancing a system in which the adult population of professionals truly represents and reflects the rapidly changing student racial demographics.

STUDENTS ORGANIZED FOR ANTI-RACISM (SOAR)

A year after I launched my Beyond Diversity seminars in the San Francisco Bay Area, Diana Levy, then principal at an alternative high school in nearby Castro Valley, contacted me with a special request. She wanted to enroll several of her students in the 2-day training. Although I was somewhat skeptical about putting students in the same room with adult educators, who often struggled through their personal racial histories and baggage, I never doubted students' ability to understand and engage with the training's content or processes. I wondered, however, if the mere presence of students would give the adults reason to be silent or, worse, to relate to the students in inauthentic and even patronizing ways. Diana's confidence in her students' ability to hold their own led me to table my concerns and approve her request. The training that followed signaled the beginning of my developing philosophy about how to engage students as leaders for racial equity in their schools.

By paying especially close attention to Diana's students and many groups of middle and high school students in subsequent trainings, I discovered several important nuances relating to adolescents' emerging racial consciousness and racial identity development. First and most critical, students are hungry for safe and meaningful opportunities to understand better how race affects their lives. With this desire comes an eagerness to say what is on their mind, sometimes without any understanding of or particular attachment to the language and intonation filters that society encourages its members to use. In other words, young people often express their truths about race in raw and piercing ways, using language that often creates heightened discomfort for the adults charged with their instruction. Another opportunity (or challenge) associated with bringing students into Courageous Conversations is that students, and particularly students of color, often bring a higher level of consciousness to the dialogue than many White adults.

The downside of engaging students in my seminars is that their earnest and honest approaches may be one of the primary reasons educators often choose *not* to engage their students in courageous conversations about race. As I discussed earlier, many White educators have lived and successfully operated with a color-blind, race-neutral mindset their entire lives. Similarly, many educators of color, although not perceiving the world to be post-racial or color-blind, have been socialized to avoid open and honest interracial interactions and dialogue. In those school and district settings where a culture of adult silence around race and racism prevails, students often feel that they do not have permission to speak publicly and openly on the matter, and getting students to speak up can be a long and painstaking process. Breaking through adults' barriers to courageous conversations about race can be extraordinarily difficult and time-consuming, but I have found that when granted permission to talk about race in a safe environment, students, both White and of color, seem to get right to it—or, at least, they seem to get to the core of the matter in much shorter time frames.

Perhaps young people approach racial issues with greater humility and velocity because they carry less accumulated baggage, both in terms of prior experience and socialization. Maybe their relative racial innocence or their seemingly innate resistance to problematic adult rules of engagement affords them greater access to and opportunity within the Courageous Conversations framework. But as an adult facilitating and supervising the interracial and intraracial discourse, during and after that first Beyond Diversity seminar with Diana Levy's students, it was hard for me not to feel hopeful about the possibility of a less racially charged and destructive future.

It is important to note, however, that students, both White and of color, have been raised and educated in a society and schools that encourage—maybe even force—them to be racially dysconscious. As a result, they sometimes mistake racial desegregation (or perhaps, integration) for racial awareness and equity. Subsequently, when students of color fail to recognize the presence and role of Whiteness or the existence of White privilege as counterforces to their success, they often unfairly blame themselves when they fall short. Similarly, White students can develop a false sense of superiority when they fail to acknowledge how their Whiteness advantages them, their culture, and their perspectives. As such, all students need opportunities to explore and expand their understandings about race. But before engaging with students in courageous conversations, educators should spend some time thinking about which aspects of the school culture and climate students might begin improving and which aspects might be addressed more appropriately by adults.

Like strategies used to transform adult educators into racial equity leaders, the process for students should first involve personal consciousness-raising followed by a focus on specific school-based race-related challenges. For example, in 2002, at one of PEG's partnering districts, Chapel Hill-Carrboro City (North Carolina) Schools, student leaders participating in the Beyond Diversity seminar were first invited to write their racial autobiographies and their emerging views on race in poetry form and share them during a "slam." (I wanted to ensure that their day away from traditional coursework would be one they could enjoy while still engaging in rigorous academic skills and knowledge development.) The students then listened to each other's poems and selected a few they believed indicated the most personality, depth of content, and stylistic precision. A poem written by 10th-grader Pablo Vega was selected as the contest winner, and his poem, "I Dream," was used to support the remaining seminar activities. It was also published in the *Courageous Conversations* field guide.

Let's take another look at Pablo's poem here. Only this time, think strategically about how it can be applied to our efforts to engage students intentionally in systemic racial equity transformation in schools.

I Dream

I am from a clash of color, from an idea of love, modeled for others' perception.
I see me as I am, but I am hidden from others' views.
I am who I am, but a living contradiction to my peers.
I see life as a blessing, a gift granted to me.
Why should my tint describe me? Why should my culture degrade me?
Why should the ignorance of another conjure my presence?
Too many times I've been disappointed by the looks,
by the sneers and misconceptions of the people who
don't get me, who don't understand why it hurts.
I dream of a place of glory and freedom, of losing the weight of
oppression on my back.
I dream of the enlightenment of people, of the opening of their eyes.
I dream for acceptance, and for the blessing of feeling special just once.
One moment of glory ... for the true virtue in my life.
For the glimmer of freedom, and a rise in real pride.

As this poem attests, not only are student voices essential to our work in eliminating the barriers to racial equity that often are unseen or overlooked by adults, their leadership can be a significant force in accelerating that transformation.

Soon after working with Pablo and his peers in Chapel Hill, I sat down to review all of the racial equity work PEG consultants and I had been doing with students since the late 1990s, beginning with Evelyn McClain's seventh and eighth graders at the Park School in suburban Baltimore County; Diana Levy's sophomores and juniors from Castro Valley; the fourth- and fifth-graders at Eastridge Elementary School in the Cherry Creek School District near Denver, Colorado; and the kids in the Scholars and Girls Growing to Greatness program, also in Cherry Creek. The first thing I realized was that all of the students we had engaged in this work were ready and willing to talk openly and honestly about race. They were curious to learn how race operates in their own and others' lives and society. At times, however, their confusion around the topic caused them to arrive at conclusions that actually diminished their racial consciousness, such as the notion that they were living in a post-racial, color-blind America and that the nation's legacy of racial injustice and inequality was a relic of the past. Interrupting students' belief that theirs is a racially just world and that, by extension, their schools are racism-free is an essential part of PEG's Framework and, more specifically, its work in student antiracism leadership development. It is also critical that students' ignorance or misinformation about race be challenged in developmentally appropriate ways that arm them with greater capacity to face and surmount the racial barriers in their lives and particularly in their schools.

In 2004, PEG began offering racial equity leadership programming specifically targeted toward middle and secondary school students. Called SOAR (Students Organized for Anti-Racism), this seminar series addresses student racial equity leadership development in three distinct phases. In the first phase, students are invited to write or voice personal narratives that depict how they experience school as racial beings. Given that many students are unversed in the specific terminology used in racial equity leadership work and often are confused in their understandings about race and how it operates, these narratives are analyzed for their qualitative value only and are not regarded as definitive or conclusive. We continue to evoke student voices throughout this and the remaining SOAR phases to track how students' understandings change and (we hope) deepen during the course of the training.

Pablo's poem is a wonderful example of how PEG engages student voices in the first phase of its SOAR training. Although organized as a contest to deepen students' understanding and engagement of racial equity, the poetry exercise clearly enabled Pablo to articulate more precisely how race and racism affected his life. This precision ultimately helped the adult educators in his district address the more salient issues relating to these topics as they were experienced by real students in their schools.

By Phase 2 of our SOAR efforts, the student leaders have gained a higher level of confidence about how to engage in courageous conversations about race and can demonstrate deeper levels of understanding about how race influences their own and others' lives. The program's emphasis then shifts to have students collaborate with adults in projects, focused efforts, and other activities aimed at addressing racial disparities in their schools and district. The quality of this work often varies widely, based on how much educators invest in developing students in Phase 1. It also varies according to the ambitiousness of the overall school and district racial equity transformation plan.

For many students of color, the second phase of SOAR offers opportunities for meaningful leadership that most had not thought was available to them in their schools or districts. Given the higher levels of relevance and meaning SOAR activities provide for these students, they often rise to the occasion, thus challenging some beliefs educators have about the students' dedication, determination, and potential to be leaders and scholars. At Prairie Middle School in Cherry Creek, Colorado, for instance, students participated in every aspect of the planning, fundraising, and execution of a weekend-long equity symposium for African American and Latino students, families, and educators in their district. This included working to bring nationally recognized speakers to the school.

SOAR's Phase 2 collaborations also provide the additional data necessary to challenge institutional complacency and unwillingness to engage with or seek understandings about under-served students of color. Providing White students with opportunities to collaborate with their peers of color as racial equity leaders helps to dispel old and ingrained notions about White students' scholastic superiority as well as harmful institutional messages about students of color. These opportunities also enable White students to develop deeper understandings about racial privilege and the specific ways society and schools inequitably support their high-level achievement and engagement at the expense of that of students of color.

Finally, using Pablo's poem to facilitate SOAR's Phase 2 equity transformation, educators and students together might explore a section of the narrative and investigate and address specific ways in which the institution is indicted. For example, a conversation could be organized around the following prompt: "How do district/school policies, programs, or practices degrade Latino students? (Identify some of the ways this takes place.)"

In SOAR's Phase 3, students have been prepared to take racial equity matters into their own hands, and most often, they also express a hunger to do so. Given that all the phases of SOAR programming are overlapping rather than linear, the adult-student equity collaborations quite often continue throughout Phase 3, as do opportunities for student racial consciousness development via professionally facilitated seminars and workshops. During this final phase, however, students may wish to challenge systemic racism in ways that have greater meaning and importance to them. For example, they may organize to coach or tutor middle school students to be racially conscious or take on various racial equity leadership roles as part of their extracurricular activities or community service projects. High school students could develop, for example, a training module for middle school students in which they invite their younger peers to read Pablo's "I Dream" poem and compare or contrast it to their own lives. By so doing, older students can help younger ones develop racial consciousness and voice. While students are not autonomous in terms of their school activities, it is critical for the adult racial equity leaders, be they educators or family/community members, to allow students to truly lead these efforts—even if it means allowing them to sometimes make mistakes—and learn from them.

It is worth reiterating that even though I view student racial equity leadership development as an integral component of systemic transformation, and thus essential to our efforts to move Courageous Conversations about race from theory to practice, we adults must be cautious about asking students to say or do that which we ourselves fear saying or doing. When students—who typically carry less racial baggage and fear—develop greater confidence and understanding to speak and challenge the racial status quo, resistant adults sometimes feel threatened and use their power to punish the students for their leadership. It behooves adult racial equity leaders to step up and ensure these students' safety and security so that their intrinsic motivation and authentic participation can grow and expand.

ESSENTIAL QUESTIONS

Think about the students in your school district as you answer these questions.

1. What evidence suggests that students in your school/district are ready and willing to engage as leaders for racial equity?

2. Which adults are fortified with the requisite will, skill, knowledge, and capacity, and thus, are qualified to lead students in your school/district in becoming leaders for racial equity?

3. How will you ensure that students are safe to develop racial consciousness and lead for racial equity in your school/district?

4. What will be your way of buffering them from known and unknown resistant adults and, perhaps, other students?

Voices From the Inside: Carla Randall

As I reflect on my personal journey to understand my own racial identity and my professional journey toward racial equity leadership, I identify several specific events that have affected me in a significant way. These events include (1) the decision by Portland Public Schools to not hire me as the principal of Jefferson High School (the only historically Black high school in Oregon); (2) an incident in which a seventh-grade Black boy was shadowed throughout his day at a middle school in Tualatin, Oregon; (3) an opportunity I missed to use my new power as chief academic officer of the Portland Public Schools to talk about race; and (4) the occasion when I read my racial autobiography to 250 Portland Public Schools leaders.

The first significant event that launched me on my journey as a leader for racial equity occurred in 2002, when I was told that instead of being hired as the principal of Jefferson High School, I was going to be placed as the principal in a seemingly suburban school in Portland with primarily White, affluent students. Let me share some background to this event. After demonstrating in my first vice principal job in Portland that I am an instructional leader with an equity focus and a continual learning ethic, who deals with performance management effectively, I was involuntarily transferred to Jefferson High School on August 25, 2001. A well-respected educator and former superintendent in Oregon had been called out of retirement to serve as the principal, and I was to be the vice principal, joining a Black vice principal who had been named 2 weeks earlier. Jefferson High School had been a failing school for decades and had been reconstituted 3 years previously. Jefferson had recently lost three Black principals, all of them leaving by November of their first year. Since 2002, Jefferson High School has lost three more Black principals.

Despite those odds, our 2001 administrative team made it through the entire year. I found a school of young, willing-to-reform teachers, and 920 students, who, with their parents, won my heart. By November, I knew that I wanted to be the principal at Jefferson High School.

I had many new experiences during my year at Jefferson. The Black vice principal refused to engage after November because he could not work with two White administrators. I had no idea what he was talking about. I observed the Black administrator being unwilling to interact with many Jefferson students because they were seemingly of a class below his own, while I was having positive interactions with many Jefferson students including smiles, conversations, and hugs. They expected to see me in hallways and in the classrooms because I had a consistent presence there. I observed that within the Black Portland community, those with lighter skin have higher status. I also watched the White principal hand out money to students at lunchtime simply because they asked for it.

I engaged in reform efforts with a primarily White staff to support students of color, and I collaborated with a team of teachers to establish freshman academies that, when implemented the following year, led to gains in student achievement. I watched a consultant from the Black community, during a meeting with the three administrators, tell the Black administrator that it was difficult for Black students to have an all-White administration. The Black administrator did not live or participate in the Jefferson neighborhood.

I learned that Black skin was not enough to make someone part of the Jefferson community. But I wasn't allowed to be the principal, even though many people believed I had the technical skills to turn the school around. Was it reverse racism? I thought so at the time, but we did not have a deep enough understanding about race.

Was it lack of experience? Experienced administrators had failed the 3 previous years, so why did I believe I could do it? Did it matter that I didn't live in the community? Other schools had principals that didn't live in their communities. Why did I have this intense emotion about not being allowed to be the principal at Jefferson High School? Did I believe I was entitled to the position?

I continued to ask these questions for 7 years, continuing to experience the intense feelings about not serving where I was most needed. I had yet to learn about Heifetz's Zone of Productive Distress or the protocols that would allow me to talk about race and discover who I am racially and what race had to do with that decision. My work with Courageous Conversations has significantly increased my understanding of White privilege. I have a deeper understanding of my White racial identity. Was it a mistake for Portland Public Schools to assign me as a strong leader to a White, affluent school rather than the lowest-performing high school in the state of Oregon?

I left Portland Public Schools in 2005, returning to the suburbs in the role of director of curriculum and instruction/director of secondary schools for the Tigard-Tualatin School District. In this role, I was introduced to Courageous Conversations at a National Staff Development Council Conference pre-session on culturally relevant teaching in 2006.

One specific event in my many racial experiences in Tigard-Tualatin occurred when as part of a District Equity Leadership Team (DELT) activity, I shadowed a seventh-grade Black boy in an attempt to understand the experiences of a Black boy in our system. I was often in classrooms in the schools I supervised, and I did not share with staff that I was shadowing this particular student. What I saw broke my heart and caused me intense distress. The principal, who served on the DELT, had a theory that our disproportional discipline data was the result of students of color accumulating experiences throughout the day in which they were dismissed or treated differently than White students in similar situations, which eventually caused them to act out. I observed this Black boy being directed throughout the day by stern-voiced White teachers. He was talking with a group of White students during class, and he was isolated and told not to speak. Nothing happened to the White students. His math teacher talked down to him constantly throughout the period, actually asking him to behave like John, a White student sitting quietly next to him. I saw an enthusiastic, likeable seventh-grade boy being treated as if he was misbehaving. He was eventually expelled, and he moved to Texas with his mother.

This experience took me beyond my limit of tolerance. I was so far in the feeling quadrant of the Courageous Conversations Compass that I questioned whether I could ever go to other corners of the Compass. I experienced intense discomfort with Whiteness and the impact it was having on the students in my schools. My initial reaction in the math classroom was to scold the teacher for her Whiteness. I did not do that, however. It is difficult to stay patient but persistent in working for change when you see a child being hurt by his experiences.

I brought my data back to the DELT, reporting what I observed so we could apply the Courageous Conversations Protocol. Others brought similar data, and we discussed the pattern for students of color as they interacted with White staff throughout the day. We listened to the staff of color on the DELT describe how it feels to be treated like this Black boy. This data informed our Equity Transformational Plan; and, in the short term, the principal began having conversations with her school equity team and staff about what had been observed in their school.

The math teacher left the district at the end of the year, and the principal continues to engage in courageous conversations about race with her staff. As someone who used to consistently enter racial conversations from the thinking quadrant of the compass, I learned that it is a good thing for me to have personal racial experiences that cause me to enter conversations from the feeling quadrant, followed by courageous conversations to move me to the remaining corners of the compass to create transformational change.

Missing my opportunity to join in a citywide conversation about race as the new chief academic officer of the Portland Public Schools is the third event that I identify to be significant in my journey as a racial equity leader. I was busy with the transition to this new position in July when I received a request to call a reporter for one of our local newspapers to discuss Courageous Conversations About Race. I had been immersed in budget and staffing conversations and assumed the reporter wanted to know what Portland Public Schools was spending for this equity work. I had not seen that budget yet, so I sent the reporter an e-mail telling her I didn't have enough information to provide her with a quote. A week later, I picked up two local papers and read two articles on racism in Portland. I experienced intense distress because I realized that I had missed an opportunity to use my new position of power to engage in a conversation about race that was citywide.

■ ■ ■

As I read the two articles, I realized that in these two lengthy articles not one person talked about the presence and role of Whiteness and its impact on racism within our systems. I was so agitated by my decision that led to this missed opportunity that I spent 3 hours on a Friday night writing an apology letter to the reporter in which I expressed my opinion about the missing perspective of Whiteness in her article. She responded immediately, asking me to rewrite the apology as an editorial opinion piece for the following week. I did as she asked, primarily because, as the new chief academic officer, I wanted the people of Portland to know my perspective that race matters. I was indicating to the community that I was claiming my Whiteness; I was planning to engage people in a conversation about race, and I was willing to take personal responsibility for institutional racism in the Portland Public Schools.

In the article I submitted, I wrote,

I have great confidence in the Courageous Conversations About Race work, because I've seen a change in the belief systems of White educators, and I've seen the experiences of people of color validated while engaging in this process.

The work is not about technical solutions. You can train teachers how to use a culturally responsive instructional strategy, but if the teacher lacks racial consciousness, students of color will know, resulting in an opportunity for a meaningful connection and appropriate teaching and learning being lost.

Community members and district staff reference my article when they come to discuss issues with me. They are waiting to see if my actions will be consistent with my words.

The final significant event I will share about my personal journey as an antiracism leader occurred when I read my updated racial autobiography to 250 district leaders as I transitioned to chief academic officer of the Portland Public Schools in August 2010. I had led the Courageous Conversations work in the Tigard-Tualatin School District, taking responsibility for designing activities for district leadership meetings that provided opportunities to apply the Agreements, Conditions, and tenets of critical race theory between training events with Pacific Educational Group. Portland Public Schools had had several starts and stops with Courageous Conversations, with fluctuating central office leadership.

Two things became apparent to me in my new role: (1) the Courageous Conversations Protocol was not being applied between training sessions with PEG, and (2) a large number of principals were reluctant to write and submit their racial autobiographies at the end of the 2010 school year because they were worried that their racial autobiographies would be used against them in a negative way in their evaluations. (Are you kidding me? We fail students of color for decades and the system worries about whether a White administrator will be identified as racist on an evaluation?)

I was tasked with designing an activity for the Executive Committee (10 people) during the August retreat. I asked people to identify where they were on the Courageous Conversations Compass, and I facilitated an activity to review the Agreements and Conditions and asked people to identify which Conditions resonated with them. As I read my own racial autobiography, I experienced unanticipated discomfort, a sure sign that I was doing the appropriate work. When we had completed the activity, participants expressed how powerful the activity was for them in terms of increasing their skill in using the Conditions. They couldn't believe how honest and vulnerable I was about my racial experiences and the development of my White racial identity. The superintendent asked me to use the same activity the following week with the District Management Team (about 70 people). I led that group in the activity, and the reaction was similar. "I can't believe you just did that," one member stated afterward. "You were willing to be so vulnerable in front of all of us," said another. Still another told me: "I understand the Conditions and Agreements on a deeper level." We engaged in deep conversations about race using the Courageous Conversations Protocol. People of color shared their own experiences within our system, which created discomfort in the room but also an amazing feeling that we were each privileged to be having this experience together. The superintendent asked me to share this activity with the entire leadership group (250 people) the following week.

Sharing my personal racial autobiography with the 250 leaders in the district caused me discomfort. I knew that I personally was in the Zone of Productive Distress and that I was facilitating others to be there as well. You could hear a pin drop as I read my racial autobiography. I was exhausted when I finished facilitating the activity, but people sought me out throughout the remainder of the day.

I heard from at least 10 White administrators that they had written their racial autobiographies but were reluctant to share with their staffs. After providing them with a protocol for the conversation and modeling, they found the will to do the same with their staff. At least five administrators of color told me that they really appreciated the courage it took for me to me read my racial autobiography. When I asked them if they were going to read theirs to their staffs, their response was, "No, it's different for me." I learned later that a group of Black administrators, in discussing the activity, expressed the following view: "Here we go again with another White person thinking she can teach about equity. She's probably not going to claim her Whiteness." But when I did provide examples of my Whiteness, my increasing awareness of my racial identity, and my self-study, which allowed me to wrestle with my own weaknesses in dealing with racism, they were surprised.

Developing the will to transform a school district into one where race is not a predictor of success begins with me taking personal responsibility for racism and for my personal journey to increase my understanding of my own racial identity. I need to continue to work at keeping myself focused on the personal, local, and immediate while examining the role and presence of Whiteness as I live my life and engage in the profession I love so much. I need to continue to read articles and books and attend conferences at which I intentionally place myself in racial situations that create discomfort for me. And when I feel that discomfort, I need to reflect and engage in courageous conversations using the Courageous Conversations Compass, Agreements, and Conditions, as well as the tenets of critical race theory to know myself better and to leave room for the missing perspective that will ultimately allow me and those I lead to arrive at an adaptive solution rather than a technical one.

Carla Randall is the chief academic officer of the Portland (Oregon) Public Schools, a PEG partnering district. She is a White American.

Voices From the Inside: Patrick Duffy and Anthony Galloway

Patrick's story

I was born and raised in the small town of Grand Marais, Minnesota. Grand Marais is the gateway to the Boundary Waters Canoe Area. It's the largest town in Cook County and a haven for city dwellers who long for a quaint, artistic atmosphere along Lake Superior when they take the ritualistic trip "up North" as so many Minnesotans do each summer. Many locals believe Grand Marais to be quite cosmopolitan, despite its size and rural location, but almost all agree that it is, as my father put it quite often, "one of the most beautiful small towns in the United States." Grand Marais was not unlike most small towns in Minnesota, however, in that it was populated almost entirely by White people.

We did not talk often about race in my hometown, but my experiences there developed my passion for developing student antiracist leaders. I was taught early about the importance of my ethnic identity. My mother, an Arab American of 100% Lebanese descent, would tell me stories about her experiences growing up in Duluth (Minnesota), often being mistaken for Jewish, where she learned from her parents the unwritten code of voluntary assimilation and, from her own experiences, the impact of oppression on those with little or no voice.

I learned much about culture and ethnic pride from my father. He was Irish Catholic, born and raised in the college town of Northfield, and he instinctively practiced culturally responsive teaching with me by letting me know I could not fail academically because of the great accomplishments and developments of "my people" from the Middle East—that is, honoring my mother and recognizing that this was a part of me that was not reflected in others in my community.

For example, while peppering me with a healthy dose of Irish pride, my father instilled in me the notion that I must succeed in mathematics because my ancestors introduced the Arabic numbers from which I was learning. He realized that subtle aspects of my Arab American ancestry would lead some to consider me somewhat of an "other" in the homogenous, rural north woods of Cook County.

I was not often conscious of my White race, but various encounters throughout my childhood led me to see that I was ethnically different from my peers. My middle name, Abalan, was not only unique but also a source of ridicule with many of my peers, once they heard it. In elementary and middle school, I often hid my middle name from others so they would not laugh at me. I was surprised that my peers did not have Lebanese sfeehas, tabouli, Syrian bread, and hushwa with their turkey, cranberries, and pumpkin pie on Thanksgiving. Once, when I was out playing at a friend's house in my neighborhood, an older kid found out I was Lebanese and pulled a knife on me, saying he was going to kill "Ahab, the Arab." In middle school, one of my social studies teachers announced to the class that I must be related to Saddam Hussein. By this time, however, I had grown more secure with my ethnic identity; still, I had a quick temper with acts of bigotry. I directed an expletive at the teacher and walked out of the room. When I shared this story with my father, I remember him asking me to wait in the hallway while he went into the classroom to give this teacher a piece of his mind.

None of this had as profound an impact on me as when a classmate said, in a group of our peers, that my mom could not "be White." His argument: "White people can't have black hair" as my mom did, so therefore she must be Black. Not only was I dumbfounded by his ignorance, but for the first time I felt an uncertainty that others might not consider me White. That uncertainty came from the unspoken messages I had learned about race, despite all of the explicit, positive messages I heard from most of my peers about my ethnic identity. I did not discuss this incident with my parents, however; I was not sure how to raise it. Despite all the conversations with my parents about ethnicity and culture, I had never had a personal conversation with them about race. Up until that point, racism to me was something from history. It was associated with a southern accent and was often accompanied with stories about the many accomplishments of the Civil Rights Movement. It was certainly not something that I ever would have considered to be a part of my personal identity development.

At the time, I was unaware of the impact that the normalization of Whiteness—that is, the color-blindness, the race neutrality, and the unearned and unconscious privileges—would have on my life and how it would continue to impact me. Throughout my formative years, a number of incidents and relationships influenced the way in which

I constructed meaning about race in my own life. In Montessori School, for example, I remember vividly my encounter with Justin Porter. The teachers had prepared the class for a new student. When Justin arrived, I, like most of the students in my all-White class, was fascinated to see a Black student. I approached him to welcome him and, on shaking his hand, noticed two things: One was that his hand felt coarser to the touch than any I had shaken before, and the other was that his hair and skin had a smell that was foreign to me. I turned and said something to one of my friends about my observations and was quickly whisked away into a corner by one of the teachers. The teacher told me that I was being racist and that she never wanted me to say anything ever again about how this boy was different. Thus, at 4 years old, it was modeled for me that I should not see difference, in particular, with people who *were* racially different from me.

■　■　■

As an undergraduate student, one of my advisers, David Roediger, taught explicitly about the social construction of Whiteness in his U.S. History class.[5] My collegiate studies thereby affirmed my thinking about the presence of a racial narrative shaping our common history and the impact of individual and collective racial and ethnic identity on our past and present. Roediger and Dionicio Valdes, my other adviser, encouraged me to take graduate classes that would allow me to explore the impact of race and privilege and how those forces affected the labor and social movements, political interactions, and foreign policy. Subsequently, as a junior undergraduate at the University of Minnesota, I audited a graduate-level class on Whiteness that was both intimidating and exhilarating; and, as a student leader at that university, I was exposed to antiracism teaching through a training course that used Lee Mun Wah's 1995 *The Color of Fear* video[6] and a simulation of the Underground Railroad that brought the history of antiracism alive through a powerful intellectual, emotional, and physical experience.

In my teaching career, both these earlier opportunities became curricular staples of my own classes and trainings for student leaders. I became fascinated by the social construction of race and developed an intellectual curiosity to find out more. I did some research on the topic and found that there had been a movement in the U.S. Congress to debunk the notion that Jesus may have been Black, which was raised by at least one scholar and which had caused quite a bit of debate in the 1980s. Then, in 1970 and 1980, the Census suggested that people of African descent (which included North Africans and Middle Easterners) were considered African American (or Black) by the U.S. government. (By 1990, however, the Census indicated that people of Middle Eastern descent fit into a category along with European Americans, who were labeled White or Caucasian.)

Thus, it seemed that my life was a personification of how race can be socially reconstructed to meet the political needs of a few in power. As I dove deeper into this phenomenon, I was surprised to find out how often the social construction of race had been shifted to maintain a racial hierarchy—that is, a caste system—in our nation. In the 1840s, I learned, I would have been considered Black not because of my Lebanese ancestry, but because of my Irish ancestry. I also discovered that numerous other groups of people in the United States have had the lines of race and ethnicity blurred to determine their citizenship, voting rights, housing, and internment. In the post-9/11 world, it came as no surprise to me that my own race was once again a point of debate by the U.S. government, in a political climate that most certainly wants to keep track of the number of Arab Americans in the country.

That is why today I often check the "Other" box on official forms and documents and welcome the opportunity to write in any explanations about the curious dichotomy between the complexity and arbitrariness of race in the United States. I never lose sight, however, of the fact that, as a visibly identifiable White male, I continue to have many unearned privileges that allow me to engage in all aspects of my life in the United States and elsewhere throughout the world far differently than my non-White peers.

Early in my professional career, I came across Beverly Tatum's book,[7] *Why Are All the Black Kids Sitting Together in the Cafeteria?* I sat on the bookstore floor between the shelves for more than 2 hours, enthralled by the themes addressed in that book and how they resonated with my own personal experiences. Over the next few years, as a social studies teacher and coach, I made a point to share not only the antiracist voices of Abraham Lincoln and Eleanor Roosevelt but also the narratives and wisdom of antiracist pioneers who received less ink in the traditional textbooks, like Frederick Douglass, Harriett Jacobs, and Chief Joseph. In doing so, I made a point to ask my students to engage in critical thinking and writing about the political, social, and economic state of our union by incorporating these diverse narratives.

In 2004, I was asked to work as a social studies teacher and equity coordinator at my high school. These roles helped me grow as a leader; they also opened the door for the most important work I had ever done. That year, an interracial group of students—inspired by seeing staff members at Midwest High School engage in dialogue around racial equity and sparked by their own intellectual curiosity—started reading Tatum's book. Indeed, I came back from the school cafeteria one day to find several of my students sitting outside my classroom door engaged in study of the book. When I asked them why they were reading that particular book, one girl replied simply, "Duh . . . we wanted to read it! We see it in classrooms all over the school, and the title looked interesting."

Around that same time, our school's Equity Team had asked the entire staff to read the book and engaged in a professional learning community dialogue about the impact of racial identity on curriculum, instruction, and school practice. The provocative title had gotten my students to take notice, but their engagement in culturally responsive instruction and racially conscious curriculum in my classes had created in them a passion for learning more about this topic. As I engaged in continued dialogue with them, I recognized that they raised many of the same questions about race that I had never had answered as an adolescent. I was inspired by their passion for change as well as their unrequited desire to engage in antiracism practice.

A few weeks after the students organized their own learning community, two interns at the local YWCA branch approached the school about piloting an antiracism curriculum in four high schools around the region. Their plan was to provide training in antiracist methods to 10 to 15 students at each school. I quickly worked with colleagues to engage some of our students with these passionate interns. As the numbers dwindled, I recognized that something more systemic was needed. Several students from my classes attended the training, but they kept coming to me afterward, asking if they could do more. I approached the original four students from my social studies classes who had been reading outside my door and asked them to work with me to develop curricula that would support systemic student leadership development. Using a model similar to the one the adults in our building were using for the same purpose, they became a sort of interracial student Equity Team.

■ ■ ■

That summer, I periodically met with these students at restaurants and at my home to develop a comprehensive, antiracist, student leadership program that could be implemented in the fall. We sent out postcards to all incoming sophomores notifying them of a one-day antiracism retreat we were planning for mid-August that would serve as the foundational training for this effort. Sixty-seven students attended the retreat, and most of them became the first "Dare 2 Be Real" student leadership group. The name of the group harkened back to the work the students had done with the YWCA interns, who asked them to dare to be real about race.

Over the course of the next 8 months, the students from this group met weekly with me to develop their will, skill, knowledge, and capacity as racial equity leaders. I recognized the importance of creating a safe space for them as they put this theory into practice. Twice a month, they would pair up and facilitate discussions and activities on racial equity in homeroom classes throughout the school. Many staff members shared their views. The student-led groups were dependent on interracial dialogue. My facilitation of those sessions focused on bringing out multiple racial perspectives, but my lone voice did not model the students' core values.

The following year, a district administrator told me to consider partnering with Anthony Galloway, whom she told me had contacted her about working with some of our students. Anthony had coordinated programming that promoted integration in various districts in the metropolitan area. Unknowingly, he and I had worked together indirectly through experiential learning programs that I had used with my classes in previous years. We soon became fast friends because of our common passion and commitment to developing the capacity of student leaders to do this work.

I invited Anthony to meet with some of the students from our equity groups after school. From the beginning, Anthony and I felt comfortable working and challenging each other because we both were interested in learning about each other's perspectives and we both recognized how our collaboration could benefit students. We spent many days visiting each other and making plans to create a program that would incorporate themes such as confronting fear, team building, mindful inquiry, antiracist scholarship, and individual and collective understandings of racial and cultural identity. I was impressed with Anthony's knack for connecting with my students and for sharing a counterstory to my own that clearly helped my students to deepen their understandings of racial perspective.

In 2008, I moved into a new school district as a school administrator. This school district was just beginning to address racial equity systemically. In my role there, I found little of the urgency needed among the staff or the community to engage in racial equity work because of the relatively small numbers of students of color and the district's reputation as one of the best in the state, if not the nation. Issues for students of color were largely invisible, but the capacity for growth among White students and staff was immense. I spent the first half of my first year there observing, discussing, and planning strategically about how to create a safe space for racial discourse. I put together a FAQ (frequently asked questions) sheet about Dare 2 Be Real and how it would benefit the school. I found that there were a number of passionate and committed racial equity leaders in the district. Equipped with information and data, I was able to get their support. I went to various staff members and asked for their input on students. Most of them had a hard time picturing White students in a group like the one I was describing, but soon I had the names of about 30 students, whom I then invited, along with a few staff, to a retreat at which Anthony and I intended to present them with information on the foundations of our leadership development work.

Over the course of the next year, our equity work gained credibility as we trained students in the Courageous Conversations Protocol and amplified their shared voice by inviting them to speak at numerous regional conferences and community forums. We also shared some videotaped images of students presenting their racial autobiographies to members of the staff. These narratives were pivotal as staff members began to understand the impact of institutional racism on all students. They also opened the door for Anthony and me to talk about racially predictable achievement at the school and throughout the region.

My collaboration with Anthony proved to be an essential and symbiotic relationship that helped move the work forward. His role as a regional leader helped keep the students and adults in my district from feeling as if they were doing this work in isolation. My success with the group, in a prominent and predominantly White school district, gave Anthony enhanced credibility in his efforts to share our model with others in the region. Combined, our interracial perspectives and blended narratives only strengthened our message and our work. We were able to model our alliance for both students and staff in other parts of the district and state.

Anthony has been a great ally for me. He challenges my thought processes and helps me to live out my mission: to work side by side with people of color to draw out and develop the skills, strengths, and brilliance of *all* children. I know that I can teach many students effectively, but as a White educator, my alliance with Anthony has helped keep me engaged in interracial discourse that gets me to challenge my discomfort and reflect on my own personal capacity to better recognize the needs of Black and Brown students.

Along the way, I have learned many lessons. For one, even though I am a racially conscious White male, I have found that it is essential to have commentary from a trusted ally of color with me in my leadership journey. In my case, a blind spot was Omar, an eighth-grade Black male student who had a reputation of being sent to my office quite regularly for disciplinary action. The day before a Dare 2 Be Real retreat, I faced a choice: either suspend Omar from school or invite him to the leadership retreat. Despite the concern of some other staff members, I invited him. After 3 hours of activity and interracial discourse, Omar told me that the retreat was one of the first times that he had really felt that people wanted him to be at school. On reflection, I wondered what had kept me from inviting him sooner. Did I feel that the group could take on only so many Omars, or that perhaps he and other students like him would turn their predicament around on their own? After the retreat, Omar showed increased classroom engagement and fewer behavior referrals, but he still failed to climb from the academic hole that had been created by our system's lack of service previous to that point. I have since recognized the need to increase the capacity of our leadership groups to engage all students who need our attention.

Anthony's story

I came into this work while I was working full time and attending college. I was your typical youth mentor/camp counselor type, having worked with performing arts summer camps, African storytelling troupes, and an organization that offers a nighttime experiential learning program called "Race to Freedom: The Underground Railroad." I participated in several poetry groups and Black student unions on campus and took on any experience that declared my Blackness to a space where I rarely see Black images in any significant measure and that addressed some of the most glaring racial disparities in employment, education, and housing. I quickly found myself in a place where I had a deep understanding of the intricacies of racial inequity and no language to express it.

I got a job with an integration district that was a partnership of 10 suburban districts and an urban center and that was working collectively on teacher training and addressing racial disparities in achievement. The district also operated two schools focused on the arts and on implementing racially equitable and culturally competent teaching strategies, and this had met with some good success. The PEG Beyond Diversity seminar was offered free to all staff, along with other staff development workshops and training, so I had a lot of support and practice early on with White voices in leadership and training, which was new to me.

My job in the district was to work with families whose children were leaving the urban center to take advantage of suburban school options. The suburban districts were going through demographic shifts that were accelerated subtly by the influx of students through the program with which I was working. As a result, I encountered a mix of gatekeepers, from well-intentioned staff charged with outreach to bus drivers (who unfairly discipline students or decide who is late by who is last to be picked up), who made it difficult for already stressed families to achieve any kind of credibility and therefore support. Although the region was engaged in very good work for the most part, I had at that point encountered only "the choir," those who had self-selected to engage in courageous conversations. I was not exposed to the reality that, in most places, those engaged in equity work were in the vanguard and hard-pressed to push or "sell" their peers on the necessity for racial equity.

At a point of frustration, I retreated to recoup some of my excitement and optimism and begin working directly with students. I was put in charge of overseeing a grant program that our district had created to fund collaborations of partnering districts to support integration and multicultural programming. To begin, I put together a list of suggestions for districts to partner around including the Underground Railroad experience, for which I was now a historian-in-residence. One of the equity and integration directors in a suburban school immediately put me in contact with a history teacher who had been taking students through the Underground Railroad experience and who was looking for some funding to support some interesting work he was doing with students.

That teacher, Patrick Duffy, invited me to his diversity seminar class to meet some of his students. He wanted me to talk to them about who I was and to share insights on the Underground Railroad experience. When I got there, the students were engaged in a deep conversation about how they were going to lead discussions about race in homeroom classes around the school. I was completely caught off-guard. Patrick's class was a diverse mix of students of different ethnic and racial backgrounds. Both students of color and White students were openly discussing race, its impacts on their schooling, and their lack of knowledge about or experience with various racial topics. What I was not aware of at the time was that these students had internalized the Six Conditions and Four Agreements of the Courageous Conversations Protocol and were running full speed to get the rest of their school on board as well. I was not expecting students to have such a deep understanding of institutional racism—I myself had just started to develop a language to describe it.

What surprised me even more was hearing the students talk about the real experiences of overt racism that they encountered regularly at the school from both their peers and their teachers. No matter what was shared, however, the students protected each other and were very clearly allies in this work. This was my first encounter with the Dare 2 Be Real leadership development group that Patrick had created.

Patrick and I quickly found not only that we have similar artistic and camp experiences, but that he had been taking students through the Underground Railroad experience that I had been leading for several years. He knew exactly who I was. He told me the story of how Dare 2 Be Real was created and of the program's need for deeper experiences and funding. We began to work together to enhance the retreat format that Patrick had been using so that it could become more intentional about growing the knowledge, skill, and will of students for racial equity work.

Patrick and I began to exhaust every opportunity we could find to fund the retreats, so we had to become more creative in our efforts. Because the grant program I oversaw required two districts to work together, we partnered his district's group with a fifth-grade class from my district to create an overnight retreat experience called "Confronting Fear." Thus, Patrick's high school group could still hold its retreat and the fifth-grade class could get high school mentors to lead its intense nighttime experience. The Dare 2 Be Real students also got to practice their facilitation and leadership skills, which they then applied to their efforts to lead smaller Courageous Conversations groups with their peers at school.

Patrick and I became a team that modeled shared interracial leadership, and we modeled it well. Patrick, as a White male, could say things that I, as a Black man, could not. Conversely, I, as a Black male, could bring a level of assumed authenticity to students of color, which helped them to open up. I sincerely believe both of us could have "gotten there" or achieved these ends, in our own way, but there was something about partnering our racial experiences that made conversations go deeper and get there faster. Then, as Patrick trained me on his framework for creating a safe space for interracial dialogue, I became a real part of his Dare 2 Be Real group and began leading conversations myself.

After Patrick and I had been working together for about a year, we began to need more opportunities for retreats and Underground Railroad experiences. I started partnering Patrick's students with high schools students from around the region to fulfill the integration district's student learning grant requirements. As these students began to engage in the Dare 2 Be Real work, their staff leaders began to inquire about starting groups of their own. About this time, Patrick took a middle school assistant principal position in one the most affluent and least diverse districts in the region; but within months of his new appointment, we were already working to establish a Dare 2 Be Real group in his new setting. This was more difficult, however, as Patrick's new district was just starting to engage in Courageous Conversations work, and the staff there seemed very skeptical about my outsider's point of view.

We began by flying in "under the radar" so as not to make the folks in the new district too uncomfortable too quickly. We also didn't want to set up Patrick's new students for adult retaliation and politics—something he had made me aware of in his work from the previous district.

■   ■   ■

It was a very interesting time, and all the while Patrick's original group in his old district was still very active. However, his new students quickly engaged in the Protocol and, in my view, kick-started the district's equity journey out of pure necessity. It helped to have an equity leader in Patrick, who had some positional power at his new site and in the district. I realized that we were forming a network of students that could help further insulate students and others from the discomfort that so many adults feel about having direct conversations about race. There was already a buzz about the new groups, and I gladly began reporting about all the groups' successes to the joint school board and my supervisors.

In addition to the original and the middle school group in Patrick's new district, I also started a chapter in the two schools my school district operated. The students in that group came from all 11 districts partnering in the integration consortium. Although I knew the basic Dare 2 Be Real framework and was familiar with the progressions of Courageous Conversations Protocol, I had a completely different experience with these two new groups. The students seemed very unimpressed by the Dare 2 Be Real model at first. What had been new and provocative at the other schools seemed merely interesting to them. They had engaged in conversations about race in some way before, had experienced fewer overtly racist encounters, and felt like their school environment, despite a few racial issues, was doing a pretty good job of honoring the experiences of all students. I decided to just follow the framework anyway and found myself running everything by Patrick to decide how to get the students more engaged. I also decided to "be real" myself and to bring my frustrations directly to the group. I even asked them if they felt the group was necessary.

The responses I received completely revitalized my will to carry on in the work. The prospect of the group, the space, not being there put every student on the defensive. One sixth-grade student stood up and stated that the group was the only place she felt like what she had to say mattered. "While it may seem like everything is OK on the surface," she said, "we all still know the stereotypes, the names, all that racist stuff we talk about in Dare 2 Be Real. It has to come from somewhere, and even if it's not here at school, we still gotta go home."

A Jewish student spoke up next. She explained that she never felt she could "be Jewish" except for in the Dare 2 Be Real sessions. I guess I had failed to realize that regardless of how unprovocative the conversation may have seemed to me, the safe space provided to these students to explore their own identities without fear was indeed important. The uninhibited student voices that came forth in the safe setting of Dare 2 Be Real sessions really helped me grow in my understanding that we needed to be intentional about sustaining a safe space, regardless of the intensity of the conversation. I was looking to engineer an experience instead of engineering a space for students to create theirs. This type of learning makes the framework sound, whether it is applied in an urban or suburban setting.

Patrick and I continued to develop retreat experiences and to form a regional approach to student antiracist leadership. From my position as a staff person of the interdistrict consortium, governed by school board members from all 11 partnering districts, I was able to tell the story often and to build regional support. This support was accelerated when a group of students came to a school board meeting to speak about why they are a part of Dare 2 Be Real. Eight students shared their experiences at that meeting, and two students in particular—one a White male student and the other a Black female—moved the board to tears with their stories of their personal experiences in Dare 2 Be Real and their demonstrations of the knowledge, skill, and will to address race and racism.

Patrick and I resolved that evening to make sure that we would always showcase students speaking about their own experiences. We realized then that the best way to highlight what creating safe spaces for interracial student dialogue can do is to share students' experiences with others. Not only because our students inspire us to do more, and not only because they can convince those in extreme discomfort to lend support to the work, but because students offer us a true litmus test as to where we really are in our equity walk.

Another recent example of this happened at a Dare 2 Be Real retreat held in a suburban district that is contiguous to the urban center. The students there had been deepening their knowledge of the development of race and had been building on their personal ethnic and racial identities. At one stage of the retreat, the students were to undergo a courage activity that involved breaking boards and bending steel. (I had learned this activity at a leadership retreat hosted by a local restaurant chain called Famous Dave's. The owner, Dave, is himself an excellent leadership trainer.)

Starting in the morning, the students wrote about their greatest fear; they were allowed to revise what they wrote throughout the day. As they began to deepen their connections to each other and as their understandings of their personal and collective understanding improved, they were allowed to cross out their original fears and replace them with deeper ones. When the time came for them to break the boards and bend the steel rods associated with this exercise, their school principal, a White male, joined the group. He wanted to observe the group and to be supportive.

As each student shared fears and the context for those fears, it became clear that all harbored deep personal pain and life experiences that most adult educators only read about. The principal, like the students' teachers and other district personnel, was able to learn firsthand about the real lived experiences of his students, and he too was moved to tears. When it came time for him to break his board, he acknowledged that his fear was that he would fail to educate all students to high academic levels. Even more, he admitted he was afraid that he would fail to educate the students who looked like those in the room.

Later, Patrick and I were able to bring four students to a PEG Summit to speak as student presenters, a common practice for our regional work. As we sat in a hotel room one evening with our students and all of our supervising staff, including the district superintendent, we had a conversation about the students' school experiences. One Black male student—who was recognized by all of his teachers as a school leader, who was the recipient of several internships and awards, and who was a junior with college prospects and great grades—shared that he had faced expulsion during his freshman year for something stupid he had done. The student looked directly at the superintendent and acknowledged that the superintendent was directly responsible for keeping him in school. This was because, he claimed, the decision about whether to expel him or not had rested solely in the superintendent's hands, and the man's refusal to expel students short of legal obligations had made all the difference in the student's life. Because that student had the language and the safe space to speak to his experiences, he was able to validate district policies that promote equity and slow down the pipeline that, in our state, too often leads Black males to prison.

This young man's and other students' stories were the result of Dare 2 Be Real's efforts to build the capacity of students in multiracial spaces to advocate for better school communities. Both Patrick and I believe that when students can speak with a language that captures their experiences and their challenges, school staff are forced to address their own practices in very real ways. But this does not happen in isolation or without the very real support of the staff and administrators who support students. Each Dare 2 Be Real group that has been successful so far has had staff who truly protect and nurture student relationships and who understand the Courageous Conversations Protocol at even its earliest stages. Each program site has principals who support the work and teachers who fight for its safe space and who safeguard it from adult politics. And because of its regional approach, Dare 2 Be Real students can reach out to their counterparts in neighboring districts for support, help, and encouragement.

Our regional network now hosts an annual summit of Dare 2 Be Real students. These summits have inspired citywide forums on race, even in communities that have remained virtually all-White after their restrictive covenants were outlawed. There have also been setbacks. As word of our success spread, one district sought to establish a Dare 2 Be Real group, but it did not want to engage fully in the Courageous Conversations Protocol or framework, nor did it want its staff or administrators to participate in the Beyond Diversity training. This resulted in a new space that was neither safe nor sustainable and that was opposed by a small but powerful group of entitled parents who were made uncomfortable by the work. In that Dare 2 Be Real group, virtually all the White male participants—who often receive the most peer pressure to leave the program, which is often seen as being solely for students of color regardless of its racial makeup—left, as did those Black males who could gain social status with Whites by denying the group's legitimacy. The remaining students did not have a multiracial cohort large enough to sustain multiple perspectives, and the group eventually unraveled. Even worse, it was seen as anti-White by those students who were made uncomfortable by some of the experiences of students of color.

■ ■ ■

While engaged in this work, Patrick conducted a critical ethnography that included suburban school student and staff participants. As evidenced by the findings of his study, student voice is an important factor in developing the will, skill, knowledge, and capacity of antiracist leaders, regardless of their position, age, or race. He found that adult leaders, in particular, developed a more positive orientation toward their work and were able to stay engaged for longer periods of time when they engaged in work with interracial groups of students, and even more so when they engaged in antiracist practices with such groups. All participants who engaged in sessions with students developed stronger will and skill to address racial inequities through their prolonged practice in interracial settings. In addition, many adult leaders shared that they felt less defensive hearing perspectives from students than from their peers or supervisors. This suggests that perhaps student antiracist leaders may be able to neutralize some of the negativity associated with adults who are struggling to share privilege and who acknowledge their complicity, albeit often unintentional, in contributing to systems that perpetuate racial inequity.

The experiences of leaders in the suburb that Patrick studied informed a model of student antiracist leadership that incorporates both safety for the students involved and the potential for the program to have the greatest impact on the individuals and the sites within which it operates. Patrick's research data indicate that this model could be transferable to similar developmental models for other stakeholders and could be replicated at other sites.

The following keys to success and student safety in the development of a systemic antiracist approach are drawn from that research and from our combined work with Dare 2 Be Real in multiple school districts throughout the region:

- Interracial groups whose membership reflects the racial demographics of the building and which are not dominated by one racial group are best suited for success. It should be noted, however, that these groups should not be developed based on racial quotas, but rather on an openness to developing racial consciousness. White participants should be particularly open to alliances with students of color. In predominantly White settings, it is essential that the group's White students and advisers not further isolate students of color, who are already historically marginalized and hypervisible within the system.
- Program staff members who will work with students should have credibility with students across all racial backgrounds and be able to practice culturally responsive teaching. They should also have an internalized understanding of critical race theory so that they can recognize racial scenarios in the group and help guide students through the leadership development process with pedagogy that fosters student growth.

- Antiracism work that is seen as happening in a silo can be dismissed more easily by groups that may have a more established voice and status within the school. It can also easily be cast as an "add-on" or fringe program by those who want to maintain the status quo. Thus, such efforts should be fully integrated into the structures and culture of the school building. This systemic integration could include scheduling program activities during the school day or horizontally aligning the student antiracist leadership group with other existing student groups (see Figure 8.1). Community support and staff guidance are also crucial, given the vulnerable nature of students; therefore, vertical integration with leadership groups such as site councils, which may have multiple adult stakeholders, can further legitimize the work of student antiracist groups.

Figure 8.1 A Structural Model for Horizontal Alignment of Student Antiracist Leadership

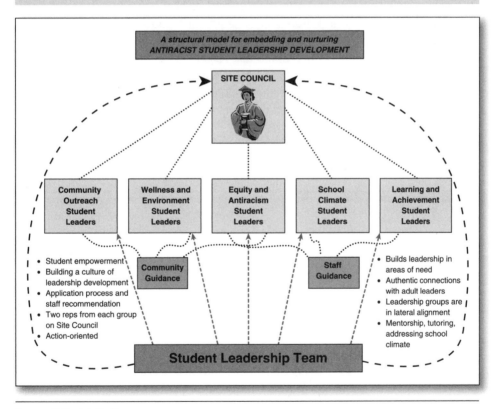

Source: © Patrick Duffy.

- Support for the program must come from the people with the most positional power. It is essential that principals, superintendents, department heads, and even school board members be made aware and supportive of the goals of the program, lest students be set up for failure or pushback.

- The focus of the group should be on students' ability to develop their own individual and collective racial identities and racial equity leadership approaches by exploring the three key themes that are the cornerstones of Dare 2 Be Real: (1) Who we were—that is: What is each student's individual racial history and what is the collective history of all the students? (2) Who we are: What aspects of the students' racial identity development intersect with other aspects of their identities? and (3) Who we want to be: What particular action-oriented movement will allow students to plan strategically for and participate in active antiracism leadership?
- To be successful, students in antiracist leadership programs must be able to share their interracial experiences in a safe setting that encourages questions and growth. These experiences can be simulations or other aspects of experiential learning, but the greatest gains result from antiracist service learning. To maximize the impact of the work and to form authentic alliances with adults who are embarking on a similar journey or greater racial consciousness, the details of student learning about race and racism should be shared with other school staff members and with the students' parents.
- Students must have a protocol for engaging in antiracist leadership activities. Students in Dare 2 Be Real programs are trained in the Courageous Conversations Protocol, Agreements, Conditions, and Compass; in Lee Mun Wah's Art of Mindful Inquiry processes, and in Judith Katz's antiracism frameworks.[8] These tools help students create a common language for leadership and provide them with opportunities for deeper analysis and action for racial equity.

Patrick Duffy is currently a principal in the Minneapolis Public Schools. He is a White American. Anthony Galloway coordinates student programming for the West Metro Education Program. He is a Black American. They have developed DARE 2 Be Real together.

NINE

Learning and Teaching for Racial Equity

From Theory to Practice

You can't teach what you don't know, and you can't lead where you won't go!

—Malcolm X

When Donna Marriott, a White, female classroom teacher at Casa de Oro Elementary School in San Diego, invited me to be her co-teacher for a semester, I was intrigued and somewhat humbled. At the time, I had barely any teaching experience. She was a celebrated reading teacher with many years of experience, recognized as a literacy expert throughout the state of California. I wondered, what did this award-winning, veteran educator, who had taught children from kindergarten through second grade with great success, think she could possibly learn from me?

Donna had participated in one of the first Beyond Diversity trainings I facilitated at the San Diego County Office of Education in the late 1990s. During that training, she shared that she was especially concerned about a few of the students of color in her class, primarily her Black boys. She worried that she was not engaging those students at the highest levels and wondered if or how her being a White female might be impeding their success.

Donna suspected that something was lacking in the way she engaged children of color in her classroom. Judging from my initial interactions with her, she seemed familiar with Black cultural styles of communication and appeared to have a healthy respect for Black culture overall. But when Donna described her Black male students as highly talented, gifted even, but as simply not engaged in their learning, I had a pretty good idea about what the problem might be. So when she contacted me about a year after Beyond

Diversity about joining her in her classroom to engage in collaborative action research focused on meeting the literacy needs of *all* her students authentically, effectively, and consistently, I jumped at the opportunity. I packed up and flew down to San Diego to begin our research effort.

Just as I had envisioned it, Donna's classroom was a welcoming and engaging physical space. The walls were covered with a good number of affirming Black male and female images and displays. Her deportment with and around her Black students, their parents, and other family members was culturally proficient and supportive. But on my first day in the classroom with Donna, I simply watched her teach or, more accurately, I watched the Black boys in her class struggle to learn.

Donna's 5-, 6-, and 7-year-old Black male students exhibited high levels of distraction, some of which, of course, was due to my presence in the room.[1] A couple of the boys also seemed to lack self-regulation skills, a trait some teachers misinterpret as aggressiveness among this population of students of color. A myriad of triggers other than Donna's story and lesson seemed to captivate their attention: other children, their clothing, sounds, and, on occasion, various details of the story Donna was reading to them.

Immediately after her class, Donna and I held a debriefing discussion. I asked her how she chose the books she read to the class and what determined where children sat in proximity to her as the teacher. She responded candidly, telling me that she strove as best she could to follow the state-required curriculum but that she also exercised a great deal of flexibility and creativity when planning reading lessons for her children.

Although Donna truly wanted me to partner with her to discover what was preventing her Black male students from achieving in her classes, deep down, I suspected that she believed some part of the boys' lack of success could be attributed to their low levels of motivation and that she wanted me to help her find out how to stimulate *them* to become more engaged rather than to show *her* how to reach them. So I then asked her to do something that I later realized was impossible for her to do: I asked her to put herself in the place of the Black males in her class and tell me if she would be happy with the day's story selection or with her ability to gain physical access to the teacher. Donna gave me a puzzled look before attempting to do what I asked of her. But, assured that I was a trustworthy colleague, she soon admitted that she had no way of knowing whether the story was of interest to the Black boys in her class. That, I suggested, was the first part of our challenge.

I reminded Donna that, for students of color and White students alike, both the instruction and the instructor must be intentional in their goal of providing relevant educational experiences to the student. Her inability to determine the relevancy of her story selection to the students in her classroom demonstrated to me that she was not being at all intentional, with respect to race—both her own and theirs—in her planning and teaching for her young Black boys. Many of the teachers I have observed in the nearly 15 years since meeting and working with Donna have demonstrated tremendous thoughtfulness and care in selecting curricular materials that show images of Black, Brown, and American Indian students. In this regard, they have been very intentional about race; yet few, I have found, have paid as much attention to how their own racial identities, both their individual and collective ones, interface with their students of color. This, too, is important.

Teachers must also pay close attention to how White children in multiracial classrooms respond to racially specific curricular materials. If they do not prepare their White students to accept or address images of people of color, for example, an illustration of a Latino doctor or an instructive video featuring a Black superhero, White students may perceive these images as foreign, inappropriate, or even frightening. Their uneducated reactions may, in turn, damage the psyche or spirit of students of color, who typically relish (or at least identify closely with) images of people who look like them.

I suggested to Donna that only through applying a deeper level of racial intentionality would she discover what works for these students and overcome the many barriers teachers construct to compromise their learning and eventually turn them off to school. I wanted her to begin using the Courageous Conversations Protocol to describe what was currently occurring in her classroom, so I asked her to reflect back on her Beyond Diversity training and her early efforts to construct and define her personal and professional meanings about race. I then asked her to talk with me about where and how race "shows up" or reveals itself in her classroom in areas besides discipline and lower achievement.

I asked several more questions to determine the scope and breadth of Donna's connections to her Black male students: Can you identify each of your Black boys by name? In what ways do they contribute to the pro-social experiences in your classes? How connected are you to their families? Can you reach out to their parents or caretakers to help you gain a better understanding of their home circumstances and to identify the activities from which they derive a sense of happiness and competence?

Many of these questions were no problem for Donna because she was already an incredibly interpersonal and relationship-oriented teacher. She also clearly realized that she needed to make her curriculum more relevant to her youngsters of color and perhaps slightly augment her already excellent repertoire of instructional practices. Deep down, however, I suspected that Donna also knew that achieving equity in her classroom depended largely on how well her already engaged and academically successful White students adjusted to any pedagogical reforms such changes would entail.

Given that she was about to make some obvious changes to how *all* her students "did school" and experienced success, Donna and I also talked about how the highest-performing White students in her classes were currently interacting with her students of color, in and outside of the classroom, and what her proposed changes might entail for her White students. Although she was convinced that exposing White children to images, perspectives, and customs of people of color would help them to operate with greater agility in multiracial settings, she wondered if those students' parents would interpret their children's struggles to learn about and gain familiarity with the ways of others as valuable or detrimental. This was indeed, a significant part of Donna's work in transforming her teaching and her classroom.

Donna and I then began planning our action research project. We agreed that I would spend about 15 to 20 hours in her classroom throughout the semester, working directly with the students as she observed me, and vice versa. We focused our attention on literacy development, beginning by placing greater racial intentionality on the literature selected for her classes. We carefully determined which of us would introduce which story and how we would process the content with all of the children, noting especially the steps we took to ensure that the boys of color advanced in meaningful participation, reading, and comprehension, and recording our success or setbacks in each area. Throughout our study, Donna maintained close contact with her Black male students' parents to get a sense of how our instructional reforms were playing out in the students' homes, specifically, to determine if the boys' experience resulted in their increased desire to talk with family members about school and to complete homework assignments.

Donna subsequently authored an article on our action research, in which she noted the following:

> Our study continued throughout the school year. Each month we studied new heroes and tackled increasingly complex issues, each week we talked about our learning, and each day we worked to make ours a classroom in which liberty and justice for all really meant for all. Still, when I reflect on the list of books we chose to study . . . , I question the titles, the number of books, and the order of their presentation. Were these the right books? Did I use enough books? Did I teach them in a sequence that made sense?
>
> But I also realize that our success had less to do with the specific texts than with our process for integrating these texts into our learning lives. The literature we chose became significant through the ways we referred to it. Our best lessons became anchor experiences on which we grew still more learning. Ruby became the referent for courage, perseverance, and youthful heroism. Harriet Tubman gave a name and face to slavery. Glenn became our eagle and encouraged each of us to spread our wings and soar.
>
> Glenn's spirit and conviction played a decisive role in the concept, design, and substance of this work. Yet, his collaboration raises an important question: Could I have done this work without him? I believe that I could have and would have. This work was my obligation and my responsibility. In truth, Glenn could not have done this work without me. While he provided many of the trigger events that defined our path and gave voice to our awareness, I constructed the daily curricula and formed the necessary relationships that supported the work before, during, and after his visits. Our daily interactions were the basis on which all this learning was founded. Liberty and justice weren't just things we read about or talked about every now and again. These concepts became part of who we were as individual and collective learners.[2]

■ ■ ■

Despite years and volumes of education reform research and hours upon hours of professional development on the key factors policymakers and practitioners agree are affecting the quality of education in the United States, little work has actually influenced the most critical leverage point: the pedagogical methods that teachers like Donna Marriott employ in their daily interactions with their lower-achieving student-of-color populations. In theory, learning and teaching for racial equity is about creating a system of educators who can demonstrate daily their understanding about, belief in, and execution of culturally relevant teaching. In practice, it is about when a community of classroom teachers can have ongoing courageous conversations about race with each other that are focused on providing the culturally rich physical environments, human relationships, and instructional methods they design, provide, and use for their most under-served students. This is possible only if the entire education system is focused on the same goals—namely, improving achievement for *all* students, narrowing the achievement gaps between racial groups, and eliminating the racial predictability and disproportionality related to which groups of students achieve in the highest- and lowest-performance categories.

Regardless of how innovative or interesting a school reform idea may be to education scholars, researchers, or practitioners, the truest litmus test for any change strategy is how effectively ordinary teachers implement it in their classroom. At the end of the day, what matters most is what happens between the teacher and the student in the classroom that results in student mastery of rigorous standards. In the long run, critical, culturally relevant, classroom-based, instructional innovations can be sustained only when entire schools and districts are dedicated to and supportive of such transformation, both in theory and in practice.

Much has been said and learned about culturally relevant teaching by way of professional learning communities. In many of the Pacific Educational Group's (PEG's) partnering districts, tremendous amounts of resources, both human and fiscal, have been and continue to be allocated to create environments in which teachers feel a responsibility for as well as the safety to engage in high-quality development of their will, skill, knowledge, and capacity to have courageous conversations about race. Indeed, committing to establishing a professional learning community culture is foundational to moving such courageous conversations from theory to practice.

I want to be careful here to make a distinction between what is often viewed in some school districts as a commitment to and focus on building and effectively using professional learning communities in theory and establishing a new and different culture. In a professional learning community *culture,* teachers are willing and able to examine racism and its impact on them personally as well as professionally—that is, on their instruction and their collaborative development with colleagues and supervisors. In a typical professional learning community, when race is placed on the table, either as an essential question related to a teacher's disposition or a student's engagement, the adult behaviors tend to veer away from the professional. As a consequence, student learning slows or halts, and the community itself experiences fracturing. Instead of pushing forth to address the essential questions about race, the tacitly agreed-upon route in these instances is to shut down rather than to deepen courageous conversations about race. The result is a twofold disaster: the so-called community remains intact, but the same children on the margins continue to be under-served and failed.

How dangerous it is when we enable educators to believe efficaciously in their own ability to learn, and yet the outcome of that learning does not produce higher achievement for Black, Brown, or American Indian children. Certainly such an approach, institutionalized over time, not only drains a district's resources, but also allows teachers and administrators to cultivate or reinforce beliefs that lower-achieving students of color lack the capability to master higher standards, even when a community of teachers has done all that they professionally know how to do. Establishing a professional learning community *culture* or ethos that intentionally and unapologetically normalizes courageous conversations about race is an initial and ongoing strategy my team at PEG and I employ when engaging with school districts that profess a commitment to achieving racial equity.

■ ■ ■

As discussed in Chapter 3, increased familiarization with and internalization of the Courageous Conversations Protocol is the only way ongoing and effective application of the Courageous Conversations Agreements, Conditions, and Compass can occur. Assuming you have theoretically mastered the Protocol and want to dramatically improve your effectiveness with students of color, let's re-examine these essential elements of the Courageous Conversations framework and their specific relationship to learning and teaching for racial equity.

It's worth restating before we begin that having continual courageous conversations about race is more than simply a way for individual teachers to come to understand themselves as racial beings and thus begin to formulate a racialized understanding of their impact on all their students. It is also a method by which communities of teachers—because they will share a specific language, meaning, and process of racial equity instructional leadership—can come together and more precisely uncover, examine, and address systemic racism at the classroom level. Moreover, as an integral component of PEG's Systemic Racial Equity Framework, the Protocol focuses on more than just the learning or teaching that happens in the classroom. For teachers, it also compels an understanding of the principles of adaptive leadership and how to empower students' family and community members as partners in sustained reform.

Recalling our conversation about adaptive leadership in Chapter 7, let's look at how the Courageous Conversations Protocol can support teachers in becoming authentic adaptive leaders in their classrooms. First, teachers wishing to raise the levels of engagement and achievement for *all* students, and especially under-served Black, Brown, and American Indian students, need to recognize their own personal and central roles, both in terms of opportunities and challenges, in creating classroom environments that work. That is, the problem of the lower performance of students of color must be viewed and addressed as essentially a *teaching* rather than a learning gap. Viewed this way, teachers gain the authority to make changes in how instruction is delivered because the responsibility for transformation truly rests within teachers' spheres of influence. This elevated sense of efficacy is not fostered when teachers can externalize the barriers to learning for their students of color.

Operating instead from a place of authority, adaptive leaders in the classroom must be willing to engage willfully in uncomfortable conversations about their own racial beliefs and corresponding practices, which stand in the way of the heightened academic engagement of students of color—indeed, *all* students. If a teacher holds low expectations about the possibility of success for Black, Brown, and American Indian students, more than likely those students will struggle to exceed those expectations. To transform the way in which curriculum is chosen and instruction is delivered dramatically and continuously, and to do so until traditionally unsuccessful students experience mastery, teachers must develop a healthy tolerance for living in the adaptive leadership model's Productive Zone of

Disequilibrium as a norm for their own professional growth and development. As cohorts of teachers authentically engage each other in courageous conversations about race and collaborations addressing their pedagogical beliefs and practices, they will arrive at adaptive learning and teaching solutions that can be tested thoughtfully in their classrooms.

One important understanding I have about adaptive leadership at the classroom-teacher level is that teachers must fend off the natural inclination to seek quick fixes to learning and teaching challenges. For example, forcing children to wear uniforms to school is a quick-fix, technical approach to improving their academic performance. Having teachers collectively surface the racial meaning about why Black, Brown, and American Indian students do not engage academically at consistently high levels in their classrooms is an effort to create an adaptive shift in their professional learning community's culture. As the late Barbara Sizemore[3]—an embattled and visionary urban school superintendent—often noted, we educators should avoid racing to implement solutions before having clearly articulated the reasons behind our existing challenges. In the language of adaptive leadership theory, we need to stay in the Zone of Productive Disequilibrium and expect/accept nonclosure if we truly want to create classrooms that are racially equitable.

■ ■ ■

When Donna Marriott faced the hard reality, corroborated by her own classroom-generated reading assessment and standardized test scores, that she was failing to reach and teach the Black boys in her literacy lessons, she instantly placed herself into a state of disequilibrium or stress. In that moment, she could have retreated from the data, falling back on excuses like a shortage of time or resources, or she could have embraced her school's pitiable collective response of blaming the students and their families for their failure, but that would have placed her beneath the threshold for learning.

According to the Courageous Conversations Protocol, had Donna chosen either of those options, she would have disengaged and resolved to establish her own comfort as a higher priority than the successful learning of her students. That Donna experienced discomfort over the racial predictability and disproportionality of her classroom data indicated that she was, indeed, staying engaged—but just barely. Had she been a member of an effective, grade-level professional learning community, at her point of discovery about her role in her Black male students' reading challenges, she might have avoided feeling that she was the only teacher who was struggling to meet the needs of the Black boys at Casa de Oro Elementary School. This sense of disconnectedness often results when teachers try to do racial equity work in isolation. Working in isolation rather than as a community and culture of educators engaged in finding a solution for struggling cohorts of students also prompts teachers to remain silent about the racial disparities in their classrooms and schools rather than to speak their truths. Being a member of a community in a caring, effective professional learning culture, can prevent teachers from progressing dangerously beyond their limits of tolerance and plunging headlong into the devastating and debilitating chasm of becoming professionally unproductive.

Once internalized in theory, teachers in particular must practice allowing the Courageous Conversations Conditions to guide their process of self-discovery, initially at the personal level and then subsequently at the professional level to help them build effective relationships with their colleagues and with their students and students' families. This practice likewise can facilitate the examination and development of teachers' instructional practice.

Rather than thinking about working through the Courageous Conversations Conditions 1 through 6 in a linear progression en route to instructional improvements, I suggest that educators approach their personal and professional development by way of the Conditions in spiraling fashion—that is, as starting with the personalization of their own home and classroom experiences through the lens of race and advancing to a larger examination of the specific impact of Whiteness on these same situations or circumstances. This focus on the presence and role of Whiteness—in ourselves; our classrooms, schools, and districts; and in our instructional practices—is critical because by doing so we educators can discover how we sometimes unconsciously and unintentionally create barriers or privileges, respectively, for students of color and White students.

When teachers examine the presence and role of race in their lives and understand it as an omnipresent factor and influence in their beliefs and behaviors, their competence in educating all children is enhanced. Just as female teachers experience some level of cultural incongruence with their male students, or middle-class teachers with their impoverished students, White teachers are positioned at a racial distance from their students of color. The presence or size of this distance does not determine a teacher's ability to teach students of color effectively, but all teachers must first recognize this incongruence and then examine when differing racial experiences and perspectives surface in their classrooms, either as physical entities or via the instruction taking place. These are the essential first steps toward achieving racial equity in learning and teaching.

Teachers of color who grew up in White-dominated contexts (refer back to Katz's Characteristics of White Culture in Chapter 3) or who have developed racial consciousnesses that are aligned more consistently with those of their White colleagues (refer back to Helms's White Racial Identity Development model, also in Chapter 3) also need to pay attention to this issue of cultural congruence. What is key, and what is derived through intentionality and practice with Condition 1 (Getting Personal, Right Here and Right Now), is teachers' ability to make race a personal, local, and immediate construct as they consider the physical environments of their classrooms, their relationships with their students and with their students' families, their relationships with their colleagues, and their instruction.

Once teachers personalize race as an omnipresent construct, the practice of examining how racial phenomena emerge can be addressed by Condition 2 (Keeping the Spotlight on Race). Granted, we educators collectively, indeed many people generally, may have to struggle to recognize the presence of elements such as race when we may not believe they actually exist. But once someone realizes and believes that race is real and a real factor in determining the scope and success of learning and teaching, developing fluency and accuracy in examining race is critical.

Asking the simple question, "What's race got to do with it?" is a good way of launching into the process of discovery and making meaning. Teachers' responses to this question might uncover overt and overwhelming racial overtones embedded in a curricular choice or instructional practice; alternately, those responses may reveal that race plays only a tiny role in a given classroom situation or circumstance. The key here is to open your mind and begin the dialogue on the realities of race in the classroom just as if you were addressing gender, class, age, or any other salient demographic factor that influences teachers' thoughts, feelings, beliefs, and actions.

■ ■ ■

A positive culture for teacher development in a professional learning community is best evidenced when teachers feel encouraged to offer multiple and often divergent perspectives about race and other matters. Establishing such a culture also lies at the heart of Condition 3. Teachers, like any other group of professionals, enter their profession with varied experiences, perspectives, talents, and abilities. Thus, their communities must offer circumstances in which they can test the validity of what they believe to be "normal" and determine how such ideologies translate into behaviors that influence student learning. I have never visited a school where one teacher has all the right answers necessary to unlock the potential of *all* children. Teachers from diverse persuasions and backgrounds must be invited into courageous conversations continuously to share their multiple perspectives about how race affects learning and teaching. The inputs of all are essential; likewise, the strategies they employ to ensure that racial differences do not have negative impacts on student achievement. In the end, what matters most is that *all* students, and especially those who are underserved, gain full access to the curriculum and can demonstrate mastery of it.

Establishing parameters that encourage and support the sharing, valuing, and implementing of multiple racial perspectives so that *all* students have greater opportunities and fewer barriers to tackle rigorous curriculum and master high academic standards is the thrust of Condition 4: Keeping Us All at the Table. This Condition calls on teachers within professional learning communities to open up and share with each other about how race has influenced (and influences still) their personal and professional lives and then to search together for the presence of racism in their curricula and instruction. I have found, however, that educators generally require support to help them listen and respond effectively to their colleagues in ways that invite deeper analysis of individual and collective challenges and, subsequently, more dramatic action steps. The tenets and tools of mindful inquiry enable teacher leaders for racial equity to support each other in uncovering, examining, and addressing racist beliefs and behaviors that influence learning and teaching.

Table 9.1 provides examples of some very basic language teachers can use to help shift the tone and nature of the dialogue on difficult racial issues from threatening to supportive using the art of mindful inquiry. This model suggests that "reflecting" teachers should not be forced to think or believe something that they are not yet prepared to embrace, such as acknowledgment of the presence of White bias in their choice of Mark Twain's *The Adventures of Huckleberry Finn* as a reading assignment. Rather, those teachers' peers should develop the skills of a "coaching educator" and use an inquiry process that encourages reflecting teachers to examine more deeply their points of view or actions and arrive at essential questions that can advance them to their own next level of effectiveness. The latter approach is far less threatening because it does not externally force change on reflecting educators but instead offers support for their internally led transformation.

Table 9.1 Listening, Inquiring, and Responding

Nine Healthy Ways to Communicate	The Art of Mindful Inquiry
1. Reflect back on what is being said. Use their words, not yours.	What I heard you say was . . .
2. Begin where they are, not where you want them to be.	
3. Be curious and open to what they are trying to say.	Tell me more what you meant by . . .
4. Notice what they are saying and what they are *not saying*.	
5. Emotionally, relate to how they are feeling. Nurture the relationship.	What angered you about what happened?
6. Notice how you are feeling. Be honest and authentic.	What hurt you about what happened?
7. Take responsibility for your part in the conflict or misunderstanding.	What's familiar about what happened?
8. Try to understand how their past affects who they are and how those experiences affect their relationship with you.	(How did it affect you? How does it affect you now?)
9. Stay with the process and the relationship, not just the solution.	What do you need/want?

Source: The Art of Mindful Facilitation by Lee Mun Wah, 2004, Berkeley, CA: Stirfry Seminars and Consulting, www.stirfryseminars.com.

Self-discovery of the ways in which one blocks or limits one's own development and expansion, and independent design of a plan for moving forward, is not only empowering; it can also be transformative and support growth for all engaged in the process. Together with a willingness to practice the Four Agreements and to place oneself in the Zone of Productive Disequilibrium, mindful inquiry can truly heighten professionalism among educators and prompt important antiracist pedagogical awakenings.

■ ■ ■

After nearly a decade of teaching at the university level, one thing I realize is that I truly need to know who my students are to appreciate them and thus to educate them effectively. This particular insight was an especially profound one for me, given that many of my own professors never took the time, nor were they afforded proper learning and teaching circumstances, to get to know me when I was in college. The presence or absence of such authentic understanding and appreciation has a lot to do with who succeeds and who fails in schools. For the vast majority of my graduate students, for example, I am the very first Black male professor they have ever experienced. With their lack of experience with Black male professors comes, in most cases, an innocent demand that I function in a way similar to their White educators. In short, their expectation is that I will "act White." Until I bring this issue to my students' attention and help them define, in racial and other terms, what they hold to be the characteristics of an outstanding professor, our communications can suffer or even break down.

This challenge presents an important opportunity for me to apply the fifth Courageous Conversations Condition in my teaching and ask the essential question: What do we mean by race? I use this to help my students uncover the salience of race, ethnicity, and nationality as it relates to them personally and to me, their professor.

I also use Condition 5 to name the specific racial and cultural lenses through which I view the physical space of my classroom, my relationships with my students, and my instructional practices. For example, I know that my classroom humor, cadence, vocabulary, and interpretations all come from a "place" of my unique racial, ethnic, and national identity and experiences. Recognizing this—and knowing that my students typically do not share similar origins of humor, cadence, vocabulary, or interpretations, nor do they spend time outside of class in similar "places"—I am aware that they generally do not have legitimate access to my curriculum or me until I grant them such meaning. However, I intentionally grant them access to both through a careful and comprehensive analysis of our collective racial, ethnic, and national identities. This sharing, in my view, is foundational with regards to my efforts to know my students authentically, and then, I hope, to appreciate them and vice versa.

■ ■ ■

Condition 6 (Let's Talk About Whiteness) is the final phase to be tackled in the ongoing struggle to examine and "de-center" Whiteness in the classroom. It is also often the most difficult aspect of the Courageous Conversations Protocol to practice and the one that presents the greatest challenge to openness and introspection among teachers and thus compromises the goal of achieving racial equity in learning and teaching.

It is essential that we begin this discussion from the premise that the public schools in the United States were never designed to educate children of color intentionally. Thus, by default, America's schools became socializing institutions grounded in the culture and consciousness of the dominant group in American society: White people of European descent. This conclusion is bolstered by the fact that certain ideals, like rugged individualism, prevail in the ethos of American schools and society today. It is reinforced further by beliefs promoted through school curricula and instruction that "effort equals reward" and that color blindness and racial neutrality are virtues. It is corroborated by falsehoods like asserting that White privilege does not exist or is a figment of the imagination of people of color. These ideals, beliefs, and falsehoods have become foundational to how school policies, programs, and practices are determined and exercised. Challenging the validity of the dominant American (White) perspective requires a yeoman's effort and unfailing resolve on behalf of racial equity leaders.

Examining the presence and role of Whiteness in the physical environment of our classrooms and schools, in the viewpoints of our instructors, and in the message and intent of our instruction is at the very heart of our efforts to challenge the presence and role of racism in education. Thus, whenever we as racial equity leaders uncover evidence of White racial biases in educational practice, such as an emphasis on individualized or "quiet" learning styles, we must be careful not to immediately label those practices as "wrong" or to dismiss them as irrelevant or inappropriate. Rather, we should investigate the degree to which such emphasis advantages or disadvantages the learning of any segment of the classroom population and determine if other cultural learning styles are also being used, especially in multiracial classrooms. Then, we should focus our efforts on decentering Whiteness and on creating space for other legitimate cultural learning styles, such as collaboration and verbal expressiveness, to be engaged for the good of *all* students.

However, teaching children of color, or White children for that matter, a single story about a person of color does not assist them in seeking the more complete truth of our nation's multiracial and multicultural heritage, nor does it alone promote the development of antiracist, intellectually curious citizens. Leaders for racial equity must learn to walk a thin line between ensuring their students' academic success within the contexts of the current system and developing within our students—*all* our students—that insight, intelligence, drive, and determination to transform the racially biased society in which we live.

CULTURALLY RELEVANT PEDAGOGY

In their exhaustive review of the literature, James Banks and his colleagues at the University of Washington Center for Multicultural Education maintain that culturally responsive teachers are "knowledgeable about the distinct cultural backgrounds of their students" and take the time and effort necessary to "acquire the skills needed to translate that knowledge into effective instruction and an enriched curriculum."[4] As Banks et al. further contend, "Making teaching culturally responsive involves strategies such as constructing and designing relevant cultural metaphors and multicultural representations to help bridge the gap between what students already know and appreciate and what they will be taught."[5] These instructional strategies, which draw heavily on students' parents and others from their communities as resources, must serve to transform that home and community information into effective classroom practice.

For the purposes of ensuring racial equity in classrooms, schools, and districts, culturally relevant pedagogy involves an attention on the part of educators to the physical environments, human relations, and instructional methods that reflect the distinct and diverse cultural backgrounds and perspectives of the students in their classrooms. Courageous Conversations provides essential tools for investigating how race and racism affect learning and teaching with regard to each of these components.

When Gloria Ladson-Billings[6] and Geneva Gay,[7] two pioneers and experts on culturally relevant teaching, ask educators to focus on assessing the physical environment, they are suggesting that we must pay close attention to the structures, images, rules, and rituals of the entire school building and specifically the classrooms in which our students spend the greatest amount of time. How do we know how the schooling setting looks, feels, and responds to students of color? How do we determine whether this setting is congruent or incongruent with physical environments more familiar to them?

Teacher leaders for racial equity often need to transform their school environments so that their students can experience an important kind of continuity between home and school. When such continuity is neither possible nor plausible, they must intentionally create a bridge between the familiar and the new. For example, in an American Indian child's home, images of tribal leadership and family may adorn the walls. Teachers who see the importance and value of cultural relevancy can re-create some of this same visual experience for their American Indian students so that there is little incongruence, from this and other standpoints, between home and school.

Donna Marriott addressed this topic in her action research article, offering the following example:

> Glenn and I made a decision to limit our inquiry into slavery because we wanted to respect the innocence of the young children we worked with and because we wanted very much to bring our study up to the here and now. Yet our time with Harriet Tubman was powerful, and its effects linger in my heart and mind, as I suspect they do for the children. The children embraced Harriet Tubman as nothing less than an icon. They played Harriet at recess—hiding in the bushes when the dogs caught their trail, dashing from safe house to safe house on their northbound journey, taking their travelers all the way to Canada, and then returning for more.
>
> During one such game, Cory said, "I am not stopping until slavery is erased." Damon, too, "played" Harriet, though in his own way. He came to school one morning with a kerchief carefully wrapped around his head. While this could have been construed as hoodlum garb, I took the time to ask Damon about his new look. He told me: "I'm covering up the cut on my head like Harriet Tubman did, and he showed me the red marker "cut" on his forehead. Kerchiefs became quite the rage in our class for a time.[8]

Much has been written about the central importance of relationships, particularly those between teachers and students, to effective schooling. Add to this an understanding of the important impact of race on learning and teaching, and you can see how essential it is for educators to understand what healthy relationships between students and teachers look like and to have a deep recognition of the patterned and predictable dynamics that emerge in interracial relations. This is critical even with regard to intraracial relations among educators and between educators and students as well as educators and parents and among students.

An additional important recognition is the understanding that race is very much associated with how, when, and with whom such relationships are formed, protected, nourished, and developed. For evidence of this, look at how much more easily very young children go about establishing friendships within and across racial lines, compared with teenagers and adults. How often have I heard younger teachers speak about having had racially diverse friendships when they were in high school or college, only to abandon or lose those relationships once they graduated and went on to their professional lives. Clearly, establishing authentic relationships across the color line continues to be a significant challenge for those who value such interactions. For those who do not place value on interracial relationships, diminishing the importance of racial distinctions in choices made about one's friends and acquaintances offers some artificial protection from the glaring reality that the adult, decision-making population in the United States continues to be extraordinarily and increasingly racially polarized.

The following findings from a recent study on racial attitudes in the United States candidly illustrate the conclusion that White people and people of color in the United States differ greatly in terms of their perceptions of race and racial inequality:

- Just 16% of whites believe that there is a lot of discrimination in America today, while 56% of blacks and 26% of Latinos believe that there is a lot of discrimination in America today.
- While many objective measures of health suggest that black Americans are in worse health overall than whites, a majority of whites believe blacks' health is "about the same" as whites. A plurality of blacks, 53%, as well as 39% of Latinos and 50% of people from other racial backgrounds, believe that blacks are in worse health overall than whites.
- 67% of blacks and 52% of Latinos believe that blacks make less money than whites, a view that tracks with official statistics on income, wealth, and unemployment. Only 37% of whites believe that blacks make less money than whites, with a narrow majority believing that blacks' and whites' incomes are about the same.
- 56% of blacks and 30% of Latinos think that the federal government treats whites better than it treats blacks. Only 9% of whites feel that the federal government treats whites better than blacks, with a majority feeling that the government treats blacks and whites about the same. One in four whites believe the U.S. government treats blacks better than whites.[9]

The implications of racial polarization are tremendous for our nation's schools. They are especially significant for White teachers positioned in multiracial classrooms who absolutely *must* form healthy and authentic relationships with their students, their students' families, their colleagues, and sometimes supervisors of color in order to ensure their own and their students' success. In my experience, the most illustrative evidence of teacher ineffectiveness is less about teachers' failures to create physical spaces that are culturally relevant for *all* students and more about teachers' inability to interact with other adults of color and, by extension, the children of color who sit in their classrooms.

White educators are implicated in this latter regard far more frequently than educators of color not only because of their overwhelming numbers in the nation's education system but also because they are more likely to be racially isolated from people of color of all ages in their personal lives. Indeed, numerous studies have shown White Americans to be the most racially isolated population in our nation. Subsequently, when newly minted White teachers arrive at multiracial schools or, even worse, schools in which the population is predominantly students and teachers of color, they often struggle to relate to these school communities in ways that are natural for them or authentic for the communities. From simple things like knowing how to offer proper greetings to more complex aspects of language usage, humor, and gesturing, White teachers who spend much of their adult nonprofessional lives primarily with other White people initially lack the cultural proficiency necessary to build effective human relations with their students of color and those students' families.

Much has been said and written about this phenomenon using a variety of softer, politically correct euphemisms, like "the challenge of suburban teachers working with urban students" or "how middle-class teachers fail to meet the needs of poor students." I call these descriptions of the profound teaching gap politically correct because they typically use language that is comfortable for politicians in federal, state, and county departments of education, right on down to the elected officials in the district board rooms. True, suburban and middle-class White educators often do struggle to understand inner-city, poor students' social, emotional, and academic needs. But even more, these same White educators continue to face conflict, frustration, and failure when working with middle-class, suburban students of color—as seen in some of the most affluent school districts across the country.

Now, I do not wish to diminish the seriousness or extent of the challenge White teachers experience in navigating across diversity borders and barriers, across a broad spectrum of intentions and sensitivities. I am simply saying that the challenges of forging authentic relations across the color line, for White educators as well as for some educators of color who lack racial consciousness and connection, is a major stumbling block to creating culturally responsive learning environments and thus achieving racial equity in our nation's schools.

Donna came to an important revelation and made a likewise important statement about this circumstance in the article depicting her classroom practice:

> A little girl who wrote, "I don't like being black," provoked me to consider the ways in which I might have contributed to her feelings of devaluation.... My teaching was silent on issues of race, and it was a silence that must have spoken loudly to my students. "Doing something" became clearer to me. I would work to end the silence—mine and theirs.[10]

Simply recognizing that the nation continues to struggle to foster meaningful and productive interracial relations and that the nation's teaching force predictably lacks the will, skills, knowledge, and capacity to do so with students is insufficient. Our teachers must be developed in a supportive, not punitive, way to form successful relationships with their students of color, many of whom have been perpetually under-served. In addition, teachers must model the qualities and characteristics of such interactions in the most explicit way possible so that White students do not inherit the interracial disabilities their adult counterparts display.

Let's "listen" again to Donna's experience and conclusions:

> At the beginning, I had many more questions than answers. Could I, white woman in the process of discovering my own complicity in a racist world, do this work? Did I know enough? Could I talk about racism with my African American students? Would I have any credibility? Where would parents come down on the issue? What material could I use? Who would support me? How would I recover from the mistakes I was bound to make? How would I justify this work in an educational and political environment focused intensely on test results? In spite of the number and complexity of the questions that confronted me, Glenn's question was always present to remind me of my responsibility. Perhaps I didn't know exactly what to do, but doing nothing was not an option.[11]

When moving Courageous Conversations from theory to practice, having a knowledge base about culturally relevant teaching, one that includes being able to understand

and recognize its key components, is essential but insufficient. Teacher leaders for racial equity must also become aware of and skilled in a process that enables deep examination of their personal racial attitudes, values, beliefs, and behaviors—aspects that typically are parlayed into their overall classroom and specific instructional decisions. Teachers need a safe and supportive place to meet and discuss the many facets of their work in schools. Even more specifically and critically, the same conditions must be established for teachers to examine something far more intimate and threatening: their curricula and instruction.

COLLABORATIVE ACTION RESEARCH FOR EQUITY (CARE)

I developed the Collaborative Action Research for Equity (CARE) program in conjunction with Donna Marriott and later Jamie Almanzán, then a gifted middle-school English as a second language teacher in the Palo Alto (California) Unified School District, to invoke a process that can enable teachers to safely and deeply examine themselves and their teaching as it relates to all children, but in particular Black, Brown, and American Indian students. For teachers in schools that lack professional learning community cultures, this type of inquiry is not only difficult—it can also be quite dangerous. In my experience, teachers who attempt to transform themselves and their teaching in a vacuum—that is, independently or in isolation from other teachers—often lack the necessary supports to deeply and safely search out their own racial blind spots. Those who may locate these unconsciously destructive beliefs and practices about learning and teaching often struggle to identify and apply alternative antiracism mindsets and pedagogies that can foster improved achievement for students of color. In Donna's case, for example, she was acting alone, without the support of her colleagues or administrators, to understand why her Black male students and other students of color were not reading on par with their White counterparts and to improve the reading skills of *all* her students. Had she not been so assured of her talents in teaching reading, however, she could never have been as open to my questioning and, at times, criticism of her practices.

Essentially, CARE creates a professional learning community culture for teachers who have received a foundational experience, such as PEG's Beyond Diversity training, and it supports them in personalizing race and Whiteness and in using the Courageous Conversations Protocol to uncover, examine, and address racial inequities in their lives and classrooms. This type of support, I believe, enables racial equity leaders-in-the-making to engage, as Roland Barth writes in *Improving Schools from Within,* in the same kinds of "continuous inquiry about teaching" that teachers in formal professional learning communities are afforded. The latter groups of teachers, Barth notes, "are researchers, students of teaching, who observe others teach, have others observe them, talk about teaching, and help other teachers. In short, they are professionals."[12] CARE provides a basic framework for professionalizing collaborative action research on equity issues through guided learning that acquaints teachers with core racial equity principles and practices, essential components of culturally relevant teaching, and a rudimentary under-standing of intrinsic motivation. In addition to exploring the cultures, histories, disposi-tions, and learning traditions of various populations of color, CARE-trained teachers are coached toward increased cultural proficiency and instructional mastery.

CARE teachers, as those who complete the training are called, are asked to select a focal group of from five to seven students who represent the particular racial demographic the teachers are struggling to educate effectively. They are charged to monitor closely these students' academic performance, affect, and engagement as they employ culturally relevant, innovative instructional modifications and approaches intentionally designed to improve the school achievement of the targeted, harder-to-reach students but implemented for all children in their classrooms. The teachers must consult with the students in the focal groups before, during, and after implementing the approaches to gauge their overall effectiveness in reaching the students. They must also monitor the impact on students in the nonfocal group, who typically are White, and ensure that they continue to experience academic success in the face of the new teaching methods.

Katharine Johnson is a CARE teacher at Irvington Elementary School in Portland, Oregon (Portland Public Schools is a PEG partnering district). She developed a writing lesson specifically designed to meet the needs of the students of color in her combined first- and second-grade classes who were not performing well in that area. The lesson, she noted, "included making a poster of smart ways to write How-To books." On the first two days of the lesson, she displayed five of her focal students' work on a poster/anchor chart so that the other members of her school's CARE team could review their work and provide her with feedback. Katharine posted the following reflections about the experience on PEG's online professional learning platform:

At the last minute I decided to include an example from a White student on the poster as well. Kim asked me, "Why did you feel you needed to include Roderick's writing?" This question has stuck with me. There are several reasons. Upon further reflection, it became clear that all of the reasons perpetuate a racist paradigm.

Part of the reason I added Roderick's paper was because I can't let go of the idea of balance. I have trained my brain to make sure I always have a student of color's work on any anchor chart or class poster. I couldn't let go this superficial balancing act when I had a poster dedicated to the work my focal students developed. Despite the fact that one of the most valuable ideas I am carrying around from the work on the CARE team is the idea that it is not only permissible, but advisable, to prioritize and highlight my students of color, I was still reluctant to follow all the way through with that idea. I couldn't just make an anchor chart representing solely the work of students of color.

Another piece of my thinking was also grounded in racist ideas. I worried that my more competent second-grade writers, who are all White, would not take the lesson seriously if all the examples were from students of color—not only students of color but also students who are perceived by their peers as lower-performing. How can I expect that perception to change unless I demonstrate their proficiency, even their excellence?

I am realizing now that even in attempting to develop an antiracist lesson plan, racism still showed up. It was still a lesson I am proud of. It was still a joy to watch Gerardo, José and Julia light up as I shared their work and they shared the smart thinking they used to create that work. But I am forever surprised at the shape-shifting nature of racism. Even when looking right at it, it can still slide through my conscious thinking and come out in my actions or thinking that is outside of my awareness. That's why the power of this group I trust is invaluable. They see what I can't.

Given that CARE teachers confront an enormous amount of new (or, more often than not, disregarded) pedagogical theories and that they are continuously and somewhat publicly examining their beliefs and behaviors related to race and schooling through a process referred to as the CARE Cycle of Inquiry (see Figure 9.1), they must become proficient in the practice and techniques of adaptive leadership. That is, CARE teachers are guided to do their most, and best, work in the Zone of Productive Disequilibrium, where they are led to seek meaning over solutions and results over rhetoric. The CARE program's Cycle of Inquiry guides teachers to Plan, Do, Reflect, and Revise—or, as Michael Fullan once described it to me, to adopt a "Ready, Fire, Aim!" approach—as a community of professional learners. Its embrace of the Courageous Conversations Protocol ensures that CARE teachers' inquiry is deep and meaningful and that it specifically challenges the very detours that have enabled teachers across the country to avoid having courageous conversations about race and essential interracial interactions. Its ultimate goal is to make responsible classroom improvements so that *all* children can experience greater success in school.

Figure 9.1 The Pacific Educational Group (PEG) Cycle of Inquiry

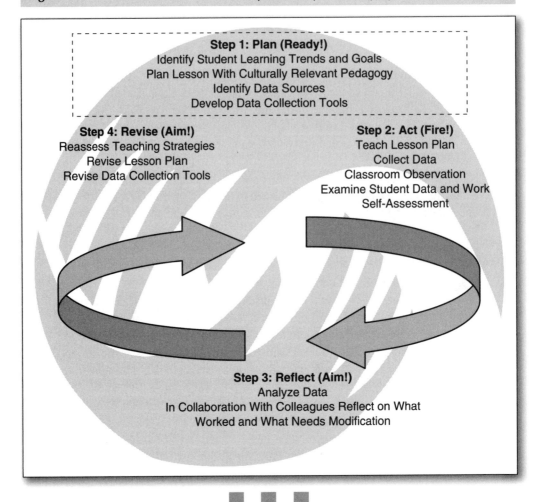

Step 1: Plan (Ready!)
Identify Student Learning Trends and Goals
Plan Lesson With Culturally Relevant Pedagogy
Identify Data Sources
Develop Data Collection Tools

Step 4: Revise (Aim!)
Reassess Teaching Strategies
Revise Lesson Plan
Revise Data Collection Tools

Step 2: Act (Fire!)
Teach Lesson Plan
Collect Data
Classroom Observation
Examine Student Data and Work
Self-Assessment

Step 3: Reflect (Aim!)
Analyze Data
In Collaboration With Colleagues Reflect on What
Worked and What Needs Modification

Donna and I together created a miniculture for true professional learning, a culture that did not exist at Casa de Oro Elementary School. However, the learning that ultimately translated into Donna's improved instruction and that prompted higher-level engagement and achievement gains for her Black male students never became a source of conversation, meaning, or reform schoolwide. Subsequently, when the boys exited Donna's classroom and advanced to third grade and beyond, some of them reverted to a pattern of failure, mainly because their successive teachers were neither equity-centered nor focused on their continuous growth, development, and improvement. Even by looping her Black boys for 3 years in a multi-age classroom, Donna could not protect them from the eventual exposure to a system that viewed them as "the problem" and their failure as "evidence."

I experienced mixed emotions when I received notice that Donna Marriott was leaving Casa de Oro elementary school to work in the San Diego Unified School's district office, where she would be supporting other teachers' literacy instructional development. On one hand, I could not help but be proud of her for being recognized as an outstanding teacher, as evidenced by her promotion. On the other hand, because Donna had so much to offer when it came to her gained ability to engage children of color and promote their highest level of reading achievement, her talents would be sorely missed. I could not help but question the wisdom of removing this talented educator from the classroom. To me, it was an indication of a systemic breakdown in the process of establishing learning environments that allow teachers to embrace their moral obligation and professional responsibility to meet the needs of *all* children.

Unlike her many colleagues at Casa de Oro who were resistant to racial equity ideas and efforts, and despite the system's overall lack of commitment to or focus on racial equity in her district, Donna chose to find meaning and then solutions to the racial equity challenges in her own classroom. Alone, she courageously disaggregated the data revealing that her Black boys were struggling academically in the classroom environments she had constructed, as a result of the inadequate relationships she had formed with her students, their families, and her colleagues of color, and because of the instructional methods and choices she had embraced. In our work together, Donna and I formed a mini-professional learning community culture in which her essential questions about race—as they related to her own race and that of the Black boys in her classes—were examined and answered.

I know that Donna left the classroom, where she was both desperately needed and uniquely effective, partly because she believed that by moving into the ranks of district administration she could help establish a culture that would benefit her colleagues at Casa de Oro and elsewhere. She also needed to leave so she would not have to witness her Black male students, whose reading and other scholastic abilities had been so amazingly elevated by the time they were promoted from her classes, experience struggle, frustration, and eventual failure in the hands of culturally destructive, unconsciously racist teachers the very next year.

ESSENTIAL QUESTIONS

Think about the makeup of your classroom and of the colleagues in your school community as you answer these questions.

1. How would you define your relationships with Black, Brown, and American Indian adults?

2. Which of these relationship characteristics most positively influences the way you think about (and act on) educating Black, Brown, and American Indian children?

3. To what degree do you believe a professional learning community culture exists in your school/district?

4. What is happening in the classrooms in your school/district that most challenges you to engage in, sustain, and deepen courageous conversations about race?

5. To what extent have you personally developed the requisite will, skill, knowledge, and capacity needed to teach lower-performing children of color effectively?

6. What personal, professional, and organizational factors challenge you in your development?

Voices From the Inside: Jackie Roehl

I teach in Edina, Minnesota, a first-ring Minneapolis suburb dominated by White, affluent residents and high-performing schools. When the school district made a commitment to ensure racial equity for all Edina Public School students, some parents, students, and even employees questioned that decision, wondering why we needed to explore race, racism, and Whiteness when our schools are consistently ranked among the top in the state and the nation. While it's true that our district boasts high graduation rates and advanced placement (AP) scores, the reality was that we suffered a significant race-based achievement gap and racial predictability in enrollment in our AP classes.

Fortunately, many community members and educators embrace the idea that to end racism in the United States and close the racial achievement gap, teachers and students must explicitly and courageously discuss issues of race, racism, and Whiteness. Even schools like mine, with a student population that is 82% White and a staff of nearly all White teachers, need to promote courageous conversations and act on equity issues. Closing the racial achievement gap in the United States is a moral and ethical imperative. Schools will do little to change the racial predictability of achievement without a major shift in teaching approaches and active social justice work. Edina is beginning to shift, and working with PEG influenced recent reforms at Edina High School that impacted teachers, students, and systems.

Having a teaching staff embrace culturally relevant pedagogy is key to closing the racial achievement gap. Teachers have long been trained to honor diversity but have also been encouraged to teach all students in the same way in the name of equality. Teachers must understand that equity is not equality because students have individual needs in terms of process and assessment—just like the vegetables in my garden have individual needs, with my tomatoes needing more water than my onions. Success in the garden comes from caring for each plant according to its needs; success in schools comes from giving each student the specific instruction she or he needs to reach high intellectual performance.

■ ■ ■

The last 8 years of my teaching career have been marked by a fierce belief that all students can achieve at high levels. Although I was committed to social justice in the past, my teaching philosophy evolved through my work with PEG and The National Urban Alliance for Effective Education (NUA). Prior to 2004, my English classroom focused on whole-class discussions about literature, where a few verbal students dominated the lessons and entertained their classmates. Although I called these discussions Socratic and believed I was teaching my students critical thinking skills, I realized that mostly my White students were reflecting my White culture back to me, and that my students of color were left out of that classroom discourse altogether. Exposure to the beliefs and practices of culturally relevant teaching helped me change my pedagogy.

I first began my journey to culturally relevant teaching with NUA and its seminars, which emphasize high intellectual performance for all students through explicit teaching strategies that stress high operational practices and lessons that consider students' cultural frames of reference. However, a piece of my pedagogy puzzle remained missing until my school district became involved with PEG in 2009. PEG seminars filled in the missing philosophical piece that is as important as having new strategies to try in class. PEG's emphasis on having courageous conversations that isolate race, and specifically, a study of critical race theory helped me reach the place that I am today—a teacher who not only incorporates culturally relevant strategies but also understands the importance of critically examining the systems of racism that prevent some students from achieving to their highest potential in school.

PEG's Beyond Diversity workshops, equity team seminars, and CARE trainings gave my colleagues and me a framework to examine the individual and systemic practices at Edina High School that limit student achievement. Debriefing equity walks allowed the team to discuss systemic issues in our school: the high frequency of Black students in our school's alternative high school, which is housed in our basement: our only Black male employees working in support positions such as security or cafeteria duty; and our Black students avoiding the school's main lunchroom during the lunch hours. As a team, we practiced the Courageous Conversations Protocol to discuss not only these equity walks but also classroom observations of focal students of color. We discussed the strategies that we could use for students who were so quiet in class that they were flying under the radar as well as those students who were engaging with the curriculum in a manner that did not fit our school's traditional White culture.

Before working with PEG, teacher conversations around classroom observations were staid and focused on the positives. Now, CARE team members are starting to speak honestly with each other about areas that need improvement regarding students of color in the classroom. These difficult conversations were the missing piece for our school to really begin systemic transformations.

■ ■ ■

In addition to the CARE team members personally changing their pedagogy, the team wanted to impact the entire staff, so we started sharing the strategies and philosophies with colleagues through equity seminars. For the last 2 years, the CARE team used staff development time and even former faculty meeting time to present to the full staff the philosophies and strategies learned from PEG and NUA. We placed an equity lens over all staff development discussions—from literacy to home-work to assessment. We even used specific readings and films from PEG seminars with our staff. For example, one 3-hour session on critical race theory and the film, *The House We Live In,* impacted many staff members, especially examining Whiteness as property, and pushed them to understand the importance of equity work at Edina High School.

Understanding critical race theory was a significant reason behind our school tak-ing another step on our equity journey—incorporating a study of critical race theory into our sophomore English classes. English teachers felt that our district's mission to give all learners the "ethical values necessary to thrive in a rapidly changing, culturally diverse, global society" could not be fully met without explicit discussions of race, rac-ism, and Whiteness. In fact, our largely White student body at our largely White school would be significantly underprepared to succeed in the world beyond the classroom if we didn't explicitly teach them about race, racism, and Whiteness before they ventured out in a world that is significantly more racially diverse than the community in which they grow up.

To that end, sophomore English classes used the theme, "The Counterstory," to frame the curriculum this past year so students could critically examine perspectives that are often left out of the canon. English teachers also encouraged students to examine the role that power has in the stories studied to get a sense of the ways Whiteness silences some voices and amplifies others. Using the Courageous Conversations Protocol with our students, we were able to guide students through difficult discussions of race, racism, and Whiteness. As a culminating essay, students used critical race theory to analyze two texts read in class.

In just 3 short years, the discussions and written reflections about race and racism in our English 10 classes have grown immensely. Three years ago, teachers across the school had little direct discussion of race. I recall the moment 3 years ago when I told my class, "Let's get a Black student's perspective" and many White students yelled at me in response: "You can't say that! That's racist!" Then, 2 years ago, English 10 incor-porated a 3-week unit on race and racism to accompany Richard Wright's memoir, *Black Boy.* I am ashamed to admit that despite the fact that *Black Boy* has been in the English 10 curriculum for 10 years, teachers previously reduced the book to a discussion of hunger and poverty, with race only briefly mentioned as part of Wright's cultural identity.

However, 2 years ago, students started to explicitly discuss race with their personal racial awakening stories and an analysis of the narratives of Blackness and Whiteness in Wright's memoir and other short selections of fiction and nonfiction. These racial awakening stories allowed students to explore the moment they first recognized race, and especially allowed White students—some for the first time—to think about Whiteness as a race. Through text-to-self connections, students were also able to discuss how Whiteness was showing up in the classrooms and hallways of Edina High School.

Even though English teachers have been able to evolve our discussions of race, racism, and Whiteness over the years to an in-depth study, some students, teachers, and parents still question why students in a school that is 82% White need to be exposed to such a course of study. Fortunately, the English teachers can courageously explain to parents and students that White students also need help exploring issues of race and racism because their own White racial identity is invisible to many, and they reduce racism to something that happened in the past to other people. Since a few vocal parents find my commitment to expanding the racial consciousness of my students troubling, parent-teacher conference days are draining and demanding. Although I have some parents who thank me for opening their children's eyes to issues of racial justice, the few parents who complain stick with me for days. One mother said that studying racism is OK, but she didn't want students to learn about Whiteness until college. Another parent asked why the race unit didn't include a discussion of the racism that White males feel from groups such as the Black Panthers. Other questions and comments are more veiled: "Wouldn't students be better served with a classic rather than *Black Boy*?" or "My daughter is looking forward to a new unit."

Although questioning parents are all too common in the education profession, answering questions about race takes a special skill set. Because of my PEG training, I was able to stay centered on the compass and explain the beliefs, thoughts, feelings, and actions behind the English curriculum.

■ ■ ■

Although incorporating a unit on race and racism was a good start compared to where my school was a few years ago, the English Department felt that educational equity could not be achieved as long as we had systemic curricular gaps between enriched and regular classes. Black and Hispanic students were overrepresented in regular classes, while White and Asian students were overrepresented in enriched classes. Although isolating race was key in our decision, we also noticed that girls were greatly overrepresented in enriched English classes, leaving overall demographics of the leveled classes skewed by race and gender.

The English Department felt the best way to address this curriculum gap was to eliminate the leveling of courses and provide the enriched curriculum to all students. Next year, this new course will launch with 12 English teachers, one special education teacher, and one English language learners teacher, working together to ensure that all students have the opportunity for a successful enriched experience. Specific structures are in place for flexible grouping based on choice books and tiered assignments that provide multiple ways for students to meet the state standards.

Overall, educators must understand that despite the fact that discussing issues of race, racism, and Whiteness is uncomfortable, they need to experience that discomfort to effect real change from the status quo that leaves so many students woefully behind. Our current system even leaves White students behind in terms of being prepared for a racially diverse global society. We need teachers who are uncomfortable with the racial predictability of enrollment in honors courses, of identification in gifted and talented programs, of academic achievement. We need teachers to be uncomfortable enough with the way things are to actively and courageously fight for a more equitable and more just education for our students.

Jackie Roehl is a tenth-grade English teacher in the Edina (Minnesota) Public Schools and Minnesota's 2012 Teacher of the Year. She is White American.

TEN

Empowering Parents and Communities of Color for Racial Equity

From Theory to Practice

When connections between school and community are weak and characterized by fear and distrust, it is more likely that the school will serve as a source of negative social capital. However, when school and a community have formed a genuine partnership based on respect and a shared sense of responsibility, positive forms of social capital can be generated.

—Pedro Noguera[1]

Hardly a day goes by in which educators, both White and those of color, fail to blame parents and other community members of color for not supporting their children's schooling success effectively. These critics often fail to realize that many of the parents and community members of color they so readily disparage often experienced racial challenges in their own education similar or identical to those their children face now. Although educators tend to shy away from empowering parents and community members of color to interact effectively with and guide the local workings of school systems, some of these same educators seem content to assign blame and responsibility for the failures of students of color to the parents and community folk in the same dysfunctional and inversely proportionate ways. They also often lose sight of the fact that the American school system was not founded to empower adults of color to serve as advocates for their children. As a result, by and large, they view these significant adults in the lives of students of color as threatening, and schools and society continue to marginalize both parents and children.

When parents and community members of color are invited "to the table" to discuss and decide on school- and education-related matters, they are asked (or forced) to contain their mixed or often downright angry and fiery emotions about the racial inequities and disparities in the education system. They are asked to function—well, as if they were White. That is, they are told to relinquish their beliefs that the system is racially biased, damaging, and perhaps hostile to them and their children and to be more submissive to the status quo and the glacial pace of change.

Such assertions of dysfunction and lack of caring, as well as demands for dispassionate dialogue, strain potentially positive future relationships between families and communities of color and school officials (the vast majority of whom are not of color). Accusations and finger pointing have not yielded improved outcomes for children of color. That is why it is my intention in this chapter to suggest that informed, appropriate parental and community support is a cornerstone for raising the achievement of *all* students, regardless of race, but it is especially critical for under-served students of color.

However, as I ask you to embark with me on this journey to a deeper analysis and understanding of what effective partnerships between school officials and families and communities of color look like, please bear in mind one important caveat: No partnership among parents, communities, and schools—no matter how effective—serves as a proxy for improving teacher quality, increasing academic rigor, or eliminating those institutional policies, programs, and practices that serve to disadvantage students of color and advantage White students. Ultimately, the challenge facing educators and racial equity leaders in schools must be viewed through the existing prism of systemic racism.

Before parents and community members of color can recognize the many good things occurring in schools that are making clear strides toward achieving racial equity, these adults must be allowed to share and shed their own school narratives, which often are steeped in generations of pain, doubt, and disappointment. This process is truly a difficult one, yet it is a hallmark of moving Courageous Conversations from theory to practice.

At Pacific Educational Group (PEG), we recognize the importance of parent and community empowerment in creating partnerships that support the academic success of students of color. Engaging the significant adults in the lives and schooling of students of color as authentic advocates on their behalf is a critical domain of PEG's Systemic Racial Equity Framework (the PEG Framework) and theory of transformation. How we go about equipping typically disenfranchised parents and community members of color with the specific skills, will, knowledge, and capacities for holding the education system and educators, as well as themselves, accountable is the focus of PEG's innovative PASS initiative: Partnerships for Academically Successful Students.

PARTNERSHIPS FOR ACADEMICALLY SUCCESSFUL STUDENTS

To engage in partnerships with adults of color in the truest sense of the word, educators must learn how to do more than merely respond to their questions and concerns relating to the "nuts and bolts" of schooling (e.g., How do you read and interpret standardized test data? What is the appropriate scope and sequence of the curriculum for my child at various grade levels? What are teachers' expectations for homework? Is there someone at the school, district, central administration, or school board who can help me address school issues and questions as they arise?). Educators must also learn to offer R-E-S-P-E-C-T to these adults—be they parents, clergy, activists, business people, or sports icons—in the diverse languages and styles that make sense to them.

This means more than merely informing parents and community members about educational policies and practices affecting their children. School officials must be able to offer authentic praise, if you will, to these real and potential advocates if they are to believe that educators sincerely recognize and understand the trials and tribulations of people and communities of color as well as their celebrations, rituals, ceremonies, recreational interests, and other aspects that greatly affect the school success of students of color. Educators must also learn how to create safe spaces for parents and community members of color to voice their counternarratives about the education they and their children have received—they must help to secure these spaces in classrooms, conference rooms, and board rooms as a primary strategy for challenging what many of these adults view as the education system's oppressive conditions.

For many educators, the PASS component of the PEG Framework is the most difficult facet to implement and thus serves as one of the greatest challenges in moving Courageous Conversations from theory to practice. Sad to say, I have found that too many educators demonstrate, and at times even verbalize, a deep-seated fear of authentically engaging with families of color. For some, this fear is grounded in an unpleasant prior experience with a parent or parents of color that they have generalized to represent all experiences. Others promote and adhere to the debilitating dominant institutional narrative that parents and community members of color are difficult to engage with; thus, they never really attempt to challenge that folklore. I characterize this narrative as folklore because typically, when some educators cultivate and perpetuate fear of engaging with adults of color, other teachers, usually in the same building, have developed wonderfully supportive relationships with these same adults.

For still other educators, partnering effectively with parents and community members of color is a struggle because the educators themselves possess an inability or unwillingness to share power with their students' home- and community-based advocates. By avoiding meaningful exchanges and interactions with parents of color, White teachers, especially, can also avoid having to examine the deficit-model beliefs and tightly embraced pedagogical theories and practices that often do not work for students of color. Suppose, for example, that a parent of color shares with his child's White teacher information on a nickname or new way of greeting the child so that the teacher can help make the child feel more welcomed and comfortable in the learning environment. If that name or greeting challenges the teacher's comfort level or sounds awkward or foreign to him or her, the teacher will most often refuse to use it and continue to greet the child in a way that is comfortable to the teacher but perhaps alienating to both the child and the parent.

The PASS process helps racial equity leaders understand what they must know and do—or not do—to engage parents and community members of color in challenging all forms of institutional racial bias in schools and education systems, removing barriers to access and opportunities for students of color, and ensuring that children of color are held to the highest standards and expectations. Five critical attributes characterize the kinds of partnerships that must be forged among educators, parents, and community-based advocates for under-served students of color. These attributes or guiding principles are represented graphically in the PASS Star (see Figure 10.1).

The five PASS principles are as follows:

Figure 10.1 The Partnerships for Academically Successful Students (PASS) Star

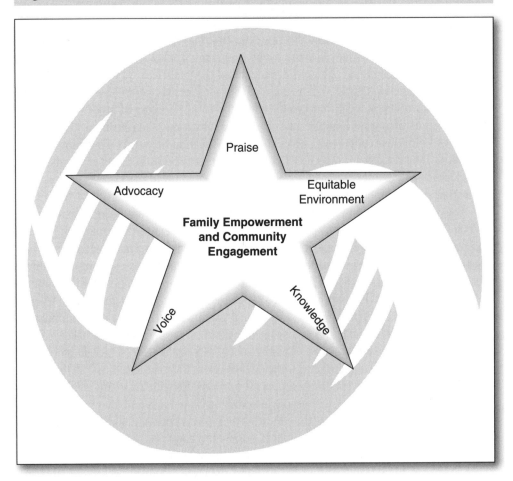

Praise. Educators must recognize and intentionally appreciate parents and community members of color, both privately and in public, for the unique energies they exude and pass on to their children and for the often amazing resilience they demonstrate in the face of social injustice and racial oppression. Mutual respect is typically the by-product of a relationship between educators and adults of color that is complete with nurturing, care, honor, and respect. In such contexts, genuine and authentic praise can bridge the racial chasm and inspire confidence among parents and community members of color that educators are sincere in their commitment to educate *all* children.

Advocacy. A parent's primary responsibility, regardless of race, is to stay actively engaged in the optimal development of his or her child. Educators and community members necessarily have a positional responsibility and moral imperative to act on behalf of *all* children, but their engagement often follows specific protocols that are institutional or culturally specific. Until educators understand, in meaningful and effective ways, just how advocacy is "done" by parents and community members of color, they might not recognize when it is present nor understand how to engage it when it is absent.

Knowledge. Educators must pay special attention to ensuring that all parents and community members of color understand important school policies and procedures and can access all available community-based educational resources. Parents and community members of color often have experienced marginalization in their own schooling, but when they are shown how to use such knowledge in identifying resources for their children, they feel empowered. Educators, in turn, must make sharing this knowledge with parents and community members of color a constitutive and intentional element of school and district transformation efforts.

Voice. Educators must construct school environments in which all educational constituencies, especially those of parents and community members of color, are able to "speak their truth." These environments likewise must be equitable and accessible because these constituencies often lack the language, knowledge, or safety to address the issues of deepest concern to them and their children. Thus, space must be created and awarded especially to them. Ultimately, the voices of parents and community members of color must emerge and influence *all* classroom-, school-, and district-level decisions made on behalf of students of color.

Equitable Environment. Welcoming institutional cultures and climates that are receptive to the voices of families and communities of color and that empower these adults to advocate effectively on behalf of their children are essential if educators are to ensure the success of students of color. In such environments, the educational system is mobilized to take action around what family and community members of color express as their priorities for the education of their children. The establishment of an equitable environment is not only an indication that the other four PASS principles have been operationalized in a school or district but also a sign that the PEG Framework is not just a theory of transformation but an actual internalized belief and practiced behavior.

It is important that educators *not* view any of the five principles in isolation; rather, they should view these essential attributes collectively, as part of an interlocking network of care and support that ensures the maximum participation, engagement, and, ultimately, empowerment of parents, community members, and students of color. Adults of color are such valuable resources and voices for the educational success of students of color, but they often cannot be enrolled and registered in efforts to advocate on behalf of their children until they experience their own personal and collective sense of validation in the schools. Once all five points of recognition in the PASS star are connected and achieved, however, I have found that parents and community members of color are much more receptive to identifying ways they can be more supportive of educators, abandoning resistive attitudes toward schools and schooling, and collaborating to ensure that students of color experience scholastic success.

The following is an excerpt from a report prepared by a member of the PEG staff who had facilitated an initial round of engagement sessions (focus groups) with parents and community members of color in one of PEG's partnering districts. Note how this report examines the personal, professional, and organizational levels of readiness among district personnel to act on what they are telling us about what strains parental relations and diminishes student performance in school.

COURAGEOUS CONVERSATIONS WITH PARENTS OF COLOR IN *[NAME OF DISTRICT]* DISTRICT

There were three main purposes for [PEG to engage in] courageous conversations with the parents of African American students in this district and with other community members of color:

1. To gather information concerning their beliefs about the causes and solutions for the academic achievement gap between underachieving African American and Latino students and their White classmates;

2. To build momentum and buy-in within the African American community for a districtwide effort to close the racial achievement gap; and,

3. To establish baseline information that will inform and support the PASS parent-engagement process as it moves forward in [the coming school year].

PEG staff conducted a total of six focus groups and five individual interviews with more than 40 parents/community members between [Date] and [Date]. The District's Community Education Department planned and organized the focus groups and interviews, with assistance from principals and a community member. Although we had set a goal of hosting 75 focus group participants, regrettably, our numbers fell short of that goal.

Individual conversations were planned for 30 minutes each, and focus groups for 60 minutes; however, all sessions went longer than the planned time, and most participants seemed eager to continue the conversations.

Because of the relatively small number of participants, the data for this report is insufficient to form conclusions about the perceived causes of and solutions for the racial achievement gap. The responses of participants did allow for the identification of several themes, which are discussed later in this report. Apart from the data collected, the process itself provided some important learning about idiosyncrasies of the [Name of District] community and organizational structure that will inform, and must be mediated through, our future parent-engagement efforts.

Two issues are noteworthy here:

- *Community infrastructure.* The sprawling geography of the district, which includes some or all of seven different cities/communities, is not conducive to having a strong community-based infrastructure that facilitates connections among people of color within the district. The absence of this infrastructure made it more difficult to mobilize people of color to participate in focus groups. Although this is presently a barrier, it is also an opportunity for the schools to fill the void by playing a more active role in building community structures that welcome and support families of color.

- *District organizational structure.* Historically in [Name of District], the Community Education Department [hereafter "Community Ed"] has been given organizational responsibility for leading and facilitating parent involvement initiatives; thus, Community Ed took the lead in organizing the data collection phase (focus groups, etc.) of our PASS work. It was not for lack of effort that this traditional method did not prove to be successful in recruiting more African American parents to the focus group meetings. We discovered, however, that the distances that may already exist between the African American parents and their schools are further aggravated when the meeting organizers (Community Ed) are yet another step removed from the schools. Teachers and principals have the closest and most natural relationships with parents of color, and this is where the connections must begin. We will heed this lesson as we form PASS teams at each school in the coming year.

Common Focus Group Themes

The following themes emerged from conversations with focus group participants led by PEG Family and Community Empowerment consultants:

1. *[Name of District] is the best district in the suburban areas for people of color.* All participants agreed that [Name of District] was the best district in suburban [Name of City]. Some had moved from district to district searching for a school community that was hospitable to African Americans. Yet, many participants felt they were not getting access to all of [Name of District]'s resources. One participant stated that "the district has everything we need, but there is no outreach to us." There was also a sense among the participants that White residents of the district were not accepting of Black youth, especially boys. A Somali participant said that counselors were not doing enough to guide students of color. "As a Somali in the system, I have never discussed college with a single counselor." There was also variation of opinion about schools within the district. The high school was viewed as being unreceptive to African American students as well as being excessively punitive and hostile toward them.

2. *The racial achievement gap is a relational issue.* Despite differences across race, class, and positional status within the district, participants had much in common as they described their beliefs concerning why the racial achievement gap exists. They identified several school-based factors as causes for the racial achievement gap: low teacher expectations of Black children; unfair treatment/punishment of Black children, especially boys; and resistance to placing Black kids in higher-level classes, especially the Challenge Program. Participants also felt that White participants tended

(Continued)

(Continued)

to focus more on the lack of parent involvement by African American and Latino parents. Participants were also very concerned about their children's status as social outsiders. Some felt educators are quicker to discipline students of color than White students (e.g., sending them out of the classroom or lowering their grades for late work; publicly shaming and disrespecting them). One parent stated, "I just don't see why teachers don't understand how difficult it is for a kid (of color) in a White system." Another parent stated that the achievement gap is "a relational issue, and they just don't know how to talk to us or our kids." In short, these participants of color felt that teachers don't understand enough about their kids' cultural and behavioral backgrounds to like them, and this causes many kids of color to feel disconnected from school.

3. *Parents spoke of a general disrespect that existed in some but not all of [Name of District]'s schools.* Parents talked about their perceptions that they were not viewed as having anything to bring to the education process. The exception was those parents who were very aggressive in advocacy for their children. They felt that if parents of color were not aggressive in staying on top of teachers, their children would not have been as successful in [Name of District] schools as they have been. Regarding the absence of respect for students, some parents remarked:

   • "They (teachers) don't talk to the parents; they tell the parents what their kids need."
   • "They will ask for you to be present, but they won't listen to what you say. They want our faces there, but not our opinions."
   • "They think we're angry when we are passionate about our children; and then, they just shut down."
   • "I was told they had enough volunteers, and I noticed that all of the volunteers were White."

4. *Parents perceive that there are different placement and punishment policies for Black kids.* Many of the parents offered specific stories that caused them to believe that educators treated their kids unfairly because of their color. As some remarked:

   • "My daughter was allowed into the Challenge Program, but when the budget was cut, she was removed."
   • "My son's teacher dragged her feet on referring him to the Challenge Program until I insisted she refer him."
   • "They suspended my son, when it was a White kid who called him 'nigger.'"
   • "Parent involvement was good during preschool, but the doors close after the 0–5 program."

Next Steps

Parents of color expressed significant interest in continuing to be engaged in courageous conversations about race as a result of their participation in these focus groups and interviews. Some have also participated in Beyond Diversity training with Community Ed. We at PEG want to build on this energy and not allow it to dissipate; however, plans for convening site-based PASS teams in [the coming year] have not come to fruition due to a variety of factors. The goal remains to do so in [2 years]. Initially, teams will include African American parents (six to eight persons), staff (two to three persons), and the principal. PASS teams will participate together in a series of trainings and will meet as school-based teams for the purpose of developing effective and sustainable community and family partnerships for academically successful students of color.

The following is a sampling of additional comments made by parents during the focus group discussions:

- "We need more Black history. Isn't it their job to teach it?"
- "We, as Black people, thought low of ourselves because we weren't told about ourselves."
- "How much is the parent's responsibility? How much is the teacher's responsibility? We need to really talk about this."
- "How do we get parents involved and engaged in their students' schooling? We have an environment in which they feel alienated."
- "As far as elementary education is concerned, the schools are doing well."
- "[Name of School] has a welcoming group. Older kids need to feel warm and welcome as well."
- "Parents do not understand the gap and/or how data is collected."
- "New math concepts? Parents don't have the 'new math.' Parents need access to information, to understand the test. Why is so much based on homework?"
- "Communications. We simply are not talked to unless something is wrong."
- "Educators and families are not hearing one another."
- "We are not giving the kids the voice to speak for themselves. They will tell you their strengths and weaknesses if you listen."
- "No representation of Blacks in history."
- "[Name of School] just started a program for African American kids, after school, on Tuesdays."
- "A kid needs a hero. We [Blacks] don't have that in the schools."
- "Our kids don't want to go to AP and be alone; then they're tardy because they need to reconnect with their boys."
- " [The state] has not yet caught up with diversity. Kids need to see walking testimonies, heroes, successful Black people. Diversity is never there. Where are the Latino and African American teachers?"
- "My 8-year-old notices the lack of diversity among teachers."
- "Kids feel isolated."
- "I'm here because kids need me here; they need to see a Black woman."

When districts call for the narratives of parents and family members of under-served students of color, quite often they are not prepared for—and thus not willing to embrace, examine, or address—the concerns expressed by these constituents. Sometimes dismissed because of their passion, language differences, or unwillingness to show up in the "White way," Black, Brown, and American Indian parents often experience a "damned if you do, damned if you don't" reaction when trying to advocate appropriately on behalf of their children. Some choose not to participate for fear of further upsetting the system, and they too are deemed to be uncaring and unresponsive. When parents of color visit with system officials, they often are viewed as inappropriate or misbehaving. Given the lack of racial acuity possessed by many educators, White educators especially, particularly with regard to their interactions with parents of color, schools are often places that marginalize parents of color just as they marginalize students of color.

PEG's process for supporting school leaders to uncover, examine, and address the authentic experiences and perspectives of Black, Brown, and American Indian parents assists educators in helping parents navigate the educational system on behalf of their children. This can only occur effectively, however, once educators are practiced in the Courageous Conversations Protocol and the school district is genuinely focused on racial equity transformation.

ENGAGING AND DEVELOPING WHITE ALLIES TO SUPPORT PARENTS AND COMMUNITY MEMBERS OF COLOR IN SCHOOLS

Over the years, we at PEG have learned a valuable lesson: that although empowering families and communities of color is key and essential to achieving racial equity in education, it is an insufficient strategy for surmounting institutionalized White privilege. Too often, transactions that lead to the creation of inequitable policies, racially biased program selections, and racially unjust instructional practices take place in sites where people of color have limited or no access such as churches (which, even in today's America, remain largely racially segregated), social clubs, and recreation and shopping centers. Because most neighborhoods in the United States (and the adult activities taking place within them) continue to be racially similar to school demographics, what may appear to be casual and seemingly harmless conversations among and between White families and school officials (e.g., board members, administrators, school-site council members, and parent-teacher leaders) in one community can lead to reforms that negatively affect students of color in another.

Now, I am not suggesting that all such conversations result in education outcomes that advantage White children and short-change Black ones, or that all important policy-making takes place away from the public eye. I am suggesting, however, that the absence of a critical mass of conscientious, informed, and empowered adult advocates of color in such conversations exacerbates the educational inequities that plague students and communities of color. The insertion of assertive, knowledgeable Black, Brown, and American Indian adult voices into these discussions has great potential for advancing more inclusive and representative dialogues at both the local and national levels.

Court orders may desegregate schools, but they have no jurisdiction to challenge de facto segregated neighborhoods. That is why the term "neighborhood schools" has come to mean "racially segregated schools" in the present-day context. Similarly, it is not enough to grant opportunities, under state policy and federal legislation such as No Child Left Behind, for parents to remove their children from failing schools and provide them with access to opportunities in higher-performing schools, even in neighboring districts, if those schools do not have space, or worse, do not feature environments that are antiracist and culturally proficient. When White families in Seattle, Washington, and Louisville, Kentucky, recently successfully petitioned the U.S. Supreme Court to block a policy that would have sent their children from predominantly White neighborhoods in to more racially plural communities to attend school, this country witnessed another challenge to the unfinished and perhaps unattainable 50-year journey to integration.

As racial equity leaders, we must not only empower families of color to voice their support for racial equity in education and hold the nation's school systems accountable for achieving it, we must also engage and develop White parents and community members as activist, racially conscious, morally assertive, and sympathetic supporters of our equity objectives. However, given all the implications of Whiteness detailed in previous chapters of this book, it is predictable that even the most socially progressive White people will struggle at some point with the concepts or methodologies of antiracism. These same people, despite their philosophical agreement with the principles of racial equity, often participate in or align themselves with the exclusive religious, civic, social, and recreation venues in which few or no people of color feel welcome. Rather than ignore these potentially powerful allies, racial equity leaders must create safe "spaces" specifically for them to uncover their own racism, which frequently is entangled in unexamined, harmful color-blind ideology.

Supporting White parents and other White activists in their quest to play a meaningful role in the struggle for racial equality is time well spent. These allies need tools and guidance to help them develop the courage they will need to intervene in the moments when racially biased and damaging language is being used and meaning constructed. Not equipping them with those tools or understandings is indeed a missed opportunity.

Moving Courageous Conversations from theory to practice is about learning how to engage effectively and in different ways with White liberals who champion social justice matters, White staunch conservatives who challenge government efforts at social programming, and White racist bigots who oppose all racial equity efforts for no other reason than to protect and perpetuate White skin privilege. Each of these factions has offered a form of resistance to efforts to ensure racial equity in education and other areas. Yet, in every historic movement to achieve racial justice, White people, even those "within the system," have played key roles, and each movement's success has depended on White individuals who lent their time, attention, and resources in support. For example, while other White citizens were violently opposed to the 1957 integration of Little Rock (Arkansas) Central High School, a small group of White teachers and administrators labored on behalf of the nine African American children chosen to take this historic stand. And one must not overlook the White women who offered to and did drive their Black domestics to and from work during the Montgomery bus boycotts. Although some race theorists may argue that many of these women were acting in their own self-interest (which I do believe was the case for some), we owe our honor and respect to those White racial allies who did so out of a belief that segregation and racism were simply unjust and inhumane.

Thus far, White parents and community members have been an untapped yet critical resource in efforts to accelerate the work of achieving racial equity in U.S. schools. However, in designing a strategy to develop and engage White parents and community members as allies in this struggle, it is important first to determine which constituencies among those populations are most likely to be sympathetic to the cause. Drawing again from history may be useful in this regard.

Entering into courageous conversations about race with those White constituencies who previously have expressed open hatred for or an unwillingness to interact with children and families of color may be noble but probably is not the most effective way to build a White, antiracist coalition of the willing. For many White people, including many White educators, embracing the full dimension of Courageous Conversations may not occur in one or even a few interactions. Internalizing the realities of White privilege and biases can be difficult for even the most progressive, liberal-minded White people. Moreover, the process of gaining a deep understanding that the fight for racial equity and against systemic racism is one that benefits White people as well as people of color is often slow and hard to digest.

The pressures on White people, in the United States and elsewhere, to deny or minimize the presence of racism and to avoid equitable interracial interactions are significant. Racism prevents many White people not only from authentically connecting with people of color, but also from understanding the fullest dimension of themselves. Adopting a mythical, color-blind posture regarding race and race relations causes White people to embrace a false sense of racial objectivity and leads them into dangerous emotional and intellectual "waters" where racial truth, their own as well as that of others, cannot be accessed or examined.

Consider, for a moment, what American society would be like if no one noticed the inequity that once existed and that still exists among men and women in this country. We as a nation would never have been able to recognize the triumph of two women having recently been appointed to the U.S. Supreme Court and of women representing, for the first time in U.S. history, fully one third of the bench. But why stop there? The significance of this goes even further, as evidenced by the words of Justice Sonya Sotomayor, whose Senate confirmation hearings were dominated not by claims that she would favor "women's issues" but by claims that she was racially biased. In response to a senator's inquiry about her ability to serve on the nation's highest court, Sotomayor stated the following: "I would hope that a wise Latina woman, with the richness of her experiences, would more often than not reach a better conclusion than a White male who hasn't lived that life." Thus, with four references to gender and only two references to race, the future justice spoke to the complexity of the struggle against inequity in our society—of its dual, even multiple heads that include those of sexism and racism.

Why did Justice Sotomayor not experience pushback for her espoused position that a woman more often will reach a better conclusion than a man? The answer: even White women who recognize institutional bias often struggle to understand the duality of their gender oppression and racial privilege. This phenomenon is what I referred to in a previous chapter as *cultural layering*, whereby, for many White educators especially, the fact that they recognize and experience oppression—due, for example, to religion, sexual orientation, or language—makes it difficult if not impossible for them to uncover, examine, and address how racial privilege somewhat defines and perhaps overshadows their perspective. For educators of color as well, layered cultural stigmatizations can lead to an irrational focus on a particular cultural aspect of one's self, someone else, or a group to the exclusion of another aspect. For the purposes of formulating a strategy for developing and engaging White allies, however, it is just this kind of difficult, delicate, and courageous conversation about race that must be had, repeatedly, until White people fully grasp their own racial truths within and engage with people of color in full-scale efforts to eliminate racial inequity.

■ ■ ■

Call me idealistic, but I refuse to accept the conjecture made by some that altruism is not an innately human characteristic. At the same time, I am not so naïve as to expect that White parents will avoid intervening with the system and offering a perspective on matters in such a way that they believe best serves their own children. Given this reality and the nature of how power is ascribed, it is imperative that White parents and community members be shown, and come to understand, the value of achieving racial equity in schools *as it relates to their own children.* Couple with this an understanding of how the U.S. educational system, as it currently operates, harms their children's development by permitting and even promoting racial inequity.

White parents and other community members must examine and address several liberal ideologies if they are to understand and embrace the philosophy that equity is good for all. A number of these problematic perspectives have to do with the distorted racial lenses through which some White people view people of color. The resulting distortions prevent White people from considering their own racial identities. They also keep White people from examining the presence and role of Whiteness in the lives of their children.

When individuals or groups have a distorted view of their own racial identity and experience, they typically have similarly distorted views of racial others—in this case, those others are students of color, their families, and their communities. Such distortions can lead White parents to construct limiting meanings about the children of color present in the school environment. Worse, they can lead White parents to view children of color as commodities or "diversity objects," there only to enrich their own children's experience. In the latter case, White parents may accommodate a relatively small number of children of color in each classroom so that their White children can "experience diversity." This mindset and its related practices, however, often exacerbate racial achievement disparities in schools, as it forces children of color to play dual roles: that of learners and racial docents.

How often I recall, in my own schooling at the elite Park School in Baltimore, not being able to focus on the lesson at hand for fear that one of my White classmates (or the teacher for that matter) might ask me to offer "the Black perspective" on an issue. This pressure to provide racial meaning in an environment in which race was generally off limits, along with the danger of having White children potentially interpret my personal meaning as a group narrative, reinforces some of the most problematic behaviors in interracial communication.

In 2010, Cable News Network (CNN) commissioned a re-creation of Kenneth and Mamie Clark's famous 1940s doll experiment. To the surprise of many (but not all, including me), the CNN study revealed that White bias, or a preference for White skin color over other colors—and, in particular, a tendency among White people to identify the color of their own skin with positive attributes and darker skin with negative attributes—is alive and well among all children, but especially among White children. After testing more than 100 Black and White children from the American North and South to establish research congruence with the original study, the 2010 study found that White children, despite the many racial advances that have occurred in recent decades, had developed neither greater acceptance nor understanding of their peers or adults of color. It further revealed that Black children continue to show some bias toward Whiteness, but far less so than White children. As CNN reported: "A white child looks at a picture of a black child and says she's bad because she's black. A black child says a white child is ugly because he's white. A white child says a black child is dumb because she has dark skin."[2] In addition, what was "really significant" to the 2010 researcher was the finding that the White children were learning and maintaining negative stereotypes about people of other races much more strongly than were the Black children.

Thus, liberal-leaning or progressive middle- and upper-income White parents who believe that because they do not allow their children to interact with blatantly racist people nor use racist slurs and epithets often also mistakenly believe that their children will grow up immune to these harmful beliefs and behaviors and that they will not perpetuate them. The findings of the CNN study suggest that this is not the case. Those findings instead underscore the critical importance for these potential White allies of racial equity to advocate for conditions in schools that will enable their children to view children of color as equally of value and virtue, as peers who can excel academically and present themselves with appropriately high levels of self-determination, self-confidence, and self-esteem. Under such circumstances, White children will experience dramatic reductions in their own White bias, which they accumulate early in life from observing the negative stereotypes of and societal biases against people of color—stereotypes and biases that typically are misrepresented as constituting equality, fairness, and justice. Studies like this provide further reason for White parents to exercise caution and not leave schools alone or society at large with responsibility for teaching their children about race and racism. Such matters are best undertaken, intentionally and repeatedly, at home and from birth.

ENGAGING WHITE ALLIES IN THE DEVELOPMENT AND RECRUITMENT OF OTHER WHITES TO THE STRUGGLE FOR RACIAL EQUITY

We will have to repent in this generation not merely for the hateful words and actions of the bad people but for the appalling silence of the good people.

—Martin Luther King Jr.

It is expected, at times inappropriately, that people of color will spend hours, days, weeks, and, for some of us, our entire lifetimes painstakingly explaining the rudimentary aspects of race and racism to our White friends, family members, and colleagues. Too often, however, racially conscious White people fail to offer the same support and guidance to other, less aware White people. In moving Courageous Conversations from theory to practice, White intraracial dialogues serve to accelerate the pace at which the education system can achieve racial equity. Large numbers of White parents, educators, and community activists already understand how to navigate the system on behalf of their own self-interest, and they already interact easily with each other in a racially polarized society. Thus, a comprehensive, well-thought-out strategy of enlisting White racial equity allies to develop and recruit other White allies makes sense.

In addition, for those White people who already believe themselves to be progressive and social justice-oriented, having other White people, rather than people of color, point out the ways in which their actions sometimes do not match their espoused beliefs results, for them, in less embarrassment, defensiveness, and, at times, resentment.

Developing White parent and community allies has other far-reaching implications, as these White constituencies often form the first line of resistance to the work required to achieve racial equity in schools—work they sometimes perceive will ultimately hurt their children's success. Racial equity leaders sometimes dismiss White parents' and community members' concerns about this, but it is not unreasonable that some White parents might arrive at this conclusion. Consider, for example, their response when, all of a sudden, detailed and protracted conversations are going on all around them about children of color, their needs, and issues, and most often in school districts and schools that were once virtually silent about or absent these students. Courageous Conversations, as praxis, means extending opportunities to White parents and community members to understand the complexities of racial equity as well as the personal and community-wide benefits of challenging racism in the schools. It also means extending these opportunities *before* dismissing the White voices that challenge them as resisters or, even worse, racists. Although it is unlikely that racial equity leaders will engage and organize 100% of White parents and community members in support of achieving racial equity in education, many White people, if given the opportunity, can emerge as critical partners and perhaps leaders in this cause.

The CNN doll study exposed the finding that White parents are often taken aback when they learn that their children are harboring dangerously racist views. They are equally baffled by the suggestion that such beliefs about race come from their homes as well as school or the media. Typically, in my experience and from the research, White parents who adopt color-blind perspectives lack membership and involvement in multiracial communities, or they operate as "racial pacifists" on key contemporary, hot-button racial issues. They thus fail to see themselves as contributing to their children's buy-in of the status quo of White privilege, White supremacy, and White cultural hegemony and domination.

The following is just one of many relatively simple exercises that can enable White school leaders to begin enlisting the support of White parents for a district's racial equity transformation efforts. Before engaging in such an exercise, it is imperative that you recognize that many White people, parents included, truly embrace the notion of antiracism in theory but have never been summoned to put their racial equity beliefs or convictions explicitly and intentionally into practice. Regardless of whether you attempt this exercise or not, you must recognize also that White families *must* be enlisted in the efforts of multiracial school districts to achieve racial equity. In the truest sense of Condition 4, all parties must be thoughtful in how the engagement of White parents and community members is structured—that is, if we are to surmount the obvious and expected resistance from this group due to tightly held yet poorly constructed, often untested, and unexamined philosophical leanings about race and racism.

EXERCISE

1. Compose a list of White parents and/or community members whom you believe would be sympathetic to the Courageous Conversations racial equity work occurring in your system.

2. Write a short narrative overview about your system's Courageous Conversations efforts. Don't forget to include your definition of racial equity and racial disparity in your narrative, along with some references to data that crystallize the system's need for improvement.

3. Schedule a time to share your narrative with one person on your list who you feel will offer you the greatest level of respect and understanding.

4. Meet and share your narrative with your potential ally. When done, solicit feedback from him or her. Be sure to ask what you could have made clearer or easier to grasp. Finally, invite your ally to help you choose and meet with the next person on your list to engage in the same type of exchange.

5. After several such conversations, arrange for all the people you have met to come together, and consider the possibility of jointly organizing to support the districts' efforts by engaging other White parents and community members in courageous conversations about race in your schools and district.

DEVELOPING AND REINVENTING SCHOOL BOARDS AS ALLIES IN THE STRUGGLE FOR RACIAL EQUITY

Many racial equity efforts at the school district level stall because of governance issues. Specifically, the reality that many school boards are composed primarily of White community members who are not professional educators adds greater challenge to the quest for racial equity. School board elections can be the most charged and sometimes undemocratic process a community undergoes. Too often, those with power in the community ensure that their voices are heard with regard to educational policies, programs, and practices by bankrolling likeminded individuals to run for and win school board seats in local elections. Such candidates learn to cater to the powerful voices in the community to gain a coveted seat on the board; then, once elected, they feel that they must be loyal to those same powerful constituencies if they aspire to future terms or other positions. In their role as policy shapers, however, these critical players, led by their superintendent and his or her executive team, must create a policy environment in which achieving racial equity operates from an expressed moral imperative as well as the legal mandates of the district. Thus, some have argued that the destruction, or conversely the triumph, of public education lies in the vision, direction, and actions taken by the leadership of that effort, be they board of education members, district administration, or teacher/staff union heads.

The establishment and implementation of sound educational policy is the backbone of effective schooling and, to that end, sound policy must be equity-centered. In most districts, however, a White superintendent of schools is selected and subsequently evaluated by a likewise White (or majority White) lay board of education. This inequitable governance structure thus diminishes the chances of leading a successful effort for racial equity. Although far from ideal, this situation is not insurmountable. With careful and strategic planning on the part of school-site and central office leaders, and with the cultivation of White parent and community members as allies, racial equity leaders not only can promote healthy, informal courageous conversations about race community-wide but also can nurture and inspire racially conscious, equity-driven White parents and other adults to seek formal leadership roles in their communities and school systems. Among the latter positions are those on local school site councils, school-based PTAs, and school boards. When leaders such as these begin to advocate for racial equity in partnership with parents and community members of color, they can become a formidable force.

So many school districts' hard-won equity victories are quickly lost because such coalitions are not developed and supported to take informed and united stands against racism. Such powerful coalition building does not happen overnight. It requires long-term investments in the nurturing and development of strategically selected White leaders. For that reason, I cannot overstate the importance of racial equity leaders cultivating alliances with school boards in which a majority understand the importance and dynamics of racial equity work and are willing to advocate on behalf of that work to the various constituencies that they represent.

Moving Courageous Conversations about race from theory to practice at the uppermost district governance levels requires that superintendents, from the outset, craft an overarching excellence and equity policy. They must then guide the school board toward ratification of that policy. This process propels that governing board to undertake deeper dialogue and forge significant understandings about racial equity. It also creates a safe space and ensures greater permanence for all the work that must take place in various places and levels within the district.

For example, after almost a year of work on developing the Portland Public Schools' (PPS) excellence and equity policy, that system's chief legal counsel and board secretary, Jollee Patterson, had this to say about the process and outcomes of his districts' racial equity work:

> When it was finally adopted by the Portland Public School Board of Education in 2011, while generally hailing the Equity & Excellence Policy as a giant step forward for the district, some believed that it was not ambitious enough. Questions about word choice surfaced as well as other, perhaps valid, yet still technical criticisms were voiced. What I feel is important to emphasize is since

its founding, PPS, like a majority of school districts in this country, never had any public statement, let alone a board policy, that spoke to equity. It is no wonder why children of color struggle in U.S. schools to reach standards proficiency at the highest levels given schools are still governed by a litany of policies crafted to educate a powerful few. Beyond crafting and adopting an "Excellence & Equity" policy, district leadership must press on to examine each and every policy to insure that it does not diminish the efforts to create school systems that effectively serve all children.

In the Chapel Hill-Carrboro City Schools, Superintendent Neil Pedersen sustained the movement of Courageous Conversations about race from theory to practice for more than 10 years and led his board of education in the development or re-crafting of equity policies that have ensured that the district will stay the course on this work long after his retirement.

Each year, PEG's consultants spend significant amounts of time attending the work sessions of state and local school boards. During these sessions, which often are open to the public and media, our consultants work with board members, coaching them in the Courageous Conversations Protocol and other PEG Framework methodologies and practices to ensure that these leaders become knowledgeable, skilled advocates for racial equity. If school leaders—superintendents, principals, central office directors, teachers and students—are to achieve racial equity, their local boards of education must be able to effectively walk their own policy talk. Both formally at the meeting tables and informally in community gatherings, school board members inform and influence families with school-age children and other voters about the importance for the community that *all* students experience success and derive opportunity to explore meaningful postsecondary options.

ESSENTIAL QUESTIONS

As you consider the larger community around your school system and the potential allies for racial equity, think about the following questions:

1. Who are the key leaders of color and White allies, embraced by their communities, whose influence, perspectives, and experiences would assist your system in its efforts to achieve racial equity and, specifically, form successful partnerships with families of color?

2. Based on what you have read in this chapter, what are some ways in which your system might initiate or strengthen existing efforts to empower parents of underserved students of color and White parent allies to give voice to inequitable schooling policies, practices, and programs?

3. What if any stand has your school board taken on issues of equity?

4. How might you support the board's development toward effectively using the Courageous Conversations Protocol to examine and revise system policies?

Voices From the Inside: Andrea Haynes Johnson

The Sixth Condition asks us to *Examine the Presence and Role of Whiteness*. As a Black woman leading this work, I had to constantly remain aware of White culture and consciousness in order to develop processes and make connections with colleagues that would support our work toward equity. The aspect of Whiteness that reared its head time and again was that of entitlement. After all, we are a high-performing, predominately White, affluent suburban school district in a liberal community that has a philanthropic history, generously donating time and money to those in need. Never mind that our disaggregated test scores revealed that our Black and Brown students were overrepresented in our discipline system while they were underperforming at rates that mirrored communities with far fewer resources. As we enter our fifth year of systemic equity work, I have found five strategies that helped me *Stay Engaged* and avoid race fatigue (*cause folks can wear on a sista' otherwise*).

1. Identify and elicit the support of White allies.

During an intense session, as I was leading a group through an activity using their racial autobiographies, a White male launched into a biting diatribe about the relationships he'd had with a variety of African Americans, including his family's servants growing up. He shared stories that literally made me want to leave the room. As the facilitator, and the only non-White person in the room, I felt the silence of Whiteness all around me and was paralyzed. No one stepped up, and I, too, sat silent as he dominated the floor and caused biting pain. On my way home, I called a White male ally and shared my truths about the incident. I asked him to facilitate the next session and work with the group to unpack the experience we'd just had. Although I participated in the session he facilitated, he was able to name some aspects of Whiteness that were in play in ways that allowed my White colleagues to accept them as truth. Through his racial experience, they were able to see the ways in which I had been marginalized and the ways that White culture prevented them from inter-rupting racism.

2. Anticipate detours and resistance, they are part of the process.

The detours came fast and furious. "Why are we only talking about race when our gay students are struggling?" "It's really an economics thing." "I have a great relationship with all of my students, it doesn't matter what color they are." Initially, I provided Jane Olson's essay, "Detour Spotting," to a small group of staff who were interested in developing their equity leadership. This allowed us to frame the detour phenomenon in a broader context. Next, we did a session on resistance with our administrative leadership team. Using materials provided by Reverend Dr. Jamie Washington, we explored Dr. Delyte D. Frost's theory of resistance in a culture of change. Through the intellectual quadrant on the Courageous Conversations Compass, we were able to place our experiences in a broader context and better manage both detours and resistance as they arose.

3. *Stick to the Courageous Conversations Protocol, it will shore you up and keep you focused on race.*

I must say this was one strategy that took me a while to embrace. However, the more I *operationalized* the protocol, the more it worked. Questioning strategies have been the most useful way of keeping the protocol alive. I was first able to practice this during one of our early in-service sessions. As the only non-White administrator, I found myself constantly aware of the elite power structure that was reinforced in the room. Time and time again, Whites in the room would veer from the Protocol and talk about the experiences of our Hispanic students, rather than honoring the agreement to *Speak Your Truth.* At first, all I could do was provide supportive eye contact to the students, parents, and staff of color as they listened to stories about "those people," knowing that many of *their* stories were being told in lieu of the stories of White folks. Then, I began to ask, "So what is your role in the situation you are describing?" "As a White educator, what do you think about...?" "So where are you on the Compass when you experience...?"

4. *Be acutely aware of "White Talk/Color Commentary."*

Circle back to the students, parents, and colleagues of color to check in and process. With so few people of color in our district, I found that the more we got involved in the work, the more distress it began to cause them. Many of them were accustomed to being guarded when it came to cross-racial conversations in public spaces. During one workshop, a teacher of color took some risks and began to express some truths that caused some real discomfort in the room. A White teacher co-opted the moment with a classic detour, "But What About Me"; "I, too, have been oppressed because of my. . . ." This brought up some familiar pain for the teacher of color, who made the decision *not* to engage in the work any longer. When we had a chance to process the incident, my colleague shared that the cost of participation in the dialogue with adults in the workplace was too high. Together, we created a space for the work to occur behind the scenes, with allies, rather than retreat completely.

5. *Connect all of the district's equity work to existing structures and frameworks.*

Although we had a good number of staff who were on board with our equity work, we still faced skeptics and dissenters. "What does this have to do with me?" "This is just one more initiative that will come and go." "I don't even teach *those kids.*" Once we embedded our equity work in structures that were familiar and held people accountable, we started to gain some real traction. First, we looked at our district's long-range plan and school improvement plan. We created an equity action plan (EAP) that was explicitly tied to both of those documents. The EAP has goals, outcomes, and specific instruments that would be used to measure progress. Next, we designed "push in" workshops for every department in the district. Each workshop was designed with the department chair and a department member to ensure that we were meeting them where they were and connecting to work that they saw as ongoing. For example, the Counseling Department workshop was a transcript analysis in which we took blind transcripts and tried to predict the race of the students by academic performance and course of study. Next, we continued to examine the transcripts to determine other patterns that emerged as we looked at the highest-performing students and the lowest-performing.

I would be remiss if I did not add that having a position at the district office, with authority, also helps me move the work along. A seat at the decision-making table as a member of the executive leadership team allows the equity lens to be a part of everything we do. Leading the work as a Black woman has its ongoing challenges. I have to be mindful of when to trudge forward and when to pull back. Even when I am faced with resistance, I risk being labeled an angry Black woman if I come on too strong. I have been accused of being one-sided, single-focused, and activist. And honestly, given the nature of the work, those words are not so bad. If we love the children we serve, we will find will, develop the skill, and build the capacity to ensure that all children achieve at the highest levels.

Andrea Haynes Johnson currently serves as the director of equity and grants in Township High School District 113. As a PEG affiliate and consultant, Johnson is trained and certified to facilitate Beyond Diversity throughout the nation. She is a Black American.

ELEVEN

Eden Prairie Schools

A Case Study

The closer you get to equity, the sooner the rules change.

—Dr. Melissa Krull, Former Superintendent,
Eden Prairie Schools

In the *Courageous Conversations* field guide, I profiled Del Roble Elementary School in San José, California, and the extraordinary leadership of then-Principal Yvette Irving and her mighty Equity and CARE Teams. At that time, while no district had shown promise of systemic transformation with respect to the Pacific Educational Group's (PEG's) Systemic Racial Equity Framework, many individual classrooms and schools throughout the nation exemplified promising practices that were coherent, consistent, and faithful with respect to our designed equity theories and practices. Seven years later, not only have several districts demonstrated such systemic and sustained focus on achieving racial equity, but some, at least for a period of time, have also posted the expected state and regional pacesetting performance results—when many educators have grown skeptical over that very possibility. One district that has impressed me in this way is Eden Prairie Schools, located in suburban Minneapolis, Minnesota.

Superintendent Melissa Krull led her district with courage and conviction. When her racial equity leaders' passion, practice, and persistence were insufficient to withstand mounting resistance from the community and internal detractors, she discovered her Personal Racial Equity Purpose (PREP) and pushed on, holding site and central office leadership accountable to her vision. Dr. Krull lived in the Zone of Productive Disequilibrium where she sought adaptive solutions to unanswered national racial equity challenges like shrinking fiscal resources, protection of (White) neighborhood schools, all-White school boards and executive leadership teams, and rapidly declining results for children of color in secondary education. She and other key Eden Prairie Schools leaders at all levels stared down fundamentalists' attacks, launched from within their community as well as from around the nation, often having to choose what works for *all* children over what will earn them public admiration and keep them employed. The following is their story of systemic racial equity transformation, told through the lens and in the words of the superintendent, Dr. Melissa Krull, and her equity coordinator, Ms. Nanette Missaghi, M.A.

EDEN PRAIRIE THEN AND NOW

Eden Prairie is a dynamic and thriving, third-ring suburb of Minneapolis, Minnesota. It is an attractive, mid-size city, home to the Minnesota Vikings football team, the Super Valu grocery store chain, the C. H. Robinson Company (trucking), ADC Telecommunications, and 2,200 other businesses. Rates of crime and unemployment are low: 0.03% for violent crimes, 2.03% for property crimes, and 4.8% unemployment (as of 2011). With its several lakes, numerous curving paths and hills, and 170 miles of scenic trails and prairies located on what was once part of the Dakota Nation, Eden Prairie was named *Money* magazine's "#1 Best Place to Live in America" in 2010.

The land on which the city now stands was taken by the U.S. government in an 1851 treaty with the Dakota and opened to American settlement immediately thereafter. The town of Eden Prairie was established in 1858 and, until the 1980s, when the area exploded with new housing developments, it was mostly a rural farming community. Today, this thriving suburb offers a diverse array of housing options, from the affluent Bear Path gated community to solidly middle-income neighborhoods to areas where most of the homes and apartments are Section 8-subsidized units.

Eden Prairie reached its highest population in 2005, at about 65,000 residents. According to the 2010 Census, the city grew from 54,901 in 2000 to 60,797 in 2010. The 2010 racial breakdown was as follows: 81.7% White, 9.5% Asian, 5.6% Black, 3% Latino, 2.3% mixed (two or more) race, and 0.2% American Indian. Figure 11.1 presents census data for the city of Eden Prairie for the years 2000 and 2010 to illustrate the changing demographics over time.

Just over 10% of Eden Prairie residents reported speaking a language at home other than English. The city also counts a significant number of people of Somali (East African) descent among its population. The exact number of Somalis has not been tabulated, but Minneapolis and St. Paul reportedly are home to the highest Somali population in North America.

Given this increasing diversity, Eden Prairie is also experiencing increasing extremes of wealth and poverty within its borders. Sarah Schewe, who, as a high school senior, wrote the winning entry in the 2006–2007 American Planning Association High School Essay Contest, titled "Affordable Housing Plan for Eden Prairie, Minnesota," details this divide as follows:

> Eden Prairie is a city of families, and 71.27% of housing is currently family housing. Yet an income divide exists between Eden Prairie's wealthier, predominantly white community (90.66%) and [its] immigrant families. While for whites the income per capita is $40,510, for Asians it falls to just $24,649 and for "Other" (which includes Somalis), it is only $12,687. This gap is growing—in the Twin Cities from1989–1999, "the average household income of the wealthiest 20 percent of Twin Cities' households rose 24 percent . . . the poorest 20 percent rose

Figure 11.1 Eden Prairie Census Demographic Data

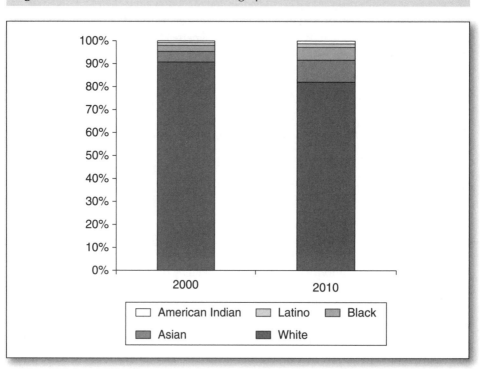

at just 16 percent."... Eden Prairie food shelves saw a dramatic increase in need from 1,500 visits in 2000 to nearly 10,000 in 2005. Meanwhile, with a median rate of $1,166 per month, Hennepin County has one of the highest mortgage costs in Minnesota. More affordable housing in Eden Prairie could help the city better support its growth and serve our immigrant families.[1]

Eden Prairie is unique in that its school district (Eden Prairies Schools, or EPS), which generally has been described as thriving, is contained within the city boundaries. The district was also viewed as fiscally responsible. It operated several large school buildings, which are cheaper to run than many smaller, neighborhood schools. It was widely presumed that *all* of the city's students were doing well, and the community was satisfied and proud.

However, student results were not disaggregated by race or service program. When those data were analyzed and revealed, the achievement and participation gaps were alarming. Not *all* EPS students were really doing well. Changes were needed for students of color and others not achieving to their highest potential.

Demographic Changes and Challenges

In the 1990s, multiple events began to challenge the status quo in Eden Prairie Schools. Community members of color were feeling dismissed by the district. An incident occurred in which two African American women stopped by the EPS central office to inquire about principal and teacher positions. After several exchanges, the women were informed that only custodial positions were available to them. They left the office feeling that they had been insulted and mistreated. As a result of this and other incidents, a number of meetings were held to address the non-White Eden Prairie community's belief that the school district did not respect diversity. One of the demands emanating from these meetings was that the district should hire a diversity coordinator. Another called for the district to hire more teachers of color.

Around that time, Minnesota's State Department of Education enacted its multicultural gender-fair rule (MCGDF), which mandated all school districts in the state to create a committee and plan to ensure that their curricula include lessons detailing the contributions of women, American Indians, Latinos, African Americans, Asian Americans, and people with disabilities. The rule also required that diversity training be provided for all district staff. In Eden Prairie, this training began as an optional, 2-hour MCGDF class for staff. Eventually, EPS, like many other school districts throughout Minnesota, got serious about making sure that its teachers understood the many facets of diversity and multicultural education.

After attending a state-sponsored Seeking Educational Equity and Diversity (SEED) training, several EPS staff members were inspired to start a local chapter of that initiative. They created the Eden Prairie SEED staff academy with the initial goal of instructing 100 EPS personnel about diversity and diverse perspectives via weekly, after-school classes. Participants could obtain credit for their attendance if they so chose. EPS's SEED classes continued for 7 years and served about 1,000 participants.

In 1990, nearly all (95% or 7,025) of EPS students were White; the 409 students of color accounted for only 5.5% of the public school population. During the 2011–2012 school year, White students made up 69.5% (6,579) and students of color 30% (2,883).

Figure 11.2 presents two other types of demographic student enrollment data. First, it shows an overall picture of student enrollment by race over a 21-year period from 1990 to 2011. Second, it shows a projection from the U.S. Census Bureau of the number of students between the ages of 5 and 19 who will be eligible to attend public schools in Eden Prairie for two Census periods (2000 and 2010). For example, in 2000, a total of 13,050 students were projected to attend: 12,190 White students and 860 students of color. In actuality, however, a combined total of 10,513 students including 9,438 White students and 1,075 students of color attended EPS district schools. In 2010, the projected total was 13,191 students: 10,797 White students and 2,394 students of color. The reality was that of the 8,983 students who enrolled, 6,158 were White students and 2,825 were students of color. In 2000, the gap between projected and actual White student enrollment was 2,752 (that is, 2,752 fewer White students enrolled than projected). That same year, students of color enrollment exceeded the projection by 215. In 2010, the projected-versus-actual enrollment gap for White students increased to 4,639 while 431 more students of color attended EPS district schools than projected. Thus, for two Census periods, the number of students of color who attend Eden Prairie Schools increased beyond the projected enrollments. However, the number of White students expected to attend declined in both periods.

Although it is difficult to be certain of the explanation, a few conclusions can be drawn as to why the White EPS student population declined while the students of color

Figure 11.2 Eden Prairie Schools Student Enrollment Analysis

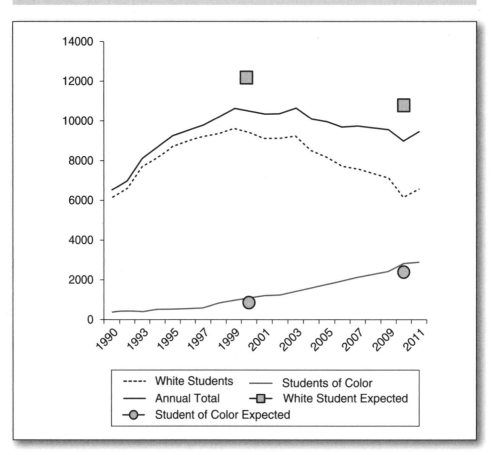

numbers remained constant and grew. Clearly, White families, more than families of color, made choices to attend schools other than Eden Prairie public schools. As in many other districts, other school options were available. Figure 11.3 illustrates the growth of the EPS district's English-language learner (ELL) population. In the late 1990s, the district's ELL population largely consisted of Russian and Vietnamese refugees. Over time, that population shifted to include mostly Somalis and Latinos from Mexico and a few other Latin American countries. The district currently serves students who speak more than 51 different languages other than English at home. The size of the district's ELL population (number of students served) has remained stable, however.

Figure 11.4 shows the trend of significantly increasing numbers of students requiring free and reduced lunch in the district. Although it is generally important that we not conflate the rising number of low-income students with the dramatically increasing number of students of color, in the case of EPS, the vast majority of students of poverty are also students of color.

Figure 11.3 District K-12 Limited English Demographics

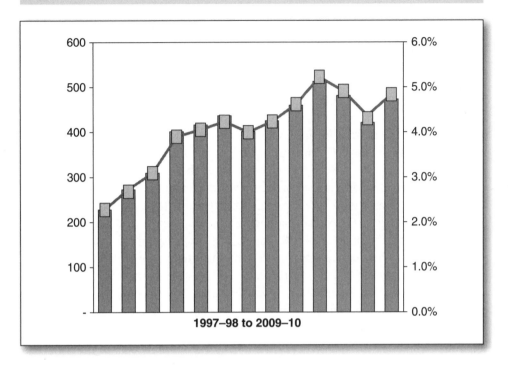

Figure 11.4 Eden Prairie Schools Free-and-Reduced-Price-Lunch Demographics

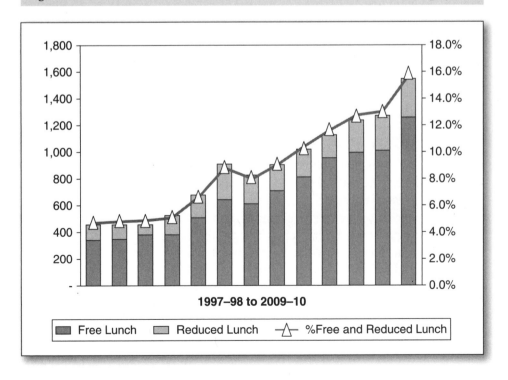

The District Responds

In 1994, EPS created a human resources and diversity coordinator position among its personnel ranks to carry forward the vision of Dr. Bill Gaslin, the superintendent at the time, who had commissioned a new strategic plan for the district in 1996. "Educating for Success in our Diverse and Changing World" was the mission statement for the district under Gaslin's tenure. His strategic plan evolved into 10 strategic initiatives that were designed to move the entire EPS system forward.

An organizational improvement committee (OIC) was established to oversee the implementation, measurement, and evaluation of the plan. Equity and diversity were embedded into two of the OIC's initiatives. Within a year, the committee launched a comprehensive, districtwide diversity assessment to establish baseline data on student achievement, program participation, staff hiring and retention, and school climate.

As the Eden Prairie workforce began to diversify and as the student of color population in the district grew, EPS worked hard to increase the number of staff of color within its ranks. District administrators knew that a diverse workforce meant better results for all students. From 1990 to 2011, while the percentage of students of color grew from about 4% in 1990 to nearly 30% in 2011, the percentage of non-administrative EPS staff of color grew from about 1% to 7% in 2011. Among the administrative staff, the percentage of people of color increased from 0% in 1990 to 16% in 2011.

Although the pace was slow, the effort was sustained. Even so, EPS survey results indicated that continued work was necessary to ensure that staff of color would be not only hired but retained. Despite all its efforts, the district faced challenges such as lack of buy-in from key staff and inadequate resources for diversity training and support. EPS staff of color continued to indicate that they did not feel welcomed by White peers and that they were being held to a higher standard. Teachers of color with foreign accents received many complaints from White parents. Principals strived to navigate the challenges of their new, more diverse workforce with little training or support. As a result, most staff of color left EPS for other opportunities. The district struggled to hold on to its remaining staff members of color.

Despite these challenges, a stream of new faces of color came and went over the years as EPS persisted in its efforts to hire and retain staff of color. Over time, two specific approaches emerged as EPS's primary strategies for diversifying its workforce. The first, called the Teacher of Color Plan, was developed to track the hiring and retaining of staff of color on a school building-by-building basis. Later, a more comprehensive approach was used, wherein the district established 5-year goals for each school, with annual benchmarks to assess the expectations for increased staff of color.

At least twice a year, all EPS building principals met with the superintendent to review their progress toward their specific hiring goals. Still, the district needed a system-wide approach, not only to address staff hiring but also to ensure academic success for *all* EPS students. If the district was serious about its equity work, it would need an overarching plan for all aspects of the system. Enter Dr. Melissa Krull.

In May 2002, the EPS board hired a new superintendent, Dr. Melissa Krull, who embraced the district's ongoing equity work and was determined to continue it. The continuing gaps in learning between White students and students of color in EPS were obvious and unacceptable to her. Thus, ensuring that all EPS teachers and other staff received professional development designed to help them eliminate those gaps became an urgent top priority districtwide.

The next year (2003–2004), Eden Prairie joined a voluntary integration district called the West Metro Education Program (WMEP), even though it did not abut any school district that was racially isolated, nor did it have a racially identifiable school. WMEP is a voluntary consortium of 11 urban and suburban school districts in the Minneapolis area. It was formed in 1989 to promote voluntary integration among the Minneapolis Public Schools (MPS) and school districts in its surrounding cities and suburbs. Its mission is to build the collective capacity of its members; to raise the achievement of all students; to eliminate the racial achievement gap; and to prepare all learners to thrive in a diverse world through regional leadership, integrated learning opportunities, shared resources, and mutual support.

The opportunity to join WMEP offered many benefits for the EPS. These included access to additional state resources (called "integration revenue"), professional development, and enrollment exchange opportunities for EPS students to attend two MPS magnet schools. Another benefit was the participation of several key EPS staff in a seminar titled Beyond Diversity, which was offered by PEG in May 2004.

A few EPS administrators decided to check out this seminar, and it proved to be especially meaningful for them. Through it, they discovered a new vehicle to propel the district's diversity mission forward. The seminar also introduced them to the Courageous Conversations About Race Protocol. Since the advent of No Child Left Behind (NCLB), they had been collecting their student achievement data, disaggregating those data, and trying to understand the huge gaps the data revealed between their White students and students of color. For years, they had struggled with the district's racial educational disparities but lacked a method to talk about it. Truth be told, they did not truly understand the disparities or the reasons behind them. Nor did they understand what the data were really telling them. Could there be something about their beliefs, their practices, or their values that was causing these challenges?

EPS administrators became increasingly curious and decided to continue on their journey by following a path not yet charted. The district recruited Glenn Singleton, PEG's CEO, to facilitate the discussion during an August 2004 retreat. Glenn's presentation was well received, and the retreat evaluations indicated that staff wanted to learn more.

But the EPS leadership understood that transformation would not happen with just administrators working on their beliefs. They knew that teachers played a big role because they were the ones delivering direct instruction to the students. About 90% of Eden Prairie's teachers were White, and most were female. Few of them had been trained to teach students from cultures and races different from their own. The leadership knew they would need new skills to teach students of color effectively. An additional benefit to WMEP membership was WMEP's partnership with the National Urban Alliance (NUA).

The NUA is a professional development company that provides onsite training for teachers. Its major focus is providing research, direct instruction, demonstration, coaching, mentoring, and feedback to teachers to help them better engage students of color in reaching their potential. NUA's focus on teacher development served as a useful complement to the early PEG work with EPS administrators. Eventually WMEP authorized PEG to design a regional equity effort called LEARN (Leaders in Equity and Anti-Racism Network), which became the initiative in which regional equity leadership teams from most member districts would be developed to craft and execute a systemic equity transformation framework, which Dr. Krull recognized as critical to her district's success with staff, students, and families of color.

THE DISTRICT DEVELOPS A CLEAR VISION OF EQUITY

After completing Beyond Diversity and six subsequent PEG-led LEARN seminars focused on developing racial equity leaders in the initial year of work, 8 of 11 participating WMEP districts were tasked to develop 5-year equity transformation plans. EPS's District Equity Leadership Team (DELT) wrote its plan over a 1 1/2-year period. The following are a few of the key points of this plan, which was formally adopted by the Eden Prairie school board in June 2007. These points illustrate the district's vision of equity:

EXCERPTS FROM EPS'S 5-YEAR EQUITY TRANSFORMATION PLAN

Eden Prairie's Commitment to Achieving Equity and Excellence

Eden Prairie Schools has always focused on the pursuit of excellence. In keeping with this tradition, we joined several neighboring districts and became active members in the WMEP (West Metro Education Program) Equity Initiative. It is the beginning of our 5-year collegial commitment to systematically address institutional racism in our schools. The goal of our work is to achieve equity; eliminate the achievement gap; and create a welcoming, inclusive, antiracist environment for everyone touched by our school system.

All of our work is rooted in solid, scientific data and research. We have carefully studied our test scores and have interviewed numerous students, employees, and parents about their experiences in our school system. In addition, we have diligently studied national findings about inequity, the achievement gap, and racism. We have found that although we have high-performing schools, not all of our students and families are reaping the benefits. And indeed, even our highest-performing students are losing out on the opportunities that come from being part of an equitable learning environment.

Background - Current Conditions - The Wake Up Call

How did Eden Prairie Schools arrive at this point of reflection by isolating race as a key factor in the achievement disparities? Data is the answer. We have had the capacity to review and analyze student achievement data for a couple of years, but had not sorted the data by race. When we did so and saw the extent of the racial disparities in the classroom, our transformation for equity began.

We now believe that we cannot rightly call ourselves a high-performing district when some of our students are "left behind" due to the color of their skin.

The district could choose to rest on its laurels of its high academic achievement average, but instead Eden Prairie has chosen the path toward equity. The gap is twofold in Eden Prairie. The first gap is program-related, whereby there is a disproportionately high number of students of color in special education and a very low number in the gifted and talented services. The second gap is between the achievement of the lowest-performing students of color and the highest-performing White students. The district is committed to eliminating that first gap of racial predictability in program participation and the second in academic achievement.

Why Are We Having Conversations About Race and Racism at Eden Prairie Schools?

The major reason we have isolated race, as an important conversation to begin at Eden Prairie Schools, is because our district student achievement data shows conclusively that students of color, especially African American students, are achieving at a significantly lower rate than white students.

We believe that we will consciously and deliberately act to eliminate the disparity between our mission of achievement for all students and the policies, practices, and structures in our school system that perpetuate inequities based on race and class. We will change the culture that is based on White privilege to be multicultural and antiracist.

We believe we will be successful at eliminating the achievement gap when every employee examines their own individual practices for ways they contribute to an environment that supports and sustains learning differences in our students of color.

The Importance of Leadership

Effective leadership is critical for the culture of an organization to change from one state of mind to another and to be sustainable over time. For Eden Prairie Schools, that means creating a new culture in which the cultures and races that differ from the dominant culture are integrated and accepted. The outcome of creating a new culture would be closing the racial achievement gap and eliminating racial predictability from the district. In order to initiate this and create a climate and environment where the conversation can begin and then take root, leadership needs to understand the critical elements involved in changing a culture.

The Important Work Begins

Early on, Eden Prairie's school board supported this equity work, so the superintendent and administrative staff moved to begin the systemic equity work with ease and clear intention. The notion of systemwide change was widely supported. The district's partnership with WMEP was under way. The superintendent was leading the effort. The principals were initiating the learning, and the entire administrative team was participating each year and throughout the year in equity training. PEG was a new innovative partner, and the NUA had joined WMEP and EPS in carrying out the equity principles in the classroom.

The longer the district kept this focus, the more systemic it became. Its intention was to systemically embrace the issue of race so that everyone who touched students and their families worked with a common language and understanding. The administrators and staff knew that the key to improving results for students was first to acknowledge that race was the common denominator; second, to engage in high-quality professional development to deeply understand race personally; and third, to take action in every aspect of the organization. They knew that systemic racism was interfering with student learning and that the need to unearth the racist practices and processes was the moral imperative. As a result, all of the district's work was viewed through the lens of race and equity. Whether it was transportation, food service, schools, administration, or board policy, everything was reviewed so that the systemic nature of the organization could be aligned with equity—ultimately serving *all* children equitably.

Creating Structures of Equity Support

Once the systemic approach modeled after PEG's Framework was under way, it became important to create structures of support for staff at all levels. It began with the DELT, formed to provide overarching leadership and accountability for the district's systemic equity transformation. Simultaneously, the NUA coaching model was designed to train teachers on NUA pedagogy and strategies. NUA coaches provided site-specific training and modeling of instructional strategies to support a cultural frame of reference for teachers and students, including strategies for student engagement and high intellectual performance. Then, Equity Teams (or E–teams), composed of a principal or department head and school staff members, were created by PEG staff to deliver equity training to all staff on topics ranging from Courageous Conversations and critical race theory to systems thinking and adaptive leadership.

Drawing once again on the PEG Systemic Racial Equity Framework and its theory of transformation, teachers were grouped into CARE (Collaborative Action Research for Equity) teams to receive support in culturally relevant teaching, which included direct instruction, curriculum selection, observation, lesson planning, and feedback from a PEG trainer/coach. The CARE process enabled teachers to address the learning needs of specific focal students of color who were underperforming in their classrooms. Finally, a DELTA (District Equity Leadership Team Advisory) group was formed to provide cultural knowledge and multiple perspectives and act as a sounding board for the DELT on specific systemic issues of equity. The work of the DELT was eventually passed on to the district's executive cabinet members. All of these structures together created an infrastructure of support and accountability in EPS, so that the equity work could directly and positively impact all students, families, and staff.

Embracing Professional Development

Both PEG's and NUA's training focused on embedding within teachers and administrators the belief that *all* children can learn with the right pedagogy. Both also focused on getting teachers and administrators to challenge their beliefs about the virtues and mythologies of color blindness and thus emerge as antiracist, culturally competent school staffs. PEG and NUA offered a radically different way of feeling, believing, thinking, and acting; and EPS's teachers and the administrators responded positively. Serious change was now under way. Over time, the entire school system, meaning every employee, would participate in PEG's Beyond Diversity training, ensuring that everyone learned a common language and protocol for negotiating race.

The district's senior-level administrators were early training targets. This meant that the superintendent; district executives, directors, and coordinators; and principals all engaged in Beyond Diversity and PEG's comprehensive equity leadership development training. Members of the school board also participated in customized training led by Glenn Singleton. As all these personnel became knowledgeable about race and internalized the language and common themes in the Beyond Diversity curriculum, their actions followed. They were then able to support their staffs, which had also begun to participate in Beyond Diversity trainings.

Superintendent Krull had asked all EPS employees to participate in Beyond Diversity. She knew that this ambitious plan would take time, but remarkably, after 7 years nearly 70% of all employees had done so, even as the district was weathering dramatic state and local cuts to education funding.

Ongoing, in-district professional development came in the form of monthly administrative team meetings focused on equity leadership, provided by the district's integration coordinator, Nanette Missaghi. Missaghi was hired in 1997 to carry out the diversity vision of then-superintendent Bill Gaslin. In her role, Missaghi also assisted in the planning and design of annual administrative retreats, school site "equity walks," and administrative year-end reflections on the equity work, facilitated by Glenn Singleton—all key professional development strategies that effected change.

Missaghi was central to the district's professional development effort. She kept district personnel consistently engaged in the equity work and brought numerous reports to the board's and superintendent's attention about how to spread this work systemwide more effectively. She kept a close eye on the training programs and ensured that EPS leaders were always at the table for WMEP regional conversations about the engagement and achievement of students of color. She kept records and data points related to progress and routinely brought forward to the superintendent and top leaders missing perspectives that were reflective of the viewpoints of staff, students, and families of color.

There was no turning back. The results would follow.

A CHANGING CLIMATE

As the system and its employees became more knowledgeable about the principles of racial equity leadership, aspects of the climate began to change. More staff of color were hired at all levels, providing new ways of thinking and doing. Discussions about race were more prevalent, and intentional changes started taking place.

Superintendent Krull engaged in frequent focused support, coaching, and guidance with Glenn Singleton. Her cabinet members spent lots of time examining all aspects of the district's functioning through the lens of racial equity, discovering how systemic racism appeared, and devising solutions for eradicating inequities. In the 2007–2008 school year, the board crafted new and revised district policy to address equitable outcomes for all students more intentionally. Superintendent Krull also began meeting with administrators of color about four times each year to hear directly from leaders of color, who offered diverse African American, American Indian, and Latino viewpoints—voices often lost in large systems that are predominantly White. She gained insights from them about how the changes, and the backlash resulting from those changes, affected them. They indicated that sometimes the effect was negative and sometimes positive, but they still encouraged her to move forward. Their inputs and multiple perspectives changed how Krull ran the district and made decisions. In turn, the administrators of color felt heard and worked in partnership with the superintendent to support the district's equity efforts.

Over time, the effects of a changing EPS climate and culture ebbed and flowed. Sometimes the change efforts seemed aligned and appeared to be advancing forward; other times, it seemed as if the whole system was slowing down or only stumbling forward. The administration learned that it would have to take bold and thoughtful approaches to make important strides toward equity. At times, these bold and unsettling strategies produced both slowdowns and setbacks, but they were precisely what were needed to make the next important shift forward.

For example, in 2010, when the state standardized results were released, an EPS elementary school, Forest Hills, was found to have made significant gains. Forest Hills was the elementary school with the largest percentage of low-income students and students of color. The gains at Forest Hills were so remarkable that many believed its successful strategies should be shared and even replicated to other schools. The 2010 data also showed that middle school results had gone down rather significantly. In fact, they had dropped to an all-time low in the district after so many years of attention and effort to bring their scores up.

During an administrative retreat that year, Singleton and the EPS equity planning team engaged in a "fishbowl" exercise to help bring to light the significance of the important gains and dramatic losses that had taken place within the system. This exercise involved creating an inner circle of discussion among administrators of color and White administrators and the two principals from the highest-performing (Forest Hills Elementary) and lowest-performing (Central Middle) schools in the district. The entire administrative leadership team was able to observe the fishbowl conversation focused on how the gains were made at Forest Hills and what factors contributed to the uncharacteristic declining achievement at the middle schools.

Tensions emerged on completion of the exercise. Even weeks afterward, the emotions of team members were found to range from fear, anger, and distrust to excitement, joy, and relief. The very thought of exposing failure was far more worrisome than many of the district's predominantly White administration felt appropriate or necessary. In follow-up discussions, a few White principals expressed anger over the way the exercise had exposed or singled out one of their colleagues. Some administrators of color, on the other hand, felt that the fishbowl exercise was the authentic and right thing to do to bring about real change in a system where losses for students, especially students of color, were so apparent.

In the year that followed the notorious fishbowl exercise, Central Middle School's administrators and staff embarked upon serious equity-improvement planning. They formed a transformation team, partnering with district racial equity leaders and the principal of Forest Hills. That team met regularly and drafted a plan that was significantly different than what had been in place in former years. They designed a strong, student-centered model that unearthed the many aspects of systemic racism and other institutional biases that perpetuated unequal opportunities for *all* students.

Later that year, when state standardized results came in, Central Middle Schools made unprecedented gains in both math and reading. The following year (AY 2010–2011), the school sustained those results and made additional small gains. Clearly, the fishbowl exercise and the district's efforts to move Courageous Conversations from theory to practice, as uncomfortable as they were, brought light and attention to a school in need of support and intervention. The key climate insight—navigating through tension transparently and openly, as opposed to isolating and shielding it—contributed to increased accountability, support, and results. In the 2011–2012 school year, Central's principal requested that his school be considered for the district's Beacon Program, so that it could be included among the schools that would receive focused support from PEG trainers to accelerate equity transformation. He was certain that his powerful and purposed E-team and CARE teams could bring on board the additional teachers and take advantage of the concentrated support and training to institutionalize their successes. That request was granted.

A Focus on Data

The intensive training taught the district administrators and staff that another key to success and change was a disciplined approach to reviewing data. Student results, discipline data, transportation data, and survey data—were all disaggregated by subgroups (race and service groups). Even though this highly scrutinized approach to data review was new to the district, it was useful—and it worked! The district continued and improved both its summative and formative assessment practices. Staff took time to study all subgroups' progress throughout the year and at key points during the year.

A concentrated study of statewide assessment results became routine. The district began using the Northwest Education Association Measurements of Academic Progress assessments for Grades K–6 and reviewing progress for students three times a year. Teachers had current data in their hands regarding student progress all year long. As a result, they were able to adjust their teaching to further affect student results. Principals began hosting "teacher talks" about data in each and every classroom. Every teacher began meeting with his or her principal at least twice a year about the results they were seeing for their focal students. Principals had firsthand knowledge of each teacher's results and knew which students were targeted for improvement. Principals were also meeting two to three times each year with the superintendent and with the district assessment director, scouring school data and establishing short-term and long-term goals for school improvement.

Subsequently, the superintendent knew which schools were moving forward rapidly and which needed more support. In the end, all schools made gains, and some made serious and significant gains. Elementary schools, in particular, made leaps and bounds forward.

EPS embraced its administrative assessment leadership, and the assessment director, Ishmael Robinson, was asked to become a central figure in its organizational leadership. Without him, many of the needed reports and data points would have been lost. He strongly valued academic achievement for all and recommended strategies for each school principal and staff that would lead them toward better results. He spent hours in schools with staff and principals teaching them how to read, use, and understand data. Robinson, a former Twin Cities integration district student himself, developed a unique way of wrapping his own compelling personal narrative around the EPS data and engendering site leaders to embrace their responsibility to support their students on the margins.

The Mental Model of Equity was created in August 2011 to illustrate graphically the foundations, connections, and benefits of the equity work being done districtwide in Eden Prairie to eliminate the student achievement gap and the predictability of racial disparities in school. This model is presented in Figure 11.5.

THE RESULTS ARE IN: PROGRESS WAS MADE

After 7 consistent years of focus and attention, the district began to see results, and the results began to show growth for *all* EPS students—and a significant narrowing of the achievement gaps between students. By the 2011–2012 school year, the gap in reading between White and Black students had narrowed by 42 percentage points. Other notable gains were a 28% gain districtwide in reading for limited English-proficient (LEP) students, with specific elementary LEP gains of 37% in reading. Simultaneously, White students' proficiency continued to grow by 4%, putting them at 90% proficiency rates overall. Nearly every subgroup saw gains and progress in achievement.

The superintendent began intentionally talking about these results openly with members of the EPS staff, board, and community. She wanted staff to know that they could seriously improve the learning of the students they taught, and she wanted the board to know that their policies were indeed transforming the system. She wanted the community to know that their school district was making gains that had not yet been seen anywhere else in the country and that Eden Prairie was one of the top districts in the state to show progress toward the elimination of achievement gaps for students while also ensuring growth for *all.*

Figures 11.6 through 11.9 are important because they reveal that nearly every subgroup saw gains and progress toward the elimination of the achievement gap. They showcase the data results from the Minnesota Comprehensive Assessments (MCA), the Minnesota Comprehensive Assessment-Modified (MCA-MOD), and the Minnesota Test of Academic Skills (MTAS) for reading and math. Each graph illustrates growth for each group. These summative measures were a means by which the district could determine if the instructional changes were making a difference in students' learning in math and reading. They also ensured that the entire system was held accountable and focused.

Figure 11.5 Eden Prairie Schools Mental Model of Systemic Equity

Eden Prairie Equity Model

The LEAVES and FRUIT are the fruits of our efforts: Eliminating student educational racial disparities and raising student achievement for all.

The BRANCHES are the best practices, such as PLCs.

The TRUNK symbolizes the pedagogy of confidence.®

The SOIL symbolizes the belief which feeds the roots of equity.

The ROOTS symbolize equity.

Source: Created by Nanette Missaghi with illustration by Shaghayegh T. Missaghi. "Pedagogy of confidence": Jackson, Y. (2011). *Pedagogy of confidence: Inspiring high intellectual performance in urban schools.* New York: Teachers College Press.

Figure 11.6 Reading Results From 2008 to 2011, by Race

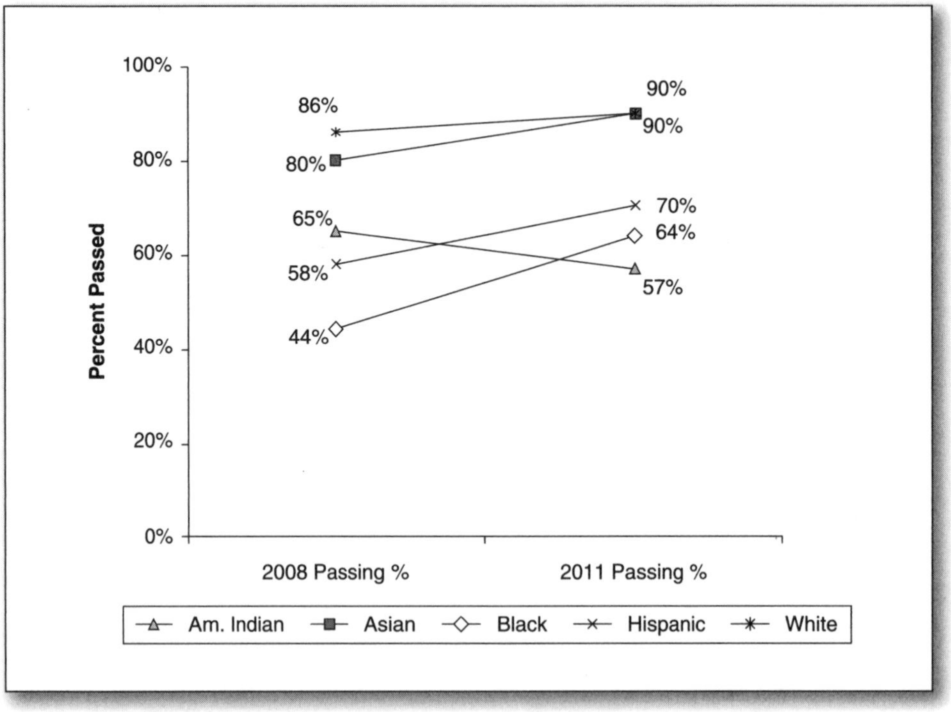

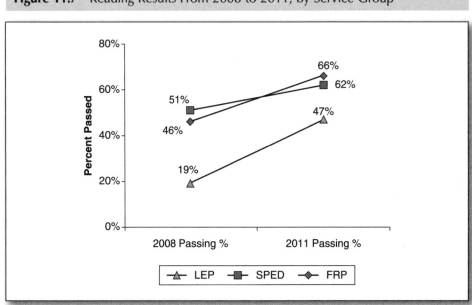

Source: Minnesota Comprehensive Assessments (MCA), the Minnesota Comprehensive Assessment-Modified (MCA-MOD), and the Minnesota Test of Academic Skills (MTAS).

Figure 11.7 Reading Results From 2008 to 2011, by Service Group

Source: Minnesota Comprehensive Assessments (MCA), the Minnesota Comprehensive Assessment-Modified (MCA-MOD), and the Minnesota Test of Academic Skills (MTAS).

Figure 11.8 Grade 3–4 Reading Results From 2008 to 2011, by Race

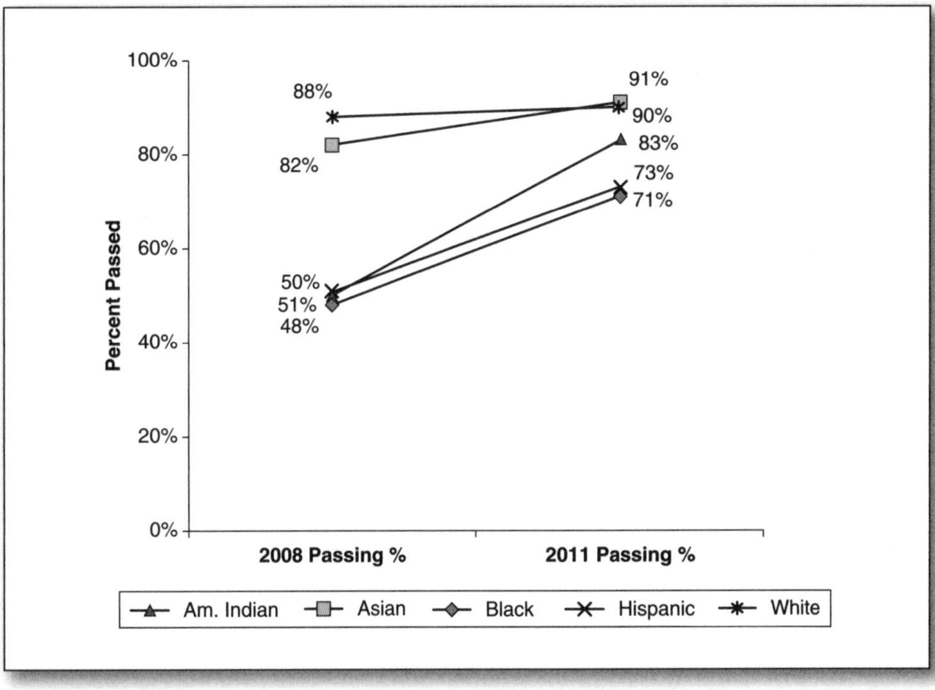

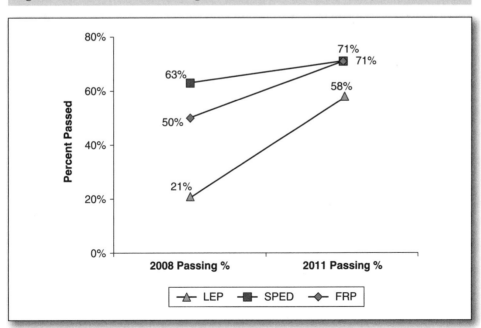

Source: Minnesota Comprehensive Assessments (MCA), the Minnesota Comprehensive Assessment-Modified (MCA-MOD), and the Minnesota Test of Academic Skills (MTAS).

Figure 11.9 Grade 3–4 Reading Results From 2008 to 2011, by Service Group

Source: Minnesota Comprehensive Assessments (MCA), the Minnesota Comprehensive Assessment-Modified (MCA-MOD), and the Minnesota Test of Academic Skills (MTAS).

Final Step: Elimination of School Segregation
While Navigating Resistance

Although serious progress was being made, new and important demographic changes continued to cause the superintendent and her staff to look closely at the racial and income balance in the district's elementary schools. Some elementary schools had low-income student enrollments between 9% and 12%, while others had numbers of these students nearing 50%. The difference between schools within the district was stark. The administration knew that the current rates of progress were noteworthy, but they also knew that it would be difficult, if not impossible, to sustain results like that without intentional elimination of the growing segregation.

Some EPS schools, they realized, were becoming increasingly segregated by student income level, while others were becoming largely White, segregated schools. Neither was good for learning. Students in schools with a high preponderance of low-income students were bound to suffer academically. The important progress that had been made was at risk unless the schools could be balanced by income.

In response, the superintendent and her team initiated a 2-year process to redraw the district's elementary school boundaries to balance the schools for space efficiency and student income level. Parents and staff were involved in this process; surveys were circulated, completed, and analyzed; and a systemwide communication plan was launched. After 2 years of study, communication, board involvement, and policy changes to support designation of the new boundaries, two maps recommended by the parents on the joint team were presented to the superintendent.

One of the two maps was chosen to present to the public for input. That map balanced the schools so that no more than a 7% difference in the number of low-income students per school would be allowed. About 1,000 students would have to change schools and attend schools that were no more than two or three miles from their current schools. Transportation costs would go down, not up, as a result.

Yet, in a community of no more than 6 square miles, where the bus rides resulting from this proposal would be, on average 22 minutes long, resistance emerged. The opposition to the plan, which was surprisingly significant, took the form of protests, petitions, lengthy board discussions, restraining orders, hostility, and lack of civility on the part of some community members. The Somali community offered a strong voice of support for the plan, however. They wanted their children to be in schools that offered the greatest opportunity. They knew that segregated schools meant less quality education for their children. The Somali voices were prominent, thoughtful, centered, and peaceful, and they persisted in expressing to the board their full support for this recommendation. The American Indian Parent Committee also wrote a letter of support to the superintendent after reviewing the map and transformation plan.

After months of board debate, media attention, lengthy public input sessions, and modifications to the proposal, the board voted 4–3 to support the decision to go forward with it. Following the vote, the superintendent and administration began the labor-intensive process of preparing for new schools that would mean greater opportunity and success for *all* students.

The boundary map went into effect fall 2011. The students were moved to their new schools without incident. Early reports indicate that the move has been a success. The kids are doing very well, and the students and families who needed the support the most won.

Key Insights

The learning gained by the EPS superintendent and administrative team about equity transformation has been invaluable. The first imperative was leadership for racial equity, which must emanate and be exercised at all levels and ranks in the system, from the board of education and superintendent all the way to the beginning teacher and clericals. The second imperative was top-notch, antiracist principal leaders, who must drive the needed changes directly into the schools. Third was establishing a strong and dedicated district equity leadership team and an equity-focused staff to keep the entire system in antiracism perspective at all times. A fourth imperative was the district's investing in outside, credible, equity consultants as partners. These included PEG and NUA, whose skilled staffs provided guidance and direction when the predicted resistance was at its most fierce. Districts that engage in such partnerships have a serious chance at transformation. A fifth imperative was keeping a constant and persistent eye on the data at every level—district, building, and classroom—to keep a watchful eye on progress.

Sixth, it was critical to ensure that the entire system was involved and that a systemic approach was applied. Every single employee was touched by and held accountable to the district's equity transformation plan. Seventh, all of the key players kept the main thing *the main thing.* That is, all saw advancing equity as the primary goal, year after year, thus contributing to the plan's long-term sustainability. Eighth, it was critical to generate as much community support and outreach as possible, especially among White parents and stakeholders, to build a safety net and added layer of engagement for equity success.

And finally but important, we never forgot, *nor will we forget,* that, as Glenn Singleton said, "This work of achieving racial equity in education is an act of love."

ESSENTIAL QUESTIONS

After reading Chapter 11, which invites understanding of the progression and key processes of equity development in Eden Prairie Schools (EPS), consider these questions:

1. What insights did you gain about the dynamics and development of racial equity leadership, learning and teaching, and family/community of color empowerment?

2. In what ways does the racial equity work currently under way in your system align or disconnect with what you now understand to have taken place in EPS?

3. What lessons learned about leading for racial equity are now apparent to you, having become familiar with the work in EPS?

Voices From the Inside: Connie Hytjan

The story I am going to tell is about the school where I am principal, Forest Hills Elementary. Forest Hills is located in the northeast quadrant of Eden Prairie, a suburban community in the western suburbs of the Minneapolis metro area. Its location lends itself to serving students in many lower- and middle-class, single-family homes as well as families who live in multi-housing complexes and rentals. In some social circles and in some instances, community members might say that the district transformation process occurred *because* of Forest Hills. In this fairly affluent community, Forest Hills was noted as "that school." We were the school identified as being the most racially and socioeconomically integrated in the district. Last spring, our demographic information indicated our population was made up of about 55% students of color, mostly Black and Brown students, and 52% students who qualified for free or reduced-price lunches. We also served a very high number of Somali students. In the 16 years I have been at Forest Hills, we likely had the highest teacher turnover and the highest number of families who chose to "open enroll" in other districts around us; we were the school that had a "tainted" reputation among neighborhood residents and community members.

I began working in Eden Prairie Schools 16 years ago—and, to be honest, I didn't even realize that I was beginning equity work when I moved here. I was hired in the district as the principal of Forest Hills.

On my first encounter with our district, I knew it was one that promoted an image of excellence and high achievement. I felt fortunate to be joining a district with such a strong and positive reputation. I soon learned, though, as I participated in administrative and other meetings that . . . we never expose the struggles or the difficult times. It was a known norm! In EPS, much like Lake Wobegon, all children were above average and life was almost perfect. There was definitely a "Minnesota Nice" culture of "When I'm angry at someone, I don't let them know. I just smile pleasantly to his or her face and then proceed to talk about them behind their back. I will most likely hold a grudge, too."

In 1996, when I arrived, our staff was made up primarily of White females, with a few White male teachers sprinkled in. Only one staff member in our school was a teacher of color; she was Asian American. Most of the teachers had 15 or more years of experience, and most of them were my age or older (at the time, I was 40). Only a few teachers were not tenured. There was very strong union representation in our school; one of the teachers had been instrumental in the strike held in the early 1970s, and he was proud to share the story with me during one of our first encounters. Most of the nonlicensed staff members were either parents with students presently in the school or parents of past students. The hiring of most of the nonlicensed staff had occurred with a "handshake" rather than a formal process for interviewing. I could tell early in my tenure at Forest Hills that varied "camps" (made up of licensed and nonlicensed staff) existed with opposing views about leadership, education, and relationships.

Following good leadership, I got acquainted with the processes and practices, both in our district and at Forest Hills. I observed and I did my own informal assessment of the culture of our school. I watched how colleagues interacted with each other, how parents were invited and welcomed, and how students were treated. I waited and gathered more and more information about our school, talking with those who had been working at Forest Hills for some time and those who had arrived only a few years earlier. I inherited my predecessor's practices and began to make a few changes that reflected my beliefs about learning, teaching, and professional responsibilities.

1. Stay balanced and centered—know yourself and the hill you will die on.

I discovered after some time that many practices and interactions in our school actually promoted low achievement and a culture of toxicity. When I arrived, our school demographics consisted of a student population of about 10% students of color and 8% students who qualified for the lunch program. While that doesn't sound very integrated today, or even at the time, it was the most integrated school in the district. Demographics over the past years had changed (and it continued to change over the many years to come), morale was low, and staff seemed to demonstrate being "victimized" by the fact that our school looked so different (demographically) from the other schools in the district. They seemed unaware of the impact that the school culture was having on their interactions, their performance, and our students' achievement.

2. Be cognizant of the present conditions.

We were faced with serious adult issues: there was a lack of trust among colleagues, administration, and parents; there were "parking-lot meetings" held regularly after staff meetings; teaching was considered a "private act" (the norm being that classroom doors were closed); little collaboration or teamwork existed; and teachers were competitive and created programs that they marketed as "better than" those of their colleagues. They displayed blatant disrespect toward each other during meetings or social times, and they regularly found excuses for their students' lack of achievement or poor behavior. Instead, they regularly blamed parents for their lack of involvement, or they blamed the child's home life. At that same time, our school continued to experience radical changes in our student demographics.

3. Be courageous . . . and don't avoid the difficult conversations.

I persevered and continued to personally reflect about "what I could do differently." I attended workshops on dealing with a difficult staff; joined a local principals' collegial organization to obtain ideas and support; read many, many books on creating a positive school climate; and consulted with the superintendent and other district colleagues. I knew I was not doing something right . . . and I tended to focus on the technical aspects of the culture, thinking that the small things I did through relationship building, being visible, writing notes of acknowledgment, and offering professional development opportunities or resources would help transform the culture of our school from one of negativity and desperation to one of optimism and hope.

One day, however, I remember thinking: "This is *absolutely* not working! The culture of our school is hurtful to our students and families. Our kids deserve better than this, and it is time I get serious in addressing the 'real issues' at hand!" I began having difficult conversations with individuals at the school. I addressed specific behaviors, conversations, and decisions I had observed and described the impact these things were having on our students, their colleagues, and the culture of the school:

- I had individual and private conversations about how this affected students (specifically students of color) by sharing the number of discipline referrals for Black boys that were coming to my office from teachers' classrooms. At one time, I can remember a teacher responding to me that I had called her a racist when I shared the data about discipline referrals coming to me from her classroom (12 of the 14 referrals made in one month were all students of color).
- I addressed teachers' negative and hurtful statements, such as "'They' (often meaning children of color) can't be in my classroom," "If only you [meaning me]

would discipline them better and change their behaviors," "If only their parents would get involved," and "Your job as the principal is to 'allow me to teach.'"

- I shared my concerns about teachers' unprofessional behaviors I observed that were unproductive to any teaching and learning environment (e.g., lashing out at their peers in public disagreement, calling someone out in front of parents).
- I had meetings with teachers who found ways to not make contact with parents who desperately needed to be consulted. Often, these teachers' excuses were, "I don't know how to use the Language Line" (that is, the parents don't speak English); "I tried calling [the parents], but they didn't call back. They won't come anyway."

All of the behaviors I observed and statements I heard I viewed as demonstrations of our staff's frustration over not being as successful as the teachers they had once been when they were teaching an entirely different demographic of students. I did know, however, that a great number of staff members were appreciative and supportive of the culture change I was attempting to make.

4. Get comfortable with being unpopular.

Needless to say, I was not popular with many staff members at our school, and there were complaints and rumors about me that seeped into the local neighborhood and parent community. Petitions for my removal were passed around, board members were called, anonymous letters were mailed to the superintendent, disrespectful notes were left on my chair, and so on. Our superintendent, Dr. Krull, and I met with parents and board members. I acknowledged that I had not done everything the "right" way, but I assured them that I was "doing the right thing" for students and staff and that students would be the primary benefactors of the culture change.

5. Challenge the systems that seem to be barriers.

Life was not getting any easier, and I was beginning to have other observations about systemic things that seemed to be questionable. When addressing these things, I may have seemed cantankerous, asking difficult questions about the distribution of Title I funds (which at the time were distributed equally among sites although our demographics were much different), use of compensatory state revenue, incestuous hiring practices, and so on—not necessarily posturing myself to be the most popular with my colleagues. I questioned the resource allocation given to the sites (based on enrollment rather than need), as I knew that funds for schools with our demographic should be available both federally and statewide. At the same time, and while all these conversations occurred, our test scores continued to fall, leaving our staff members even more frustrated and angry. I was beginning to feel isolated and alone, wondering how district officials would help a potentially failing school.

Many of my difficult conversations with staff resulted in staff leaving. A couple resigned, but many of them asked to transfer to other schools where they thought they could be more successful and no longer bothered by a principal who had the reputation of "asking for too much." To this day, I feel bad that those teachers left, and I feel failure in that I wasn't able to lead teachers who are challenged with change or feeling a lack of competency. I was not proud of the fact that I was not able to support them in a way that they needed.

The teacher transfers only increased the Forest Hills community's wonderment of me. Questions arose, like, "Who is this principal that no one can work for?" and "Why are all the *good* teachers leaving?" It was said that my expectations were "unreasonable, that I asked too much of my staff," and that I openly talked about conflicts and concerns (and even directed staff to try solving their own conflicts before coming to me). It was definitely a culture clash for Eden Prairie and Forest Hills, specifically, where things like this were *not* talked about at this time.

6. *Surround yourself with excellence.*

That some staff left provided me with an opportunity to begin hiring. I sought to hire staff of color (not an easy task in this suburban community). My goal was to increase our staff of color in hopes of one day having a staff demographic matching that of our student demographic. I knew it was an ambitious goal, but I recognized it to be a very important one.

I hired a young Hmong teacher, and immediately, this action met with resistance. Both parents and the new teacher's colleagues soon reported to me that her accent was too strong and she wouldn't be a good role model for children learning to read; her grammar was not proper and she was modeling inappropriate language; and her classroom reflected her culture (beautiful Hmong art and artifacts hung in her room), which was interpreted by some as "not American." If I could only remember the number of parents who requested their children be moved out of her classroom as well as the number of staff who came to me with their "concerns" about this teacher, who said they were only trying to give me a "heads up" of what other people in the community were saying.

These concerns were not so secret to our Hmong teacher, and I was very worried that she would leave. With coaching from me and mentoring from our veteran Asian American teacher, she remained at Forest Hills and flourished. At the present time, she is considered a very high-performing teacher-leader in our district. Two years ago, she was one of ten finalists for the Minnesota Teacher of the Year award.

So, the story continues. As a next step and as a response to the community's concern about Forest Hills, Dr. Krull and the school board hired a consultant to help Forest Hills "get healthy." This consultant held focus groups and consulted with me, sharing with me all my flaws of leadership, suggesting to me that I "stay curious," and encouraging me to create "safe places" for staff members to share their perspectives. Our staff participated, I participated, some engaged, and many others not so much. The consultant helped in that she provided me with a forum to share my feelings and emotions. Although I knew I was doing the right thing, it did not seem all that right at the moment. My emotions were on edge and I was becoming very worried.

I contemplated leaving our district, wondering if I could really ever help our school community overcome the "adult mess" that had been created. I continued to be concerned about our students, specifically the students of color, and the impact all these adult issues were having on their achievement. Our test scores were at an all-time low and the worst in the district. Parents and community members were concerned. They were calling me, meeting with me, waiting for answers about what we were going to do to turn this cycle around.

During this time, only the "loyals" and the "believers" stood by me, watching, waiting, and supporting. Those who had, in the past, been formally silenced—started speaking out. They who used to enable "unprofessional behavior" stopped enabling it. Those who were lacking in understanding about why the changes were necessary started noticing some positive results from the few changes that had been made. They were beginning to become convinced. Unfortunately, there were still those who remained challenged by the changes or by the drama of it. They continued their quest to keep the culture the same as it had been.

More teachers voluntarily transferred, and the buzz in the community got stronger. During my performance review that year, Dr. Krull and I agreed that no more teachers would transfer. I even had a performance goal indicating that!

7. Hire well and tell the new hires why they were hired.

In the meantime, I continued the work at Forest Hills—the work that I knew would make the most positive difference for students. I worked to find and hire teachers and staff who wanted to be at Forest Hills. I searched for professionals who reflected the demographics of our student population, who had high expectations for *all* students, and who had the heart for the work. I sought candidates who had the experiences that would contribute to our school community's success, the beliefs that would foster positive relationships with students and colleagues, and the passion and persistence it takes to work with a multiracial and multicultural demographic of students. By this time, about 30% of our student populations consisted of students of color.

As I hired, I continued to look for the "right people" in all roles in the school who shared a vision and beliefs that all students can learn and that it is up to the teachers and staff to create the conditions to ensure that they do. I readily continued to share my expectations of our work, the staff's role in the work, and our student focus. At this moment, our work as a team really began. In addition, staff members within the district who had been watching from afar began asking for transfers into Forest Hills. They were ready to join in on our journey.

Staff members who remained at Forest Hills became more open to sharing their expertise, were more collaborative, and began to assume leadership roles. Ideas were shared willingly, and when there were different perspectives, they were accepted rather than challenged disrespectfully. We absolutely experienced growing pains, and things were far from perfect, but it was becoming evident to all who remained that the culture of our school was influential to the success of its members.

8. Understand the power of people.

Many of our staff persevered and stayed the course with me, believing in the power of collaboration, relationships, partnerships, and high expectations. Attitudes over time shifted from "we can't do this" to "how can we do it, and when should we begin?" Students truly became the focus of our work. Adults became selfless in their work, recognizing their role as stewards and servers of students.

The really apparent part in our "new direction" was that we didn't have all the systems in place to ensure that students had what they needed to be successful. It became clear that disparities in achievement between our White students and students of color still existed. Equity became a focus of learning and conversation for our staff, and our work with Glenn Singleton became foundational. An Equity Team was established and "intentional conversations" about race, the achievement gap, and culturally responsive teaching started happening. Still working rather independently, we recognized that we needed to do something different to make a bigger difference.

9. Staying the course: The courage to act.

Forest Hills School did not "turn around" overnight. Our test scores remained flat, and our parent community was struggling—lacking volunteers, working hard to promote a school with a negative reputation, having conversations with their neighbors who were hesitant about enrolling in our school, worrying about our fundraising abilities as compared to the other schools—and they begged that boundary lines be redrawn so we could basically "start over." When a new Spanish Immersion school opened in our district, more White families left our school believing that their children would have more opportunity to attend with other students who looked like them (and with whom they could relate better) than they would at Forest Hills. Our student of color population percentage continued to increase. In the winter of 2007, the school board recognized Forest Hills's demographic differences and, under the superintendent's recommendation, charged Forest Hills with redesigning itself; the board also provided much-needed resources to accomplish the task. Immediately, we began a strategic planning process.

10. Know when to lead and when to follow...

The last 5 years have been a whirlwind. Our staff has embraced more changes than one can imagine. They are more introspective and reflective than any staff I could ever aspire to have had the privilege of working with. They are innovative, passionate about our students, stubborn about ensuring their success, and energized. We have put into place unbelievable programs—for teachers, for students, and for parents—and developed an inordinate number of teacher leaders. We have spent the last 5 years engaged in professional development, honing our skills as learners first so as to better serve our students as teachers. We have researched best practices, collaborated with colleagues and parents, analyzed data, confronted our weaknesses, and focused on our relationships with students. We recognize the importance of teamwork and persistence. We don't take "No" for an answer, and we won't let students fail. We recognize the importance of student goal setting and high student engagement. We value literacy and numeracy and the importance of social and emotional learning. We ensure that no student is isolated, and we engage in courageous conversations about race and the influence of White privilege. We take our students and their parents as they come—with little or no judgment, providing them what they need to be successful. And, we are still learning! One more important thing to note: We know we aren't perfect or doing everything right!

I can't take personal credit for any of this, but I am more than proud to share credit. As an outcome of our strategic planning, Forest Hills now:

- Has a consistent literacy model in place with common language and practices (including progress monitoring, encompassing a Response To Intervention

(RTI) framework; access to nonfiction, leveled text; scientifically based interventions; technology-based instruction, etc.);

- Has common classroom and consistent schoolwide protocols and practices (based on Responsive Classroom and Positive Behavior Intervention Systems);
- Regularly participates in teacher talks with me, program specialists, and other teacher leaders to talk about their classroom data, interventions, and programs;
- Has a well-developed social and emotional learning program and aligned practices in place, along with a coordinator to oversee the program;
- Has a family service center in place for families to come to participate in ESL classes, book clubs, and volunteer opportunities. The staff in that center is intentional about welcoming families to our school, ensuring that they have everything they need to be successful and involved (including child care so they can come to volunteer);
- Has extended-day experiences (both academic and co-curricular) for all students—with transportation provided—to ensure that *all* students have access to programs and experiences;
- Engages in common practices for student goal setting and frequent celebrations for student's individual and collective success;
- Participates in frequent Equity Walks to help inform us of the work yet to be done, specifically for our students of color.

11. *Be humbly arrogant.*

In the spring of 2011, morale continues to be high at Forest Hills, and our students are doing well. We knew that the topic of Forest Hills becoming a "racially identifiable" school in our district continued to be discussed by the school board. We also knew that the students at Forest Hills were greatly benefiting from our integration, and we knew from our work with Glenn and our Equity Walks that students in the other elementary schools, while doing well, are experiencing some isolation and lesser achievement gains. For that reason and many more, our superintendent and administration began advocating for a district transformation—meaning boundary changes—to better balance the demographics of our schools. After much controversy, debate, discussion, and education, our board approved the boundary changes and called for the replication of Forest Hills programs. The day following the decision, the work of preparing for the transformation began.

12. *Students first . . .*

Our staff had very mixed feelings about this. While they recognized the value of our demographic, they were also a little worried and sad. They mourned the loss of our students, hoping that their success would continue in their new schools. We prepared our many students for the changes to their new school, supporting them and reinforcing how good this would be for them to meet new friends and how excited their new teachers and friends will be to have them join them.

Meanwhile, angst and a spirit of resistance was felt in our community, and many of the families scheduled to come to Forest Hills and other elementary schools left the district to attend other community schools. Our staff did an amazing job of marketing our school, reaching out to the community (and our new families) to share our programs and meet our staff. Many of the families who agreed to come to Forest Hills from other elementary schools came with reservation, knowing of our past test scores and community's perception.

13. *Acknowledge, celebrate, and remain optimistic: The work is never done.*

In the end, we lost over half of our students to other schools. While excited to invite our new students into Forest Hills, our staff misses our former students. As a staff, we continue to be excited about our work, approaching this new school year as an opportunity for our new learning as well as that of our students. We continue to focus on relationships as a foundational component in our work and promote a culture of high expectations, collaboration, and respect.

State testing results recently were published. As expected, our students did well and our school made Adequate Yearly Progress in all cells (although we all know that test scores are only one part of true student success). From 2008 to 2011, our reading scores for students in Grades 3 and 4 increased from 49% proficient to 73% proficient for Black students. At the same time, all subgroups, including White students showed gains. At Grade 4, our reading scores showed only a 12% gap between White students and Black students (with 39 Black students achieving at 82% proficiency and 65 White students achieving at 94% proficiency). It's true—our scores look pretty good—but we aren't done!

It has been quite a journey. I have learned a lot about leadership when engaged in equity work and about the things that must be in place for students of color to be successful in *any* school.

Connie Hytjan is currently the principal of Forest Hills Elementary School in Eden Prairie (Minnesota) Schools. She is White American.

ADDENDUM

The following overview was developed in 2008 to convey to EPS district leaders a schematic representation of the vision of equity with its accompanying goals and structures of support.

Eden Prairie Schools Vision of Equity: District Overview 9.28.11

District Mission:

Eden Prairie Schools Goal:

To ensure the high academic performance of *all* learners

Eden Prairie Schools Board Results Policies:

All students will achieve academic excellence without racial predictability and graduate prepared for postsecondary options.

WMEP/LEARN—Lead Regional Equity Work

DELT: Eden Prairie District Equity Leadership Team

Executive Cabinet

Role: To lead, oversee, learn, and manage the dynamic processes of system-wide transformational change.

Purpose: The guiding team ensures successful systemic transformation. The team examines district policies, practices, structures, climate, and culture that may be barriers to equity and excellence and leads systemic change efforts that result in high levels of achievement for students of all races. It is also responsible for aligning and embedding the framework into the existing strategic plan and board goals to ensure all efforts are streamlined for optimal student achievement results.

DELTA: Eden Prairie District Equity Leadership Team Advisory

Role: Serve as an advisory group that provides multiple perspectives to DELT, innovative ideas/programs, and Equity Team support.

Purpose: The advisory team to ensure successful systemic transformation.

Site E-Teams	*Department E-Teams*
All school sites	Facilities and Safety, Food Service, Technology, Transportation, and ASC
Members—Principal and site members	Members—Department directors and site members
Role—Antiracist school leaders, led by the principal, who design and deliver professional development activities, which shift the culture of the school toward embracing schoolwide equity transformation	Role—Antiracist leaders who design and deliver professional development activities, which shift the culture of the department/site toward embracing districtwide equity transformation
Tasks—To practice courageous conversations, analyze achievement data, school improvement planning, create vision and establish goals, staff meeting facilitation, faculty/staff study group facilitation, literature circle facilitation, parent/student focus group facilitation, equity walk-through participation, develop equity "local" team and provide mutual support and appreciation	Tasks—To practice courageous conversations, analyze department data, climate improvement planning, create vision and establish goals, staff training facilitation, faculty/staff study group facilitation, literature circle facilitation, develop equity "local" team and provide mutual support and appreciation

TWELVE

Beyond Passion, Practice, and Persistence . . .

A Purpose for Achieving Equity!

Not everything that is faced can be changed, but nothing can be changed until it is faced.

—James Baldwin

Like Melba Pattillo Beals and the eight other brave Black children who integrated Little Rock's Central High School in 1957, I believe the universe chose me at a very young age and presented me with this quest for racial equity as my life's mission. And although I often wonder why it chose me to be a warrior in this struggle, I have never regretted being chosen.

Strange as it may seem to some (but not to others), my personal quest for racial equity, at a conscious level, began one crisp Saturday morning in fall 1975 when my mother informed me that I would not be going outside to play with my usual circle of friends, some of whom were my classmates from Hilton Elementary School in Baltimore. Instead, she said, I would be traveling with her, all the way out to Brooklandville, Maryland, to take the entrance examination for the private school she hoped I would be able to attend that next fall. Of course, none of what she was telling me made any sense to me at the time, but I got up and dutifully put on my school clothes to prepare for the long ride from Baltimore City to The Park School in the heart of Baltimore County.

I was an obedient child who rarely challenged the orders given to me by family members or other "grown folks" in my neighborhood, including my teachers, clergy members, and my parents' adult friends. And I received a steady diet of racial consciousness development from those adults during my childhood by listening in on the grownups' conversation as they shared tale upon tale about their daily efforts to navigate the unjust racial terrains of their workplaces, municipal service centers, and sites of leisure and recreation. Despite the many challenges that often faced my family's working-class household, I always felt as though I lived a blessed life. I was surrounded by adults who loved and cared for me. I could trust the guidance of those elders and the wisdom they passed down to me from the ancestors who came before them. But the 2-month period between the first time I sat down in that room full of White children, unrehearsed, for the entry exam, and the day my mother and I were called back to the middle-school principal's office and informed of my probationary admission status was like a long intake of breath before my life took on a whole new direction.

Probationary admission, Principal Dick Peyton explained to my mother and me, meant that my invitation to enter Park School's seventh grade was contingent on my successful completion of that institution's summer school program. Now, in all my years of schooling up to that point, I had never been required to attend summer school. In fact, with the exception of receiving an occasional 3 for conduct (because I often talked too much in class), my academic performance had always been near the top of my class. Summer school, in my youthful experience, was for the "slow" kids, not for those who, like me, were doing well and who were well behaved.

So I did not know what to make of this summer school requirement, and neither did my mother. But impressed as she was with the invitation for me to attend this prestigious school, and armed with the realization that I had scored well enough on the test to be admitted, my mother was confident that I was ready. She accepted Park's invitation on my behalf, and that was it.

During summer school, Principal Peyton told us, I would receive refresher courses in math and English. To my surprise and dismay summer school was not a refresher—it was all new learning! Approximately 15 of us—I was one of a few students of color—took classes in pre-algebra and English grammar and literature such as we had never seen the likes of before. I soon realized that Hilton Elementary simply had not prepared me for academics at the level of rigor that The Park School required. The most eye-opening instruction for me, however veiled, was that which attempted to teach us that White schools and White students and White culture and White norms were simply superior, academically and otherwise.

My summer school experience also brought with it some other brand new feelings. One of these was that of inferiority. While most of my new classmates would be White, some carried with them a distinction, such as being a child of a Park School alumnus or coming from a very wealthy family. Very few of them received the invitation to attend summer school, however. I met them when the regular school year began in the fall. Others—and this category included the majority of students of color at Park—were invited to join the student body because they were outstanding athletes, or fulfilled the school's vision for diversity, labels that I later realized virtually mandated their need for refresher coursework.

Because Park School was located in a wealthy suburban enclave nearly 10 miles away from my comparatively urban Baltimore neighborhood, my long-time childhood friend, Jimmy Smith—who was also among those of us invited to attend Park—and I were driven back and forth to middle school every day by our parents, before and after their work day began and ended. And almost daily, I would come home virtually shell-shocked by some new concept—be it academic, cultural, or social—that I had to struggle to comprehend while my White classmates seemingly mastered it instantaneously. For nearly 2 hours each evening, after sports and other extracurricular activities had concluded, the handful of Black students from all grade levels at Park would wait in the school lobby for our working parents to pick us up from school. There we would compare notes on our successes, but most often our failures, in navigating the White, Jewish, upper-class culture and climate of our school.

Sometimes I felt hopeful as I listened to the upper-school Black students express growing confidence and competence in their efforts to excel and fit in. Other times, it was clear to me that, as Black students, we just never could quite gain entry into the exclusive White preserve known as the private school. Yet, it was at the predominantly White and Jewish Park School where my foundational and conscious work as a racial equity leader commenced. As a child, however, I simply could not envision how significant a leader for racial equity I was to become.

I also realize now that the parallels between my experiences at Park and President Obama's schooling at the elite Punnahou School in Honolulu are astounding. With his Black friend and classmate Ray, Obama came to discover the rules of Whiteness and the lack of racial justice in the world, just as my best friend Jimmy and I did here on the mainland. In his autobiographical work, *Dreams From My Father*, Obama repeatedly alludes to his early racial lessons, noting:

> We were always playing on the white man's court, Ray had told me, by the white man's rules. . . .
>
> . . . And the final irony: Should you refuse this defeat and lash out at your captors, they would have a name for that, too, a name that could cage you just as good. Paranoid. Militant. Violent. Nigger . . .
>
> . . . Only Malcolm X's autobiography seemed to offer something different.[1]

I mention this to stress that my work to move Courageous Conversations About Race from theory to practice is not something that began when I founded the Pacific Educational Group (PEG) exactly 20 years ago. My calling and purpose to elevate the constructive racial consciousness of White people and people of color through the power of conversation, as a way of improving our society, began nearly four decades ago. And it has evolved ever since into a more than full-time occupation.

■ ■ ■

In the *Courageous Conversations* field guide, I indicated that racial equity leaders need passion, practice, and persistence to be successful in their endeavors. Add to this that we must also be firmly grounded in purpose—our own personal racial equity purpose—for this morality is what will sustain us when the going gets really tough.

Case in point: Early in my professional career, when I was establishing a reputation as a diversity trainer, I believed that helping White educators recognize and address the many biases and harmful beliefs around the various human differences would enable *all* students to achieve at higher levels. My earliest diversity trainings did not require White educators to engage in examination of their own personal, local, and immediate racial attitudes and beliefs. I quickly noticed, however, that this theory of change contained two critical design flaws that ultimately doom it to failure. First, it requires already marginalized people to bare their souls about the impact of race and racism on their lives, while allowing those with power—that is, those who do the marginalizing—to sit back and assess the validity and significance of their victims' narratives as if they, the perpetrators, were somehow detached from or "objective" reviewers of the marginalizing circumstances.

Second, this theory is challenged especially with regard to race and racial matters. That is, when the narratives of the marginalized focus on issues relating to economic class, gender, or even sexual orientation differences, the marginalizers are often more likely to address those issues with laser-like focus and a relative willingness to develop new understandings. When the topic of race literally walks in the door, so to speak, either intentionally but more often than not unintentionally, logic and focus figuratively jump out of the window. Moreover, even those from targeted and oppressed groups other than the racially marginalized seem challenged to engage willingly in courageous conversations about race from their places of truth. Simply put, my life and lived experiences have shown me that White peoples' struggle to discover the truths about race, which requires that they listen to, truly hear, and constructively address the racial narratives of people of color—let alone examine their own racial experiences—is the most formidable stumbling block of all to achieving racial equity.

After several years of attempting to make my diversity training approach work, I decided that a new model was needed. As a person of color, I wanted to find a way to engage White educators in courageous conversations about race such that they and all other parties involved could feel empowered, valued, and energized. Simultaneously and more critically, I sought to craft a method that would not further injure people of color, but instead beckon us to join a much needed process of racial healing and emancipation. This dual focus then became my vision and purpose for proficient practice in racial equity leadership.

As I progressed along this path, I noticed that, in their efforts to help move Courageous Conversations from theory to practice, White educational leaders often search for routes to effectiveness that do not involve or require them to engage people of color at all. Indeed, many see it as entirely acceptable to focus on how to train all-White administrative teams and faculties in all-White settings to lead for racial equity without addressing why these monoracial groups and environments are completely devoid of racial diversity in the first place. A preferable and more effective first step is to recognize that authentic, antiracist equity work inextricably involves engaging and empowering people of color in those efforts. Complacency in challenging the racism inherent in all-White leadership teams, staffs, or settings is, in and of itself, a perpetuation of racism.

Now, I know some readers may be thinking: Well, what if we just don't *have* any team or staff members of color? To this, I say that your first act of antiracism must be to implement Condition 3 of the Courageous Conversations Protocol: to engage multiple racial perspectives in your racial equity work. When schools and districts accept the fact that they have failed to attract, hire, develop, or promote educators of color, yet proceed with "business as usual"—even if that business is racial equity transformation work—then they are essentially expressing a lack of concern about the plight of people of color and failing to see a need to enlist them in equity efforts. I challenge these systems to go out and find credible educators of color to help them formulate, implement, monitor, evaluate, and sustain an effective racial equity plan. Secure the involvement of competent, capable educators and other leaders of color in meaningful and enduring ways. Inclusion of their voices is essential to achieve true understanding about how race is socially constructed and differentially lived, and these members of the profession and society can bring much-needed authenticity and diversity of perspective to the table. The next challenge, of course, is to create an environment in which educators of color can be productive and thrive.

Similarly, I have noticed that a growing number of educators of color have absorbed and internalized the protocols and designs for reifying White supremacy, which often equates to self-preservation in education systems that destroy the life opportunities for and spirits of children of color. When educators of color fluctuate in and out of racial consciousness and antiracist activism, thus alternately displaying anger and numbness, they do not encourage their White counterparts to be consistently accountable, nor require families and community members of color to face up to and embrace their responsibility in meeting the educational needs of their own children. When people of color are invited into the conversation, or better, when we demand our seat at the table, it is our moral obligation to speak our truth and walk our talk.

In the almost 2 years since I first began imagining this book, I have witnessed more backlash and organized resistance against racial equity work than in any years previously. A handful of superintendents in PEG's partnering districts have moved on or been removed due to a lack of support for this work from their school boards and other powerful White parents' and citizens' groups. Many more have told me that they are facing imminent threats to their leadership, just as their equity efforts are beginning to yield irrefutable quantitative and qualitative gains. One example of this has taken place in the suburban Eden Prairie Schools (EPS).

In Chapter 11, two EPS administrators described the remarkable racial equity work being done in that district. Their narrative confirmed that after almost a decade of efforts informed by PEG's Systemic Racial Equity Framework, EPS (and a few other of PEG's partnering districts across the nation in cities like Portland, Oregon, and San Leandro, California) has proved that dramatically decreasing racial disparities systemwide is not beyond the reach of passionate, practicing, persistent, and purposeful educators. Besides realizing improved academic achievement of more EPS students and unprecedented acceleration in the learning and skills acquisition of Black, Brown, English language learners, special education, and low-socioeconomic-status students in that district, EPS has witnessed a greatly improved climate and culture with respect to learning and teaching. Their powerful process of transformation, marked by improved performance results for most subgroups, also revealed that the district has yet to provide adequate relevance and support for American Indian children and still relegates them to virtual invisibility. EPS had discovered how to achieve racial equity and was blazing a path toward educational equality.

Yet, as this manuscript begins its final journey toward publication, the local school board in Eden Prairie, yielding to the demands of a powerful contingent of White parents and community members, has violated its own equity policy, disregarded its previous equity decisions, and taken actions that run counter to its established equity principles.

Two months after she completed critical work outlined in Chapter 11, EPS Superintendent Melissa Krull was stripped of her leadership authority, offered a hefty contract buy-out package, and shown the door. An interim White male superintendent, with limited if any knowledge of or experience in leading for racial equity, was hired to quiet the White, anti-equity voices that had called so vehemently for Krull's removal and to extinguish the district's racial equity transformation progress, which was, by then, a national success story in the making.

The board's actions to dismantle EPS's racial equity efforts included but were not limited to the following:

- Failure to collectively oppose a well-funded and successful campaign to unseat school board members who supported the district's racial equity work and to replace them with anti-equity-focused White members
- The selection of an outside firm (headed by an outspoken critic of racial equity work in general and PEG in particular) to lead the search for a new superintendent .
- The orchestrating of a strategy intended to lure back to EPS those White families who had moved their children to neighboring districts in protest of the district's equity work
- The launching of planning efforts to establish a new program for gifted and talented children—which, in this and other cases, overwhelmingly exist to serve affluent White students
- The decision to reduce or eliminate support for equity professional development for school leaders, including defunding work previously provided by PEG
- An attempt to restore previous racially disproportionate school boundaries and school configurations

A similar assault on the principles of democratic education and racial equity took place in Wake County, North Carolina. Through a referendum to end busing passed in 2010, powerful White groups essentially turned back the clock of progress in that region to the days of the 1896 Supreme Court decision in *Plessy v. Ferguson,* which mandated separate-but-equal facilities, including schools, for White people and people of color in the United States. These and other challenges to racial equity progress are certain to rise to the highest level of legality, given the escalating racial polarization and tension in our country.

Despite these setbacks, the biggest question on my mind as I come to the end of writing this second *Courageous Conversations* book has little to do with what, technically, needs to happen in districts, schools, and classrooms to eliminate racial achievement disparities. Although the process of developing teachers, administrators, and other staff members as racial equity leaders will continue to be a work in progress, much has been achieved. Our more significant challenge in realizing racially equitable schools is truly an adaptive one. That is, how do our most effective educators survive the process of racial equity transformation in their systems? I am troubled and puzzled today mostly by what will happen to those bold, dedicated chief school officers who have committed to work with PEG to bring about racial equity, now that the disparities in their districts have begun to lessen dramatically and the promise of equity has come into sight. In seemingly progressive, well-resourced communities like Eden Prairie, Rochester, Minnesota, or San Leandro, California, I am left wondering why record gains in proficiency for their underserved students of color and other marginalized students were not enough to bring those communities together in celebration rather than to divide them further. I am hard-pressed to understand why the Eden Prairie school board and a powerful yet vocal minority of White parents and community members voted to see fewer rather than more students meeting high standards and achieving in their schools. Actually, the only explanation I can find is simple: racism. My own productive disequilibrium is prompted by my unquenched thirst for a solution that effectively opposes these forces.

A similar scenario was playing out in the Pulaski County School District of Little Rock, Arkansas, with another former PEG partner, as I was wrapping up this book. As I see it, the Arkansas state government, aligned with other district leadership entities, the business community, and, again, with White community brokers, engaged in dealings to force the removal of Pulaski County's equity-focused African American superintendent, Charles Hopson, before he could even execute his first-year plan to address his district's financial challenges and long-unanswered desegregation mandates, some of which dated back to the late 1950s and early 1960s. On the record, the State Department of Education indicated that it took over district management because of board and superintendent ineffectiveness in dealing with its system's fiscal distress. Perhaps, Superintendent Hopson's plan to block any further marginalization and miseducation of the district's large Black population had more to do with the state's hostile takeover. You can refer back to Hopson's story in his own "Voice" captured in Chapter 5.

PEG was contracted to provide racial equity leadership training to principals in the Pulaski district, but that was the easy part. The harder part was making sure that Little Rock's Black schoolchildren got what was owed to them nearly 60 years after the U.S. Supreme Court's *Brown v. Board of Education* ruling. Prior to Hopson's arrival, many of that district's Black public school students were still assigned to crumbling facilities and subjected to a rigor-less curriculum, even while influential White school board members and their appointed interim superintendent diverted larger and larger shares of district resources toward the shrinking population of White students. For this latter group of students, a brand new, state-of-the-art high school was being built in the "far-White" reaches of the district.

In the 2 years since I signed the contract for this second *Courageous Conversations* book, I believe I have witnessed and read about some of the worst racial transgressions in U.S. education since the late 1950s. Indeed, the outright unethical (and perhaps illegal) assaults on equity reforms and racial equity-focused leadership that have taken place in school districts across the country have been demoralizing. In those 2 years, I have spent hours, days, weeks, and months worrying about how our tiny, yet mighty army of racial equity leaders would withstand the vicious attacks and outright lies that have been lodged against us, our ideals, and our programs from boardrooms and media outlets across the land. How, I wondered, would we ever be able to keep our eyes on the prize—improved achievement for *all* students—while weathering such attacks?

Writing a book as these multiple challenges unfolded was not only personally and professionally difficult for me but also spiritually demoralizing. The very act of writing, however—of clarifying and sharing my evolving thoughts on the Courageous Conversations About Race ideal—helped immensely. It enabled me to lift myself out of the morose, painful, and unpalatable experience of seeing racial equity progress replaced by racial injustice, and it caused me to focus even more intensely on providing educators with the tools and narratives they need to move those conversations more purposefully from theory to practice. Composing these thoughts and words and seeing them transformed into pages of manuscript and ultimately this book was, in itself, uplifting.

I was aided in this effort not only by the dedication and fortitude of my colleagues and peers in school classrooms and district offices nationwide but also by a "higher power." That is, I must have listened to Barack Obama's awe-inspiring presidential acceptance speech a dozen times in the past 2 years. Over and over again, our new president's words gave me the strength to carry on, to keep my talented and dedicated staff at PEG moving forward, and to provide the critical supports and resources for the courageous leaders in our partnering districts, independent schools, and institutions of higher education. President Obama's example of hope, faith, and the steadfast (albeit sometimes, for obvious reasons, masked) commitment he and his administration have shown to the cause of racial equity have given me all the proof and courage I need.

■ ■ ■

I recall my mentor, Dr. Asa Hilliard, once saying, not too long before he transitioned, "When you begin to do things that raise the achievement of the poorest and disenfranchised students, you may not always get applause. You need to be ready for that." I wish I could converse with Dr. Hilliard now and tell him about all the horrible and mean-spirited activities I have seen in response to the success of my work and that of PEG. I would love to hear from him and from other of my activist ancestors about how we might more formidably face the vociferous and mainly White opposition that refuses to accept or support racial equity—even when it results in academic growth, higher achievement, and broader and more diverse perspectives and experiences for their own children. I also would benefit from his perspective surrounding how we can move forward when an increasing number of educators allow fear of losing their job to stand in their way of effectively serving children. I also wonder what Dr. Hilliard's strategy would be as White community members become increasingly litigious in confronting advocates for racial equity. I wonder what activist and visionary ancestors from Latino and American Indian communities would recommend that we do to counter the community coalitions led by nationally recognized fundamentalists and their efforts to derail our progress?

To me—born in 1964, merely a few years after the first violent struggle to improve education for people of color—the national fray has never seemed more tumultuous than in the past couple of years. I must admit that these circumstances caused me to experience a great deal of trepidation, but they have never caused me to doubt my purpose. Instead, they have caused me to embrace even more tightly the very tools that have prompted growth and gains in PEG's partnering districts. They have also forced me to focus on practicing more expertly my use of those tools.

During the summer of 2011, finding myself at a spiritual low given the negative reaction against my and PEG's equity work in schools, I read Melba Beals's epic *Warriors Don't Cry*.[2] The book offered me some critical insights and understandings about African

Americans' centuries-long struggle to achieve racial equality through education. I admired Beals's courage to stand up to a violent and resistant White community that had organized to oppose integration, both inside and outside of Little Rock Central High School. As a 15-year-old Black student, she was taunted, battered, ridiculed, disqualified, and dismissed by her White classmates, but she never let their hatred get the best of her. Instead, she stayed the course, sometimes quite wearily. Even though she and her family were in grave jeopardy, Beals remained focused on her purpose: to ensure that the Black students of Little Rock received the same access to quality education to which their White counterparts had grown accustomed. Beals's words, like President Obama's, gave me inspiration and hope.[3]

Moved by Dr. Beals's story of courage, I traveled to an undisclosed location in the western part of the United States to meet with her personally. We had to meet somewhat secretly because even then, more than 50 years since she acted on her purpose in Arkansas, her life is still threatened. Beals frightened me when she warned me never to return to Little Rock, and certainly not without protection, but she congratulated me on my purpose. She also encouraged me to continue to struggle in the quest to emancipate *all* children from a racist educational system—and to *complete this book!*

■ ■ ■

It was time to "seal the deal." My manuscript for *More Courageous Conversations About Race* was long overdue. I needed to pick myself up out of the national toxicity and plop myself down in a supportive, healing community to write. Armed with my computer and an armful of text resources, I logged thousands of miles to find places and spaces where I could relax my mind and concentrate on putting into words that which would truly assist equity-centered educators in achieving their goals for our nation's classrooms, schools, and districts. In each setting, I learned something more about myself as a proud, racially conscious Black American and about the racial equity purpose I shared with other leaders in my field. In each, I uncovered, examined, and addressed more and more of the insidious and blatant manifestations of systemic racism that deprive all children of the freedom to learn.

Initially, the thought of spending 2 weeks in a cabin in California's Tahoe National Forest, without television or cell phone coverage, frightened me. But deep down, I knew that I needed to unplug not only those gadgets but also myself in order to focus on the task at hand. Absent the creature comforts of home and the big-city conveniences, my daily routines of writing, exercising, writing, cooking, writing, eating, writing, cleaning, writing, reading, resting and more writing proved to be fruitful. I must admit that my fear of a visit from one of California's brown bears instilled in me some extra discipline to stay inside with the lights on after the sun went down and to keep my mind alert. When writer's block would set in, I entertained myself with one-sided conversations on topics such as the virtual absence of people of color in the forest and why enjoying the outdoors is so often depicted as a White cultural norm and not as something people of color typically do. When I was not worried about the bears, I did some of my finest thinking and composing in that little cabin in the forest.

After Tahoe, my fall 2011 journey to Australia offered me a second inspirational boost toward completing this project. While in Perth, I reflected on my work with White, East

Indian, and Aboriginal educators at the University of Western Australia and Curtin University. The biggest gift I derived from that assignment was having my eyes and heart opened authentically to the plight of the indigenous people there, revelations that soon extended to my understandings about and interactions with native people here in the United States. And, of course, I was forever changed by the acceptance and teaching of my Aboriginal friends, including Marion and Dawn.

I escaped to the Big Island of Hawaii over the Thanksgiving recess after Summit 2011 to complete the third leg of this writing project. Simply the thought of my time there continues to rejuvenate me and ignite my passion for racial equity work. I found peace of mind there, working in a tropical environment populated by indigenous people who exude a deep sense of healing, humanity, and oneness with nature despite the continued dispossession of their land and appropriation of their culture. Also there, a personal introduction to Shamanism via Stewart Blackburn helped me to heal from the physical wounding that this writing project, and my racial equity purpose more generally, offers me. A month later, I travelled to Salvador da Bahia, to complete the first draft among (and sometimes be mistaken for one of) the inhabitants of Brazil's so-called "capital of happiness." The Afro-Brazilian dialect, music, food, samba, and overall festive atmosphere were invigorating and inspiring.

On my final night in Bahia, however, while sitting on the dock with my newest group of Brazilian friends, who were singing songs of hope in a tongue unrecognizable to me, a young Black boy scurried past us and ducked under the boardwalk beneath us. Not one of my companions stopped their revelry to stare, as I did, in disbelief and dismay as the boy, who couldn't have been more than 14, lifted what appeared to be a crack pipe to his mouth and began drawing deeply on the acrid fumes.

My spirits quickly dampened when I realized that none of the singing adults seemed fazed by the boy's actions. My Brazilian friends shouted to me, "Forget about him! He's just a street child. He's nothing!" Not one chose to intervene; none even seemed to care one way or another about the plight of that child. Not one bit.

The boy soon staggered out from under the boardwalk and wandered back into the late-night streets, leaving me to wonder how I had managed to structure my American life in such a way that I was a neophyte witness to such horrible circumstances. I instantly became depressed and went back to my hotel to pack. I left Brazil the next day, experiencing mixed emotions of joy and pain.

Yet, in my paralyzing moment of despair on the dock in Bahia that evening, I felt a connection to the U.S. educators who may find discussions and actions around issues of racial equity as shocking and revelatory as I found my bitter discovery about Brazil's so-called "disposable children" and the callous responses of the adults around them. I thought about how overwhelming their sense of guilt and helplessness must be; how conflicted they must feel when they are confronted, for the first time in many cases, with the reality—and the immensity—of the racial equity challenges before them.

I thought too about how alone an educator who wants to make change—who wants to do more than simply have courageous conversations about race but to move racial equity considerations from theory to practice—must feel. In that moment, the issue at hand for me was as clear and pronounced as ever: to finish this book and advance the process of systemic equity transformation in our schools. This contribution cannot be viewed as the definitive answer to our adaptive equity challenges, but another bold step along the pathway to discovery.

By the time this book makes its way to print, the United States will be nearing the end of yet another critical presidential election battle. Many will wonder how the incumbent, if re-elected, or his opponent can guide the country out of reportedly some of the toughest economic times since the Great Depression. Others will be watching closely to see how the opposing parties will reframe the gigantic issues affecting the nation such as health care reform, taxation, immigration, war, and especially unemployment. Perhaps a few will recognize that the shift in balance on the Supreme Court that could result from the appointment of just one additional conservative justice, as opposed to the appointment of one who is truly focused on racial equity and social justice, might alter the course of schooling in America for the next several decades. Still others will be braced for what is certain to be a whirlwind of racial posturing, with racist insults being hurled at people of color by racially unconscious and dysconscious White people from the Far Right to "What's Left" of the political spectrum.

Regardless of who is elected, my expectation is that this nation will refuse to recognize the tremendous strides that its first Black president has made as commander-in-chief. It will be quick to blame Obama for not being able to fully clean up the economic, political, and moral messes that he inherited from his predecessors, who openly and unapologetically put the interests of White, wealthy men and corporations over the needs of poor people, of working- and middle-class people of all races, and especially people of color, who continue to hunger for equitable educational and professional access and opportunity.

Like any leader, President Obama, if re-elected, will need to analyze carefully the plans, strategies, actions, and results of his first term and determine what he might have done differently to yield more positive outcomes. This is obviously a necessary step forward for the leader of any ailing nation. Unfortunately, however, what I believe he will never be able to do, until perhaps he leaves office, is to have an open and frank conversation about how the legislative, judicial, and executive branches and groups of American people dealt differentially and "deficitly" with him due to the color of his skin. Only then perhaps will he be able to assess the impact of these dealings on his ability to lead and foster meaningful change in the health and well-being of the country.

It was Shaman Stewart who helped me to reposition myself when once again I slipped into sadness while witnessing our country stumbling over the presidential racial issues at hand without a protocol to address them. Once believing I would be depressed and perhaps flee the country should racism and corruption alter the results of election 2012, instead I now see that racial truth will prevail regardless of the contest's outcome. Never have I witnessed our country so racially polarized and yet so silent on these obvious racial matters. A second term for Obama is certain to usher in opportunities for this Black president to address critical racial nondiscussables that are prohibitive to his quest for re-election. Just as the election of Romney will restore wealthy White leadership in the White House, supported by a racially uncaring and out-of-touch White populous, in an age when a larger and larger share of the U.S. population is people of color. That is, regardless of who wins, Obama or Romney, this country will necessarily take a giant step closer to confronting our lived racial dis-ease.

Despite the racial-truth paralysis evident at the highest levels of our government, we, the people, can and should still engage in similar types of courageous conversations about race—conversations that can provide a rich source of data about the state of U.S. race relations and racism in the 21st-century. Understanding and owning up to our racial state of being is a first and critical step to our truly becoming a *racist nation in recovery*. Yet, the great tragedy of this nation does not rest solely in the fact that racism is still alive and well within our boundaries. A far greater tragedy is that we have yet to develop a national culture and climate that gives Americans of all races permission to discuss race in humane and productive ways.

The fear among White Americans of being labeled racist when they notice or mention our society's racial disparities, much less when they offer their often underdeveloped racialized perspectives, is as potent and debilitating today as it was in 1976 when I entered the all-White Park School. Likewise disabling is the fear of a growing number of middle-class people of color, who worry justifiably about professional retribution and personal retaliation from their White supervisors, co-workers, colleagues, and friends, should they speak their own truths about race in interracial settings. Our collective silence on these matters is the greatest source of our national demise.

■ ■ ■

What I love most about the Courageous Conversations concept and how it empowers those educators who serve as the foot soldiers for racial equity across this country and around the world is that it engages, sustains, and deepens interracial discourse about race, race relations, and racism as a primary strategy for improving student achievement. But even beyond that, the practice of racial equity leadership allows the nation's educators to fulfill an essential yearning for personal and interpersonal integrity. It is about making sure that our moral, emotional, intellectual, and relational quadrants are each aligned and that they offer congruent meaning when responding to a racialized event in a classroom, school, school community, or school district office setting. It is also about ensuring that educators' beliefs and behaviors about and in response to race are consistent with one another, for only from that place of consistency can we find the courage to "walk our walk" and "talk our talk." Thus, Courageous Conversations is about supporting us, adults inside the education profession and throughout the community, to answer the summons to place the future of our children over our own past and present opportunities.

Only from that place of integrity and truth can we fulfill our desire to offer ourselves unconditionally and unapologetically, to the best service of humankind on behalf of its most vulnerable populations: our children. Only from there can we disrupt any and all of the blatant and covert movements that challenge the educational emancipation of our most needy students. For indeed, if the truth sets us free, and I believe it does, then when we challenge systemic racism, from the classroom to the boardroom, from the community streets to the school corridors, daily and directly, *all* students will be freed to achieve at a higher level.

Moving Courageous Conversations from theory to practice requires that those of us who are committed to racial equity rededicate ourselves to continuous learning about our field and reinvent ourselves daily as more effective activists for racial justice. That some of us may waver in the face of growing resistance is not a sign of weakness—rather, it is a sign of our humanity. But to abandon this cause, when we are all painfully reminded daily of the moral imperative to act—through the news media, by our interactions with disengaged youth, or in the swelling ranks of the unemployed and incarcerated—and when we have witnessed so many successes is conversely inhumane.

As illuminated by the many powerful and purposed "voices from the inside" presented in this book, those educators who have moved Courageous Conversations successfully from theory to practice have seen unprecedented results and improvements in educational outcomes for *all* students, but especially the students of color who have been so long under-served by traditional schools. That outcome confirms the reality that systemic racism is the most devastating factor contributing to the diminished capacity of *all* children. It also further challenges our once firmly held core beliefs about the seeming permanence of racial disparities and gaps in educational achievement.

This is change we can believe in.

Yes.

We.

Can.

But will we?

Notes

Foreword

1. *Maggie's American Dream: The Life and Times of a Black Family*, by James Comer, 1989, New York: Plume.
2. "Stereotype Threat and the Intellectual Test Performance of African-Americans," by C. M. Steele and J. Aronson, 1995, *Journal of Personality and Social Psychology, 1,* 26–37.

Chapter 1

1. "The Other America," speech by Martin Luther King Jr., Grosse Point High School, March 14, 1968.
2. "Carter Again Cites Racism as Factor in Obama's Treatment," *CNN Politics/African-American,* September 19, 2009, retrieved from http://articles.cnn.com/2009–09–15/politics/carter.obama_1_president-jimmy-carter-president-obama-health-care-plan?_s=PM:POLITICS
3. *The Maroon Within Us: Selected Essays on African American Community Socialization* (p. 194), by Asa G. Hilliard III, 1995, Baltimore: Black Classic Press.
4. "My Pedagogic Creed," *The early works of John Dewey: Vol. 5. 1882–1898: Early Essays, 1895–1898 (The Collected Works of John Dewey, 1882–1953),* John Dewey, 2008. Carbondale: Southern Illinois University Press.

Chapter 2

1. *Ethical Ambition: Living a Life of Meaning and Worth* (p. 23), by Derrick Bell, 2003, New York: Bloomsbury Publishing US.

Chapter 3

1. *Because of Race: How Americans Debate Harm and Opportunity in Our Schools* (p. 178), by Micah Pollack, 2008, Princeton, NJ: Princeton University Press.
2. "The Myth About Boys," by David Von Drehle, *Time,* July 26, 2007.
3. "Rodrigo's Reconsideration: Intersectionality and the Future of Critical Race Theory," by Richard Delgado, *Iowa Law Review, 96,* 1263.
4. "White Is a Color," by Glenn Singleton, unpublished manuscript, San Francisco: Pacific Educational Group.
5. "Whiteness as Property," by Cheryl I. Harris, *Harvard Law Review, 8* (June 1993), 1771.

6. Truthdig, "Chris Hedges's Columns: The Obama Deception: Why Cornel West Went Ballistic," by Chris Hedges, *Truthdig*, May 16, 2011, retrieved from http://www.truthdig.com/report/item/the_obama_deception_why_cornel_west_went_ballistic_20110516

7. Ibid.

Chapter 4

1. "The Freedom to Learn" (p. 255), by W. E. B. Du Bois, in *W. E. B. Du Bois Speaks*, edited by P. S. Foner, 1970, New York: Pathfinder Books.

2. *Leading for Equity: The Pursuit of Excellence in the Montgomery County Public Schools* (p. 120), by Stacey M. Childress, Denis P. Doyle, and David A. Thomas, 2009, Cambridge, MA: Harvard University Press.

3. "Levels of Racism: A Theoretical Framework and a Gardener's Tale," by Camara Phyllis Jones, 2000, *American Journal of Public Health, 8*, 1212–1215.

4. Ibid., p. 1212.

5. Ibid., p. 1213.

6. Ibid., p. 1212.

7. *Courageous Conversations About Race: A Field Guide for Achieving Equity in Schools* (p. 31), by Glenn Singleton and Curtis Linton, 2005, Thousand Oaks, CA: Corwin.

8. "Address Real Cause of Cheating," by Bob Schaeffer, *USA Today*, March 10, 2011, retrieved from http://www.usatoday.com/NEWS/usaedition/2011-03-11-editorial11_ST1_U.htm

9. *No Longer Separate, Not Yet Equal: Race and Class in Elite College Admission and Campus Life* (p. 1431 n.7), by Thomas J. Espenshade and Alexandria Walton Radford, 2009, Princeton, NJ: Princeton University Press.

10. "Effective Schools for the Urban Poor" (p. 23), by Ronald Edmonds, *Educational Leadership* (October 1979).

11. *The Right to Learn: A Blueprint for Creating Schools That Work*, by Linda Darling-Hammond, 2001, New York: Jossey-Bass.

12. *The New Jim Crow: Mass Incarceration in the Age of Colorblindness*, by Michelle Alexander, 2012, New York: The Free Press.

13. *Leading for Equity*, Childress et al., p. 127.

14. "Digital Natives, Digital Immigrants," by Marc Prensky, October 2001, *On the Horizon, 5*, retrieved from http://www.marcprensky.com/writing/Prensky%20-%20Digital%20Natives,%20Digital%20Immigrants%20-%20Part1.pdf

15. *Do It Afraid: Obeying God in the Face of Fear*, by Joyce Meyer, 1996, Fenton, MO: Warner Faith.

Chapter 5

1. *Unnatural Causes: Is Inequality Making Us Sick?* (documentary series), presented by the National Minority Consortia of Public Television, 2008, San Francisco: California Newsreel, retrieved from http://www.unnaturalcauses.org/

2. Statistics and a variety of helpful information about American Indians and diabetes may be found at the website of the National Diabetes Information Clearinghouse, http://diabetes.niddk.nih.gov/dm/pubs/americanindian/

3. *The Pedagogy of Confidence: Inspiring High Intellectual Performance in Urban Schools* (p. 49), by Yvette Jackson, 2011, New York: Teachers College Press.

4. "'So When It Comes Out, They Aren't That Surprised That It Is There': Using Critical Race Theory as a Tool of Analysis of Race and Racism in Education" (p. 29), by Jessica De Cuir and Adrienne Dixon, June-July 2004, *Educational Researcher, 33.* Reprinted with permission.

5. *The Dangers of NOT Speaking About Race: A Summary of Research Affirming the Merits of a Color-Conscious Approach to Racial Communication and Equity* (p. 2), by Phillip Mazzocco, 2006, Columbus: The Ohio State University, Kirwan Institute for the Study of Race and Ethnicity, retrieved from http://www.pacificeducationalgroup.org/library/

6. Ibid.

7. *A Race Is a Nice Thing to Have: A Guide to Being a White Person or Understanding the White Persons in Your Life,* by Janet E. Helms, 1992, Topeka, KS: Content Communications.

8. "When Are WE Going to Get Over It?" by Andrew M. Manis, 2009, *EUR This N That/ Urban Black News Blog,* retrieved from http://www.eurthisnthat.com/2009/08/28/andrew-m-manis-asks-when-are-we-white-people-going-to-get-over-it

9. *Racism Without Racists: Color-Blind Racism and the Persistence of Racial Inequality in the United States,* by Eduardo Bonilla-Silva, 2003, Lanham, MD: Rowman & Littlefield.

10. *The Dangers of NOT Speaking About Race,* Mazzocco, p. 4.

11. *Other People's Children: Cultural Conflict in the Classroom* (p. 73), by Lisa Delpit, 1995, New York: The New Press.

12. *The Souls of Black Folk* (pp. 6–7), by W. E. B. Du Bois, 1904/2012, Charleston, SC: CreateSpace.

13. Ibid., pp. 6–7.

14. "Beyond Love: A Critical Race Ethnography of the Schooling of Black Males," by Garrett Duncan, 2002, *Equity and Excellence in Education, 2,* 131–143.

15. *Bad Boys: Public Schools in the Making of Black Masculinity (Law, Meaning, and Violence),* by Ann Arnett Ferguson, 2001, Ann Arbor: University of Michigan Press.

16. "The Trouble with Black Boys: The Role and Influence of Environmental and Cultural Factors on the Academic Performance of African American Males," by Pedro Noguera, July 2003, *Urban Education, 4,* 436.

17. *Yes We Can: The 2010 Schott 50 State Report on Public Education and Black Males,* by Schott Foundation for Public Education, 2010, Cambridge, MA: Author.

18. *Transforming School Culture: How to Overcome Staff Division,* by Anthony Muhammad, 2009, Bloomington, IN: Solution Tree.

19. My thanks to Nanette Missaghi of Eden Prairie (MN) Schools for helping me locate, understand, and articulate Dr. Muhammad's theory.

Chapter 6

1. *Towards a New Consciousness* (p. 99), by Gloria Anzaldúa, 1999, San Francisco, CA: Aunt Lute Books.

2. "Dysconscious Racism: Ideology, Identity, and the Miseducation of Teachers," by Joyce E. King, 1991, *Journal of Negro Education, 2,* 135.

3. *The Practice of Adaptive Leadership: Tools and Tactics for Changing Your Organization and the World,* by Ronald A. Heifetz, Alexander Grashow, and Martin Linsky, 2009, Cambridge, MA: Harvard Business School Press.

4. "White Privilege: Unpacking the Invisible Knapsack," by Peggy McIntosh, in *Race, Class, and Gender: An Anthology* (pp. 103–107), edited by Margaret L. Andersen and Patricia Hill Collins, 1989, Belmont, CA: Wadsworth/Thomson Learning.

5. *Handbook of Adult Resilience,* by John W. Reich, Alex J. Zautra, and John Stuart Hall, 2010, New York: Guilford Press.

6. "An Examination of How a Culturally Appropriate Definition of Resilience Affects the Physical and Mental Health of Aboriginal People," by Marion G. Kickett, October 11, 2011, PhD diss., University of Western Australia School of Population Health, Faculty of Medicine, Dentistry, and Health Sciences, Perth, Australia.

7. As noted by Barbara Palmer in the *Stanford Report:* "Now the largest student-run powwow in the country, the Stanford Powwow was started in 1971 by the newly organized Stanford American Indian Organization to offer an alternative to the image of Native American cultures depicted by the university's mascot at the time, a caricature of an Indian. A year later, then-President Richard W. Lyman recommended that Stanford drop the mascot, in response to a petition signed by 55 Native American students and staff, who called it demeaning and degrading. The actions and 'pseudo-traditional costume' worn by 'Prince Lightfoot,' a Yurok named Timm Williams who danced at football and basketball games, was particularly insulting to Plains Indian students and made a mockery of traditional practices, the petitioners wrote. 'The students have been raised to have a great deal of respect for the dancers who have earned the honor of performing tribal rites … we cannot and will not accept the demeaning, insulting ways in which this symbol distorts the image of the Native American and prostitutes the religious aspects of all tribes in general.'" (May 15, 2002, http://news.stanford.edu/news/2002/may15/powwow-515.html)

8. Ogbu has a body of work around this topic. One item that speaks directly to these findings is "Voluntary and Involuntary Minorities: A Cultural-Ecological Theory of School Performance with Some Implications for Education," by John Ogbu and Herbert D. Simons, 1988, *Anthropology and Education Quarterly, 2,* 155–188.

9. "Abusers Used School in Poor L.A. Area as Stalking Grounds," by William M. Welch and Marisol Bello, February 10, 2012, *USA Today,* retrieved from http://www.usatoday.com/news/education/story/2012-02-09/miramonte-school-sex-abuse-case/53034154/1

10. Ibid.

11. *Child Abuse and Culture: Working With Diverse Families,* by Lisa Aronson Fontes, 2005, New York: Guilford Press.

12. "Abusers Used School," Welch and Bello.

13. *The Latino Threat: Constructing Immigrants, Citizens, and the Nation,* by Leo R. Chavez, 2008, Stanford, CA: Stanford University Press.

14. Readers who would like to address this subject in more detail are invited to read: *School Effectiveness for Language Minority Students,* by W. Thomas and V. Collier, 1997, Washington, DC: National Clearinghouse for Bilingual Education; *Language, Power, and Pedagogy: Bilingual Children in the Crossfire,* by J. Cummins, 2000, Clevedon, UK: Multilingual Matters; *Dual Language Instruction: A Handbook for Enriched Education,* by Nancy Cloud, Fred Genesee, and Else Hamayan, 2000, Boston: Heinle & Heinle; and *Dual Language Education,* by Kathryn J. Lindholm-Leary, 2001, Philadelphia: Multilingual Matters.

Chapter 7

1. *100 Native American Quotes,* by Crazy Horse/Tashunkewitko, retrieved from http://www.circleofexistence.com/quotes/crazyhorse.php

2. To read more about Linda Darling-Hammond's *The Right to Learn: A Blueprint for Creating Schools That Work,* by Linda Darling-Hammond, 2001, New York: Jossey-Bass.

3. "'So When It Comes Out, They Aren't That Surprised That It Is There': Using Critical Race Theory as a Tool of Analysis of Race and Racism in Education" (p. 29), by Jessica De Cuir and Adrienne Dixon, June-July 2004, *Educational Researcher, 33.*

4. *The Fifth Discipline: The Art & Practice of the Learning Organization*, by Peter M. Senge, 1994, New York: Doubleday.

5. "The Culture Builder," by Roland S. Barth, 2002, *Educational Leadership, 8*, 6–11.

6. *The Fifth Discipline*, Senge.

7. Ibid.

8. The Ladder of Inference is found in *The Fifth Discipline Fieldbook: Strategies and Tools for Building a Learning Organization*, by Peter M. Senge, Art Kleiner, Charlotte Roberts, and Rick Ross, 1994, New York: Crown Business. The Iceberg is found in *Schools That Learn: A Fifth Discipline Fieldbook for Educators, Parents, and Everyone Who Cares About Education*, by Peter M. Senge, 2000, New York: Crown Business.

9. *Leadership on the Line: Staying Alive Through the Dangers of Leading*, by Ronald A. Heifetz and Martin Linsky, 2002, Cambridge, MA: Harvard Business Review Press.

10. Ibid.

11. "What is Adaptive Leadership? Technical & Adaptive," by Cambridge Leadership Associates, retrieved from http://www.cambridge-leadership.com/index.php/adaptive_leadership

12. Ibid.

13. *Leadership on the Line* (p. 31), Heifetz and Linsky. See also *The Practice of Adaptive Leadership: Tools and Tactics for Changing Your Organization and the World*, by Ronald A. Heifetz, Alexander Grashow, and Marty Linsky, 2009, Cambridge, MA: Harvard Business Review Press.

14. *Leadership on the Line* (p. 49), Heifetz and Linsky.

15. *Leadership on the Line*, Heifetz and Linsky, see the chapter, "Think Politically," pp. 75–100.

16. "Helping Without Bias: Narcissistic Altruism," by Kim Anderson, May 11, 2012, retrieved from http://www.helpingwithoutbias.com/apps/blog/tag/narcissistic-altruism

17. The name of Bellevue Community College was changed to Bellevue College in 2009, when the institution began awarding bachelor's degrees.

Chapter 8

1. *The Fire Next Time* (p. 9), by James Baldwin, 1964/1992, New York: Vintage.

2. *A Race Is a Nice Thing to Have: A Guide to Being a White Person or Understanding the White Persons in Your Life*, by Janet E. Helms, 1992, Topeka, KS: Content Communications; "An Update of Helms's White and People Of Color Racial Identity Models," by Janet E. Helms, 1995, in *Handbook of multicultural counseling* (pp. 181–198), edited by J. G. Ponterotto, J. M. Casas, L. A. Suzuki, & C. M. Alexander, Thousand Oaks, CA: Sage.

3. "Dysconscious Racism," by Joyce E. King, 1991, *Journal of Negro Education, 2*, 133–146.

4. *Shades of Black: Diversity in African-American Identity*, by William E. Cross Jr., 1991, Philadelphia: Temple University Press.

5. Roediger's early published works include *Black on White: Black Writers on What It Means to Be White*, New York: Schocken, 1999; *The Wages of Whiteness: Race and the Making of the American Middle Class*, London & New York: Verso, 1999; and *Colored White: Transcending the Racial Past*, Los Angeles: University of California Press, 2002. Valdez is the author of *Mexicans in Minnesota*, St. Paul: Minnesota Historical Society Press, 2005.

6. *The Color of Fear* (documentary), by Lee Mun Wah, 1995, Berkeley, CA: StirFry Seminars and Consulting.

7. *Why Are All the Black Kids Sitting Together in the Cafeteria? and Other Conversations About Race*, by Beverly Daniel Tatum, 1997, New York: Basic Books.

8. These approaches are detailed in Chapters 1 and 2 of this book.

Chapter 9

1. Given that fewer than 2% of teachers nationwide—less than 1 in 50—are African American men, it is not unusual for Black boys to go through their entire school careers and have little or no interaction with a Black male teacher, counselor, or administrator. My presence as an observer certainly created a stir among these Black boys, who seemed both genuinely excited and mystified to see me.

2. "Tackling Racism: Ending the Silence," by Donna M. Marriott, March 2003, *Phi Delta Kappan, 7,* 500.

3. *Walking in Circles: The Black Struggle for School Reform,* by Barbara Sizemore, 2008, Chicago: Third World Press.

4. *Diversity Within Unity: Essential Principles for Teaching and Learning in a Multiculture Society,* by James A. Banks, Peter Cookson, Geneva Gay, Willis D. Hawley, Jacqueline Jordan Irvine, Sonia Nieto, and Walter G. Stephan, 2000, Seattle: University of Washington, College of Education, Center for Multicultural Education.

5. Ibid.

6. "But That's Just Good Teaching! The Case for Culturally Relevant Pedagogy," by Gloria Ladson-Billings, 1995, *Theory into Practice, 3,* 159–165.

7. "Preparing for Culturally Responsive Teaching," by Geneva Gay, 2002, *Journal of Teacher Education, 2,* 106–116.

8. "Tackling Racism: Ending the Silence" (pp. 499–500), by Donna M. Marriott, 2003, *Phi Delta Kappan, 7,* 496–501.

9. *Post-Racial? Americans and Race in the Age of Obama* (p. 4), by Daniel Byrd and Bruce Mirken, 2011, Berkeley, CA: The Greenlining Institute, retrieved from http://www.greenlining.org/resources/pdfs/AmericansandRaceinAgeofObama.pdf

10. *Tackling Racism,* Marriott, p. 496.

11. *Tackling Racism,* Marriott, pp. 496–497.

12. *Improving Schools From Within: Teachers, Parents, and Principals Can Make the Difference,* by Roland S. Barth, 1991, Hoboken, NJ: Jossey-Bass.

Chapter 10

1. "Urban Schools Must Start Empowering—and Stop Blaming—Parents," *In Motion,* by Pedro Noguera, June 1, 2011, retrieved from http://www.inmotionmagazine.com/er11/pn_compt.html

2. "Study: White and Black Children Biased Toward Lighter Skin," *CNN U.S.,* May 13, 2010, retrieved from http://articles.cnn.com/2010–05–13/us/doll.study_1_black-children-pilot-study-white-doll?_s=PM:US

Chapter 11

1. *Affordable Housing Plan in Eden Prairie,* by Sarah Schewe, 2007, retrieved from http://www.planning.org/essay/previous.htm?print=true.

Chapter 12

1. *Dreams From My Father: A Story of Race and Inheritance* (p. 85), by Barack Obama, 2004, New York: Three Rivers Press.

2. *Warriors Don't Cry: A Searing Memoir of the Battle to Integrate Little Rock's Central High,* by Melba Patillo Beals, 1995, New York: Washington Square Press.

3. In addition to Dr. Beals, I am deeply appreciative to Dr. Yvette Jackson for her timely book, *The Pedagogy of Confidence,* which made my understanding of the physiological impacts of racism accessible. Dr. Jackson's book gave me the language to explain, on a personal scale, what was shutting down my ability to write this book and prohibiting under-served students of color from realizing their true cognitive potentials in school. Unlike the children, however, I could remove myself, at least temporarily, from a national stage that, in my mind, was growing more racially hostile and relocate myself to settings that nurtured my spirit, soothed my soul, and prompted my clearer thinking.

Recommended Reading

Alexander, Michelle. (2012). *The new Jim Crow: Mass incarceration in the age of colorblindness.* New York: The Free Press.

Anderson, Kim. (2012, May 11). *Helping without bias: Narcissistic altruism.* Retrieved from http://www.helpingwithoutbias.com/apps/blog/tag/narcissistic-altruism

Baldwin, James. (1992). *The fire next time.* New York: Vintage. (Original work published in 1962)

Banks, James A. (Ed.). (2012). *Encyclopedia of diversity in education.* Thousand Oaks, CA: Sage.

Banks, James A., Cookson, Peter, Gay, Geneva, Hawley, Willis D., Irvine, Jacqueline Jordan, Nieto, Sonia, & Stephan, Walter G. (2000). *Diversity within unity: Essential principles for teaching and learning in a multiculture society.* Seattle: University of Washington, College of Education, Center for Multicultural Education.

Barth, Roland S. (1991). *Improving schools from within: Teachers, parents, and principals can make the difference.* Hoboken, NJ: Jossey-Bass.

Barth, Roland S. (2002). The culture builder. *Educational Leadership, 8,* 6–11.

Beals, Melba Patillo. (1995). *Warriors don't cry: A searing memoir of the battle to integrate Little Rock's Central High.* New York: Washington Square Press.

Bonilla-Silva, Eduardo. (2003). *Racism without racists: Color-blind racism and the persistence of racial inequality in the United States.* Lanham, MD: Rowman & Littlefield.

Byrd, Daniel, & Mirken, Bruce. (2011). *Post-Racial? Americans and race in the age of Obama.* Berkeley, CA: The Greenlining Institute. Retrieved from http://www.greenlining.org/resources/pdfs/AmericansandRaceinAgeofObama.pdf

Childress, Stacey M., Doyle, Denis P., & Thomas, David A. (2009). *Leading for equity: The pursuit of excellence in the Montgomery County Public Schools.* Cambridge, MA: Harvard University Press.

Cloud, Nancy, Genesee, Fred, & Hamayan, Else. (2000). *Dual language instruction: A handbook for enriched education.* Boston: Heinle & Heinle.

Cross, William E., Jr. (1991). *Shades of black: Diversity in African-American identity.* Philadelphia: Temple University Press.

Cummins, J. (2000). *Language, power, and pedagogy: Bilingual children in the crossfire.* Clevedon, UK: Multilingual Matters.

Darling-Hammond, Linda (2001). *The right to learn: A blueprint for creating schools that work.* New York: Jossey-Bass.

De Cuir, Jessica, & Dixon, Adrienne. (2004). "So when it comes out, they aren't that surprised that it is there": Using critical race theory as a tool of analysis of race and racism in education. *Educational Researcher, 33,* 26–31.

Delgado, Richard. (2011). Rodrigo's reconsideration: Intersectionality and the future of critical race theory. *Iowa Law Review, 96,* 1247–1287.

Delpit, Lisa. (1995). *Other people's children: Cultural conflict in the classroom.* New York: The New Press.

Dewey, John. (2008). *The early works of John Dewey:* Vol. 5. *1882—1898: Early Essays, 1895–1898 (The Collected Works of John Dewey, 1882-1953).* Carbondale: Southern Illinois University Press.

Du Bois, W. E. B. (1903). *The souls of Black folk.* Chicago: A. C. McClurg.

Du Bois, W. E. B. (2012). *The souls of Black folk.* Charleston, SC: CreateSpace. (Original work published 1904)

Duncan, Garrett. (2002). Beyond love: A critical race ethnography of the schooling of Black males. *Equity and Excellence in Education, 2,* 131–143.

Edmonds, Ronald. (1979, October). Effective schools for the urban poor. *Educational Leadership,* 15–24.

Espenshade, Thomas J., & Radford, Alexandria Walton. (2009). *No longer separate, not yet equal: Race and class in elite college admission.* Princeton, NJ: Princeton University Press.

Ferguson, Ann Arnett. (2001). *Bad boys: Public schools in the making of Black masculinity (law, meaning, and violence).* Ann Arbor: University of Michigan Press.

Foner, P. S. (Ed.). (1970). *W. E. B. Du Bois speaks.* New York: Pathfinder Books.

Fontes, Lisa Aronson. (2005). *Child abuse and culture: Working with diverse families.* New York: Guilford Press.

Fordham, Signithia, & Ogbu, John. (1986). Black students' school success: Coping with the burden of "acting White." *Urban Review, 18,* 176–206.

Gay, Geneva. (2002). Preparing for culturally responsive teaching. *Journal of Teacher Education, 2,* 106–116.

Giovanni, Nikki. (1999). *Those who ride the night winds.* New York: Harper Perennial.

Harris, Cheryl I. (1993). Whiteness as property. *Harvard Law Review, 8,* 1707–1791. Retrieved from http://papers.ssrn.com/sol3/cf_dev/AbsByAuth.cfm?per_id=329292

Heifetz, Ronald A., Grashow, Alexander, & Linsky, Martin. (2009). *The practice of adaptive leadership: Tools and tactics for changing your organization and the world.* Cambridge, MA: Harvard Business Review Press.

Heifetz, Ronald A., & Linsky, Martin. (2002). *Leadership on the line: Staying alive through the dangers of leading.* Cambridge, MA: Harvard Business Review Press.

Helms, Janet E. (Ed.). (1990). *Black and White racial identity: Theory, research, and practice.* Westport, CT: Greenwood.

Helms, Janet E. (1992). *A race is a nice thing to have: A guide to being a White person or understanding the White persons in your life.* Topeka, KS: Content Communications.

Helms, Janet E. (1995). An update of Helms's White and people of color racial identity models. In J. G. Ponterotto, J. M. Casas, L. A. Suzuki, & C. M. Alexander (Eds.), *Handbook of multicultural counseling* (pp. 181–198). Thousand Oaks, CA: Sage.

Hilliard, Asa G., III. (1995). *The maroon within us: Selected essays on African American community socialization.* Baltimore: Black Classic Press.

Jackson, Yvette. (2011). *The pedagogy of confidence: Inspiring high intellectual performance in urban schools.* New York: Teachers College Press.

Jones, Camara Phyllis. (2000). Levels of racism: A theoretical framework and a gardener's tale. *American Journal of Public Health, 8,* 1212–1215.

Katz, Judith H. (2003). *White awareness: Handbook for anti-racism training.* Tulsa: University of Oklahoma Press. (Original work published 1978).

Katz, Judith H. (2009). *White culture and racism: Working for organizational change in the United States.* Roselle, NJ: Crandall, Dostie, & Douglass Books. Retrieved from http://www.cddbooks.com/Bookstore/DetailPage.asp?item=WP003

Kickett, Marion G. *An examination of how culturally appropriate definitions of resilience affect the physical and mental health of Aboriginal people.* Unpublished PhD dissertation, University of

Western Australia School of Population Health, Faculty of Medicine, Dentistry, and Health Sciences, Perth, Australia.

King, Joyce E. (1991). Dysconscious racism. *Journal of Negro Education, 2,* 133–146.

Ladson-Billings, Gloria. (1995). But that's just good teaching! The case for culturally relevant pedagogy. *Theory into Practice, 3,* 159–165.

LeMoine, Noma. (2001). Language variation and literacy acquisition in African American students. In Joyce L. Harris, Alan G. Kamhi, & Karen E. Pollock (Eds.), *Literacy in African American communities* (pp. 169–194). Mahwah, NJ: Lawrence Erlbaum.

LeMoine, Noma, & Hollie, Sharroky. (2007). Developing academic English for standard English learners. In H. Samy Alim & John Baugh (Eds.), *Talkin Black talk: Language, education, and social change* (pp. 43–55). New York: Teachers College Press.

LeMoine, Noma, & Los Angeles Unified School District. (1999). *English for your success: A language development program for African American students—curriculum guide for Grades 2–3.* Maywood, NJ: Peoples Publishing Group.

Lindholm-Leary, Kathryn J. (2001). *Dual language education.* Philadelphia: Multilingual Matters.

Manis, Andrew M. (2009). When are WE going to get over it?" EUR This N That/Urban Black News Blog. Retrieved from http://www.eurthisnthat.com/2009/08/28/andrew-m-manis-asks-when-are-we-white-people-going-to-get-over-it/

Marriott, Donna M. (2003). Tackling racism: Ending the silence. *Phi Delta Kappan, 7,* 496–501.

Mazzocco, Phillip. (2006). *The dangers of NOT speaking about race: A summary of research affirming the merits of a color-conscious approach to racial communication and equity.* Columbus: The Ohio State University, Kirwan Institute for the Study of Race and Ethnicity. Retrieved from http://www.pacificeducationalgroup.org/library/

McIntosh, Peggy. (1989). White privilege: Unpacking the invisible knapsack." In Margaret L. Andersen & Patricia Hill Collins (Eds.), *Race, class, and gender: An anthology* (pp. 103–107). Belmont, CA: Wadsworth/Thomson Learning.

Meyer, Joyce. (1996). *Do it afraid: Obeying God in the face of fear.* Fenton, MO: Warner Faith.

Mosedale, Mike. (2004, February 18). The mall of Somalia. *City Pages.* Retrieved from http://www.citypages.com/2004–02–18/news/the-mall-of-somalia

Muhammad, Anthony. (2009). *Transforming school culture: How to overcome staff division.* Bloomington, IN: Solution Tree.

Mun Wah, Lee. (2004). *The art of mindful facilitation.* Berkeley, CA: StirFry Seminars and Consulting.

National Minority Consortia of Public Television. (2008). *Unnatural causes: Is inequality making us sick?* San Francisco: California Newsreel. Retrieved from http://www.unnaturalcauses.org/

Noguera, Pedro. (2003). The trouble with Black boys: The role and influence of environmental and cultural factors on the academic performance of African American males. *Urban Education, 38,* 431–459.

Ogbu, John, & Simons, Herbert D. (1988). Voluntary and involuntary minorities: A cultural-ecological theory of school performance with some implications for education. *Anthropology and Education Quarterly, 2,* 155–188.

Pollack, Micah. (2008). *Because of race: How Americans debate harm and opportunity in our schools.* Princeton, NJ: Princeton University Press.

Prensky, Marc. (2001, October). Digital natives, digital immigrants. *On the Horizon, 5.* Retrieved from http://www.marcprensky.com/writing/Prensky%20-%20Digital%20Natives,%20Digital%20Immigrants%20-%20Part1.pdf

Reich, John W., Zautra, Alex J., & Hall, John Stuart. (2010). *Handbook of adult resilience.* New York: Guilford Press.

Schaeffer, Bob. (2011, March 10). Address real cause of cheating. *USA Today*. Retrieved from http://www.usatoday.com/NEWS/usaedition/2011–03–11-editorial11_ST1_U.htm

Schewe, Sarah. (2007). *Affordable housing plan in Eden Prairie*. http://www.planning.org/essay/previous.htm?print=true.

Schott Foundation for Public Education. (2010). *Yes we can: The 2010 Schott 50 state report on public education and Black males*. Cambridge, MA: Author.

Senge, Peter M. (1994). *The fifth discipline: The art & practice of the learning organization*. New York: Doubleday.

Senge, Peter M. (2000). *Schools that learn: A fifth discipline fieldbook for educators, parents, and everyone who cares about education*. New York: Crown Business.

Senge, Peter M., Kleiner, Art, Roberts, Charlotte, & Ross, Rick. (1994). *The fifth discipline fieldbook: Strategies and tools for building a learning organization*. New York: Crown Business.

Singham, Mano. (2005). *The achievement gap in U.S. education: Canaries in the mine*. Lanham, MD: R&L Education.

Singleton, Glenn, & Linton, Curtis. (2006). *Courageous conversations about race: A field guide for achieving equity in schools*. Thousand Oaks, CA: Corwin.

Sizemore, Barbara. (2008). *Walking in circles: The Black struggle for school reform*. Chicago: Third World Press.

Thomas, Wayne P., & Collier, Virginia (1997). *School effectiveness for language minority students*. Washington, DC: National Clearinghouse for Bilingual Education.

Von Drehle, David. (2007). The myth about boys. *Time*, July 26.

West, Cornel. (1994). *Race matters*. New York: Vintage.

Index

Aboriginal population, 137–141, 310–311

Achievement gap, 75–81, 76 (figure), 77 (figure), 133 (figure), 134 (figure), 246, 286, 288 (figure), 289 (figure)

Adaptive challenges, 172–175

Adaptive Leadership, 170–175, 171 (figure), 196–197

Administrative support, 196–202

Adultification, 113

Advocacy, 254, 254 (figure)

Affirmative action, 81–82, 108

African American population, 99, 100, 145

African American students
  classroom environment, 232–233
  educational opportunities, 114–115, 116, 119–120, 170, 179
  language challenges, 306
  out-of-school suspensions, 119–120
  parental involvement, 260
  professional learning communities, 232–233, 242
  racially specific curricular materials, 228
  special education programs, 119–120
  student achievement data, 75–76, 76 (figure), 77 (figure), 133 (figure), 134 (figure), 169, 288 (figure), 289 (figure)
  Systemic Racial Equity Framework, 163, 164 (figure)
  systemic racism, 74
  university enrollment, 82

Akbar, Na'im, 98

Alexander, Devon, 63–66

Alexander, Michelle, 86, 87–88, 322

Almanzán, Jamie, 242

American Indians
  Eden Prairie, Minnesota, 274 (figure)
  government subsidies, 99–100
  health considerations, 99, 100
  historical discrimination, 155–157

American Indian students
  academic achievement, 76, 77 (figure), 131–136, 134 (figure), 142, 169, 288 (figure), 289 (figure)
  classroom environment, 232–233
  cultural identity, 141–142, 318
  educational opportunities, 116, 170, 179
  parental involvement, 260
  professional learning communities, 232–233, 242
  racially specific curricular materials, 228
  special education programs, 119–120
  stereotypical portrayals, 131
  Systemic Racial Equity Framework, 163, 164 (figure)
  systemic racism, 74
  university enrollment, 82

Anderson, Kim, 183, 322

Angelou, Maya, 67

Ann Arbor, Michigan, 161

Antiracism training, 17–20, 112, 164

Anzaldúa, Gloria, 129

Art of mindful inquiry, 45–47, 235–236, 236 (table)

Asian Americans, 274 (figure)

Asian students
  academic achievement, 76 (figure), 77 (figure), 80–81, 133 (figure), 134 (figure), 288 (figure), 289 (figure)
  university enrollment, 82

CORWIN

A SAGE Company

The Corwin logo—a raven striding across an open book—represents the union of courage and learning. Corwin is committed to improving education for all learners by publishing books and other professional development resources for those serving the field of PreK–12 education. By providing practical, hands-on materials, Corwin continues to carry out the promise of its motto: "Helping Educators Do Their Work Better."